Born on November 24, 1888, in Maryville, Missouri, DALE CARNEGIE was a farmer's son who completed his education from the State Teachers College in Warrensburg. As a sales representative, Carnegie worked for Armour & Company for a considerable time, until he quit sales in 1911 to pursue his dream of becoming a lecturer. He also attended the American Academy of Dramatic Arts in New York but did not earn much success as an actor. As an author, some of his published works include Abraham Lincoln's biography, titled *Lincoln the Unknown*, self-help books like *How to Stop Worrying and Start Living, How to Win Friends and Influence People, The Quick & Easy Way To Effective Speaking, Develop Self-Confidence, Improve Public Speaking, How To Enjoy Your Life And Your Job* and *Little Known Facts About Well Known People* to name a few. He has also co-authored several books on the art of public speaking.

DALE CARNEGIE
OMNIBUS

Om Books International

Reprinted in 2020

Om Books International

Corporate & Editorial Office
A-12, Sector 64, Noida 201 301
Uttar Pradesh, India
Phone: +91 120 477 4100
Email: editorial@ombooks.com
Website: www.ombooksinternational.com

Sales Office
107, Ansari Road, Darya Ganj,
New Delhi 110 002, India
Phone: +91 11 4000 9000
Fax: +91 11 2327 8091
Email: sales@ombooks.com
Website: www.ombooks.com

ISBN: 978-93-84625-50-4

Printed in India

10 9 8 7 6 5 4 3 2

Contents

The Quick & Easy Way To Effective Speaking

PART I
BASIC PRINCIPLES OF EFFECTIVE SPEAKING

PART II
TECHNIQUES OF EFFECTIVE SPEAKING

PART III
THE THREE ASPECTS OF EVERY SPEECH

PART IV

THE TWO METHODS OF DELIVERING A TALK

Develop Self-Confidence, Improve Public Speaking

How To Enjoy Your Life and Your Job

PART I: WIN FRIENDS AND INFLUENCE PEOPLE

PART II: STOP WORRYING

THE QUICK & EASY WAY TO EFFECTIVE SPEAKING

PART I

BASIC PRINCIPLES OF EFFECTIVE SPEAKING

1

Acquiring The Basic Skills

I started teaching classes in public speaking in 1912, the year the Titanic went down in the icy waters of the North Atlantic.

Over the years, at these classes, people are given the opportunity of sharing what they hope to gain from this training. Naturally, the phraseology varies; but the central desire, the basic want in the vast majority of cases, remains surprisingly the same: "When I am called upon to stand up and speak, I become so self-conscious, so frightened, that I can't think clearly, can't concentrate, can't remember what I intended to say. I want to gain self-confidence, poise, and the ability to think on my feet. I want to get my thoughts together in logical order, and I want to be able to talk clearly and convincingly before a business or social group."

Does this sound familiar? Have you experienced these same feelings of inadequacy? Would you give a small fortune to have the ability to speak convincingly and persuasively in public? The very fact that you have begun reading the pages of this book is proof of your interest in acquiring the ability to speak effectively.

I know what you are going to say, what you would say if you could talk to me: "But Mr. Carnegie, do you really think I could develop the confidence to get up and face a group of people and address them in a coherent, fluent manner?"

I have spent nearly all my life helping people get rid of their fears and develop courage and confidence. I could fill many books with the stories of the miracles that have taken place in my classes. It is not, therefore, a question of my *thinking*. I *know* you can, if you practice the directions and suggestions that you will find in this book.

Is there the faintest shadow of a reason why you should not be able to think as well in a perpendicular position before an audience as you can sitting down? Is there any reason why you should play host to butterflies in your stomach and become a victim of the "trembles" when you get up to address an audience? Surely, you realize that this condition can be remedied, that training and practice will wear away your audience fright and give you self-confidence.

This book will help you to achieve that goal. It is not an ordinary textbook. It is not filled with rules concerning the mechanics of speaking. It does not dwell on the physiological aspects of vocal production and articulation. It is the distillation of a lifetime spent in training adults in effective speaking. It starts with you as you are, and from that premise works naturally to the conclusion of what you want to be. All you have to do is co-operate—follow the suggestions in this book, apply them in every speaking situation, and persevere.

In order to get the most out of this book, and to get it with rapidity and dispatch, you will find these four guideposts useful:

FIRST
Take Heart From Others' Experience

There is no such animal, in or out of captivity, as a born public speaker. In those periods of history when public speaking was a refined art that demanded close attention to the laws of rhetoric and the niceties of delivery, it was even more difficult to be born a public speaker. Now we think of public speaking as a kind of enlarged conversation. Gone forever is the old grandiloquent style and the stentorian voice. What we like to hear at our dinner meetings, in our church services, on our TV sets and radios, is straightforward speech, conceived in common sense and dedicated to the proposition that we like speakers to talk with, and not at, us.

Despite what many school texts would lead us to believe, public speaking is not a closed art, to be mastered only after years of perfecting the voice and struggling with the mysteries of rhetoric. I have spent almost all of my teaching career proving to people that it is *easy* to speak in public, provided they follow a few simple, but important, rules. When I started to teach at the 125th Street YMCA in New York City back in 1912, I didn't know this any more than my first students knew it. I taught those first classes pretty much the way I had been taught in my college years in Warrensburg, Missouri. But I soon discovered that I was on the wrong track; I was trying to teach adults in the business world as though they were college freshmen. I saw the futility of using Webster, Burke, Pitt, and O'Connell as examples to imitate. What the members of my classes wanted was enough courage to stand on their hind legs and make a clear, coherent report at their next business meeting. It wasn't long before I threw the textbooks out the window, got right up there on the podium and, with a few simple ideas, worked with those fellows until they could give their reports in a convincing manner. It worked, because they kept coming back for more.

I wish I could give you a chance to browse through the files of testimonial letters in my home or in the offices of my representatives in various parts of the world. They come from industrial leaders whose names are frequently mentioned in the business section of *The New York Times* and *The Wall Street Journal*, from governors of states and members of parliaments, from college presidents, and from celebrities in the world of entertainment. There are thousands more from housewives, ministers, teachers, young men and women whose names are not well known yet, even in their own communities, executives and executive trainees, laborers, skilled and unskilled, union men, college students, and business women. All of these people felt a need for self-confidence and the ability to express themselves acceptably in public. They were so grateful for having achieved both that they took the time to write me letters of appreciation.

Of the thousands of people I have taught, one example comes to mind as I write because of the dramatic impact it had on me at the time. Some years ago, shortly after he joined my course, D. W. Ghent, a successful businessman in Philadelphia, invited me to lunch. He leaned across the table and said: "I have sidestepped every opportunity to speak to various gatherings, Mr. Carnegie, and there have been many. But now I am chairman of a board of college trustees.

I must preside at their meetings. Do you think it will be possible for me to learn to speak at this late date in life?"

I assured him, on the basis of my experience with men in similar positions who had been members of my classes, that there was no doubt in my mind that he would succeed.

About three years later we lunched together again at the Manufacturers' Club. We ate in the same dining room and at the very same table we had occupied at our first meeting. Reminding him of our former conversation, I asked him whether my prediction had come true. He smiled, took a little red-backed notebook out of his pocket, and showed me a list of speaking engagements for the next several months. "The ability to make these talks," he confessed, "the pleasure I get in giving them, the additional service I can render in the community—these are among the most gratifying things in my life."

But that was not all. With a feeling of justifiable pride, Mr. Ghent then played his ace card. His church group had invited the prime minister of England to address a convocation in Philadelphia. And the Philadelphian selected to make the introduction of the distinguished statesman, on one of his rare trips to America, was none other than Mr. D. W. Ghent.

This was the man who had leaned across that same table less than three years before and asked me whether I thought he would ever be able to talk in public!

I have seen thousands of similar miracles worked in my courses. I have seen men and women whose lives were transformed by this training, many of them receiving promotions far beyond their dreams or achieving positions of prominence in their business, profession, and community. Sometimes this has been done by means of a single talk delivered at the right moment. Let me tell you the story of Mario Lazo.

Years ago, I received a cable from Cuba that astonished me. It read: "Unless you cable me to the contrary, I am coming to New York to take training to make a speech." It was signed: "Mario Lazo." Who was he? I wondered! I had never heard of him before.

When Mr. Lazo arrived in New York, he said: "The Havana Country Club is going to celebrate the fiftieth birthday of the founder of the club; and I have been invited to present him with a silver cup and to make the principal talk of the evening. Although I am an attorney, I have never made a public talk in my life. I am terrified at the thought of speaking. If I fail, it will be deeply embarrassing to my wife and myself socially; and, in addition, it might lower my prestige with my clients. That is why I have come all the way from Cuba for your help. I can stay only three weeks."

During those three weeks, I had Mario Lazo going from one class to another speaking three or four times a night. Three weeks later, he addressed the distinguished gathering at the Havana Country Club. His address was so outstanding that *Time* magazine reported it under the head of foreign news and described Mario Lazo as a "silver-tongued orator."

Sounds like a miracle, doesn't it? It is a miracle—a twentieth-century miracle of conquering fear.

SECOND
Keep Sight Of Your Goal

When Mr. Ghent spoke of the pleasure his newly acquired skill in public speaking gave him, he touched upon what I believe (more than any other one factor) contributed to his success. It's true he followed the directions and faithfully did the assignments. But I'm sure he did these things because he wanted to do them, and he wanted to do them because he saw himself as a successful speaker. He projected himself into the future and then worked toward bringing that projection into reality. That is exactly what you must do.

Concentrate your attention on what self-confidence and the ability to talk more effectively will mean to you. Think of what it may mean to you socially, of the friends it will bring, of your increased capacity to be of service in your civic, social, or church group, of the influence you will be able to exert in your business. In short, it will prepare you for leadership.

In an article entitled "Speech and Leadership in Business," S. C. Allyn, Chairman of the Board of the National Cash Register Company and Chairman of UNESCO, wrote in the *Quarterly Journal of Speech*: "In the history of our business, many a man has drawn attention to himself by a good job done on the platform. A good many years ago a young man, who was then in charge of a small branch in Kansas, gave a rather unusual talk, and is today our vice-president in charge of sales." I happen to know that this vice-president is now the president of the National Cash Register Company.

There is no predicting how far the ability to speak on your feet will take you. One of our graduates, Henry Blackstone, President of the Servo Corporation of America, says, "The ability to communicate effectively with others and win their co-operation is an asset we look for in men moving to the top."

Think of the satisfaction and pleasure that will be yours when you stand up and confidently share your thoughts and feelings with your audience. I have traveled around the world several times, but I know of few things that give greater delight than holding an audience by the power of the spoken word. You get a sense of strength, a feeling of power. "Two minutes before I begin," said one of my graduates, "I would rather be whipped than start; but two minutes before I finish, I would rather be shot than stop."

Begin now to picture yourself before an audience you might be called upon to address. See yourself stepping forward with confidence, listen to the hush fall upon the room as you begin, feel the attentive absorption of the audience as you drive home point after point, feel the warmth of the applause as you leave the platform, and hear the words of appreciation with which individual members of the audience greet you when the meeting is over. Believe me, there is a magic in it and a never-to-be forgotten thrill.

William James, Harvard's most distinguished professor of psychology, wrote six sentences that could have a profound effect on your life, six sentences that are the open sesame to Ali Baba's treasure cave of courage: "In almost any subject, your passion for the subject will save you. If you care enough for a result, you will most certainly attain it. If you wish to be good, you will be good. If you wish to be rich, you will be rich. If you wish to be learned, you will be learned. Only then you must really wish these things and wish them with exclusiveness and not wish one hundred other incompatible things just as strongly."

Learning to speak effectively to groups brings other benefits than merely the ability to make formal public speeches. As a matter of fact, if you never give a formal public speech in your life, the benefits to be derived from this training are manifold. For one thing, public speaking training is the royal road to self-confidence. Once you realize that you can stand up and talk intelligently to a group of people, it is logical to assume that you can talk to individuals with greater confidence and assurance. Many men and women have taken my course in Effective Speaking primarily because they were shy and self-conscious in social groups. When they found they were capable of speaking on their feet to their fellow class members without having the roof fall in, they became aware of the ridiculousness of self-consciousness. They began to impress others, their families, friends, business associates, customers, and clients, with their newly found poise. Many of our graduates, like Mr. Goodrich, were impelled to take the course by the remarkable change in the personalities of those around them.

This type of training also affects the personality in ways that are not immediately apparent. Not long ago, I asked Dr. David Allman, the Atlantic City surgeon and former president of the American Medical Association, what in his opinion were the benefits of public speaking training in terms of mental and physical health. He smiled and said he could best answer that question by writing a prescription that "no drugstore can fill. It must be filled by the individual; if he thinks he can't, he is wrong."

I have the prescription on my desk. Every time I read it, I am impressed. Here it is, just as Dr. Allman jotted it down:

Try your best to develop an ability to let others look into your head and heart. Learn to make your thoughts, your ideas, clear to others, individually, in groups, in public. You will find, as you improve in your effort to do this, that you—your real self—are making an impression, an impact, on people such as you never made before.

You can reap a double benefit from this prescription. Your self-confidence strengthens as you learn to speak to others, and your whole personality grows warmer and better. This means that you are better off emotionally, and if you are better off emotionally, you are better off physically. Public speaking in our modern world is for everybody, men and women, young and elderly. I do not know personally about its advantages to one in business or industry. I only hear that they are great. But I do know its advantages in health. Speak when you can, to a few or to many; you will do it better and better, as I have found out, myself; and you will feel a buoyancy of spirit, a sense of being a whole, rounded person, such as you never felt before.

It is a wonderful sense to have, and no pill ever made can give it to you.

The second guidepost, then, is to picture yourself as successfully doing what you fear to do, and to concentrate on the benefits you will receive through your ability to talk acceptably before groups. Remember the words of William James: "If you care enough for a result, you will most certainly attain it."

THIRD
Predetermine Your Mind To Success

I was asked once, on a radio program, to tell in three sentences the most important lesson I have ever learned. This is what I said: "The biggest lesson I have ever learned is the stupendous importance of what we think. If I knew what you think, I would know what you are, for your thoughts make you what you are. By changing our thoughts, we can change our lives."

You have set your sights on the goal of increased confidence and more effective communication. From now on, you must think positively, not negatively, about your chances to succeed in this endeavor. You must develop a buoyant optimism about the outcome of your efforts to speak before groups. You must set the seal of determination upon every word and action that you devote toward the development of this ability.

Here is a story that is dramatic proof of the need for resolute determination on the part of anyone who wants to meet the challenge of more expressive speaking. The man

I am writing about has come up the management ladder so far that he has become a big business legend. But the first time he stood up to speak in college, words failed him. He couldn't get beyond the middle of the five-minute talk his teacher had assigned. His face went white, and he hurried off the platform in tears.

The man who had that experience as a young student didn't let that failure frustrate him. He determined to become a good speaker and didn't stop in that determination until he became a world-respected economic consultant to the government. His name is Clarence B. Randall. In one of his thoughtful books, *Freedom's Faith,* he has this to say about public speaking: "I have service stripes all the way up one sleeve and all the way down the other from appearances before luncheons and dinners of manufacturers' associations, Chambers of Commerce, Rotary Clubs, fund-raising campaigns, alumni organizations, and all the rest. I talked myself into World War I by a patriotic address in Escanaba, Michigan; I have barnstormed for charity with Mickey Rooney, and for education with President James Bryant Conant of Harvard and Chancellor Robert M. Hutchins of the University of Chicago; and I have even made an after-dinner speech in very bad French.

"I think I know something about what an audience will listen to, and how they want it said. And there is nothing whatever about it that a man worthy to bear important business responsibility cannot learn if he will."

I agree with Mr. Randall. The will to succeed must be a vital part of the process of becoming an effective speaker. If I could look into your mind and ascertain the strength of your desire and the light and shadow of your thought, I could foretell, almost with certainty, the swiftness of your progress toward your goal of improved communicative skills.

In one of my classes in the Middle West, a man stood up the first night and unabashedly said that as a builder of homes he wouldn't be content until he became a spokesman for the American Home Builders' Association. He wanted nothing more than to go up and down this country and tell everybody he met the problems and achievements of his industry. Joe Haverstick meant what he said. He was the kind of class member that delights an instructor: he was in dead earnest. He wanted to be able to talk, not on local issues only, but on national ones, and there was no half-heartedness about his desires. He prepared his talks thoroughly, practiced them carefully, and never missed a single session, though it was the busy season of the year for men in his business. He did precisely what such a class member always does—he progressed at a rate that surprised him. In two months he had become one of the outstanding members of the class. He was voted its president.

The instructor handling that class was in Norfolk, Virginia, about a year later, and this is what he wrote: "I had forgotten all about Joe Haverstick back in Ohio when, one morning while I was having breakfast, I opened *Virginia Pilot*. There was a picture of Joe and a write-up about him. The night before, he had addressed a large meeting of area builders, and I saw that Joe was not just a spokesman for the National Home Builders Association; he was its president."

So, to succeed in this work, you need the qualities that are essential in any worthwhile endeavor: desire amounting to enthusiasm, persistence to wear away mountains, and the self-assurance to believe you will succeed.

When Julius Caesar sailed over the channel from Gaul and landed with his legions in what is now England, what did he do to insure the success of his army? A very clever thing: he halted his soldiers on the chalk cliffs of Dover; and, looking down over the waves two hundred feet below, they saw red tongues of fire consume every ship in which they had crossed. In the enemy's country, with the last link with the Continent gone, the last means of retreat burned, there was but one thing left for them to do: to advance, to conquer. That is precisely what they did.

Such was the spirit of the immortal Caesar. Why not make it yours, too, as you set out to conquer your fear of audiences? Throw every shred of negative thought into the consuming fires and slam doors of steel upon every escape into the irresolute past.

FOURTH

Seize Every Opportunity To Practice

The course I gave in the 125th Street YMCA before World War I has been changed almost beyond recognition. Every year, new ideas are woven into the sessions and old ones cast away. But one feature of the course remains unchanged. Every member of every class must get up once, and in the majority of cases, twice, and give a talk before his fellow members. Why? Because no one can learn to speak in public without speaking in public any more than a person can learn to swim without getting in the water. You could read every volume ever written about public speaking—including this one—and still not be able to speak. This book is a thorough guide. But you must put its suggestions into practice.

When George Bernard Shaw was asked how he learned to speak so compellingly in public, he replied: "I did it the same way I learned to skate—by doggedly making a fool of myself until I got used to it." As a youth, Shaw was one of the most timid persons in London. He often walked up and down the Embankment for twenty minutes or more before venturing to knock at a door. "Few men," he confessed, "have suffered more from simple cowardice or have been more horribly ashamed of it."

Finally, he hit upon the best and quickest and surest method ever yet devised to conquer timidity, cowardice, and fear. He determined to make his weak point his strongest asset. He joined a debating society. He attended every meeting in London where there was to be a public discussion, and he always arose and took part in the debate. By throwing his heart into the cause of socialism, and by going out and speaking for that cause, George Bernard Shaw transformed himself into one of the most confident and brilliant speakers of the first half of the twentieth century.

Opportunities to speak are on all sides. Join organizations and volunteer for offices that will require you to speak. Stand up and assert yourself at public meetings, if only to second a motion. Don't take a back seat at departmental meetings. Speak up! Teach a Sunday School class. Become a Scout leader. Join any group where you will have an opportunity to participate actively in the meetings. You have but to look around you to see that there is scarcely a single business, community, political, professional, or even neighborhood activity that does not challenge you to step forward and speak up. You will never know what progress you can make unless you speak, and speak, and speak again.

"I know all about that," a young business executive once said to me, "but I hesitate to face the ordeal of learning."

"Ordeal!" I replied. "Put that thought out of your mind. You've never thought of learning in the right—the conquering—spirit."

"What spirit is that?" he asked.

"The spirit of adventure," I told him, and I talked to him a little about a path to success, through public speaking, and the warming up, the unfolding, of one's personality.

"I'll give it a try," he finally said. "I'll head into this adventure."

As you read on in this book, and as you put its principles into practice, you, too, will be heading into adventure. You will find it is an adventure in which your power of self-direction and your vision will sustain you. You will find it is an adventure that can change you, inside and out.

Don't wait for a huge platform before you give your best performance.

—Bernard Kelvin Clive

~

Act enthusiastic and you will be enthusiastic.

—Dale Carnegie

2

Develop Confidence

"Five years ago, Mr. Carnegie, I came to the hotel where you were conducting one of your demonstrations. I walked up to the door of the meeting room and then stopped. I knew if I entered that room and joined a class, sooner or later, I'd have to make a speech. My hand froze on the doorknob. I couldn't go in. I turned my back and walked out of the hotel.

"If I had only known then how you make it easy to conquer fear, the paralyzing fear of an audience, I wouldn't have lost these past five years."

The man who spoke these revealing words wasn't talking across a table or a desk. He was directing his remarks to an audience of some two hundred people. It was the graduation session of one of my courses in New York City. As he gave his talk, I was particularly impressed by his poise and self-assurance. Here was a man, I thought, whose executive skills will be tremendously increased by his newly acquired expressiveness and confidence. As his instructor, I was delighted to see that he had dealt a death blow to fear, and I couldn't help thinking how much more successful, and what is more, how much happier this man would have been if his victory over fear had come five or ten years before.

Emerson said, "Fear defeats more people than any other thing in the world." Oh, how I have been made aware of the bitter truth of that statement. And how grateful I am that during my life I have been able to rescue people from fear. When I started to teach my course in 1912, little did I realize that this training would prove to be one of the best methods ever devised to help people eliminate their fears and feelings of inferiority. I found that learning to speak in public is nature's own method of overcoming self-consciousness and building up courage and self-confidence. Why? Because speaking in public makes us come to grips with our fears.

In years of training men and women to speak in public, I have picked up some ideas to help you quickly overcome stage fright and develop confidence in a few short weeks of practice.

FIRST

Get The Facts About Fear Of Speaking In Public

You are not unique in your fear of speaking in public. Surveys in colleges indicate that eighty to ninety per cent of all students enrolled in speech classes suffer from stage fright at the beginning of the course. I am inclined to believe that the figure is higher among adults at the start of my course, almost one hundred per cent.

A certain amount of stage fright is useful! It is nature's way of preparing us to meet unusual challenges in our environment. So, when you notice your pulse beating faster and your respiration speeding up, don't become alarmed. Your body, ever alert to external stimuli, is getting ready to go into action. If these physiological preparations are held within limits, you will be capable of thinking faster, talking more fluently, and generally speaking with greater intensity than under normal circumstances.

Many professional speakers have assured me that they never completely lose all stage fright. It is almost always present just before they speak, and it may persist through the first few sentences of their talk. This is the price these men and women pay for being like race horses and not like draft horses. Speakers who say they are "cool as a cucumber" at all times are usually as thick-skinned as a cucumber and about as inspiring as a cucumber.

The chief cause of your fear of public speaking is simply that you are unaccustomed to speak in public. For most people, public speaking is an unknown quantity, and consequently one fraught with anxiety and fear factors. For the beginner, it is a complex series of strange situations, more involved than, say, learning to play tennis or drive a car. To make this fearful situation simple and easy: practice, practice, practice. You will find, as thousands upon thousands have, that public speaking can be made a joy instead of an agony, merely, by getting a record of successful speaking experiences behind you.

The story of how Albert Edward Wiggam, the prominent lecturer and popular psychologist, overcame his fear, has been an inspiration to me ever since I first read it. He tells how terror-struck he was at the thought of standing up in high school and delivering a five-minute declamation.

"As the day approached," he writes, "I became positively ill. Whenever the dreadful thought occurred to me, my whole head would flush with blood and my cheeks would burn so painfully that I would go out behind the school building and press them against the cold brick wall to try to reduce their surging blushes. It was the same way with me in college.

"On one occasion, I carefully memorized a declamation beginning, 'Adam and Jefferson are no more.' When I faced the audience, my head was swimming, so I scarcely knew where I was. I managed to gasp out the opening sentence, stating that 'Adam and Jefferson have passed away.' I couldn't say another word, so I bowed...and walked solemnly back to my seat amid great applause. The president got up and said, 'Well, Edward, we are shocked to hear the sad news, but we will do our best to bear up under the circumstances.' During the uproarious laughter that followed, death would surely have been a welcome relief. I was ill for days afterward.

"Certainly, the last thing on earth I ever expected to become was a public speaker."

A year after he left college, Albert Wiggam was in Denver. The political campaign of 1896 was raging over the issue of Free Silver. One day he read a pamphlet explaining the proposals of the Free Silverites; he became so incensed over what he considered the errors and hollow promises of Bryan and his followers, that he pawned his watch for enough money to get back to his native Indiana. Once there, he offered his services to speak on the subject of sound money. Many of his old school friends were in the audience. "As I began," he writes, "the picture of my Adam and Jefferson speech in college swept over me. I choked and stammered and all seemed to be lost. But, as Chauncey Depew often said, both the audience and I managed somehow to live through the introduction; and encouraged by this tiny success, I went on talking for what I thought was about fifteen minutes. To my amazement, I discovered I had been talking an hour and a half.

"As a result, within the next few years, I was the most surprised person in the world to find myself making my living as a professional public speaker.

"I knew at first hand what William James meant by the habit of success."

Yes, Albert Edward Wiggam learned that one of the surest ways of overcoming the devastating fear of speaking before groups is to get a record of successful experiences behind you.

You should expect a certain amount of fear as a natural adjunct of your desire to speak in public, and you should learn to depend on a limited amount of stage fright to help make you give a better talk.

If stage fright gets out of hand and seriously curtails your effectiveness by causing mental blocks, lack of fluency, uncontrollable tics, and excessive muscular spasm, you should not despair. These symptoms are not unusual in beginners. If you make the effort, you will find the degree of stage fright soon reduced to the point where it will prove a help and not a hindrance.

SECOND

Prepare In The Proper Way

The principal speaker at a New York Rotary Club luncheon several years ago was a prominent government official. We were looking forward to hearing him describe the activities of his department.

It was obvious almost at once that he had not planned his speech. At first he tried to talk impromptu. Failing in that attempt, he pulled out of his pocket a sheaf of notes which evidently had no more order than a flatcar full of scrap iron. He fumbled awhile with these, all the time becoming more embarrassed and inept in his delivery. Minute by minute he became more helpless, more bewildered. But he kept on floundering, apologizing, trying to make some semblance of sense out of his notes and raising a glass of water with a trembling hand to his parched lips. He was a sad picture of a man completely overcome by fright, due to almost total lack of preparation. He finally sat down, one of the most humiliated speakers I have ever seen. He made his talk as Rousseau says a love letter should be written: he began without knowing what he was going to say, and finished without knowing what he had said.

Since 1912, it has been my professional duty to evaluate over five thousand talks a year. From that experience, one great lesson stands out like Mount Everest, towering above all the others: *only the prepared speaker deserves to be confident.* How can anyone ever hope to storm the fortress of fear if he goes into battle with defective weapons, or with no ammunition at all? "I believe," said Lincoln, "that I shall never be old enough to speak without embarrassment when I have nothing to say."

If you want to develop confidence, why not do the one thing that will give you security as a speaker? "Perfect love," wrote the Apostle John, "casteth out fear." So does perfect preparation. Daniel Webster said he would as soon think of appearing before an audience half-clothed as half-prepared.

Never memorize word for word: By "perfect preparation" do I mean that you should memorize your talk? To this question I give back a thunderous NO. In their attempts to protect their egos from the dangers of drawing a mental blank before an audience, many speakers fall headlong into the trap of memorization. Once a victim of this type of mental dope addiction, the speaker is hopelessly bound to a time-consuming method of preparation that destroys effectiveness on the platform.

When H.V. Kaltenborn, the dean of American news commentators, was a student at Harvard University, he took part in a speech contest. He selected a short story entitled "Gentlemen, the King." He memorized it word for word and rehearsed it hundreds of times. The day of the contest he announced the title, "Gentlemen, the King." Then his mind went blank. It not only went blank; it went black. He was terrified. In desperation he started telling the story in his own words. He was the most surprised boy in the hall when the judges gave him first prize. From that day to this, H. V. Kaltenborn has never read nor memorized a speech. That has been the secret of success in his broadcasting career. He makes a few notes and talks naturally to his listeners without a script.

The man who writes out and memorizes his talks is wasting his time and energy, and courting disaster. All our lives we have been speaking spontaneously. We haven't been thinking of words. We have been thinking of ideas. If our ideas are clear, the words come as naturally and unconsciously as the air we breathe.

Even Winston Churchill had to learn that lesson the hard way. As a young man, Churchill wrote out and memorized his speeches. Then one day, while delivering a memorized talk before the British Parliament, he stopped dead in his mental tracks. His mind went blank. He was embarrassed, humiliated! He began his last sentence all over again. Again his mind went blank and his face scarlet. He sat down. From that day to this, Winston Churchill has never attempted to deliver a memorized talk.

If we memorize our talk word for word, we will probably forget it when we face our listeners. Even if we do not forget our memorized talk, we will probably deliver it in a mechanical way. Why? Because it will not come from our hearts, but from our memories. When talking with people privately, we always think of something we want to say, and then we go ahead and say it without thinking of words. We have been doing that all our lives. Why attempt to change it now? If we do write out and memorize our talks, we may have the same experience that Vance Bushnell had.

Vance was a graduate of the Beaux Arts School in Paris, and later became vice president of one of the largest insurance companies in the world—the Equitable Lite Assurance Society. Years ago, he was asked to address a conference of two thousand Equitable Life representatives from all over America at a meeting in White Sulphur Springs, West Virginia. At that time, he had been in the life insurance business for only two years, but he had been highly successful, so he was scheduled to make a twenty-minute talk.

Vance was delighted to do so. He felt it would give him prestige. But, unfortunately, he wrote out and memorized his talk. He rehearsed forty times in front of a mirror. He had everything down pat: every phrase, every gesture, every facial expression. It was flawless, he thought.

However, when he stood up to deliver his address, he was terrified. He said: "My part in this program is...." His mind went blank. In his confusion, he took two steps backward and tried to start all over again. Again, his mind went blank. Again he took two steps back and tried to start. He repeated this performance three times. The platform was four feet high; there was no railing at the back; and there was a space five feet wide between the back of the platform and the wall. So, the fourth time he stepped back, he toppled backwards off the platform and disappeared into space. The audience howled with laughter. One man fell off his chair and rolled in the aisle. Never before nor since in the history of the Equitable Life Assurance Society has anyone ever given such a comic performance. The astonishing part of the story is that the audience thought it was really an act. The old-timers of the Equitable Life are still talking about his performance.

But what about the speaker, Vance Bushnell? Vance Bushnell himself told me it was the most embarrassing occasion of his life. He felt so disgraced that he wrote out his resignation.

Vance Bushnell's superiors persuaded him to tear up his resignation. They restored his self-confidence; and Vance Bushnell, in later years, became one of the most effective speakers in his organization. But he never memorized a talk again. Let us profit by his experience.

I have heard countless scores of men and women try to deliver memorized talks, but I don't remember even one speaker who wouldn't have been more alive, more effective, more human, if he had tossed his memorized talk into the waste basket. If he had done that, he might have forgotten some of his points. He might have rambled, but at least he would have been human.

Abraham Lincoln once said: "I don't like to hear a cut-and-dried sermon. When I hear a man preach, I like to see him act as if he were fighting bees." Lincoln said he wanted to hear a speaker cut loose and get excited. No speaker ever acts as if he were fighting bees when he is trying to recall memorized words.

Assemble And Arrange Your Ideas Beforehand: What, then, is the proper method of preparing a talk? Simply this: search your background for significant experiences that have taught you something about life, and assemble *your* thoughts, *your* ideas, *your* convictions, that have welled up from these experiences. True preparation means brooding over your topics. As Dr. Charles Reynold Brown said some years ago in a memorable series of lectures at Yale University: "Brood over your topic until it becomes mellow and expansive...then put all these ideas down in writing, just a few words, enough to fix the idea...put them down on scraps of paper—you will find it easier to arrange and organize these loose bits when you come to set your material in order." This doesn't sound like such a difficult program, does it? It isn't. It just requires a little concentration and thinking to a purpose.

Rehearse Your Talk: Should you rehearse your talk after you have it in some kind of order? By all means. Here is a sure-fire method that is easy and effective. Use the ideas you have selected for your talk in everyday conversation with your friends and business associates. Instead of going over the ball scores, just lean across the luncheon table and say something like this: "You know, Joe, I had an unusual experience one day. I'd like to tell you about it." Joe will probably be happy to listen to your story. Watch him for his reactions. Listen to his response. He may have an interesting idea that may be valuable. He won't know that you are rehearsing your talk, and it really doesn't matter. But he probably will say that he enjoyed the conversation.

Allan Nevins, the distinguished historian, gives similar advice to writers: "Catch a friend who is interested in the subject and talk out what you have learned at length. In this way you discover facts of interpretation that you might have missed, points of arguments that had been unrealized, and the form most suitable for the story you have to tell."

THIRD

Predetermine Your Mind To Success

In the first chapter, you remember, this sentence was used in reference to building the right attitude toward public speaking training in general. The same rule applies to the specific task, now, facing you, that of making each opportunity to speak a successful experience. There are three ways to accomplish this:

Lose Yourself In Your Subject: After you have selected your subject, arranged it according to plan, and rehearse it by "talking it out" with your friends, your preparation is not ended. You must sell yourself on the importance of your subject. You must have the attitude that has inspired all the truly great personages of history—a belief in your cause. How do you fan the fires of faith in your message? By exploring all phases of your subject, grasping its deeper meanings, and asking yourself how your talk will help the audience to be better people for having listened to you.

Keep Your Attention Off Negative Stimuli: For instance, thinking of yourself making errors of grammar or suddenly coming to an end of your talk somewhere in the middle of it is certainly a negative projection that could cancel confidence before you started. It is especially important to keep your attention off yourself just before your turn to speak. Concentrate on what the other speakers are saying, give them your wholehearted attention and you will not be able to work up excessive stage fright.

Give Yourself A Pep Talk: Unless he is consumed by some great cause to which he has dedicated his life, every speaker will experience moments of doubt about his subject matter. He will ask himself whether the topic is the right one for him, whether the audience will be interested in it. He will be sorely tempted to change his subject. At times like these, when negativism is most likely to tear down self-confidence completely, you should give yourself a pep talk. In clear, straightforward terms, tell yourself that your talk is the right one for you, because it comes out of your experience, out of your thinking about life. Say to yourself that you are more qualified than any member of the audience to give this particular talk and, by George, you are going to do your best to put it across. Is this old-fashioned teaching? It may be, but modern experimental psychologists now agree that motivation based on autosuggestion is one of the strongest incentives to rapid learning, even when simulated. How much more powerful, then, will be the effect of a sincere pep talk based on the truth?

FOURTH
Act Confident

The most famous psychologist that America has produced, Professor William James, wrote as follows: "Action seems to follow feeling, but really action and feeling go together; and by regulating the action, which is under the direct control of the will, we can indirectly regulate the feeling, which is not.

"Thus the sovereign voluntary path to cheerfulness, if our spontaneous cheerfulness be lost, is to sit up cheerfully and to act and speak as if cheerfulness were already there. If such conduct does not make you feel cheerful, nothing else on that occasion can.

"So, to feel brave, act as if you were brave, use all of your will to that end, and a courage fit will very likely replace the fit of fear."

Apply Professor James' advice. To develop courage when you are facing an audience, act as if you already had it. Of course, unless you are prepared, all the acting in the world will avail but little. But granted that you know what you are going to talk about, step out briskly and take a deep breath. In fact, breathe deeply for thirty seconds before you ever face your audience. The increased supply of oxygen will buoy you up and give you courage. The great tenor, Jean de Reszke, used to say that when you had your breath so you "could sit on it", nervousness vanished.

Draw yourself up to your full height and look your audience straight in the eyes, and begin to talk as confidently as if every one of them owed you money. Imagine that they do. Imagine that they have assembled there to beg you for an extension of credit. The psychological effect on you will be beneficial.

If you doubt that this philosophy makes sense, take the word of an American who will always be a symbol of courage. Once he was the most timorous of men; by practicing self-assurance, he became one of the boldest; he was the trust-busting, audience-swaying, Big-Stick-wielding President of the United States, Theodore Roosevelt.

"Having been a rather sickly and awkward boy," he confesses in his autobiography, "I was, as a young man, at the first both nervous and distrustful of my powers. I had to train myself painfully and laboriously not merely as regards my body but as regards my soul and spirit."

Fortunately, he has disclosed how he achieved the transformation. "When a boy," he wrote, "I read a passage in one of Marryat's books which always impressed me. In this passage, the captain of some small British man-of-war is explaining to the hero how to acquire the quality of fearlessness. He says that at the outset almost every man is frightened when he goes into action, but that the course to follow is for the man to keep such a grip on himself that he can act just as if he were not frightened. After this is kept up long enough, it changes from pretense to reality, and the man does in very fact become fearless by sheer dint of practicing fearlessness when he does not feel it.

"This was the theory upon which I went. There were all kinds of things of which I was afraid at first, ranging from grizzly bears to mean horses and gunfighters; but by acting as if I were not afraid I gradually ceased to be afraid. Most men can have the same experience if they choose."

Overcoming fear of public speaking has a tremendous transfer value to everything that we do. Those who answer this challenge find that they are better persons because of it. They find that their victory over fear of talking before groups has taken them out of themselves into a richer and fuller life.

A salesman wrote: "After a few times on my feet before the class, I felt that I could tackle anyone. One morning I walked up to the door of a particularly tough purchasing agent, and before he could say 'no,' I had my samples spread out on his desk, and he gave me one of the biggest orders I have ever received."

A housewife told one of our representatives: "I was afraid to invite the neighbors in for fear that I wouldn't be able to keep the conversation going. After taking a few sessions and getting up on my feet, I took the plunge and held my first party. It was a great success. I had no trouble stimulating the group along interesting lines of talk."

At a graduating class, a clerk said: "I was afraid of the customers, I gave them a feeling that I was apologetic. After speaking to the class a few times, I found that I was speaking up with more assurance and poise, I began to answer objections with authoritativeness. My sales went up forty-five per cent the first month after I started to speak to this class."

They discovered that it was easy to conquer other fears and anxieties and to be successful where before they may have failed. You, too, will be able to meet the problems and conflicts of life with a new sense of mastery. What has been a series of insoluble situations can become a bright challenge to increased pleasure in living.

> *To be yourself in a world that is constantly trying to make you something else is the greatest accomplishment.*
>
> —Ralph Waldo Emerson

3

Speak Effectively, The Quick And Easy Way

I seldom watch television in the daytime. But a friend recently asked me to listen to an afternoon show that was directed primarily to housewives. It enjoyed a very high rating, and my friend wanted me to listen because he thought the audience-participation part of the show would interest me. It certainly did. I watched it several times, fascinated by the way the master of ceremonies succeeded in getting people in the audience to make talks in a way that caught and held my attention. These people were obviously not professional speakers. They had never been trained in the art of communication. Some of them used poor grammar and mispronounced words. But all of them were interesting. When they started to talk they seemed to lose all fear of being on camera and they held the attention of the audience.

Why was this? I know the answer because I have been employing the techniques used in this program for many years. These people, plain, ordinary men and women, were holding the attention of viewers all over the country; they were talking about themselves, about their most embarrassing moments, their most pleasant memory, or how they met their wives or husbands. They were not thinking of introduction, body, and conclusion. They were not concerned with their diction or their sentence structure. Yet, they were getting the final seal of approval from the audience—complete attention in what they had to say. This is dramatic proof of what to me is the first of three cardinal rules for a quick and easy way to learn to speak in public:

FIRST

Speak About Something You Have Earned The Right To Talk About Through Experience Or Study

The men and women whose live flesh-and-blood stories made that television program interesting were talking from their own personal experience. They were talking about something they knew. Consider what a dull program would have resulted if they had been asked to define communism or to describe the organizational structure of the United Nations. Yet, that is precisely the mistake that countless speakers make at countless meetings and banquets. They decide they must talk about subjects of which they have little or no personal knowledge and to which they have devoted little or no attention. They pick a subject like Patriotism, or Democracy, or Justice, and then, after a few hours of frantic searching through a book of quotations or a speaker's handbook for all occasions, they hurriedly throw together some generalizations vaguely remembered from a political science course they once took in college, and proceed to give a talk distinguished for nothing other than its length. It never occurs to these speakers that the audience might be interested in factual material bringing these high-flown concepts down to earth.

At an area meeting of Dale Carnegie instructors in the Conrad Hilton Hotel in Chicago some years ago, a student speaker started like this: "Liberty, Equality, Fraternity. These are the mightiest ideas in the dictionary of mankind. Without liberty, life is not worth living. Imagine what existence would be like if your freedom of action would be restricted on all sides."

That is as far as he got, because he was wisely stopped by the instructor, who then asked him why he believed what he was saying. He was asked whether he had any proof or personal experience to back up what he had just told us. Then, he gave us an amazing story.

He had been a French underground fighter. He told us of the indignities he and his family suffered under Nazi rule. He described in vivid language how he escaped from the secret police and how he finally made his way to America. He ended by saying: "When I walked down Michigan Avenue to this hotel today, I was free to come or go, as I wished. I passed a policeman and he took no notice of me. I walked into this hotel without having to present an identification card, and when this meeting is over, I can go anywhere in Chicago I choose to go. Believe me, freedom is worth fighting for." He received a standing ovation from that audience.

TELL US WHAT LIFE HAS TAUGHT YOU

Speakers who talk about what life has taught them never fail to keep the attention of their listeners. I know from experience that speakers are not easily persuaded to accept this point of view—they avoid using personal experiences as too trivial and too restrictive. They would rather soar into the realms of general ideas and philosophical principles, where unfortunately the air is too rarefied for ordinary mortals to breathe. They give us editorials when we are hungry for the news. None of us is averse to listening to editorials, when they are given by a man who has earned the right to editorialize—an editor or publisher of a newspaper. The point, though, is this: Speak on what life has taught you and I will be your devoted listener. It was said of Emerson that he was always willing to listen to any man, no matter how humble his station, because he felt he could learn something from every man he met. I have listened to more adult talks, perhaps, than any other man west of the Iron Curtain, and I can truthfully say that I have never heard a boring talk when the speaker related what life had taught him, no matter how slight or trivial the lesson may have been.

To illustrate: Some years ago, one of our instructors conducted a course in public speaking for the senior officers of New York City banks. Naturally, the members of such a group, having many demands upon their time, frequently found it difficult to prepare adequately, or to do what they conceived of as preparing. All their lives they had been thinking their own individual thoughts, nurturing their own personal convictions, seeing things from their own distinctive angles, living their own original experiences. They had spent forty years storing up material for talks. But it was hard for some of them to realize that.

One Friday, a certain gentleman connected with an uptown bank—for our purposes we shall designate him as Mr. Jackson—found four-thirty had arrived, and what was he to talk about? He walked out of his office, bought a copy of *Forbes Magazine* at a newsstand, and in the subway coming down to the Federal Reserve Bank where the class met, he read an article entitled, "You Have Only Ten Years to Succeed." He read it, not because he was interested in the article especially, but because he had to speak on something to fill his quota of time.

An hour later, he stood up and attempted to talk convincingly and interestingly on the contents of this article.

What was the result, the inevitable result?

He had not digested, had not assimilated what he was trying to say. "Trying to say"—that expresses it precisely. He was *trying.* There was no real message in him seeking for an outlet; and his whole manner and tone revealed it unmistakably. How could he expect the audience to be any more impressed than he himself was? He kept referring to the article, saying the author said so and so. There was a surfeit of *Forbes Magazine* in it, but regrettably little of Mr. Jackson.

After he finished his talk, the instructor said, "Mr. Jackson, we are not interested in this shadowy personality who wrote that article. He is not here. We can't see him. But we are interested in you and your ideas. Tell us what you think, personally, not what somebody else said. Put more of Mr. Jackson in this. Would you take this same subject next week? Read this article again, and ask yourself whether you agree with the author or not. If you do, illustrate the points of agreement with observations from your own experience. If you don't agree with him, tell us why. Let this article be the starting point from which to launch your own talk."

Mr. Jackson reread the article and concluded that he did not agree with the author at all. He searched his memory for examples to prove his points of disagreement. He developed and expanded his ideas with details from his own experience as a bank executive. He came back the next week and gave a talk that was full of his own convictions, based on his own background. Instead of a warmed-over magazine article, he gave us ore from his own mine, currency coined in his own mint. I leave it to you to decide which talk made a stronger impact on the class.

LOOK FOR TOPICS IN YOUR BACKGROUND

Once a group of our instructors were asked to write on a slip of paper what they considered was the biggest problem they had with beginning speakers. When the slips were tallied, it was found that "getting beginners to talk on the right topic" was the problem most frequently encountered in early sessions of my course.

What is the right topic? You can be sure you have the right topic for you if you have lived with it, made it your own through experience and reflection. How do you find topics? By dipping into your memory and searching your background for those significant aspects of your life that made a vivid impression on you. Several years ago, we made a survey of topics that held the attention of listeners in our classes. We found that the topics most approved by the audience were concerned with certain fairly defined areas of one's background:

Early Years And Upbringing: Topics that deal with the family, childhood memories, school days, invariably get attention, because most of us are interested in the way other people met and overcame obstacles in the environment in which they were reared.

Whenever possible, work into your talks, illustrations and examples from your early years. The popularity of plays, movies, and stories that deal with the subject of meeting the challenges of the world in one's early years attests to the value of this area for subject matter of talks. But how can you be sure anyone will be interested in what happened to you when you were young? There's one test. If something stands out vividly in your memory after many years have gone by, that almost guarantees that it will be of interest to an audience.

Early Struggles To Get Ahead: This is an area rich in human interest. Here again, the attention of a group can be held by recounting your first attempts to make your mark on the world. How did you get into a particular job or profession? What twist of circumstances accounted for your career? Tell us about your setbacks, your hopes, your triumphs when you were establishing yourself in the competitive world. A real-life picture of almost anyone's life—if told modestly—is almost surefire material.

Hobbies And Recreation: Topics in this area are based on personal choice and, as such, are subjects that command attention. You can't go wrong talking about something you do out of sheer enjoyment. Your natural enthusiasm for your particular hobby will help get this topic across to any audience.

Special Areas Of Knowledge: Many years of working in the same field have made you an expert in your line of endeavor. You can be certain of respectful attention if you discuss aspects of your job or profession based on years of experience or study.

Unusual Experiences: Have you ever met a great man? Were you under fire during the war? Have you gone through a spiritual crisis in your life? These are experiences that make the best kind of speech material.

Beliefs And Convictions: Perhaps you have given a great deal of time and effort to thinking about your position on vital subjects confronting the world today. If you have devoted many hours to the study of issues of importance, you have earned the right to talk about them. But when you do, be certain that you give specific instances for your convictions.

Audiences do not relish a talk filled with generalizations. Please don't consider the casual reading of a few newspaper articles sufficient preparation to talk on these topics. If you know little more about a subject than the people in your audience, it is best to avoid it. On the other hand, if you have devoted years of study to some subject, it is undoubtedly a topic that is made to order for you. By all means, use it.

~

As was pointed out in Chapter Two, the preparation of a talk does not consist merely in getting some mechanical words down on paper, or in memorizing a series of phrases. It does not consist in lifting ideas secondhand from some hastily read book or newspaper article. But it does consist in digging deep into your mind and heart and bringing forth some of the essential convictions that life has stored there. Never doubt that the material is there. It is! Rich stores of it, waiting for you to discover it. Do not spurn such material as too personal, too slight for an audience to hear. I have been highly entertained and deeply moved by such talks, more entertained and more moved than I have been by many professional speakers.

Only by talking about something you have earned the right to talk about will you be able to fulfill the second requirement for learning to speak in public quickly and easily. Here it is:

SECOND

Be Sure You Are Excited About Your Subject

Not all topics that you and I have earned the right to talk about make us excited. For instance, as a do-it-yourself devotee, I certainly am qualified to talk about washing dishes. But somehow or other I can't get excited about this topic. As a matter of fact, I would rather forget about it altogether. Yet I have heard housewives—household executives, that is—give superb talks about this same subject. They have somehow aroused within themselves such a fury of indignation about the eternal task of washing dishes, or they have developed such ingenious methods of getting around this disagreeable chore, that they have become really excited about it. As a consequence, they have been able to talk effectively about this subject of washing dishes. Here is a question that will help you determine the suitability of topics you feel qualified to discuss in public: if someone stood up and directly opposed your point of view, would you be impelled to speak with conviction and earnestness in defense of your position? If you would, you have the right subject for you.

Recently, I came across some notes I had written in 1926 after I had visited the Seventh Session of the League of Nations in Geneva, Switzerland. Here is a paragraph: "After three or four lifeless speakers read their manuscripts, Sir George Foster of Canada took the floor. With immense satisfaction I noted that he had no papers or notes of any kind. He gestured almost constantly. His heart was in what he was saying. He had something he very much wanted to get across. The fact that he was earnestly trying to convey to the audience certain convictions that he cherished in his own heart was as plain as Lake Geneva outside the windows. Principles I have been advocating in my teaching were beautifully illustrated in that talk."

I often recall that speech by Sir George. He was sincere; he was earnest. Only by choosing topics which are felt by the heart as well as thought out by the mind will this sincerity be made manifest. Bishop Fulton J. Sheen, one of America's most dynamic speakers, learned this lesson early in life.

"I was chosen for the debating team in college," he wrote in his book, *Life Is Worth Living,* "and the night before the Notre Dame debate, our professor of debating called me to his office and scolded me."

"'You are absolutely rotten. We have never had anybody in the history of this college who was a worse speaker than yourself.'"

"'Well,' I said, trying to justify myself, 'if I am so rotten, why did you pick me for the team?'

"'Because,' he answered, 'you can think; not because you can talk. Get over in that corner. Take a paragraph of your speech and go through it.' I repeated a paragraph over and over again for an hour, at the end of which he said, 'Do you see any mistake in that?' 'No.' Again an hour and a half, two hours, two and a half hours, at the end of which I was exhausted. He said, 'Do you still not see what is wrong?'

"Being naturally quick, after two hours and a half, I caught on. I said, 'Yes, I am not sincere. I am not myself. I do not talk as if I meant it.'

At this point, Bishop Sheen learned a lesson he always remembered; *he put himself into his talk.* He became excited about his subject matter. Only then the wise professor said, "Now, you are ready to speak!"

When a member of one of our classes says, "I don't get excited about anything, I lead a humdrum sort of life," our instructors are trained to ask him what he does in his spare time. One goes to the movies, another bowls, and another cultivates roses. One man told his instructor that he collected books of matches. As the instructor continued to question him about this unusual hobby, he gradually became animated. Soon he was using gestures as he described the cabinets in which he stored his collection. He told his instructor that he had match books from almost every country in the world. When he became excited about his favorite topic, the instructor stopped him. "Why don't you tell us about this subject? It sounds fascinating to me." He said that he didn't think anyone would be interested! Here was a man who had spent years in pursuit of a hobby that was almost a passion with him; yet, he was negative about its value as a topic to speak about. This instructor assured this man that the only way to gauge the interest value of a subject was to ask yourself how interested you are in it. He talked that night with all the fervor of the true collector, and I heard later that he gained a certain amount of local recognition by going to various luncheon clubs and talking about match book collecting.

This illustration leads directly to the third guiding principle for those who want a quick and easy way to learn to speak in public.

THIRD
Be Eager To Share Your Talk With Your Listeners

There are three factors in every speaking situation: the speaker, the speech or the message, and the audience. The first two rules in this chapter dealt with the interrelationships of the speaker to a speech. Up to this point there is no speaking situation. Only when the speaker relates his talk to a living audience will the speaking situation come to life. The talk may be well prepared; it may concern a topic which the speaker is excited about; but for complete success, another factor must enter into his delivery of the talk. He must make his listeners feel that what he has to say is important to them. He must not only be excited about his topic, but he must be eager to transfer this excitement to his listeners. In every public speaker of note in the history of eloquence, there has been this unmistakable quality of salesmanship, evangelism, call it what you will. The effective speaker earnestly desires his listeners to feel what he feels, to agree with his point of view, to do what he thinks is right for them to do, and to enjoy and relive his experience with him. He is audience-centered and not self-centered. He knows that the success or failure of his talk is not for him to decide—it will be decided in the minds and hearts of his hearers.

I trained a number of men in the New York City Chapter of the American Institute of Banking to speak during a thrift campaign. One of the men in particular wasn't getting across to his audience. The first step in helping that man was to fire up his mind and heart with zeal for his subject. I told him to go off by himself and to think over this subject until he became enthusiastic about it. I asked him to remember that the Probate Court Records in New York show that more than 85 per cent of the people leave nothing at all at death; that only 3.3 per cent leave $10,000 or over. He was to keep constantly in mind that he was not asking people to do him a favor or something that they could not afford to do. He was to say to himself: "I am preparing these people to have meat and bread and clothes and comfort in their old age, and to leave their wives and children secure." He had to remember he was going out to perform a great social service. In short, he had to be a crusader.

He thought over these facts. He burned them into his mind. He aroused his own interest, stirred his own enthusiasm, and came to feel that he, indeed, had a mission. Then when he went out to talk, there was a ring to his words that carried conviction. He sold his listeners on the benefits of thrift because he had an eager desire to help people. He was no longer just a speaker armed with facts; he was a missionary seeking converts to a worthwhile cause.

At one time in my teaching career I relied considerably on the textbook rules of public speaking. In doing this I was merely reflecting some of the bad habits that had been instilled into me by teachers who had not broken away from the stilted mechanics of elocution.

I shall never forget my first lesson in speaking. I was taught to let my arm hang loosely at my side, with the palm turned to the rear, fingers half-closed and thumb touching my leg. I was drilled to bring the arm up in a picturesque curve, to give the wrist a classical turn, and then to unfold the forefinger first, the second finger next, and the little finger last. When the whole aesthetic and ornamental movement had been executed, the arm was to retrace the course of the curve and rest again by the side of the leg. The whole performance was wooden and affected. There was nothing sensible or honest about it.

My instructor made no attempt to get me to put my own individuality into my speaking; no attempt to have me speak like a normal, living human being conversing in an energetic manner with my audience.

Contrast this mechanistic approach to speech training with the three primary rules I have been discussing in this chapter. They are the basis of my entire approach to training in effective speaking. You will come across them again and again in this book.

A speaker should approach his preparation not by what he wants to say, but by what he wants to learn.

—Todd Stocker

~

For better or worse, you must play your own instrument in the orchestra of life.

—Dale Carnegie

PART II

TECHNIQUES OF EFFECTIVE SPEAKING

4

Introducing Speakers, Presenting And Accepting Awards

When you are called upon to speak in public, you may introduce another speaker or make a longer talk to inform, entertain, convince, or persuade. Perhaps you are program chairman of a civic organization or a member of a women's club and you face the task of introducing the main speaker at your next meeting, or perhaps you are looking forward to the time when you will address the local PTA, your sales group, a union meeting, or a political organization. In Chapter Thirteen, I will give you hints on preparing the longer type of talk, and this chapter will help you to prepare a speech of introduction. I shall also give you some valuable hints on presenting and accepting awards.

John Mason Brown, the writer and lecturer, whose lively talks have won audiences everywhere in the country, was speaking one night with the man who was to introduce him to his audience.

"Stop worrying about what you are going to say," the man told Mr. Brown. "Relax. I don't believe in preparing a speech. Nope, preparation's no good. Spoils the charm of the thing;

kills gaiety. I just wait for the inspiration to come to me when I'm on my feet—and it never fails."

These reassuring words let Mr. Brown look forward to a fine introduction, he recalls in his book, *Accustomed As I Am*. But when the man arose to make it, it came out this way:

Gentlemen, may I have your attention, please? We have bad news for you tonight. We wanted to have Isaac F. Marcosson speak to you, but he couldn't come. He's sick. (Applause.) Next, we asked Senator Bledridge to address you...but he was busy. (Applause.) Finally, we tried in vain to get Doctor Lloyd Grogan of Kansas City to come down to speak to you. (Applause.) So, instead, we have—John Mason Brown. (Silence.)

Mr. Brown, recalling this disaster, said only: "At least my friend, that inspirationalist, got my name correctly."

Of course you can see that this man, who was so sure his inspiration would carry him through, couldn't have done much worse if he had tried to do so. His introduction violated every obligation he had both to the speaker whom he was introducing and to the audience which was to hear the speaker. There aren't many of these obligations, but they are important, and it is astonishing how many program chairmen fail to realize this.

The speech of introduction serves the same purpose as a social introduction. It brings the speaker and the audience together, establishes a friendly atmosphere, and creates a bond of interest between them. The man who says, "You don't have to make a speech, all you have to do is introduce the speaker," is guilty of understatement. No speech is more mangled than the speech of introduction, probably, because it is looked upon as unimportant by many chairmen who are entrusted with the duty of preparing and delivering it.

An introduction—that term was fashioned from two Latin words, *intro,* to the inside, and *ducere,* to lead—ought to lead us to the inside of the topic sufficiently to make us want to hear it discussed. It ought to lead us to the inside facts regarding the speaker, facts that demonstrate his fitness for discussing this particular topic. In other words, an introduction ought to "sell" the topic to the audience and it ought to "sell" the speaker. And it ought to do these things in the briefest amount of time possible.

That is what it ought to do. But does it? Nine times out of ten, no—emphatically *no.* Most introductions are poor affairs, feeble and inexcusably inadequate. They do not have to be. If the speaker making the introduction realizes the importance of his task and goes about doing it in the right way he will soon be in demand as a chairman or master of ceremonies.

Here are some suggestions to help you make a well-organized speech of introduction.

FIRST

Thoroughly Prepare What You Are Going To Say

Even though the introductory talk is short, hardly ever exceeding one minute, it demands careful preparation. First, you must gather your facts. These will center around three items: the subject of the speaker's talk, his qualifications to speak on that subject, and his name. Often, a fourth item will become apparent—why the subject chosen by the speaker is of special interest to the audience.

Be certain that you know the correct title of the talk and something about the speaker's development of the subject matter. There is nothing more embarrassing than for the speaker to take exception to the introduction by disclaiming part of it as untrue of his stand on the subject. This can be obviated by making sure you know what the speaker's subject is and refraining from trying to predict what he will say. But, your duty as introducer demands that you give the title of the speaker's talk correctly and point out its relevance to the audience's interests. If at all possible, try to get this information directly from the speaker. If you have to rely on a third party, a program chairman, for instance, try to get the information in writing and check with the speaker just before the meeting.

But perhaps most of your preparation will involve getting the facts on the speaker's qualifications. In some cases you will be able to get an accurate listing from *Who's Who* or a comparable work, if your speaker is nationally or regionally well known. On the local level, you can appeal to the public relations or personnel office of the concern where he works, or in some cases verify your facts by calling a close friend or a member of his family. The main idea is to get your biographical facts correct. People close to your speaker will be glad to furnish you with material.

Of course, too many facts will become boring, especially when one degree implies the speaker's acquisition of lesser degrees. To say that a man received a B.S. and an M.A. degree is superfluous when you indicate that he is a Doctor of Philosophy. Likewise, it is best to indicate the highest and most recent offices a man has held rather than to string out a catalogue of the positions he has held since leaving college. Above all, do not pass over the most distinguished achievements of a man's career instead of the less important.

For example, I heard a well-known speaker—a man who ought to have known better—introduce the Irish poet W. B. Yeats. Yeats was to read his own poetry. Three years prior to that he had been awarded the Nobel Prize in Literature, the highest distinction that can be bestowed upon a man of letters. I am confident that not ten per cent of that particular audience knew of the award or its significance. Both ought, by all means, to have been mentioned. They ought to have been announced even if nothing else were said. But what did the chairman do? He utterly ignored these facts, and wandered off into talking about mythology and Greek poetry.

Above all, be certain of the speaker's name and begin at once to familiarize yourself with its pronunciation. John Mason Brown says that he has been introduced as John Brown Mason and even John Smith Mason. In his delightful essay, "We Have With Us Tonight," Stephen Leacock, the distinguished Canadian humorist, tells of one introduction he received in which the introducer said:

There are many of us who have awaited Mr. Learoyd's coming with the most pleasant anticipations. We seemed from his books to know him already as an old friend. In fact, I do not think I exaggerate when I tell Mr. Learoyd that his name in our city has long been a household word. I have very, very great pleasure in introducing to you—Mr. Learoyd.

The main purpose of your research is to be specific, for only by being specific will the introduction achieve its purpose—to heighten the audience's attention and make it receptive to the speaker's talk. The chairman who comes to a meeting poorly prepared usually comes up with something as vague and soporific as this:

Our speaker is recognized everywhere as an authority on his subject. We are interested in hearing what he has to say on this subject, because he comes from a great distance. It gives me great pleasure to present, let's see now, oh, here it is, Mr. Blank.

By taking a little time to prepare we can avoid the sad impression such an introduction makes upon both speaker and audience.

SECOND

Follow The T-I-S Formula

For most introductions, the T-I-S formula serves as a handy guide in organizing the facts you have collected in your research:

1. T stands for Topic. Start your introduction by giving the exact title of the speaker's talk.
2. I stands for Importance. In this step, you bridge over the area between the topic and the particular interests of the group.
3. S stands for Speaker. Here, you list the speaker's outstanding qualifications, particularly those that relate to his topic. Finally, you give his name, distinctly and clearly.

There is plenty of room in this formula for using your imagination. The introduction need not be cut and dried. Here is an example of an introduction that follows the formula without giving the effect of a formula at all. It was given by a New York City editor, Homer Thorne, when he introduced a New York Telephone Company executive, George Wellbaum, to a group of newspaper men and women:

"Our speaker's topic is 'The Telephone Serves You.'"

It seems to me that one of the world s big mysteries—like love and a horse player's persistence—is the mystery of what happens when you make a telephone call.

Why do you get a wrong number? Why can you sometimes make a call from New York to Chicago quicker than from your own home town to another town just over the hill? Our speaker knows the answers, and all the others to telephone questions. For twenty years it has been his job to digest all sorts of details about the telephone business and to make this business clear to other people. He is a telephone company executive who has earned his title by work.

He will speak to us now about the ways his company serves us. If you are feeling friendly toward the service today, look on him as a patron saint. If you've recently been annoyed by your telephone, let him be a spokesman for the defense.

Ladies and Gentlemen, the vice-president of the New York Telephone Company, Mr. George Wellbaum."

Notice how cleverly the introductory speaker gets the audience thinking about the telephone. By asking questions, he excites their curiosity and then indicates that the speaker will answer these questions and any others the audience may have.

I doubt that this introduction was written out or memorized. Even on paper it sounds conversational and natural. An introduction should never be memorized. Cornelia Otis Skinner was once introduced by a chairman of the evening whose memorized words she forgot as she began. She took a deep breath and then said: "Due to the exorbitant price of Admiral Byrd, we have with us this evening, Miss Cornelia Otis Skinner."

The introduction should be spontaneous, seemingly arising out of the occasion, not strait-laced and severe.

In the introduction of Mr. Wellbaum, quoted above, there are no cliches, such as, 'it gives me great pleasure,' and 'it is a great privilege to introduce to you.' The best way to present a speaker is to give his name or to say, 'I present,' and give his name.

Some chairmen are guilty of talking too long and making the audience restive. Others indulge in flights of oratorical fancy in order to impress the speaker and the audience with a sense of their importance. Still others make the sad error of dragging in "canned jokes," sometimes not in the best taste, or of using humor that patronizes or deprecates the speaker's profession. All of these faults should be avoided by the man who is desirous of achieving the purposes of an effective introduction.

Not many years ago it was a kind of oratorical fashion to over-praise the speaker in the introduction. Bouquets of flowers were heaped upon the speaker by the chairman. The poor speaker was often overwhelmed by the heavy odor of flattery.

A popular humorist, Tom Collins, of Kansas City, Missouri, told Herbert Prochnow, author of *The Toastmaster's Handbook,* that "it is fatal to a speaker who intends to be humorous to promise his audience they soon will be rolling in the aisles with uncontrollable mirth. When a toastmaster begins to mumble about Will Rogers, you know you might just as well cut your wrists and go home, because you are ruined."

On the other hand, don't under-praise either. Stephen Leacock recalls the time he had to respond to introductory remarks that ended in this manner:

> This is the first of our series of lectures for this winter. The last series, as you all know, was not a success. In fact, we came out at the end of the year with a deficit. So this year, we are starting a new line and trying the experiment of cheaper talent. May I present Mr. Leacock.

Mr. Leacock dryly comments: "Judge how it feels to crawl out in front of the audience labelled cheaper talent."

THIRD

Be Enthusiastic

In making an introduction of a speaker, manner is quite as important as matter. You should try to be friendly, and instead of saying how happy you are, be genuinely pleasant making your talk. If you give the introduction with a sense of building to a climax at the end when you announce the speaker's name, the sense of anticipation will be increased and the audience will applaud the speaker more enthusiastically. This display of the audience's good feeling will in turn help to stimulate the speaker to do his best.

When you do pronounce the speaker's name at the very end of the introduction, it is well to remember the words, 'pause', 'part', and 'punch'. By *pause, it* is meant that a little silence just before the name is given will give an edge to anticipation; by *part* is meant that the first and last names should be separated by a slight pause so that the audience gets a clear impression of the speaker's name; by *punch* it meant that the name should be given with vigor and force.

There is one more caution: please, I beg of you, when you do enunciate the speaker's name, don't turn to him, but look out over the audience until the last syllable has been uttered; *then* turn to the speaker. I have seen countless chairmen give fine introductory speeches that were ruined at the end because they turned toward the speaker, pronouncing his name for him alone and leaving the audience in total ignorance of his identity.

FOURTH
Be Warmly Sincere

Be sure to be sincere. Do not indulge in deprecatory remarks or snide humor. A tongue-in-cheek type of introduction is often misinterpreted by some members of the audience. Be warmly sincere, because you are in a social situation that demands the highest kind of finesse and tact. You may be on familiar terms with the speaker, but the audience isn't, and some of your remarks, innocent though they be, may be misconstrued.

FIFTH
Thoroughly Prepare The Talk Of Presentation

"It has been proved that the deepest yearning of the human heart is for recognition—for honor!"

When Margery Wilson, the author, wrote this she expressed a universal feeling. We all want to get along well in life. We want to be appreciated. Someone else's commendation, if it is only a word—let alone a gift presented at a formal affair—lifts the spirit magically.

Althea Gibson, the tennis star, managed to get this "yearning of the human heart" most aptly into the title of her autobiography. She called it, *I Wanted To Be Somebody.*

When we make a speech of presentation, we reassure the recipient that he really is *somebody.* He has succeeded in a certain effort. He is deserving of honor. We have come together to pay him this honor. What we have to say should be brief but we should give it careful thought. It may not mean much to those who are used to receiving honors, but to others less fortunate it may be something to be remembered brightly all the rest of a lifetime.

We, therefore, should give serious consideration to our choice of words in presenting the honor. Here is a time-tested formula:

1. Tell why the award is made. Perhaps it is for long service, or for winning a contest, or for a single notable achievement. Explain this simply.
2. Tell something of the group's interest in the life and activities of the person to be honored.
3. Tell how much the award is deserved and how cordially the group feels toward the recipient.
4. Congratulate the recipient and convey everyone's good wishes for the future.

Nothing is so essential to this little talk as sincerity. Everyone realizes this, perhaps without saying so. So if you have been chosen to make a speech of presentation, you as well as the recipient have been honored. Your associates know you can be trusted with the task that demands a heart as well as a head. This must not tempt you to make certain mistakes that some speakers make. They are mistakes concerned with exaggeration.

At a time such as this, it is easy to exaggerate someone's virtues far beyond their real measure. If the award is deserved, we must say so, but we should not add words of over-praise. Exaggerated praise makes the recipient uncomfortable and it doesn't convince an audience which knows better.

We also should avoid exaggerating the importance of the gift itself. Instead of stressing its intrinsic value, we should emphasize the friendly sentiments of those who are giving it.

SIXTH

Express Your Sincere Feelings In The Talk Of Acceptance

This should be even shorter than the speech of presentation. It certainly shouldn't be anything we have memorized: yet, being ready to make it will be an advantage. If we know we are to be given a present, with a speech of presentation, we shouldn't be at a loss for words of acknowledgment that will be a credit to us.

Just to mumble, "thank you" and "greatest day in my life" and "most wonderful thing that ever happened to me," is not very good. Here, as in the speech of presentation, a danger of exaggeration lurks. "Greatest day" and "most wonderful thing" take in too much territory. You can express heartfelt gratitude better in more moderate terms. Here is a suggested format:

1. Give a warmly sincere "thank you" to the group.
2. Give credit to others who have helped you, your associates, employers, friends, or family.
3. Tell what the gift or award means to you. If it is wrapped, open it and display it. Tell the audience how useful or decorative it is and how you intend to use it.
4. End with another sincere expression of your gratitude.

In this chapter, we have discussed three special types of talks, any one of which you may be called upon to give in the course of your work or your affiliation with some organization or club.

I urge you to follow these suggestions carefully when making any of these talks and you will have the satisfaction that comes from saying the right thing at the right time.

Oratory is the highest form of music.

—Agona Apell

~

Fear doesn't exist anywhere except in the mind.

—Dale Carnegie

5

Organizing The Longer Talk

No sane man would start to build a house without some sort of plan; but why will he begin to deliver a talk without the vaguest notion of what he wishes to accomplish?

A talk is a voyage with a purpose, and it must be charted. The man who starts nowhere, generally gets there.

I wish that I could paint this saying of Napoleon's in flaming letters of red a foot high over every doorway on the globe where students of effective speaking gather: "The art of war is a science in which nothing succeeds which has not been calculated and thought out."

That is just as true of speaking as of shooting. But do speakers realize it—or, if they do, do they always act on it? They do not. Many a talk has just a trifle more plan and arrangement than a bowl of Irish stew.

What is the best and most effective arrangement for a given set of ideas? No one can say until he has studied them. It is always a new problem, an eternal question that every speaker must ask and answer himself again and again. No infallible rules can be given; but we can, at any rate, indicate the three major phases of the longer talk to get action: the attention step, the body, and conclusion. There are some time-tested methods of developing each phase.

FIRST

Get Attention Immediately

I once asked Dr. Lynn Harold Hough, formerly president of Northwestern University, what was the most important fact his long experience as a speaker has taught him. After pondering a moment, he replied, "To get an arresting opening, something that will seize favorable attention immediately." Dr. Hough struck at the heart of the matter of all persuasive speaking: how to get the audience 'tuned in' right from the speaker's first words. Here are some methods which, if applied, will give high attention value to your opening phrases.

BEGIN YOUR TALK WITH AN INCIDENT

Lowell Thomas, who has made a world-wide reputation as a news analyst, lecturer, and motion picture producer, began a talk on Lawrence of Arabia with this statement:

"I was going down Christian Street in Jerusalem one day when I met a man clad in the gorgeous robes of an oriental potentate. At his side hung the curved gold sword worn only by the descendants of the prophet Mohammed..."

And he was off—off with a *story* from *his experience.* That is what hooks attention. That kind of opening is almost foolproof. It can hardly fail. It moves, it marches. We follow because we identify ourselves as part of a situation and we want to know what is going to happen. I know of no more compelling method of opening a talk than by the use of a story. One of my own talks which I have given many times begins with these words:

"Just after I had finished college, I was walking one night down a street in Huron, South Dakota, and I saw a man standing on a box talking to a crowd of people. I was curious, so I became part of the group listening to him. 'Do you know,' the speaker was saying, 'that you never see a bald-headed Indian? Or you never see a bald-headed woman, do you? Now, I'm going to tell you why....'"

No stalling. No 'warm-up' statements. By launching directly into an incident, you can make it easy to capture an audience's attention.

A speaker who begins a talk with a story from his experience is on safe ground, for there is no groping for words, no loss of ideas. The experience he is relating to is his, a re-creation, as it were, of part of his life, the very fiber of his being. The result? A self-assured, relaxed manner which will help a speaker establish himself on a friendly basis with an audience.

AROUSE SUSPENSE

Here is the way Mr. Powell Healy began a talk at the Penn Athletic Club in Philadelphia:

"Eighty-two years ago, there was published in London a little volume, a story, which was destined to become immortal. Many people have called it 'the greatest little book in the world'. When it first appeared, friends meeting one another on the Strand or Pall Mall asked the question, 'Have you read it?' The answer invariably was: 'Yes, God bless him, I have'.

The day it was published, a thousand copies were sold. Within a fortnight, the demand had consumed fifteen thousand. Since then it has run into countless thousands of editions and has been translated into every language under heaven. A few years ago, J.P. Morgan purchased the original manuscript for a fabulous sum and it now reposes among the priceless treasures in his magnificent art gallery. What is this world famous book? It is..."

Are you interested? Are you eager to know more? Has the speaker captured the favorable attention of his listeners? Do you feel this opening has held your attention, heightened your interest as it progressed? Why? Because it aroused your curiosity and held you in suspense.

Curiosity! Who is not susceptible to it?

Perhaps you, too! You are asking just who *is* the author and what is the book mentioned above? To satisfy your curiosity, here is the answer. The author is Charles Dickens, the book: *A Christmas Carol.*

Creating suspense is a sure-fire method of getting your listeners interested. Here is how I try to arouse suspense in my lecture on "How To Stop Worrying And Start Living." I begin like this: "In the spring of 1871, a young man who was destined to become a world-famous physician, William Osier, picked up a book and read twenty-one words that had a profound effect upon his future."

What were the twenty-one words? And how did these words affect his future? These are the questions your listeners will want answered.

STATE AN ARRESTING FACT

Clifford R. Adams, director of the Marriage Counseling Service of the Pennsylvania State College, began an article in *The Reader's Digest,* entitled "How to Pick a Mate," with these startling facts—facts that make you gasp, facts that make an arresting opener:

"Today, the chances that our young people will find happiness through marriage are slim indeed. The rise of our divorce rate is frightening. One marriage in five or six landed on the rocks in 1940. By 1946, it is expected to be one in four. And if long-range trends continue, the rate in fifty years will be one in two."

Here are two other examples of "arresting facts" openers:

"The War Department predicts that, in the first night of an atomic war, twenty million Americans will be killed."

"A few years ago, the Scripps-Howard newspapers spent $176,000 on a survey to discover what customers disliked about retail stores. It was the most costly, the most scientific, the most thorough survey ever made of retail selling problems. Questionnaires were sent into 54,047 homes in sixteen different cities. One of the questions was: 'What do you dislike about the stores in this town?'

"Almost two-fifths of all the answers to that question were the same: Discourteous clerks!"

This method of making startling statements at the beginning of a talk is effective in establishing contact with the listener because it jars the mind. It is a kind of 'shock technique' that enlists attention by using the unexpected to focus attention upon the subject matter of the talk.

One of our class members in Washington, D. C. used this method, arousal of curiosity, as effectively as anyone I have ever heard. Her name, Meg Sheil. Here is her opening:

"I was a prisoner for ten years. Not in an ordinary prison, but in one whose walls were worry about my inferiority and whose bars were the fear of criticism." Don't you want to know more about this true-life episode?

A danger of the startling opener must be avoided, that is, the tendency to be over-dramatic or too sensational. I remember one speaker who started his talk by shooting a pistol into the air. He got attention all right, but he also blasted the eardrums of his listeners.

Make your opening conversational in manner. An efficient way to discover whether you have an opener that is conversational is to try it out across the dinner table. If the way you open your talk isn't conversational enough to be spoken across the dinner table, it probably won't be conversational enough for an audience either.

Frequently, however, the opening of the talk that is supposed to get the listeners' interest is, in reality, the dullest part of the talk. For example, I recently heard a speaker begin like this: "Trust in the Lord and have faith in your own ability...A preachy, obvious way to begin a talk! But note his second sentence; it is interesting; it has heart throb in it. "My mother was left a widow in 1918 with three children to support, and no money..." Why, oh *why*, didn't that speaker begin in his first sentence by telling about the struggles of his widowed mother with three little children to support!

If you want to interest your listeners, don't begin with an introduction. Begin by leaping right into the heart of your story.

That is what Frank Bettger does. He is the author of *How I Raised Myself From Failure To Success In Selling.* He is an artist when it comes to creating suspense in his first sentence. I know, because he and I traveled together all over the United States giving talks on selling under the auspices of the United States Junior Chamber of Commerce. I always admired the superb way he opened his talk on enthusiasm. No preaching. No lecturing. No sermonizing. No general statements. Frank Bettger leaped right into the heart of his subject in his first sentence. He began his talk on enthusiasm like this:

"Shortly after I started out as a professional baseball player, I got one of the biggest shocks of my life."

What effect did this opening have on his audience? I know, I was there. I saw the reaction. He had everyone's attention instantly. Everyone was eager to hear why and how he was shocked, and what he did about it.

ASK FOR A SHOW OF HANDS

A splendid way to get interested attention is to ask the audience to raise their hands in answer to a question. For example, I have opened my talk on "How to Prevent Fatigue" with this question:

"Let's see your hands. How many of you get tired more quickly than you feel you ought to?"

Note this point: When you ask for a show of hands, usually give the audience some warning that you are going to do so. Do not open a talk with: "How many people here believe the income tax should be lowered? Let's see your hands." Give the audience a chance to be ready for the vote by saying, for instance: "I am going to ask for a show of hands on a question of importance to you. This is the question: 'How many of you believe that trading stamps benefit the consumer?'"

The technique of asking for a show of hands gets a priceless reaction known as "audience participation." When you use it, your talk is no longer a one-sided affair. The audience is participating in it now. When you ask, "How many of you get tired more quickly than you feel you ought to?" everyone starts thinking of his favorite topic: himself, his aches, his fatigue. He lifts his hand and possibly looks around to see who else has his hand up. He forgets that he is listening to a talk. He smiles. He nods to a friend sitting next to him. The ice is broken. You, the speaker, are at ease, and so is the audience.

PROMISE TO TELL THE AUDIENCE HOW THEY CAN GET SOMETHING THEY WANT

An almost unfailing way to get alert attention is to promise to tell your listeners how they can get what they want by doing what you suggest. Following are some illustrations of what I mean:

"I am going to tell you how to prevent fatigue. I am going to tell you how to add one hour a day to your waking life."

"I'm going to tell you how you can materially increase your income."

"I promise that, if you will listen to me for ten minutes, I'll tell you one sure way to make yourself more popular."

The "promise" type of opener is sure to get attention because it goes straight to the self-interests of the audience. All too often speakers neglect to tie their topics to the vital interests of their hearers. Instead of opening the door to attention, they slam it shut with dull openings that trace the history of the subject matter or laboriously dwell upon the background necessary to an understanding of the topic.

I remember one talk I heard a few years ago on a topic which, in itself, was important to the audience: the necessity of periodic health examinations. How did the speaker begin his talk? Did he add to the natural attractiveness of his subject by an effective opening? No. He started with a colorless recital of the history of his topic and the audience began to lose interest in him and in his subject. An opening built around the "promise" technique would have been admirably appropriate. For instance:

Do you know how long you are expected to live? Life insurance companies can predict this by means of life expectancy tables which have been compiled from the lives of millions of persons. You can expect to live two-thirds of the time between your present age and eighty.

Now, is this long enough for you to live? No, no! We are all passionately eager to live longer and we want to prove that this prediction is wrong. But how, you ask, can this be done? How can I extend my life beyond the shockingly small number of years statisticians say remain for me? Well, there is an answer, a possible way this can be done, and I shall tell you how to do this...

I leave it to you to decide whether this type of opening captures your interest, if it compels you to listen to the speaker. You *must* listen to him because he not only is talking about you, about your life, but he has promised to tell you something of the most intense personal value to you. No dull recital of impersonal facts here! Such an opening as this is almost impossible to resist.

USE AN EXHIBIT

Perhaps the easiest way in the world to gain attention is to hold up something for people to look at. Almost any creature, from the simplest to the most complex, will give heed to that kind of stimulus. It can be used sometimes with effectiveness before the most dignified audience. For example, Mr. S. S. Ellis, of Philadelphia, opened one of his talks in one of our classes by holding a coin between his thumb and forefinger, and high above his shoulder. Naturally everyone looked. Then he inquired: "Has anyone here ever found a coin like this on the sidewalk? It announces that the fortunate finder will be given a lot free in such and such a real estate development. He has but to call and present this coin". Mr. Ellis then proceeded to condemn the misleading and unethical practices involved.

All of the foregoing methods are commendable. They may be used separately or they may be combined. Recognize that how you open a talk largely determines whether the audience is going to accept you and your message.

SECOND

Avoid Getting Unfavorable Attention

Please, please, I urge you, remember that you must not only capture the attention of your audience, but you must capture their *favorable* attention. Please note that I said *favorable* attention. No rational person would begin a talk by insulting his audience or by making any obnoxious or disagreeable statement that would turn them against him and his message. Yet how frequently speakers begin talks by attracting attention through the use of one of the following devices.

DO NOT OPEN WITH AN APOLOGY

To begin a talk with an apology does not get you off to a good start either. How often we all have heard speakers begin by calling the attention of the audience to their lack of preparation or their lack of ability. If you are not prepared, the audience will probably discover it without your assistance. Why insult your audience by suggesting that you did not think them worth preparing for, that just any old thing you had on the fire was good enough to serve them? No, we don't want to hear apologies; we want to be informed and interested—to be *interested:* remember that. Let your opening sentence capture the interest of your audience. Not the second sentence. Not the third sentence. The *first!*

AVOID THE "FUNNY" STORY OPENING

You may have noticed that there is one method of opening a talk, and one much favored by speakers, that is not recommended here: the so-called "funny" story opening. For some lamentable reason, the novice feels that he ought to "lighten up" his talk by telling a joke; he assumes that the mantel of Mark Twain has descended upon his shoulders. Do not fall into this trap; you will discover to your embarrassment the painful truth that the "funny" story is more often pathetic than funny—and the story may be known to persons in your audience.

A sense of humor, though, is a prized asset for any speaker. A talk need not begin, nor be, heavy-footed, elephantine, and excessively solemn. Not at all. If you have the ability to tickle the risibilities of your audience by some witty reference to a local situation or to something arising out of the occasion or the remarks of a previous speaker, then by all means do so. Observe some incongruity. Exaggerate it. That type of humor is more likely to succeed than stale jokes about Pat and Mike, or mothers-in-law, or shaggy dogs, because it is *relevant* and because it is original.

Perhaps the easiest way to create merriment is to tell a story on yourself. Depict yourself in some ridiculous and embarrassing situation. That gets down to the very essence of humor, Jack Benny has used this device for years. He was one of the first major radio comedians to "poke fun" at himself. By making himself the butt of jokes concerning his ability to play the violin, his miserliness, and his age, Jack Benny works a rich vein of humor that keeps his ratings high from year to year.

Audiences open their hearts, as well as their minds, to speakers who deliberately deflate themselves by calling attention to some deficiency or failing on their part, in a humorous sense, of course. On the other hand, creating the image of the "stuffed shirt" or the visiting expert with all the answers leaves an audience cold and unreceptive.

THIRD
Support Your Main Ideas

In the longer talk to get action you will have several points; the fewer the better, but all of them will require support material. In Chapter Seven we discussed one method of supporting the point of a talk, which is what you want the audience to do, by illustrating it with a story, an experience out of your life. This type of example is popular because it appeals to a basic drive in people, summed up by the slogan, "Everybody Loves a Story." An incident or happening is the kind of example most often used by the average speaker, but it is by no means the only way your point can be supported. You might also use statistics, which are nothing more than illustrations scientifically grouped, expert testimony analogies, exhibits, or demonstrations.

USE STATISTICS

Statistics are used to show the proportion of instances of a certain kind. They can be impressive and convincing, especially as evidence where an isolated example might not do as well. The effectiveness of the Salk antipoliomyelitis vaccine program was measured by statistics gathered in all parts of the country. Isolated cases of ineffectiveness were the exceptions that proved the rule. A talk based on one of these exceptions would not, therefore, convince a parent that the Salk vaccine program would not protect his child.

Statistics, of themselves, can be boring. They should be judiciously used, and when used they should be clothed in a language that makes them vivid and graphic.

Here is an example of how statistics can be impressive by comparing them with things familiar to us. In backing up his point that a vast amount of time is lost by New Yorkers' neglecting to answer telephones promptly an executive said:

Out of each one hundred telephone connections made, seven show a delay of more than a minute before the person called answers. Every day 280,000 minutes are lost in this way. In the course of six months, this minute delay in New York is about equal to all the business days that have elapsed since Columbus discovered America.

Mere numbers and amounts, taken by themselves, are never very impressive. They have to be illustrated; they ought, if possible, to be put in terms of our experiences. I remember listening to a lecture by a guide in the vast power room under Grand Coulee Dam. He could have given us the square-foot figures of the room's size, but that would not have been so convincing as the method he used. He told us that the room was large enough for a crowd of 10,000 people to view a football game on a regulation field and, in addition, there would be room left over for several tennis courts at each end!

Many years ago, a student in my course at the Brooklyn Central YMCA told in a talk the number of houses destroyed by fire during the previous year. He further said that, if these burned buildings had been placed side by side, the line would have reached from New York to Chicago, and that if the people who had been killed in those fires had been placed half a mile apart, that gruesome line would reach back again from Chicago to Brooklyn.

The figures he gave I forgot almost immediately but years have passed, and, without any effort on my part, I can still see that line of burning buildings stretching from Manhattan Island to Cook County, Illinois.

USE THE TESTIMONY OF EXPERTS

Frequently you can effectively back up the points you want to make in the body of your talk by the use of the testimony of an expert. Before using testimony it should be tested by answering these questions:

1. Is the quotation I am about to use accurate?
2. Is it taken from the area of the mans expert knowledge? To quote Joe Louis on economics would obviously be exploiting his name but not his forte.
3. Is the quotation from a man who is known and respected by the audience?
4. Are you sure that the statement is based on firsthand knowledge, not personal interest or prejudice?

USE ANALOGIES

An analogy, according to Webster, is a "relation of likeness between two things... consisting in the resemblance not of the things themselves but of two or more attributes, circumstances, or effects."

The use of an analogy is a fine technique for supporting a main idea. Here is an excerpt from a talk on "The Need for More Electric Power," by C. Girard Davidson when he was Assistant Secretary of the Interior. Note how he employs a comparison, an analogy, to back up his point:

A prosperous economy has to keep moving forward or it goes into a tailspin. There is a parallel with the airplane, which is a useless collection of nuts and bolts standing still on the ground. When moving forward in the air, however, it comes into its own and serves as a useful function. To stay up, it has to keep going forward. If it doesn't move, it sinks—and it can't move backward.

Here is another, perhaps one of the most outstanding analogies in the history of eloquence; it was used by Lincoln in answer to his critics during a crucial period of the Civil War:

Gentlemen, I want you to suppose a case for a moment. Suppose that all the property you were worth was in gold, and you had put it in the hands of Blondin, the famous rope-walker, to carry across the Niagara Falls on a tightrope. Would you shake the rope while he was passing over it, or keep shouting to him, "Blondin, stoop a little more! Go a little faster!" No, I am sure you would not. You would hold your breath as well as your tongue, and keep your hands off until he was safely over. Now the government is in the same situation. It is carrying an immense weight across a stormy ocean. Untold treasures are in its hands. It is doing the best it can. Don't badger it! Just keep still, and it will get you safely over.

USE A DEMONSTRATION WITH OR WITHOUT AN EXHIBIT

When executives of the Iron Fireman firm were talking to dealers, they needed some way of dramatizing the fact that fuel should be fed into a furnace from the bottom rather than from the top. So they hit on this simple but striking demonstration. The speaker lights a candle. Then he says:

See how clearly the flame burns—how tall it is. Since virtually all the fuel is being converted into heat, it gives off practically no smoke.

The fuel of the candle is fed in from below, just as the Iron Fireman feeds fuel into a furnace.

Suppose that this candle was fueled from above, as hand-stoked furnaces are. *(Here the speaker turns the candle upside down.)*

Notice how the flame dies down. Smell the smoke. Hear it sputter. See how red the flame is because of incomplete combustion. And finally the flame goes out, as a result of inefficient fueling from above.

Some years ago, Henry Morton Robinson wrote an interesting article on "How Lawyers Win Cases" for *Your Life* magazine. In it, he describes how a lawyer named Abe Hummer is credited with a telling dramatic demonstration of showmanship while representing an insurance company in a damage suit. The plaintiff, a Mr. Postlerhwaite, stated that as a result of falling down an elevator shaft his shoulder had been so severely injured that he was unable to raise his right arm.

Hummer appeared to be gravely concerned. "Now Mr. Postlethwaite," he said confidently, "show the jury how high you can raise your arm." Gingerly Postlethwaite brought his arm up to ear level. "Now show us how high you could raise it before you were injured," urged Hummer. "as high as this." said the plaintiff, shooting his arm at full length over his head

You may draw your own conclusion regarding the reaction of the jury to this demonstration.

In the longer talk to secure action you might make three, or at most, four points. They could be uttered in less than a minute. To recite them to an audience would be dull and boring. What makes these points come alive? It is the support material you use. This is what gives sparkle and interest to your talk. By the use of incidents, comparisons and demonstrations, you make your main ideas clear and vivid; by the use of statistics and testimony you substantiate the truth and emphasize the importance of your main points.

FOURTH

Appeal For Action

I dropped in to talk a few minutes one day with George F. Johnson, the industrialist and humanitarian. He was President of the great Endicott-Johnson Corporation at the time. More interesting to me, though, was the knowledge that he was a speaker who could make his hearers laugh, and sometimes cry, and often remember for a long time what he said.

He didn't have a private office. He had a corner of a big, busy factory, and his manner was as unpretentious as his old wooden desk.

"You've come at a good time," he said as he stood up to greet me. "I've just got a job out of the way. I've jotted down what I want to say at the end of a talk I'm going to give to the workers tonight."

"It's always a relief to get a talking shape in your mind from beginning to end," I told him.

"Oh, I haven't got it all in mind yet," he said. "Just the general idea and the specific way I want to finish it."

He was not a professional speaker. He never went in for ringing words or fine phrases. From experience, however, he had learned one of the secrets of successful communication. He knew that if a talk is to go over well, it has to have a good ending. He realized that the conclusion of a talk is the part toward which all that precedes it must reasonably move if an audience is to be impressed.

The close is really the most strategic point in a talk, what one says last, the final words left ringing in the ears when one ceases—these are likely to be remembered longest. Unlike Mr. Johnson, beginners seldom appreciate the importance of this; their endings often leave much to be desired.

What are their most common errors? Let us discuss a few and search for remedies.

First, there is the man who finishes with: "That is about all I have to say on the matter, so I guess I shall stop." This speaker usually throws a smoke screen over his inability to end a talk satisfactorily by lamely saying "thank you." That is not an ending. That is a mistake. It reeks of the amateur. That is almost unpardonable. If that is all you have to say, why not round *off* your talk, and promptly take your seat and stop without talking about stopping. Do that, and the inference that that is all you have to say may, with safety and good taste, be left to the discernment of the audience.

Then, there is the speaker who says all he has to say, but he does not know how to stop. I believe it was Josh Billings who advised people to take the bull by the tail instead of the horns, since it would be easier ro let go. This speaker has the bull by the frontal extremities, and wants to part company with him, but try as hard as he will, he can't get near a friendly fence or tree. So he finally thrashes about in a circle, covering the same ground, repeating himself, leaving a bad impression.

The remedy? An ending has to be planned sometime, doesn't it? Is it the part of wisdom to try to do it after you are facing an audience, while you are under the strain and stress of talking, while your mind must be intent on what you are saying? Or does common sense suggest the advisability of doing it quietly, calmly, beforehand?

How do you go about bringing your talk to a climactic close? Here are a few suggestions:

SUMMARIZE

In the longer talk a speaker is very apt to cover so much ground that at the close the listeners are a little hazy about all his main points. However, few speakers realize that. They are misled into assuming that because these points are crystal clear in their own minds, they must be equally lucid to their hearers. Not at all. The speaker has been pondering over his ideas for some time. But his points are all new to the audience; they are flung at the audience like a handful of shot. Some may stick, but most are liable to roll off in confusion. The hearers are liable, in the words of Shakespeare, to "remember a mass of things but nothing distinctly."

Here is a good example. The speaker, a traffic manager for one of Chicago's railways, ends his talk with this summary:

In short, gentlemen, our own back-door yard experience with this block device; the experience in its use in the East, in the West, in the North; the sound operating principles underlying its operation; the actual demonstration in the money saved in one year in wreck prevention—move me most earnestly and unequivocally to recommend its immediate installation on our Southern branch.

You see what he has done? You can see it and feel it without having heard the rest of the talk. He has summed up in a few sentences, in sixty-two words, practically all the points he had made in the entire talk.

Don't you feel that a summary like that helps? If so, make that technique your own.

ASK FOR ACTION

The closing just quoted is also an excellent illustration of the ask-for-action ending. The speaker wanted something done: a block device installed on the Southern branch of his road. He based his request for action on the money it would save, on the wrecks it would prevent. The speaker wanted action, and he got it. This was not a mere practice talk. It was delivered before the board of directors of a railway, and it secured the installation of the block device for which it asked.

In your final words of a talk to secure action the time has come to ask for the order. So ask for it! Tell your audience to join, contribute, vote, write, telephone, buy, boycott, enlist, investigate, acquit, or whatever it is you want them to do. Be sure to obey these caution signs, however:

Ask Them To do Something Specific: Don't say, "Help the Red Cross." That's too general. Say, instead, "Send your enrollment fee of one dollar tonight to the American Red Cross, 125 Smith Street in this city."

Ask The Audience For Some Response That Is Within Their Power To Give: Don't say, "Let us cast our ballot against the Demon Rum." It can't be done. At the moment, we aren't ballotting on the Demon Rum. You could, instead, ask them to join a temperance society or to contribute to some organization which is fighting for prohibition.

Make It As Easy As You Can For Your Audience To Act On Your Appeal: Don't say, "Write your congressman to vote against this bill." Ninety-nine per cent of your listeners won't do it. They are not vitally interested; or it is too much trouble; or they will forget. So make it easy and pleasant to act. How? By writing a letter yourself to your congressman, saying, "We, the undersigned, urge you to vote against Bill No. 74321." Pass the letter around with a fountain pen, and you will probably get a lot of signers—and perhaps lose your fountain pen.

90% of how well the talk will go is determined before the speaker steps on the platform.

—Somers White

~

Only the prepared speaker deserves to be confident.

—Dale Carnegie

6

Applying What You Have Learned

At the fourteenth session of my course I have often heard with pleasure students tell how they used the techniques in this book in their everyday lives. Salesmen point to increased sales, managers to promotions, executives to a widened span of control, all due to the increased skill with which they gave instructions and solved problems using the tools of effective speech.

As N. Richard Diller wrote in *Today's Speech:* "Talk, the type of talk, the amount of talk, and the atmosphere for such talk...can act as the very life blood of an industrial communication system." R. Fred Canaday. in charge of the General Motors Dale Carnegie Course in Effective Leadership, wrote in the same magazine: "One of the basic reasons we at General Motors are interested in speech training is our recognition that every supervisor is a teacher to a greater or lesser degree. From the time he interviews a prospective employee, through the orientation phase of early employment, on through regular assignment and possible promotion, a supervisor is continually called upon to explain, describe, reprimand, inform, instruct, review, and discuss myriads of subjects with each person in his department."

As we proceed up the ladder of oral communication to those areas that come closest to public speaking—discussions, decision-making, problem-solving and policy-formulating conferences—we see again how the skills of effective speaking as taught in this book can be transferred to everyday speech activities. The rules for effective speaking before groups are directly applicable to conference participation and conference leadership.

Organization of the idea to be presented, the choice of the right words to launch it, the earnestness and enthusiasm used in delivering it are elements that will guarantee the idea's life in the final stage of solution. All these elements have been thoroughly discussed in this book. It remains for the reader to apply what he has learned in every conference in which he participates.

Perhaps you are wondering when to begin applying what you have learned in the previous thirteen chapters of this book. You may be surprised if I answer that query by one word: Immediately.

Even though you are not planning to make a speech in public for some time, if at all, I am certain you will find that the principles and techniques in this book are applicable every day. When I say start using these techniques *now,* I mean in the very next speaking situation in which you find yourself.

If you analyze the speaking that you do every day, you will be amazed by the similarity of purpose between your daily speaking and the type of formal communication discussed in these pages.

In Chapter Seven, you were urged to keep in mind one of four general purposes when you speak before groups; you may want to give them information, entertain them, convince them that your position is right, or persuade them to take action of some kind. In public speaking we cry to keep these purposes distinct, both as to the content of the talk and the manner of our delivery.

In daily speaking, these purposes are fluid, merging with one another and constantly changing through the course of the day. At one moment we may be indulging in friendly chit-chat and then suddenly we may be using speech to sell a product or persuade a child to put his spending money in the bank. By applying the techniques described in this book to everyday conversation we can make ourselves more effective, get our ideas across more efficiently, and motivate others with skill and fact.

FIRST

Use Specific Detail In Everyday Conversation

Take just one of these techniques, for instance. Remember in Chapter Four, I appealed to you to put detail in your talk. In that way you make your ideas come alive, in a vivid and graphic way. Of course I was thinking mainly of speaking before groups. But isn't the use of detail just as important in everyday conversation? Just think for a moment of the really interesting conversationalists of your acquaintance. Aren't they the ones who fill their talk with colorful, dramatic details, who have the ability to use picturesque speech?

Before you can begin to develop your conversational skills you must have confidence. So almost all that was said in the first three chapters of this book will be useful in giving you the security to mix with others and to voice your opinions in an informal social group. Once you are eager to express your ideas even on a limited scale, you will begin to search your experience for material that can be converted to conversation. Here a wonderful thing happens—your horizons begin to expand and you see your life take on new meaning.

Housewives, whose interests may have become somewhat restricted, have been most enthusiastic in reporting what happens when they begin to apply their knowledge of speaking techniques to small conversational groups. "I realize that my newly found confidence gave me courage to speak up at social functions," Mrs. R. D. Hart told her classmates in Cincinnati, "and I began taking an interest in current events. Instead of withdrawing from the give and take of the group, I eagerly joined it. Not only that, but everything I did became grist for the conversational mill and I found myself becoming interested in a host of new activities."

To an educator there is nothing new in Mrs. Hart's grateful report. Once the drive to learn and to apply what has been learned is stimulated, it starts a whole train of action and interaction that vivifies the entire personality. A cycle of achievement is set up and, like Mrs. Hart, one gets the feeling of fulfillment, all through putting into practice just one of the principles taught in this book.

Though few of us are professional teachers, all of us use speech to inform others on many occasions during the day. As parents instructing our children, as neighbors explaining a new method of pruning roses, as tourists exchanging ideas on the best route to follow, we constantly find ourselves in conversational situations that require clarity and coherence of thought, vitality and vigor of expression. What was said in Chapter Eight in relation to the talk to inform is applicable in these situations as well.

SECOND
Use Effective Speaking Techniques In Your Job

Now we enter the area of the communicative process as it affects our jobs. As salesmen, managers, clerks, department heads, group leaders, teachers, ministers, nurses, executives, doctors, lawyers, accountants, and engineers, we are all charged with the responsibility of explaining specialized areas of knowledge and giving professional instructions. Our ability to make these instructions in clear, concise language may often be the yardstick used by our superiors in judging our competence. How to think quickly and verbalize adroitly is a skill acquired in presenting speeches of information, but this skill is by no means limited to formal speaking—it can be used every day by every one of us. The need for clarity in business and professional speech today is highlighted by the recent spate of oral communications courses in industry, government, and professional organizations.

THIRD
Seek Opportunities To Speak In Public

In addition to using the principles of this book in everyday speech, where incidentally you will reap the greatest rewards, you should seek every opportunity to speak in public. How do you do this? By joining a club where public speaking of some sort goes on. Don't just be an inactive member, a mere looker-on. Pitch in and help by doing committee work. Most of these jobs go begging. Get to be program chairman. That will give you an opportunity to interview good speakers in your community, and you certainly will be called upon to make speeches of introduction.

As soon as possible, develop a twenty to thirty minute talk. Use the suggestions in this book as a guide. Let your club or organization know that you are prepared to address them. Offer your services to a speaker's bureau in your town. Fund raising campaigns are looking for volunteers to speak for them. They provide you with a speaker's kit which will be of great help in preparing your talk. Many speakers of consequence have begun in this way. Some of them have risen to great prominence. Take Sam Levenson, for example, the radio and TV star and a speaker whose services are sought all over the country. He was a high school teacher in New York. Just as a sideline he began making short talks about what he knew best, his family, relatives, his students, and the unusual aspects of his job. These talks took fire, and he was soon asked to address so many groups it began to interfere with his teaching chores. But, by this time he was a guest on network programs and it wasn't long before Sam Levenson transferred his talents entirely to the entertainment world.

FOURTH
You Must Persist

When we learn any new thing, like French or golf or speaking in public, we never advance steadily. We do not improve gradually. We do it by waves, by abrupt starts and sudden stops. Then we remain stationary a time, or we may even slip back and lose some of the ground we have previously gained. These periods of stagnation, or retrogression, are well known by all psychologists; they have been named "plateaus in the curve of learning." Students of effective speaking will sometimes be stalled, perhaps for weeks, on one of these plateaus. Work as hard as they may, they cannot seem to get off it. The weak ones give up in despair. Those with grit persist, and they find that suddenly, almost overnight, without knowing how or why it has happened, they have made great progress. They have lifted from the plateau like an airplane. Abruptly they have acquired naturalness, force, and confidence in their speaking.

You may always, as has been stated elsewhere in these pages, experience some fleeting fear, some shock, some nervous anxiety, the first few moments you face an audience. Even the greatest musicians have felt it in spite of their innumerable public appearances. Paderewski always fidgeted nervously with his cuffs immediately before he sat down at the piano. But as soon as he began to play, all of his audience-fear vanished quickly like a mist in August sunshine.

His experience will be yours. If you will but persevere, you will soon eradicate everything, including this initial fear; and that will be initial fear, and nothing more. After the first few sentences, you will have control of yourself. You will be speaking with positive pleasure.

One time a young man who aspired to study law wrote to Lincoln for advice. Lincoln replied: "If you are resolutely determined to make a lawyer of yourself, the thing is more than half done already.... Always bear in mind that your own resolution to succeed is more important than any other one thing."

Lincoln knew. He had gone through it all. He had never, in his entire life, had more than a total of one year's schooling. And books? Lincoln once said he had walked and borrowed every book within fifty miles of his home. A log fire was usually kept going all night in the cabin. Sometimes he read by the light of that fire. There were cracks between the logs in the cabin, and Lincoln often kept a book sticking there. As soon as it was light enough to read in the morning, he rolled over on his bed of leaves, rubbed his eyes, pulled out the book and began devouring it.

He walked twenty and thirty miles to hear a speaker and, returning home, he practiced his talks everywhere—in the fields, in the woods, before the crowds gathered at Jones' grocery at Gentryville; he joined literary and debating societies in New Salem and Springfield, and practiced speaking on the topics of the day. He was shy in the presence of women; when he courted Mary Todd he used to sit in the parlor, bashful and silent, unable to find words, listening while she did the talking. Yet that was the man who, by faithful practice and home study, made himself into the speaker who debated with the most accomplished orator of his day, Senator Douglas. This was the man who, at Gettysburg, and again in his second inaugural address, rose to heights of eloquence that have rarely been attained in all the annals of mankind.

Small wonder that, in view of his own terrific handicaps and pitiful struggle, Lincoln wrote: "If you are resolutely determined to make a lawyer out of yourself, the thing is more than half done already."

An excellent picture of Abraham Lincoln hangs in the Presidents office in the White House. "Often when I had some matter to decide," said Theodore Roosevelt, "something involved and difficult to dispose of, something where there were conflicting rights and interest, I would look up at Lincoln, try to imagine him in my place, try to figure out what he would do in the same circumstances. It may sound odd to you, but, frankly, it seemed to make my troubles easier of solution."

Why not try Roosevelt's plan? Why not, if you are discouraged and feeling like giving up the fight to make a more effective speaker of yourself, why not ask yourself what he would do under the circumstances? You know what he would do. You know what he did do. After he had been beaten by Stephen A. Douglas in the race for the U.S. Senate, he admonished his followers not to "give up after one or one hundred defeats."

FIFTH

Keep The Certainty Of Reward Before You

How I wish I could get you to prop this book open on your breakfast table every morning until you had memorized these words from Professor William James: Let no youth have any anxiety about the upshot of his education, whatever the line of it may be. If he keeps faithfully busy each hour of the working day, he may safely leave the final result to itself. He can, with perfect certainty, count on waking up some fine morning to find himself one of the competent ones of his generation, in whatever pursuit he may have singled out.

~

And now, with the renowned Professor James to fall back upon, I shall go so far as to say that if you keep right on practicing intelligently, you may confidently hope to wake up one fine morning and find yourself one of the competent speakers of your city or community.

Regardless of how fantastic that may sound to you now, *it is true as a general principle*. Exceptions, of course, there are. A man with an inferior mentality and personality, and with nothing to talk about, is not going to develop into a local Daniel Webster; but, *within reason*, the assertion is correct.

Let me illustrate: former Governor Stokes of New Jersey attended the closing banquet of one of our classes at Trenton. He remarked that the talks he had heard that evening were as good as the speeches that he had heard in the House of Representatives and Senate at Washington. These Trenton "speeches" were made by businessmen who had been tongue-tied with audience-fear a few months previously. They were not incipient Ciceros, these New Jersey businessmen; they were typical of the businessmen one finds in any American city. Yet they woke up one fine morning to find themselves among the competent speakers of their city, and probably in the country.

I have known and carefully watched literally thousands of persons trying to gain self-confidence and the ability to talk in public. Those that succeeded were, in only a few instances, persons of unusual brilliancy. For the most part, they were the ordinary run of businessmen you will find in your own home town. But they kept on. More exceptional men sometimes got discouraged or too deeply immersed in money-making, and they did not get very far; but the ordinary individual with grit and singleness of purpose, at the end of the road, was at the top.

That is only human and natural. Don't you see the same tiling occurring all the time in commerce and the professions? John D. Rockefeller, Sr., said that the first essential for success in business was patience and the knowledge that reward is ultimately certain. It is likewise one of the first essentials for success in effective speaking.

A few summers ago, I started out to scale a peak in the Austrian Alps called the *Wilder Kaiser.* Baedaker said that the ascent was difficult, and a guide was essential for amateur climbers. A friend and I had none, and we were certainly amateurs; so a third party asked us if we thought we were going to succeed. "Of course," we replied.

"What makes you think so?" he inquired.

"Others have done it without guides," I said, "so I know it is within reason, and *I never undertake anything thinking defeat.*"

That is the proper psychology for anything from speaking to an assault on Mt. Everest.

How well you succeed is largely determined by thoughts you have prior to speaking. See yourself in your imagination talking to others with perfect self-control.

It is easily in your power to do this. Believe that you will succeed. Believe it firmly, and you will then do what is necessary to bring success about.

During the Civil War, Admiral Dupont gave half a dozen excellent reasons why he had not taken his gunboat into Charleston harbor. Admiral Farragut listened intently to the recital. "But there was another reason that you have not mentioned," he replied.

"What is that?" questioned Admiral Dupont.

The answer came: "You did not believe you could do it."

The most valuable thing that most members acquire from training in our classes is an increased confidence in themselves, an additional faith in their ability to achieve. What is more important for one's success in almost any undertaking?

Emerson wrote, "Nothing great was ever achieved without enthusiasm." That is more than a well-turned literary phrase; it is the road map to success.

William Lyon Phelps was probably the most beloved and the most popular professor ever to teach at Yale University. In his book *The Excitement of Teaching,* he states, "With me, teaching is more than an art or an occupation. It is a passion.

I love to teach, as a painter loves to paint, as a singer loves to sing, as a poet loves to write. Before I get out of bed in the morning, I think with ardent delight of my group of students."

Is there any wonder a teacher so filled with enthusiasm for his job, so excited about the work ahead of him, achieved success? Billy Phelps exerted a tremendous influence on his students, largely by the love and excitement, by the enthusiasm, he put into his teaching.

If you put enthusiasm into learning how to speak more effectively you will find that the obstacles in your path will disappear. This is a challenge to focus all your talent and power on the goal of effective communication with your fellow men. Think of the self-reliance, the assurance, the poise that will be yours, the sense of mastery that comes from being able to hold the attention, stir the emotions, and convince a group to act. You will find that competence in self-expression will lead to competence in other ways as well, for training in effective speaking is the royal road to self-confidence in all the areas of working and living.

In the manual for the guidance of instructors who teach the Dale Carnegie Course are these words: "When class members discover that they can hold the attention of an audience and receive an instructor's praise, and the applause of the class—when they are able to do that, they develop a sense of inner power, courage, and calm that they have never before experienced. The result? They undertake and accomplish things that they never dreamed possible. They find themselves longing to talk before groups, they take active parts in business and professional and community activities, and become leaders."

The word "leadership" has been used often in the chapters that have gone before this one. Clear, forceful, and emphatic expressiveness is one of the marks of leadership in our society. This expressiveness must govern all the utterances of the leader from private interview to public pronouncements. Properly applied, the material in this book will help to develop leadership—in the family, the church group, the civic organization, the corporation, and the government.

The most precious things iti speech are the pauses.

—Sir Ralph Richardson

~

Speakers who talk about what life has taught them never fail to keep the attention of their listeners.

—Dale Carnegie

PART III

THE THREE ASPECTS OF EVERY SPEECH

7

Earning The Right To Talk

Many years ago, a Doctor of Philosophy and a rough-and ready fellow who had spent his youth in the British Navy were enrolled in one of our classes in New York. The man with the degree was a college professor; the ex-star was the proprietor of a small side-street trucking business. His talks were far better received by the class than those given by the professor. Why? The college man used beautiful English. He was urbane, cultured, refined. His talks were always logical and clear. But they lacked one essential—concreteness. They were vague and general. Not once did he illustrate a point with anything approaching a personal experience. His talks were usually nothing more than a series of abstract ideas held together by a thin string of logic.

On the other hand, the trucking firm proprietor's language was definite, concrete, and picturesque. He talked in terms of everyday facts. He gave us one point and then backed it up by telling us what happened to him in the course of his business. He described the people he had to deal with and the headaches of keeping up with regulations. The virility and freshness of his phraseology made his talks highly instructive and entertaining.

I cite this instance, not because it is typical of college professors or of men in the trucking business, but because it illustrates the attention-compelling power of rich, colorful details in a talk.

There are four ways to develop speech material that guarantees audience attention. If you follow these four steps in your preparation you will be well on the way to commanding the eager attention of your listeners.

FIRST
Limit Your Subject

Once you have selected your topic, the first step is to stake out the area you want to cover and stay strictly within those limits. Don't make the mistake of trying to cover the open range. One young man attempted to speak for two minutes on the subject of "Athens from 500 B.C. to the Korean War." How utterly futile! He barely had gone beyond the founding of the city before he had to sit down, another victim of the compulsion to cover too much in one talk. This is an extreme example, I know; I have heard thousands of talks, less encompassing in scope, that failed to hold attention for the same reason—they covered far too many points. Why? Because it is impossible for the mind to attend to a monotonous series of factual points. If your talk sounds like the World Almanac you will not be able to hold attention very long. Take a simple subject, like a trip to Yellowstone Park. In their eagerness to leave nothing out, most people have something to say about every scenic view in the Park. The audience is whisked from one point to another with dizzying speed. At the end, all that remains in the mind is a blur of waterfalls, mountains, and geysers. How much more memorable such a talk would be if the speaker limited himself to one aspect of the Park, the wildlife or the hot springs, for example. Then there would be time to develop the kind of pictorial detail that would make Yellowstone Park come alive in all its vivid color and variety.

This is true of any subject, whether it be salesmanship, baking cakes, tax exemptions, or ballistic missiles. You must limit and select before you begin, narrow your subject down to an area that will fit the time at your disposal.

In a short talk, less than five minutes in duration, all you can expect is to get one or two main points across. In a longer talk, up to thirty minutes, few speakers ever succeed if they try to cover more than four or five main ideas.

SECOND

Develop Reserve Power

It is far easier to give a talk that skims over the surface than to dig down for facts. But when you take the easy way you make little or no impression on the audience. After you have narrowed your subject, then the next step is to ask yourself questions that will deepen your understanding and prepare you to talk with authority on the topic you have chosen: "Why do I believe this? When did I ever see this point exemplified in real life? What precisely am I trying to prove? Exactly how did it happen?"

Questions like these call for answers that will give you reserve power, the power that makes people sit up and take notice. It was said of Luther Burbank, the botanical wizard, that he produced a million plant specimens to find one or two superlative ones. It is the same with a talk. Assemble a hundred thoughts around your theme, then discard ninety.

"I always try to get ten times as much information as I use, sometimes a hundred times as much," said John Gunther not long ago. The author of the bestselling *Inside* books was speaking of the way he prepared to write a book or give a talk.

On one occasion in particular, his actions bore out his words. In 1956, he was working on a series of articles on mental hospitals. He visited institutions, talked to supervisors, attendants, and patients. A friend of mine was with him, giving some small assistance in the research, and he told me they must have walked countless miles up stairs and down, along corridors, building to building, day after day. Mr. Gunther filled notebooks. Back in his office, he stacked up government and state reports, private hospital reports, and reams of committees' statistics.

"In the end," my friend told me, "he wrote four short articles, simple enough and anecdotal enough to make good speeches. The paper on which they were typed weighed, perhaps, a few ounces. The filled notebooks, and everything else he used as the basis for the few ounces of product, must have weighed twenty pounds."

Mr. Gunther knew that he was working with pay dirt He knew he couldn't overlook any of it. An old hand at this sort of thing, he put his mind to it, and he sifted out the gold nuggets.

A surgeon friend of mine said: "I can teach you in ten minutes how to take out an appendix. But it will take me four years to teach you what to do if something goes wrong." So it is with speaking: Always prepare so that you are ready for any emergency, such as a change of emphasis because of a previous speaker's remarks, or a well-aimed question from the audience in the discussion period following your talk.

You, too, can acquire reserve power by selecting your topic as soon as possible. Don't put it off until a day or two before you have to speak. If you decide on the topic early you will have the inestimable advantage of having your subconscious mind working for you. At odd moments of the day when you are free from your work, you can explore your subject, refine the ideas you want to convey to your audience. Time ordinarily spent in reverie while you are driving home, waiting for a bus, or riding the subway, can be devoted to mulling over the subject matter of your talk. It is during this incubation period that flashes of insight will come, just because you have determined your topic far in advance and your mind subconsciously works over it.

Norman Thomas, a superb speaker who has commanded the respectful attention of audiences quite opposed to his political point of view, said: "If a speech is to be of any importance at all, the speaker should live with the theme or message, turning it over and over in his mind. He will be surprised at how many useful illustrations or ways of putting his case will come to him as he walks the street, or reads a newspaper, or gets ready for bed, or wakes up in the morning. Mediocre speaking very often is merely the inevitable and the appropriate reflection of mediocre thinking, and the consequence of imperfect acquaintance with the subject in hand."

While you are involved in this process you will be under strong temptation to write your talk out, word for word. Try not to do this, for once you have set a pattern, you are likely to be satisfied with it, and you may cease to give it any more constructive thought. In addition, there is the danger of memorizing the script. Mark Twain had this to say about such memorization: "Written things are not for speech;

their form is literary; they are stiff, inflexible, and will not lend themselves to happy effective delivery with the tongue. Where their purpose is merely to entertain, not to instruct, they have to be limbered up, broken up, colloquialized, and turned into the common form of unpremeditated talk; otherwise they will bore the house—not entertain it."

Charles F. Kettering, whose inventive genius sparked the growth of General Motors, was one of America's most renowned and heartwarming speakers. Asked if he ever wrote out any part or all of his talks, he replied: "What I have to say is, I believe, far too important to write down on paper. I prefer to write on my audience's mind, on their emotions, with every ounce of my being. A piece of paper cannot stand between me and those I want to impress."

THIRD
Fill Your Talk With Illustrations And Examples

In the *Art of Readable Writing,* Rudolf Flesch begins one of his chapters with this sentence: "Only stories are really readable." He then shows how this principle is used by *Time* and *Reader's Digest.* Almost every article in these top-circulation magazines either is written as pure narrative or is generously sprinkled with anecdotes. There is no denying the power of a story to hold attention in talking before groups as well as writing for magazines.

Norman Vincent Peale, whose sermons have been heard by millions on radio and television, says that his favorite form of supporting material in a talk is the illustration or example. He once told an interviewer from the *Quarterly Journal of Speech* that "the true example is the finest method I know of to make an idea clear, interesting, and persuasive. Usually, I use several examples to support each major point."

Readers of my books are soon aware of my use of the anecdote as a means of developing the main points of my message. The rules from *How To Win Friends And Influence People* can be listed on one and a half pages. The other two hundred and thirty pages of the book are filled with stories and illustrations to point up how others have used these rules with wholesome effect.

How can we acquire this most important technique of using illustrative material? There are five ways of doing this: Humanize, Personalize, Specify, Dramatize, and Visualize.

HUMANIZE YOUR TALK

I once asked a group of American businessmen in Paris to talk on "How to Succeed." Most of them merely listed a lot of abstract qualities and gave preachments on the value of hard work, persistence, and ambition.

So I halted this class, and said something like this: "We don't want to be lectured to. No one enjoys that. Remember, you must be entertaining or we will pay no attention whatever to what you are saying. Also remember that one of the most interesting things in the world is sublimated, glorified gossip. So tell us the stories of two men you have known. Tell why one succeeded and why the other failed. We will gladly listen to that, remember it, and possibly profit by it."

There was a certain member of that course who invariably found it difficult to interest either himself or his audience. This night, however, he seized the human interest suggestion and told us of two of his classmates in college. One of them had been so conservative that he had bought shirts at the different stores in town, and made charts showing which ones laundered best, wore longest, and gave the most service per dollar invested. His mind was always on pennies; yet, when he was graduated—it was an engineering college—he had such a high opinion of his own importance that he was not willing to begin at the bottom and work his way up, as the other graduates were doing. Even when the third annual reunion of the class came, he was still making laundry charts of his shirts, while waiting for some extraordinarily good thing to come his way. It never came. A quarter of a century has passed since then, and this man, dissatisfied and soured on life, still holds a minor position.

The speaker then contrasted with this failure the story of one of his classmates who had surpassed all expectations. This particular chap was a good mixer. Everyone liked him. Although he was ambitious to do big things later, he started as a draftsman. But he was always on the lookout for opportunity. Plans were then being made for the New York World's Fair. He knew engineering talent would be needed there, so he resigned from his position in Philadelphia and moved to New York. There he formed a partnership and engaged immediately in the contracting business. They did considerable work for the telephone company, and this man was finally taken over by that concern at a large salary.

I have recorded here only the bare outline of what the speaker told. He made his talk interesting and illuminating with a score of amusing and human interest details. He talked on and on—this man who could not ordinarily find material for a three-minute speech—and he was surprised to learn, when he stopped, that he had held the floor on this occasion for ten minutes. The speech had been so interesting that it seemed short to everyone. It was his first real triumph.

Almost everyone can profit by this incident. The average speech would be far more appealing if it were rich with human interest stories. The speaker should attempt to make only a few points and to illustrate them with concrete cases. Such a method of speech building can hardly fail to get and hold attention.

Of course, the richest source of such human interest material is your own background. Don't hesitate to tell us about your experiences because of some feeling that you should not talk about yourself. The only time an audience ob jects to hearing a person talk about himself is when he does it in an offensive, egotistical way. Otherwise, audiences are tremendously interested in the personal stories speakers tell. They are the surest means of holding attention; don't neglect them.

PERSONALIZE YOUR TALK BY USING NAMES

By all means, when you tell stories involving others, use their names, or, if you want to protect their identity, use fictitious names. Even impersonal names like "Mr. Smith" or "Joe Brown" are far more descriptive than "this man" or "a person." The label identifies and individualizes. As Rudolf Flesch points out, "Nothing adds more realism to a story than names; nothing is as unrealistic as anonymity. Imagine a story whose hero has no name."

If your talk is full of names and personal pronouns you can be sure of high listenability, for you will have the priceless ingredient of human interest in your speech.

BE SPECIFIC, FILL YOUR TALK WITH DETAIL

You might say at this point, "this is all very fine, but how can I be sure of getting enough detail into my talk?" There is one test. Use the 5-W formula every reporter follows when he writes a news story: answer the questions When? Where? Who? What? and Why? If you follow this formula your examples will have life and color. Let me illustrate this with an anecdote of my own, one that was published by the *Reader's Digest:*

"After leaving college, I spent two years traveling through South Dakota as a salesman for Armour and Company. I covered my territory by riding on freight trains. One day I had to lay over in Redfield, S. D., for two hours to get a train going south. Since Redfield was not in my territory I couldn't use the time for making sales. Within a year I was going to New York to study at the American Academy of Dramatic Arts, so I decided to use this spare time practicing speaking. I wandered down through the train yards and began rehearsing a scene for *Macbeth.* Thrusting out my arms, I cried dramatically: 'Is this a dagger which I see before me, the handle toward my hand? Come, let me clutch thee: I have thee not, and yet I see thee still.'

"I was still immersed in the scene when four policemen leaped upon me and asked why I was frightening women. I couldn't have been more astounded if they had accused me of robbing a train. They informed me that a housewife had been watching me from behind her kitchen curtains a hundred yards away. She had never seen such goings-on. So she called the police, and when they approached they heard me ranting about daggers.

"I told them I was practicing Shakespeare,' but I had to produce my order book for Armour and Company before they let me go."

Notice how this anecdote answers the questions posed in the 5-W formula above.

Of course, too much detail is worse than none. All of us have been bored by lengthy recitals of superficial, irrelevant details. Notice how in the incident about my near-arrest in a South Dakota town there is a brief and concise answer to each of the 5-W questions. If you clutter your talk with too much detail, your audience will blue-pencil your remarks by refusing to give you their complete attention. There is no blue pencil more severe than inattentiveness.

DRAMATIZE YOUR TALK BY USING DIALOGUE

Suppose you want to give an illustration of how you succeeded in calming down an irate customer by using one of the rules of human relations. You could begin like this:

"The other day a man came into my office. He was pretty mad because the appliance we had sent out to his house only the week before was not working properly. I told him that we would do all we could to remedy the situation. After a while he calmed down and seemed satisfied that we had every intention to make things right." This anecdote has one virtue—it is fairly specific—but it lacks names, specific details, and, above all, the actual dialogue which would make this incident come alive. Here it is with these added qualities:

"Last Tuesday, the door of my office slammed and I looked up to see the angry features of Charles Blexam, one of my regular customers. I didn't have time to ask him to take a seat. 'Ed, this is the last straw,' he said, 'you can send a truck right out and cart that wash machine out of my basement.'

"I asked him what was tip. He was too willing to reply." It won't work,' he shouted, the clothes get all tangled, and my wife's sick and tired of it.'

"I asked him to sit down and explain it in more detail." 'I haven't got time to sit down. I'm late for work and I wish I'd never come in here to buy an appliance in the first place.

Believe me, I'll never do it again.' Here he hit the desk with his hand and knocked over my wife's picture.

"'Look, Charley,' I said, 'if you will just sit down and tell me all about it, I promise to do whatever you want me to do.' With that, he sat down, and we calmly talked it over." It isn't always possible to work dialogue into your talk, but you can see how the direct quotation of the conversation in the excerpt above helps to dramatize the incident for the listener. If the speaker has some imitative skill and can get the original tone of voice into the words, dialogue can become more effective. Also, dialogue gives your speech the authentic ring of everyday conversation. It makes you sound like a real person talking across a dinner table, not like a pedant delivering a paper before a learned society or an orator ranting into a microphone.

VISUALIZE BY DEMONSTRATING WHAT YOU ARE TALKING ABOUT

Psychologists tell us that more than eighty-five per cent of our knowledge comes to us through visual impressions.

No doubt this accounts for the enormous effectiveness of television as an advertising as well as entertainment medium. Public speaking, too, is a visual as well as auditory art.

One of the best ways to enrich a talk with detail is to incorporate visual demonstration into it. You might spend hours just telling me how to swing a golf club, and I might be bored by it. But get up and show me what you do when you drive a ball down the fairway and I am all eyes and ears. Likewise, if you describe the erratic maneuvers of an airplane with your arms and shoulders, I am more intent on the outcome of your brush with death.

I remember a talk given in an industrial class that was a masterpiece of visual detail. The speaker was poking good-natured fun at inspectors and efficiency experts. His mimicry of the gestures and bodily antics of these gentlemen as they inspected a broken-down machine was more hilarious than anything I have ever seen on television. What is more, visual detail made that talk memorable—I for one shall never forget it, and I am sure the other members of that class are still talking about it.

It is a good idea to ask yourself, "How can I put some visual detail into my talk?" Then proceed to demonstrate, for, as the ancient Chinese observed, one picture is worth ten thousand words.

FOURTH
Use Concrete, Familiar Words That Create Pictures

In the process of getting and holding attention, which is the first purpose of every speaker, there is one aid, one technique, that is of the highest importance. Yet, it is all but ignored. The average speaker does not seem to be aware of its existence. He has probably never consciously thought about it at all. I refer to the process of using words that create pictures. The speaker who is easy to listen to is the one who sets images floating before your eyes. The one who employs foggy, commonplace, colorless symbols sets the audience to nodding.

Pictures, Pictures. Pictures. They are as free as the air you breathe. Sprinkle them through your talks, your conversation, and you will be more entertaining, more influential.

Herbert Spencer, in his famous essay on the "Philosophy of Style," pointed out long ago the superiority of terms that call forth bright pictures:

"We do not think in generals but in particulars. We should avoid such a sentence as:

"'In proportion as the manners, customs, and amusements of a nation are cruel and barbarous, the regulations of their penal code will be severe!'

"And in place of it, we should write:

"'In proportion as men delight in battles, bull fights, and combats of gladiators, will they punish by hanging, burning, and the rack.'"

Picture-building phrases swarm through the pages of the Bible and through Shakespeare like bees around a cider mill. For example, a commonplace writer would have said that a certain thing would be "superfluous," like trying to improve the perfect. How did Shakespeare express the same thought? With a picture phrase that is immortal: "To gild refined gold, to paint the lily, to throw perfume on the violet."

Did you ever pause to observe that the proverbs that are passed on from generation to generation are almost all visual sayings? "A bird in the hand is worth two in the bush." "It never rains but it pours." "You can lead a horse to water but you can't make him drink." And you will find the same picture element in almost all the similes that have lived for centuries and grown hoary with too much use: "Sly as a fox." "Dead as a doornail." "Flat as a pancake." "Hard as a rock."

Lincoln continually talked in visual terminology. When he became annoyed with the long, complicated, red-tape reports that came to his desk in the White House, he objected to them, not with colorless phraseology, but with a picture phrase that it is almost impossible to forget. "When I send a man to buy a horse," he said, "I don't want to be told how many hair the horse has in his tail. I wish only to know his points."

Make your eye appeals definite and specific. Paint mental pictures that stand out as sharp and clear as a stag's antlers silhouetted against the setting sun. For example, the word "dog" calls up a more or less definite picture of such an animal—perhaps a cocker spaniel, a Scottish terrier, a St. Bernard, or a Pomeranian. Notice how much more distinct an image springs into your mind when a speaker says "bulldog"—the term is less inclusive. Doesn't "a brindle bulldog" call up a still more explicit picture? Is it not more vivid to say "a black Shetland pony" than to talk of "a horse"? Doesn't "a white bantam rooster with a broken leg" give a much more definite and sharp picture than merely the word "fowl"?

In *The Elements of Style*, William Strunk, Jr., states: "If those who have studied the art of writing are in accord on any one point, it is on this: the surest way to arouse and hold the attention of the reader is by being specific, definite, and concrete. 'The greatest writers—Homer, Dante, Shakespeare—are effective largely because they deal in particulars and report the details that matter. Their words call up pictures." This is as true of speaking as of writing.

I once devoted a session years ago in my course in Effective Speaking to an experiment in being factual. We adopted a rule that in every sentence the speaker must put either a fact or a proper noun, a figure, or a date. The results were revolutionary. The class members made a game of catching one another on generalities; it wasn't long before they were talking, not the cloudy language that floats over the head of an audience, but the clear-cut, vigorous language of the man on the street.

"An abstract style," said the French philosopher, Alain, "is always bad. Your sentences should be full of stones, metals, chairs, tables, animals, men, and women."

This is true of everyday conversation as well. In fact, all that has been said in this chapter about the use of detail in talks before groups applies to general conversation. It is detail that makes conversation sparkle. Anyone who is intent upon making himself a more effective conversationalist may profit by following the advice contained in this chapter. Salesmen, too, will discover the magic of detail when applied to their sales presentations. Those in executive positions, housewives, and teachers will find that giving instructions and dispensing information will be greatly improved by the use of concrete, factual detail.

If you can't write your message in a sentence, you can't say it in an hour.

—Dianna Booher

~

Tell the audience what you're going to say, say it; then tell them what you've said.

—Dale Carnegie

8

Vitalizing The Talk

Right after the First World War, I was in London working with Lowell Thomas, who was giving a series of brilliant lectures on Allenby and Lawrence of Arabia to packed houses. One Sunday I wandered into Flyde Park to the spot near Marble Arch entrance where speakers of every creed, color, and political and religious persuasion are allowed to air their views without interference from the law. For a while I listened to a Catholic explaining the doctrine of the infallibility of the Pope, then I moved to the fringes of another crowd, intent upon what a Socialist had to say about Karl Marx. I strolled over to a third speaker, who was explaining why it was right and proper for a man to have four wives! Then I moved away and looked back at the three groups.

Would you believe it? The man who was talking about polygamy had the fewest number of people listening to him! There was only a handful. The crowds around the other two speakers were growing larger by the minute. I asked myself why? Was it the disparity of topics? I don't think so. The explanation, I saw as I watched, was to be found in the speakers themselves. The fellow who was talking about the advantages of having four wives didn't seem to be interested in having four wives himself. But the other two speakers,talking from almost diametrically opposed points of view, were wrapped up in their subjects. They talked with life and spirit. Their arms moved in impassioned gestures. Their voices rang with conviction. They radiated earnestness and animation.

Vitality, aliveness, enthusiasm—these are the first qualities I have always considered essential in a speaker. People cluster around the energetic speaker like wild turkeys around a field of autumn wheat.

How do you acquire this vital delivery that will keep the attention of your audience? In the course of this chapter I will give you three sovereign ways to help you put enthusiasm and excitement into your speaking.

FIRST

Choose Subjects You Are Earnest About

Chapter Three stressed the importance of feeling deeply about your subject. Unless you are emotionally involved in the subject matter you have chosen to talk about, you cannot expect to make your audience believe in your message. Obviously, if you select a topic that is exciting to you because of long experience with it, such as a hobby or recreational pursuit, or because of deep reflection or personal concern about it (as, for instance, the need for better schools in your community), you will have no difficulty in talking with excitement. The persuasive power of earnestness was never more vividly demonstrated to me than in a talk made before one of my classes in New York City more than two decades ago. I have heard many persuasive talks, but this one, which I call the Case of Blue Grass *vs.* Hickory Wood Ashes, stands out as a kind of triumph of sincerity over common sense.

A top-flight salesman of one of the best-known selling organizations in the city made the preposterous statement that he had been able to make blue grass grow without the aid of seeds or roots. He had, according to his story, scattered hickory wood ashes over newly plowed ground. Presto! Blue grass had appeared! He firmly believed that the hickory wood ashes, and the hickory wood ashes alone, were responsible for the blue grass.

Commenting on his talk, I gently pointed out to him that his phenomenal discovery would, if true, make him a millionaire, for blue grass seed was worth several dollars a bushel. I also told him that it would make him the outstanding scientist of all history. I informed him that no man, living or dead, had ever been able to perform the miracle he claimed to have performed: no man had ever been able to produce life from inert matter.

I told him that very quietly, for I felt that his mistake was so palpable, so absurd, as to require no emphasis in the refutation. When I had finished, every other member of the course saw the folly of his assertion; but he did not see it, not for a second. He was in earnest about his contention, deadly in earnest. He leaped to his feet and informed me that he was *not* wrong. He had not been relating theory, he protested, but personal experience. He *knew* whereof he spoke. He continued to talk, enlarging on his first remarks, giving additional information, piling up additional evidence, sincerity and honesty ringing in his voice.

Again I informed him that there was not the remotest hope in the world of his being right or even approximately right or within a thousand miles of the truth. In a second he was on his feet once more, offering to bet me five dollars and to let the U. S. Department of Agriculture settle the matter.

And do you know what happened? Several members in the class were won over to his side. Many others were beginning to be doubtful. If I had taken a vote I am certain that more than half of the businessmen in that class would not have sided with me. I asked them what had shaken them from their original position. One after another said it was the speaker's earnestness, his belief, so energetically stated, that made them begin to doubt the common sense viewpoint.

Well, in the face of that display of credulity I had to write the Department of Agriculcure. I was ashamed, I told them, to ask such an absurd question. They replied, of course, that it was impossible to get blue grass or any other living thing from hickory wood ashes, and they added that they had received another letter from New York asking the same question. That salesman was so sure of his position that he sat down and wrote a letter, too!

This incident taught me a lesson I'll never forget. *If a speaker believes a thing earnestly enough and says it earnestly enough, he will get adherents to his cause,* even though he claims he can produce blue grass from dust and ashes. How much more compelling will our convictions be if they are arrayed on the side of common sense and truth!

Almost all speakers wonder whether the topic they have chosen will interest the audience. There is only one way to make sure that they will be interested: stoke the fires of your enthusiasm for the subject and you will have no difficulty holding the interest of a group of people.

A short time ago, I heard a man in one of our classes in Baltimore warn his audience that if the present methods of catching rock fish in Chesapeake Bay were continued the species would become extinct. And in a very few years! He felt his subject. It was important. He was in real earnest about it. Everything about his matter and manner showed that. When he arose to speak, I did not know that there was such a creature as a rock fish in Chesapeake Bay. I imagine that more of the audience shared my lack of knowledge and lack of interest. But before the speaker finished, all of us would probably have been willing to sign a petition to the legislature to protect the rock fish by law.

Richard Washburn Child, the former American Ambassador to Italy, was once asked the secret of his success as an interesting writer. He replied: "I am so excited about life that I cannot keep still. I just have to tell people about it." One cannot keep from being enthralled with a speaker or writer like that.

I once went to hear a speaker in London; after he was through, one of our party, Mr. E. E Benson, a well-known English novelist, remarked that he enjoyed the last part of the talk far more than the first. When I asked him why, he replied: "The speaker himself seemed more interested in the last part, and I always rely on the speaker to supply the enthusiasm and interest."

Here is another illustration of the importance of choosing your topics well.

A gentleman, whom we shall call Mr. Flynn, was enrolled in one of our classes in Washington, D. C. One evening early in the course, he devoted his talk to a description of the capital city of the United States. He had hastily and superficially gleaned his facts from a booklet issued by a local newspaper. They sounded like it—dry, disconnected, undigested. Though he had lived in Washington for many years, he did not present one personal instance of why he liked the city. He merely recited a series of dull facts, and his talk was as distressing for the class to hear as it was agonizing for him to give.

A fortnight later, something happened that touched Mr. Flynn to the core: an unknown driver had smashed into his new car while it was parked on the street and had driven away without identifying himself. It was impossible for Mr. Flynn to collect insurance and he had to foot the bill himself. Here was something that came hot out of his experience. His talk about the city of Washington, which he laboriously pulled out sentence by sentence, was painful to him and his audience; but when he spoke about his smashed-up car, his talk welled up and boiled forth like Vesuvius in action. The same class that had squirmed restlessly in their seats two weeks before now greeted Mr. Flynn with a heart warming burst of applause.

As I have pointed out repeatedly, you cannot help but succeed if you choose the right topic for you. One area of topics is sure-fire: talk about your convictions! Surely you have strong beliefs about some aspect of life around you. You don't have to search far and wide for these subjects—they generally lie on the surface of your stream of consciousness, because you often think about them.

Not long ago, a legislative hearing on capital punishment was presented on television. Many witnesses were called to give their viewpoints on both sides of this controversial subject. One of them was a member of the police department of the city of Los Angeles, who had evidently given much thought to this topic. He had strong convictions based on the fact that eleven of his fellow police officers had been killed in gun battles with criminals. He spoke with the deep sincerity of one who believed to his heart's core in the righteousness of his cause. The greatest appeals in the history of eloquence have all been made out of the depths of someone's deep convictions and feelings. Sincerity rests upon belief, and belief is as much a matter of the heart and of warmly feeling what you are saying as it is of the mind and coldly thinking of what to say. "The heart has reasons that the reason does not know." In many classes I have had frequent occasions to verify Pascal's trenchant sentence. I remember a lawyer in Boston who was blessed with a striking appearance and who spoke with admirable fluency, but when he finished speaking people said: "Clever chap." He made a surface impression because there never seemed to be any feeling behind his glittering facade of words. In the same class, there was an insurance salesman, small in stature, unprepossessing in appearance, a man who groped for a word now and then, but when he spoke there was no doubt in any of his listeners' minds that he felt every word of his talk. It is almost a hundred years since Abraham Lincoln's assassination in the presidential box of Ford's Theatre in Washington, D. C., but the deep sincerity of his life and his words still lives with us. As far as knowledge of law is concerned, scores of other men of his time outstripped him. He lacked grace, smoothness, and polish. But the honesty and sincerity of his utterances at Gettysburg, Cooper Union, and on the steps of the Capitol in Washington, have not been surpassed in our history.

You may say, as one man once did, that you have no strong convictions or interests. I am always a little surprised at this, but I told this man to get busy and get interested in something. "What, for instance?" he asked. In desperation I said, "Pigeons." "Pigeons?" he asked in a bewildered tone. "Yes," I told him, "pigeons. Go out on the square and look at them, feed them, go to the library and read about them, then come back here and talk about them." He did. When he came back there was no holding him down. He started to talk about pigeons with all the fervor of a fancier. When I tried to stop him he was saying something about forty books on pigeons and he had read them all. He gave one of the most interesting talks I have ever heard.

Here is another suggestion: Learn more and more about what you now consider a pretty good topic. The more you know about something the more earnest and excitedly enthusiastic you will become. Percy H. Whiting, the author of the *Five Great Rules of Selling,* tells salesmen never to stop learning about the product they are selling. As Mr. Whiting says, "The more you know about a good product, the more enthusiastic you become about it." The same thing is true about your topics—the more you know about them, the more earnest and enthusiastic you will be about them.

SECOND

Relive The Feelings You Have About Your Topic

Suppose you are telling your audience about the policeman who stopped you for going one mile over the speed limit. You can tell us that with all the cool disinterestedness of an onlooker, but it happened to you and you had certain feelings which you expressed in quite definite language. The third-person approach will not make much of an impression on your audience. They want to know exactly how you felt when that policeman wrote out that ticket. So, the more you relive the scene you are describing, or recreate the emotions you felt originally, the more vividly you will express yourself.

One of the reasons why we go to plays and movies is that we want to hear and see emotions expressed. We have become so fearful of giving vent to our feelings in public that we have to go to a play to satisfy this need for emotional expression.

When you speak in public, therefore, you will generate excitement and interest in your talk in proportion to the amount of excitement you put into it. Don't repress your honest feelings; don't put a damper on your authentic enthusiasms. Show your listeners how eager you are to talk about your subject, and you will hold their attention.

THIRD
Act In Earnest

When you walk before your audience to speak, do so with an air of anticipation, not like a man who is ascending the gallows. The spring in your walk may be largely put on, but it will do wonders for you and it gives the audience the feeling that you have something you are eager to talk about. Just before you begin, take a deep breath. Keep away from furniture or from the speaker's stand. Keep your head high and your chin up. You are about to tell your listeners something worthwhile, and every part of you should inform them of that clearly and unmistakably. You are in command, and as William James would say, act as if you are. If you make an effort to send your voice to the back of the hall, the sound will reassure you. Once you begin making gestures of any kind, they will help to stimulate you.

This principle of "warming up our reactivity," as Donald and Eleanor Laird describe it, can be applied to all situations that demand mental awareness. In their book *Techniques for Efficient Remembering,* the Lairds point to President Theodore Roosevelt as a man who "breezed through life with a bounce, vigor, dash, and enthusiasm which became his trademark. He was absorbingly interested, or effectively pretended he was, in everything he tackled." Teddy Roosevelt was a living exponent of the philosophy of William James: "Act in earnest and you will become naturally earnest in all you do."

Above all, remember this: acting in earnest will make you feel earnest.

If you don't know what you want to achieve in your presentation your audience never will.

—Harvey Diamond

~

There are always three speeches, for every one you actually gave. The one you practiced, the one you gave, and the one you wish you gave.

—Dale Carnegie

9

Delivering The Talk

Would you believe it? There are four ways, and only four ways, in which we have contact with the world. We are evaluated and classified by these four contacts: what we do, how we look, what we say, and how we say it. This chapter will deal with the last of these—how we say it.

When I first started to teach public speaking classes, I spent a great deal of time on the use of vocal exercises to develop resonance, increase the range of voice, and enhance inflectional agility. It wasn't long, however, before I began to see the utter futility of teaching adults how to project their tones into the upper sinuses and how to form "liquid" vowels. This is all very fine for those who can devote three or four years to improving themselves in the art of vocal delivery. I realized that my students would have to settle for the vocal equipment they were born with. I found that if I expended the time and energy I formerly devoted to helping class members to "breathe diaphragmatically" and worked on the far more important objectives of freeing them from their inhibitions and general reluctance to let themselves go, I would achieve quick and lasting results that were truly amazing. I thank God I had the sense to do this.

FIRST
Crash Through Your Shell Of Self-Consciousness

In my course there are several sessions that have as their purpose the freeing of tightly bound and tense adults. I got down on my knees, literally, to implore my class members to come out of their shells and find out for themselves that the world would treat them with cordiality and welcome when they would do so. It took some doing, I admit, but it was worth it. As Marshal Foch says of the art of war, "It is simple enough in its conception, but unfortunately complicated in its execution." The biggest stumbling block, of course, is stiffness, not only of the physical, but of the mental as well, a kind of hardening of the categories that comes with growing up.

It is not easy to be natural before an audience. Actors know that. When you were a child, say, four years old, you probably could have mounted a platform and talked naturally to an audience. But when you are twenty-and-four, or forty-and-four, what happens when you mount a platform and start to speak? Do you retain that unconscious naturalness that you possessed at four? You may, but it is dollars to doughnuts that you will become stiff and stilted and mechanical, and draw back into your shell like a snapping turtle.

The problem of teaching or of training adults in delivery is not one of superimposing additional characteristics; it is largely one of removing impediments, of getting them to speak with the same naturalness that they would display if someone were to knock them down.

Hundreds of times I have stopped speakers in the midst of their talks and implored them to "talk like a human being." Hundreds of nights I have come home mentally fatigued and nervously exhausted from trying to drill members of my classes to talk naturally. No, believe me, it is not so easy as it sounds.

In one of the sessions of my course I ask the class to act out portions of dialogue, some of which is in dialect. I ask them to throw themselves into these dramatic episodes with abandon. When they do, they discover to their amazement that, though they may have acted like a fool, they didn't feel badly when they were doing it. The class too is amazed at the dramatic ability some of the class members display. My point is that once you let your hair down before a group you are not likely to hold yourself back when it comes to the normal, everyday expression of your opinions whether to individuals or before groups.

The sudden freedom you feel is like a bird taking wing after being imprisoned in a cage. You see why it is that people flock to the theater and the movies—because there they see their fellow human beings act with little or no inhibition, there they see people wearing their emotions prominently displayed on their sleeves.

SECOND

Don't Try To Imitate Others—Be Yourself

We all admire speakers who can put showmanship into their speaking, who are not afraid to express themselves, not afraid to use the unique, individual, imaginative way of saying what they have to say to the audience.

Shortly after the close of the First World War, I met two brothers in London, Sir Ross and Sir Keith Smith. They had just made the first aeroplane flight from London to Australia to win a fifty-thousand-dollar prize offered by the Australian government. They had created a sensation throughout the British Empire and had been knighted by the King.

Captain Hurley, a well-known scenic photographer, had flown with them over a part of their trip, taking motion pictures; so I helped them prepare an illustrated travel talk of their flight and trained them in the delivery of it. They gave it twice daily for four months in Philharmonic Hall, London, one speaking in the afternoon, the other at night.

They had had identically the same experience, they had sat side by side as they flew halfway around the world, and they delivered the same talk, almost word for word. Yet, somehow it didn't sound like the same talk at all.

There is something besides the mere words in a talk which counts. It is the flavor with which they are delivered. It is not so much just what you say as how you say it.

Brulloff, the great Russian painter, once corrected a pupil's study. The pupil looked in amazement at the altered drawing, exclaiming: "Why, you have touched it only a tiny bit, but it is quite another thing." Brulloff replied, "Art begins where the tiny bit begins." That is as true of speaking as it is of painting and of Paderewski's playing.

The same thing holds true when one is touching words. There is an old saying in the English Parliament that everything depends upon the manner in which one speaks and not upon the matter. Quintilian said it long ago, when England was one of the outlying colonies of Rome.

"All Fords are exactly alike," their maker used to say, but no two men are just alike. Every new life is a new thing under the sun; there has never been anything just like it before, and never will be again. A young man ought to get that idea about himself; he should look for the single spark of individuality that makes him different from other folks, and develop that for all he is worth. Society and schools may try to iron it out of him; their tendency is to put us all in the same mold but, I say, don't let that spark be lost; it's your only real claim to importance.

All that is doubly true of effective speaking. There is no other human being in the world like you. Hundreds of millions of people have two eyes and a nose and a mouth; but none of them looks precisely like you; and none of them has exactly your traits and methods and cast of mind. Few of them will talk and express themselves just as you do when you are speaking naturally. In other words, you have an individuality. As a speaker, it is your most precious possession. Cling to it. Cherish it. Develop it. It is the spark that will put force and sincerity into your speaking. "It is your only real claim to importance." Please, I beg you, do not attempt to force yourself in a mold and thereby lose your distinctiveness.

THIRD

Converse With Your Audience

Let me give you an illustration that is typical of the fashion in which thousands of persons talk. I happened on one occasion to be stopping in Murren, a summer resort in the Swiss Alps. I was living at a hotel operated by a London company; and they usually sent out from England a couple of lecturers each week to talk to the guests. One of them was a well-known English novelist. Her topic was "The Future of the Novel." She admitted that she had not selected the subject herself; and the long and short of it was that she had nothing she cared to say about it to make it worthwhile expressing. She had hurriedly made some rambling notes; and she stood before the audience, ignoring her hearers, not even looking at them, staring sometimes over their heads, sometimes at her notes, sometimes at the floor. She unreeled words into the primeval void with a far-away look in her eyes and a far-away ring in her voice.

That isn't delivering a talk at all. It is a soliloquy. It has no *sense of communication*. And that is the first essential of good talking: a *sense of communication*. The audience must feel that there is a message being delivered straight from the mind and heart of the speaker to their minds and their hearts. The kind of talk I have just described might as well have been spoken out in the sandy, waterless wastes of the Gobi desert. In fact, it sounded as if it were being delivered in some such spot rather than to a group of living human beings.

An enormous amount of nonsense and twaddle has been written about delivery. It has been shrouded in rules and rites and made mysterious. Old-fashioned "elocution" has often made it ridiculous. The businessman, going to the library or book shop, has found volumes on "oratory" that were utterly useless. In spite of progress in other directions, in almost every state in the Union today, schoolboys are still being forced to recite the ornate "oratory of 'orators'"—a thing that is as useless as a squirrel-headed tire pump, as out-of-date as a quill pen.

An entirely new school of speaking has sprung up since the twenties. In keeping with the spirit of the times, it is as modem and as practical as the automobile, direct as a telegram, businesslike as a telling advertisement. The verbal fireworks that were once the vogue would no longer be tolerated by an audience today.

A modern audience, regardless of whether it is fifteen people at a business conference or a thousand people under a tent, wants the speaker to talk just as directly as he would in a chat, and in the same general manner he would employ in speaking to one of them in conversation , in the same *manner,* but with greater force or energy. In order to appear natural, he has to use much more energy in talking to forty people than he does in talking to one, just as a statue on top of a building has to be of heroic size in order to make it appear of lifelike proportions to an observer on the ground. At the close of one of Mark Twain's lectures in a Nevada mining camp, an old prospector approached him and inquired: "Be them your natural tones of eloquence?"

That is what the audience wants: "Your natural tones of eloquence," enlarged a bit. The only way to acquire the knack of this enlarged naturalness is by practice. And, as you practice, if you find yourself talking in a stilted manner, pause and say sharply to yourself mentally: "Here! What is wrong? Wake up! Be human." Then mentally pick out a person in the audience, someone in the back or the least attentive person you can find, and talk to this person. Forget there is anyone else present at all. *Converse* with this person. Imagine that he has asked you a question and that you are answering it, and that you are the *only* one who can answer it. If he were to stand up and talk to you, and you were to talk back to him, that process would immediately and inevitably make your speaking more conversational, more natural, more direct. So, imagine that is precisely what is taking place.

You may go so far as actually to ask questions and answer them. For example, in the midst of your talk, you may say, "and you ask what proof have I for this assertion? I have adequate proof and here it is..." Then proceed to answer the question. That sort of thing can be done very naturally. It will break up the monotony of one's delivery; it will make it direct and pleasant and conversational.

Speak to the Chamber of Commerce just as you would to John Henry Smith. What is a meeting of the Chamber of Commerce, after all, but a collection of John Henry Smiths? Won't the same methods that are successful with those men individually be successful with them collectively?

Earlier in this chapter was described the delivery of a certain novelist. In the same ballroom in which she had spoken, we had the pleasure, a few nights later, of hearing Sir Oliver Lodge. His subject was "Atoms and Worlds." He had devoted to this subject more than half a century of thought and study and experiment and investigation. He had something that was essentially a part of his heart and mind and life, something that he wanted very much to say. He forgot that he was trying to make a "speech." That was the least of his worries. He was concerned only with telling the audience about atoms, telling us accurately, lucidly, and feelingly. He was earnestly trying to get us to see what he saw and to feel what he felt.

And what was the result? He delivered a remarkable talk. It had both charm and power. It made a deep impression. He was a speaker of unusual ability. Yet I am sure he didn't regard himself in that light. I am sure that few people who heard him ever thought of him as a "public speaker" at all.

If you speak in public so that people hearing you will suspect that you have had training in public speaking, you will not be a credit to your instructor, especially an instructor in one of my courses. He desires you to speak with such intensified naturalness that your audience will never dream that you have been "formally" trained. A good window does not call attention to itself. It merely lets in the light. A good speaker is like that. He is so disarmingly natural that his hearers never notice his manner of speaking: they are conscious only of his matter.

FOURTH

Put Your Heart Into Your Speaking

Sincerity and enthusiasm and high earnestness will help you, too. When a man is under the influence of his feelings, his real self comes to the surface. The bars are down. The heat of his emotions has burned all barriers away. He acts spontaneously. He talks spontaneously. He is natural.

So, in the end, even this matter of delivery comes back to the thing which has already been emphasized repeatedly in these pages: namely, *put your heart into your talks.*

"I shall never forget," said Dean Brown in his Lectures on Preaching before the Yale Divinity School, "the description given by a friend of mine of a church service which he once attended in the city of London. The preacher was George MacDonald; he read for the Scripture lesson that morning the eleventh chapter of Hebrews. When the time came for the sermon, he said: 'You have all heard about these men of faith. I shall not try to tell you what faith is. There are theological professors who could do that much better than I could do it. I am here to help you believe.' Then followed such a simple, heartfelt, and majestic manifestation of the man's own faith in those unseen realities which are eternal, as to beget faith in the minds and hearts of all his hearers. *His heart was in his work, and his delivery was effective because it rested upon the genuine beauty of his own inner life.*"

"His heart was in his work." That is the secret. Yet I know that advice like this is not popular. It seems vague. It sounds indefinite. The average person wants foolproof rules, something definite, something he can put his hands on, rules as precise as the directions for operating a car.

That is what he wants; that is what I would like to give him. It would be easy for him and it would be easy for me. There are such rules, and there is only one little thing wrong with them: they just don't work. They take all the naturalness and spontaneity and life and juice out of a man's speaking. I know. In my younger days, I wasted a great deal of energy trying them. They won't appear in these pages for, as Josh Billings observed in one of his lighter moments: "There ain't no use in knowin' so many things that ain't so."

Edmund Burke wrote speeches so superb in logic and reasoning and composition that they are today studied as classic models of oratory in the colleges of the land; yet Burke, as a speaker, was a notorious failure. He didn't have the ability to deliver his gems, to make them interesting and forceful; so he was called "the dinner bell" of the House of Commons. When he arose to talk, the other members coughed and shuffled and either went to sleep or went out in droves.

You can throw a steel-jacketed bullet at a man with all your might, and you cannot make even a dent in his clothing. But put powder behind a tallow candle and you can shoot it through a pine board. Many a tallowcandle speech with powder makes, I regret to say, more of an impression than a steel-jacketed talk with no force, no excitement, behind it.

FIFTH

Practice Making Your Voice Strong And Flexible

When we are really communicating our ideas to our listeners we are making use of many elements of vocal and physical variety. We shrug our shoulders, move our arms, wrinkle our brows, increase our volume, change pitch and inflection, and talk fast or slow as the occasion and the material may dictate. It is well to remember that all these are effects and not causes. The so-called variables, or modulations of tone, are under the direct influence of our mental and emotional state. That is why it is so important that we have a topic we know and a topic we are excited about when we go before an audience. That is why we must be so eager to share that topic with our listeners. Since most of us lose the spontaneity and naturalness of youth as we grow older, we tend to slip into a definite mold of physical and vocal communication. We find ourselves less ready to use gestures and animation; we rarely raise or lower our voices from one pitch to another. In short, we lose the freshness and spontaneity of true conversation. We may get into the habit of talking too slowly or too rapidly, and our diction, unless carefully watched, tends to become ragged and careless. In this book you have been repeatedly told to act natural, and you may suppose that I therefore condone poor diction or monotonous delivery provided it is natural. On the contrary, I say that we should be natural in the sense that we express *our* ideas and express them with spirit. On the other hand, every good speaker will not accept himself as incapable of improvement in breadth of vocabulary, richness of imagery and diction, and variety and force of expression. These are areas in which everyone interested in self-improvement will seek to improve.

It is an excellent idea to evaluate oneself in terms of volume, pitch variation, and pace. This can be done with the aid of a tape recorder. On the other hand, it would be useful to have friends help you make this evaluation. If it is possible to secure expert advice, so much the better. It should be remembered, however, that these are areas for practice away from the audience. To concern yourself with technique when you are before an audience will prove fatal to effectiveness. Once there, pour yourself into your talk, concentrate your whole being on making a mental and emotional impact on your audience, and nine chances out of ten you will speak with more emphasis and force than you could ever get from books.

> *Best way to conquer stage fright is to know what you're talking about.*
>
> —Michael H. Mescon

> *There are four ways, and only four ways, in which we have contact with the world. We are evaluated and classified by these four contacts: what we do, how we look, what we say, and how we say it.*
>
> —Dale Carnegie

10

Sharing The Talk With The Audience

Russell Conwell's famous lecture, "Acres of Diamonds," was given nearly six thousand times. You would think that a talk repeated so often would become set in the speaker's mind, that no word or intonation would vary in delivery. That was not the case. Dr. Conwell knew that audiences differ. He recognized that he had to make each successive audience feel that his talk was a personal, living thing created for it, and it alone. How did he succeed in keeping this interrelationship between speaker, speech, and audience alive from one speaking engagement to the next? "I visit a town or city," he wrote, "and try to arrive there early enough to see the postmaster, the barber, the hotel manager, the principal of the schools, some of the ministers, and then go into the stores and talk with people, and see what has been their history and what opportunities they had. Then I give my lecture and talk to those people about the subjects that apply to them locally."

Dr. Conwell was thoroughly aware that successful communication depends upon how well the speaker can make his talk a part of the listeners and the listeners a part of the talk. That is why we have no true copy of "Acres of Diamonds," one of the most popular talks ever given from a lecture platform. With his clever insight into human nature and his painstaking industry, Dr. Conwell did not give the same lecture twice, although he addressed almost six thousand different audiences on the same subject. You can profit from his example by making certain that your talks are always prepared with a specific audience in mind. Here are some simple rules that will help you to build up a strong feeling of rapport with your listeners.

FIRST

Talk In Terms Of Your Listeners' Interests

That is exactly what Dr. Conwell did. He made a point of working into his lecture plenty of local allusions and examples. His audiences were interested because his talk concerned them, their interests, their problems. This linkage with what your listners are most interested in, namely, themselves, will insure attention and guarantee that the lines of communication will remain open. Eric Johnston, former head of the United States Chamber of Commerce and now president of the Motion Picture Association, uses this technique in almost every talk he gives. Note how resourcefully he employed local interests in a commencement address at the University of Oklahoma:

> You Oklahomans are well acquainted with goose-pimple peddlers. You don't have to think back too far to remember when they were writing Oklahoma off the books as a hopeless risk forever.
>
> Why, in the 1930s, all the ravens of despair were telling the crows to bypass Oklahoma unless they could pack along their own rations.

> They consigned Oklahoma to an everlasting future as part of a new American desert. Nothing would ever bloom again—they said. But in the 1940s, Oklahoma was a garden spot—and the toast of Broadway. For, once again, there was "waving wheat that sure smells sweet when the wind comes right behind the rain."
>
> In one short decade, the dustbowl was smothered with corn stalks as high as the elephant's eye.
>
> Here was a pay-off for faith—and calculated risk...
>
> But it is always possible to see our own times in better perspective against the backdrop of yesterday.
>
> So I looked up the files of the *Daily Oklahoman* for the spring of 1901 in preparation for my visit here. I wanted to sample the flavor of life in the territory fifty years ago.
>
> And what did I discover?
>
> Why I found the big accent was all on Oklahoma's future. The big stress was on hope.

Here is an excellent example of talking in terms of audience interest. Eric Johnston used instances of calculated risk right out of his listeners' backyards. He made them feel that his talk was no mimeographed copy—it was freshly created for them. No audience can withhold attention from a speaker who talks in its interests.

Ask yourself how knowledge of your subject will help the members of your audience solve their problems and achieve their goals. Then proceed to show them that, and you will have their complete attention. If you are an accountant and you start your talk by saying something like this, "I am going to show you how to save from fifty to a hundred dollars on your tax return," or you are a lawyer and you tell your listeners how to go about making a will, you will be certain to have an interested audience. Surely, there is some topic in your special fund of knowledge that can be of real help to members of your audience.

When asked what interests people, Lord Northcliffe, the William Randolph Hearst of British journalism, replied, "themselves." He built a newspaper empire on that single truth.

In *Mind in the Making,* James Harvey Robinson describes reverie as "a spontaneous and favorite kind of thinking." He goes on to say that, in reverie, we allow our ideas to take their own course, and this course is determined by our hopes and fears, our spontaneous desires, their fulfillment or frustration; by our likes and dislikes, our loves, hates, and resentments. There is nothing so interesting to ourselves as ourselves.

Harold Dwight, of Philadelphia, made an extraordinarily successful talk at a banquet which marked the final session of our course. He talked about each person in turn around the entire table, how he had spoken when the course started, how he had improved; he recalled the talks various members had made, the subjects they had discussed; he mimicked some of them, exaggerated their peculiarities, had everyone laughing, had everyone pleased. With such material, he could not possibly have failed. It was absolutely ideal. No other topic under the blue dome of heaven would have so interested that group. Mr. Dwight knew how to handle human nature.

Some years ago I wrote a series of articles for the *American Magazine,* and I had the opportunity of talking with John Siddall, who was then in charge of the Interesting People Department.

"People are selfish," he said. "They are interested chiefly in themselves. They are not very much concerned about whether the government should own the railroads; but they do want to know how to get ahead, how to draw more salary, how to keep healthy. If I were editor of this magazine," he went on, "I would tell them how to take care of their teeth, how to take baths, how to keep cool in summer, how to get a position, how to handle employees, how to buy homes, how to remember, how to avoid grammatical error, and so on. People are always interested in human interest stories, so I would have some rich man tell how he made a million in real estate. I would get prominent bankers and presidents of various corporations to tell the stories of how they battled their ways up from the ranks to power and wealth."

Shortly after that, Siddall was made editor. The magazine then had a small circulation. Siddall did just what he said he would do. The response? It was overwhelming. The circulation figures climbed up to two hundred thousand, three, four, half a million. Here was something the public wanted. Soon a million people a month were buying it, then a million and a half, finally two million. It did not stop there, but continued to grow for many years. Siddall appealed to the self-interests of his readers.

The next time you face an audience, visualize them as eager to hear what you have to say—as long as it applies to them. Speakers who fail to take this essential egocentricity of their listeners into account are apt to find themselves facing a restless audience, one squirming in boredom, glancing at wristwatches, and looking hopefully toward the exit doors.

SECOND

Give Honest, Sincere Appreciation

Audiences are composed of individuals, and they react like individuals. Openly criticize an audience and they resent it. Show your appreciation for something they have done that is worthy of praise, and you win a passport into their hearts. This often requires some research on your part. Such fulsome phrases as "this is the most intelligent audience I have ever addressed," are resented as hollow flattery by most audiences.

In the words of a great speaker, Chauncey M. Depew, you have to "tell them something about themselves that they didn't think you could possibly know." For example, a man who spoke before the Baltimore Kiwanis Club recently could find nothing unusual about that club except that it had in its membership a past international president and an international trustee. This was no news to the members of the club. So he tried to give it a new twist. He started his talk with this sentence: "The Baltimore Kiwanis Club is one club in 101,898!" The members listened. This speaker was certainly wrong—because there were only 2,897 Kiwanis Clubs in the world. The speaker then went on:

> Yes, even if you don't believe it, it is still a fact that your club, mathematically at least, is one in 101,898. Not one club in 100,000 or one in 200,000, but just exactly one in 101,898.
>
> How do I figure that out? Kiwanis International has only 2,897 member clubs. Well, the Baltimore club has a past president of Kiwanis International and an international trustee. Mathematically, the chances that any Kiwanis club will have both a past

president and an international trustee at the same time are one in 101,898—and the reason I know its right is that I got a Johns Hopkins Ph.D. in mathematics to figure it out for me.

Be exactly one hundred per cent sincere. An insincere statement may occasionally fool an individual, but it never fools an audience. "This highly intelligent audience..." "This exceptional gathering of the beauty and chivalry of Ho-Ho-Kus, New Jersey..." "I'm glad to be here because I love each one of you." No, no, no! If you can't show sincere appreciation, don't show any!

THIRD

Identify Yourself With The Audience

As soon as possible, preferably in the first words you utter, indicate some direct relationship with the group you are addressing. If you are honored by being asked to speak, say so. Wien Harold Macmillan spoke to the graduating class at De Pauw University in Greencastle, Indiana, he opened up the lines of communication in his first sentence.

"I am very grateful for your kind words of welcome," he said, "For a Prime Minister of Great Britain to be invited to your great university is an unusual occasion. But I feel that my present office was not the only nor, indeed, perhaps the main reason for your invitation."

Then he mentioned that his mother was an American, born in Indiana, and that her father had been one of De Pauw's first graduates.

"I can assure you that I am proud to be associated with De Pauw University," he said, "and to renew an old family tradition."

You may be sure that Macmillan's reference to an American school and to the American way of life which his mother and her pioneer father knew made friends for him at once.

Another way to open the lines of communication is to use the names of people in the audience. I once sat next to the main speaker at a banquet and I was amazed at his curiosity concerning various people in the hall. All through the meal he kept asking the master of ceremonies who the person in the blue suit at one table was, or what was the name of the lady in the flowered hat. When he arose to speak, it became evident at once why he was curious. He very cleverly wove some of the names he had learned into his talk, and I could see the evident pleasure on the faces of the persons whose names were used and I sensed the warm friendliness of the audience that this simple technique won for the speaker.

Notice how Frank Pace, Jr., speaking as the president of the General Dynamics Corporation, worked in a few names to advantage. He was speaking at an annual dinner of Religion in American Life, Inc., in New York:

"This has been a delightful and meaningful evening for me in many ways," he said. "First, I have my own minister, the Reverend Robert Appleyard, here in the audience. By his words, deeds, and leadership he has been an inspiration to me personally, to my family, and to our entire congregation... Secondly, to sit between Lewis Strauss and Bob Stevens, men whose interest in religion has been amplified by their interest in public service...is again a source of great personal pleasure..."

One word of caution: If you are going to work strange names into your talk, having learned them through inquiries made for the occasion, be sure you have them exactly right; be sure you understand fully the reason for your use of the names; be sure you mention them only in a favorable way; and use them in moderation.

Another method of keeping the audience at peak attentiveness is to use the pronoun "you" rather than the third-person "they." In this way you keep the audience in a state of self-awareness, which I have pointed out earlier cannot be overlooked by the speaker if he is to hold the interest and attention of his listeners. Here are some excerpts from a talk on Sulphuric Acid by one of our students in a New York City class:

> Sulphuric acid touches you in your life in a score of ways. If it were not for sulphuric acid, your car would stop, for it is used extensively in the refining of kerosene and gasoline. The electric lights that illuminate your office and your home would not be possible without it.
>
> When you turn on the water for your bath, you use a nickel-plated faucet, which requires sulphuric acid in its manufacture. The soap you use has possibly been made from greases or oils that have been treated with the acid. The bristles in your hairbrush and your celluloid comb could not have been produced without it. Your razor, no doubt, has been pickled in it after annealing.
>
> You come down to breakfast. The cup and saucer, if they are other than plain white, could not have come into being without it. Your spoon, knife and fork have seen a bath of sulphuric acid if they are silver-plated. And so on through the whole day sulphuric acid affects you at every turn. Go where you will, you cannot escape its influence.

By skillfully using "you" and inserting his listeners into the picture, this speaker was able to keep attention alive and glowing. There are times, however, when the pronoun "you" is dangerous, when it may establish a cleavage between speaker and audience rather than a bridge. This occurs when it might seem as though we were talking down to our audience or lecturing it. Then it is better to say "we" instead of "you."

Dr. W.W. Bauer, Director of Health Education of the American Medical Association, often used this technique in his radio and television talks. "We all want to know how to choose a good doctor, don't we?" he said in one of his talks. "And if we are going to get the best service from our doctor, don't we all want to know how to be good patients?"

FOURTH

Make Your Audience A Partner In Your Talk

Did it ever occur to you that you can keep an audience hanging on every word by using a little showmanship? The moment you choose some member of the audience to help you demonstrate a point or dramatize an idea, you will be rewarded by a noticeable rise in attention. Being aware of themselves as an audience, the members of it are keenly conscious of what happens when one of its own is brought into "the act" by the speaker. If there is a wall between the man on the platform and the people out there, as many speakers say, the use of audience participation will break that wall down. I remember a speaker who was explaining the distance it takes to stop a car after the brakes have been applied. He asked one of his listeners in the front row to stand and help demonstrate how this distance varied with the speed of the car. The man in the audience took the end of a steel tape measure and carried it forty-five feet down the aisle, where he stopped on a signal from the speaker. As I watched this procedure I couldn't help but notice how the whole audience became engrossed in the talk. I said to myself that the tape measure, in addition to being a graphic illustration of the speakers point, was certainly a line of communication between that speaker and this audience. Without that touch of showmanship the audience might still be concerned with what it was going to have for dinner or what programs would be on TV that evening.

One of my favorite methods of getting audience participation is simply to ask questions and to get responses, I like to get the audience on its feet, repeating a sentence after me, or answering my questions by raising their hands. Percy H. Whiting, whose book *How to Put Humor in Your Speaking and Writing* contains some valuable advice on the subject of audience participation, suggests having your listeners vote on something, or inviting them to help you solve a problem. "Get yourself in the right state of mind," says Mr. Whiting, "a state of mind that recognizes that a speech is unlike a recitation—that it is designed to get audience reaction—to make the audience a partner in the enterprise." I like that description of the audience as "a partner in the enterprise." It is the key to what this chapter is all about. If you use audience participation you confer the rights of partnership on your listeners.

FIFTH
Play Yourself Down

Of course, nothing will take the place of sincerity in this speaker-audience relationship. Norman Vincent Peale once gave some very useful advice to a fellow minister who was having great difficulty keeping the audience intent upon his sermons. He asked this minister to question his feelings about the congregation he addressed each Sunday morning—did he like them, did he want to help them, did he consider them his intellectual inferiors? Dr. Peale said that he never ascended the pulpit without feeling a strong sense of affection for the men and women he was about to face. An audience is quick in taking the measure of a speaker who assumes that he is superior in mental accomplishment or in social standing. Indeed, one of the best ways for a speaker to endear himself to an audience is to play himself down.

Edmund S. Muskie, then U.S. Senator from Maine, demonstrated this when he spoke to the American Forensic Association in Boston.

"I approach my assignment this morning with many doubts," he said. "In the first place, I am conscious of the professional qualifications of this audience, and question the wisdom of exposing my poor talents to your critical view. In the second place, this is a breakfast meeting—an almost impossible time of day for a man to be on guard effectively; and failure in this respect can be fatal to a politician. And thirdly, there is my subject—the influence which debating has had on my career as a public servant. As long as I am active politically, there is likely to be a sharp division of opinion among my constituents as to whether that influence has been good or bad.

"Facing these doubts, I feel very much like the mosquito who found himself unexpectedly in a nudist colony. I don't know where to begin."

Senator Muskie went on, from there, to make a fine address.

Adlai E. Stevenson played himself down at the beginning of a commencement exercise address at Michigan State University. He said:

"My feeling of inadequacy on these occasions brings to mind Samuel Butler's remark when he was once asked to talk about how to make the most out of life. I think his reply was: 'I don't even know how to make the most out of the next fifteen minutes.' And I feel that way about the next twenty minutes."

The surest way to antagonize an audience is to indicate that you consider yourself to be above them. When you speak, you are in a showcase and every facet of your personality is on display. The slightest hint of braggadocio is fatal. On the other hand, modesty inspires confidence and good will. You can be modest without being apologetic. Your audience will like and respect you for suggesting your limitations as long as you show you are determined to do your best.

The world of American television is a demanding one, and every season top-rated performers fall under the withering fire of competition. One of the survivors who comes back year after year is Ed Sullivan, who is not a television professional, but a newspaper man. He is an amateur in this fiercely competitive field and he survives because he doesn't presume to be anything but an amateur. Some of his mannerisms on camera would have been handicaps for anyone with less natural appeal. He cups his chin in his hand, hunches his shoulders, tugs at his necktie, stumbles over words. But these failings are not fatal for Ed Sullivan. He doesn't resent people for criticizing these faults. At least once a season he hires the services of a talented mimic who caricaturizes him to perfection, exaggerating all his faults. Ed Sullivan laughs as unaffectedly as everyone else when this performer holds the mirror up to nature. He welcomes criticism, and audiences love him for it. Audiences like humility. They resent the show-off, the egotist.

Henry and Dana Lee Thomas, in their book *Living Biographies of Religious Leaders,* said of Confucius:

"He never tried to dazzle people with his exclusive Knowledge. He merely tried to enlighten them with his inclusive sympathy." If we have this inclusive sympathy, we have the key that unlocks the door to the audiences' heart.

> *They may forget what you said, but they will never forget how you made them feel.*
>
> —Carl W. Buechner

~

> *You can make more friends in two months by becoming interested in other people than you can in two years by trying to get other people interested in you.*
>
> —Dale Carnegie

PART IV

THE TWO METHODS OF DELIVERING A TALK

11

The Short Talk To Get Action

A famous English bishop, during World War I, spoke to the troops at Camp Upton. They were on their way to the trenches; only a very small percentage of them had any adequate idea why they were being sent. I know; I questioned them. Yet the Lord Bishop talked to these men about "International Amity," and "Serbia's Right to a Place in the Sun." Why, half of them did not know whether Serbia was a town or a disease. He might just as well have delivered a learned disquisition on the nebular hypothesis. However, not a single trooper left the hall while he was speaking; military police were stationed at every exit to prevent their escape.

I do not wish to belittle the bishop. He was every inch a scholar, and before a body of churchmen he would probably have been powerful; but he failed with these soldiers, and he failed utterly. Why? He evidently knew neither the precise purpose of his talk nor how to accomplish it.

What do we mean by the purpose of a talk? Just this: every talk, regardless of whether the speaker realizes it or not, has one of four major goals. What are they?

1. To persuade or get action.
2. To inform.

3. To impress and convince.
4. To entertain.

Let us illustrate these by a series of concrete examples from Abraham Lincoln's speaking career.

Few people know that Lincoln once invented and patented a device for lifting stranded boats off sand bars and other obstructions. He worked in a mechanic's shop near his law office making a model of his apparatus. When friends came to his office to view the model, he took no end of pains to explain it. The main purpose of those explanations was to inform.

When he delivered his immortal oration at Gettysburg, when he gave his first and second inaugural addresses, when Henry Clay died and Lincoln delivered a eulogy on his life—on all these occasions, Lincoln's main purpose was to impress and convince.

In his talks to juries, he tried to win favorable decisions. In his political talks, he tried to win votes. His purpose, then, was action.

Two years before he was elected president, Lincoln prepared a lecture on inventions. His purpose was to entertain. At least, that should have been his goal; but he was evidently not very successful in attaining it. His career as a popular lecturer was, in fact, a distinct disappointment. In one town, not a person came to hear him.

But he succeeded notably in his other speeches, some of which have become classics of human utterance. Why? Largely because in those instances he knew his goal, and he knew how to achieve it.

Because so many speakers fail to line up their purpose with the purpose of the meeting at which they are speaking, they often flounder and come to grief.

For example: A United States congressman was once hooted and hissed and forced to leave the stage of the old New York Hippodrome, because he had—unconsciously, no doubt, but nevertheless, unwisely—chosen to make an informative talk. The crowd did not want to be instructed. They wanted to be entertained. They listened to him patiently, politely, for ten minutes, a quarter of an hour, hoping the performance would come to a rapid end. But it didn't. He rambled on and on; patience snapped; the audience would not stand for more. Someone began to cheer ironically. Others took it up. In a moment, a thousand people were whistling and shouting. The speaker, obtuse and incapable as he was of sensing the temper of his audience, had the bad taste to continue. That aroused them. A battle was on. Their impatience mounted to ire. They determined to silence him. Louder and louder grew their storm of protest. Finally, the roar of it, the anger of it, drowned his words—he could not have been heard twenty feet away. So he was forced to give up, acknowledge defeat, and retire in humiliation.

Profit by his example. Fit the purpose of your talk to the audience and the occasion. If the congressman had decided in advance whether his goal of informing the audience would fit the goal of the audience in coming to the political rally, he would not have met with disaster. Choose one of the four purposes only after you have analyzed the audience and the occasion which brings them together.

To give you guidance in the important area of speech construction, this entire chapter is devoted to the short talk to get action. The next three chapters will be devoted to the other major speech purposes: to inform, to impress and convince, and to entertain. Each purpose demands a different organizational pattern of treatment, each has its own stumbling blocks that must be hurdled. First, let's get down to the brass tacks of organizing our talks to get the audience to act.

Is there some method of marshaling our material so that we will have the best chance for successful follow-through on what we ask the audience to do? Or is it just a matter of hit-and-miss tactics?

I remember discussing this subject with my associates back in the thirties when my classes were beginning to catch on all over the country. Because of the size of our groups we were using a two-minute limit on the talks given by class members. This limitation did not affect the talk when the purpose of the speaker was merely to entertain or inform. But when we came to the talk to actuate, that was something else. The talk to get action just didn't get off the ground when we used the old system of introduction, body, and conclusion—the organizational pattern followed by speakers since Aristotle. Something new and different was obviously needed to provide us with a sure-fire method of obtaining results in a two-minute talk designed to get action from the listeners.

We held meetings in Chicago, Los Angeles, and New York. We appealed to all our instructors, many of them on the faculties of speech departments in some of our most respected universities. Others were men who held key posts in business administration. Some were from the rapidly expanding field of advertising and promotion. From this amalgam of background and brains, we hoped to get a new approach to speech organization, one that would be streamlined, and one that would reflect our age's need for a psychological as well as a logical method for influencing the listener to act.

We were not disappointed. From those discussions came the Magic Formula of speech construction. We began using it in our classes and we have been using it ever since. What is the Magic Formula? Simply this: Start your talk by giving us the details of your Example, an incident that graphically illustrates the main idea you wish to get across. Second, in specific clearcut terms give your Point, tell exactly what you want your audience to do; and third, give your Reason, that is, highlight the advantage or benefit to be gained by the listener when he does what you ask him to do.

This is a formula highly suited to our swift-paced way of life. Speakers can no longer afford to indulge in long, leisurely introductions. Audiences are composed of busy people who want whatever the speaker has to say in straightforward language. They are accustomed to the digested, boiled-down type of journalism that presents the facts straight from the shoulder. They are exposed to hard-driving Madison Avenue advertising that shoots the message in forceful, clear terms from signboard, television screen, magazine, and newspaper. Every word is measured and nothing is wasted. By using the Magic Formula you can be certain of gaining attention and focusing it upon the main point of your message. It cautions against indulgence in vapid opening remarks, such as: "I didn't have time to prepare this talk very well," or "When your chairman asked me to talk on this subject, I wondered why he selected me." *Audiences are not interested in apologies or excuses, real or simulated.* They want *action.* In the Magic Formula you give them action from the opening word.

The formula is ideal for short talks, because it is based upon a certain amount of suspense. The listener is caught up in the story you are relating but he is not aware of what the point of your talk is until near the end of the two- or three-minute period. In cases where demands are made upon the audience, this is almost necessary for success. No speaker who wants his audience to dig deep in their pocketbooks for a cause, no matter how worthy, will get very far by starting like this: "Ladies and gentlemen. I'm here to collect five dollars from each of you." There would be a scramble for the exits. But if the speaker describes his visit to the Children's Hospital, where he saw a particularly poignant case of need, a little child who lacked financial help for an operation in a distant hospital, and then asks for contributions, the chances of getting support from his audience would be immeasurably enhanced. It is the story, the *Example,* that prepares the way for the desired action.

Note how the incident-example is used by Leland Stowe to predispose his audience to support the United Nations' Appeal for Children:

> I pray that I'll never have to do it again. Can there be anything much worse than to put only a peanut between a child and death? I hope you'll never have to do it, and live with the memory of it afterward. If you had heard their voices and seen their eyes, on that January day in the bomb-scarred workers' district of Athens...Yet all I had left was a half-pound can of peanuts. As I struggled to open it, dozens of ragged kids held me in a vise of frantically clawing bodies. Scores of mothers, with babes in their arms, pushed and fought to get within arm's reach. They held their babies out toward me. Tiny hands of skin and bone stretched convulsively. I tried to make every peanut count.

> In their frenzy they nearly swept me off my feet. Nothing but hundreds of hands: begging hands, clutching hands, despairing hands; all of them pitifully little hands. One salted peanut here, and one peanut there. Six peanuts knocked from my fingers, and a savage scramble of emaciated bodies at my feet. Another peanut here, and another peanut there. Hundreds of hands, reaching and pleading; hundreds of eyes with the light of hope flickering out. I stood there helpless, an empty blue can in my hand.... Yes, I hope it will never happen to you.

The Magic Formula can be used also in writing business letters and giving instructions to fellow employees and subordinates. Mothers can use it when motivating their children, and children will find it useful when appealing to their parents for a favor or privilege. You will find it a psychological tool that can be used to get your ideas across to others every day of your life.

Even in advertising, the Magic Formula is used every day. Eveready Batteries recently ran a series of radio and television commercials built upon this Formula. In the Example step, the announcer told of someone's experience of being trapped, for instance, in an overturned car late at night. After giving the graphic details of the accident, he then called upon the victim to finish the story by telling how the beams of the flashlight, powered by Eveready Batteries, brought help in time. Then the announcer went on to the Point and Reason: "Buy Eveready Batteries and you may survive a similar emergency." These stories were all true experiences out of the Eveready Battery Company's files.

I don't know how many Eveready Batteries this particular advertising series sold, but I do know that the Magic Formula is an effective method of presenting what you want an audience to do, or to avoid. Let us take up the steps, one at a time.

FIRST

Give Your Example, An Incident From Your Life

This is the part of your talk that will take up the major portion of your time. In it you describe an experience that taught you a lesson. Psychologists say we learn in two ways: one, by the Law of Exercise, in which a series of similar incidents leads to a change of our behavioral patterns; and two, by the Law of Effect, in which a *single* event may be so startling as to cause a change in our conduct. All of us have had this type of unusual experience. We do not have to search long for these incidents because they lie close to the surface of our memories. Our conduct is guided to a large extent by these experiences. By vividly reconstructing these incidents we can make them the basis of influencing the conduct of others. We can do this because people respond to words in much the same way that they respond to real happenings. In the Example part of your talk, then, you must recreate a segment of your experience in such a way that it tends to have the same effect upon your audience as it originally had upon you. This places upon you the obligation to clarify, intensify, and dramatize your experiences in a way that will make them interesting and compelling to your listeners. Below are a number of suggestions which will help to make the Example step of your action talk clear, intense, and meaningful.

BUILD YOUR EXAMPLE UPON A SINGLE PERSONAL EXPERIENCE

The incident type of example is particularly powerful when it is based upon a single event that had a dramatic impact upon your life. It may not have taken more than a few seconds, but in that short span of time you learned an unforgettable lesson. Not long ago a man in one of our classes told of a terrifying experience when he tried to swim to shore from his overturned boat. I am sure that everyone in his audience made up his mind that, faced with a similar situation, he would follow this speaker's advice and stay with the capsized boat until help came. I remember another example of a speaker's harrowing experience involving a child and an overturned power mower. That incident was so graphically etched in my mind that I will always be on guard when children are hovering near my power mower. Many of our instructors have been so impressed by what they have heard in their classes that they have acted promptly to prevent similar accidents around their homes. One keeps a fire extinguisher handy in his kitchen, for instance, because of a talk he heard which vividly recreated a tragic fire that started from a cooking accident. Another has labeled all bottles containing poison, and has seen to it that they are out of the reach of his children. This action was prompted by a talk detailing the experience of a distraught parent when she discovered her child unconscious in the bathroom with a bottle of poison clutched in her hand.

A single personal experience that taught you a lesson you will never forget is the first requisite of a persuasive action talk. With this kind of incident you can move audiences to act—if it happened to you, your listeners reason, it can happen to them, and they had better take your advice by doing what you ask them to do.

START YOUR TALK WITH A DETAIL OF YOUR EXAMPLE

One of the reasons for starting your talk with the Example step is to catch attention at once. Some speakers fail to get attention with their opening words because all too often these words consist only of repetitious remarks, cliches, or fragmentary apologies that are of no interest to the audience. "Unaccustomed as I am to public speaking," is particularly offensive, but many other commonplace methods of beginning a talk are just as weak in attention-getting value. Going into the details of how you came to choose the subject, revealing to the audience that you are not too well prepared (they will discover that fact soon enough), or announcing the topic or theme of your talk like a preacher giving the text of the sermon are all methods to avoid in the short talk to get action.

Take a tip from top-flight magazine and newspaper writers: begin right in your example and you will capture the attention of your audience immediately.

Here are some opening sentences that drew my attention like a magnet: "In 1942, I found myself on a cot in a hospital"; "Yesterday at breakfast my wife was pouring the coffee and..."; "Last July I was driving at a fast clip down Highway 42..."; "The door of my office opened and Charlie Vann, our foreman, burst in"; "I was fishing in the middle of the lake; I looked up and saw a motorboat speeding toward me."

If you start your talk with phrases that answer one of the questions, Who? When? Where? What? How? or Why?, you will be using one of the oldest communication devices in the world to get attention—the story. "Once upon a time" are the magic words that open the floodgates of a child's imagination. With this same human interest approach you can captivate the minds of your listeners with your first words.

FILL YOUR EXAMPLE WITH RELEVANT DETAIL

Detail, of itself, is not interesting. A room cluttered with furniture and bric-a-brac is not attractive. A picture filled with too many unrelated details does not compel the eyes to linger upon it. In the same way, too many details—unimportant details—make conversation and public speaking a boring test of endurance. The secret is to select only those details that will serve to emphasize the point and reason of the talk. If you want to get across the idea that your listeners should have their cars checked before going on a long trip, then all the details of your Example step should be concerned with what happened to you when you failed to have your car checked before taking a trip. If you tell about how you enjoyed the scenery or where you stayed when you arrived at your destination, you will only succeed in clouding the point and dissipating attention.

But relevant detail, couched in concrete, colorful language, is the best way to recreate the incident as it happened and to picturize it for the audience. To say merely that you once had an accident because of negligence is bald, uninteresting, and hardly likely to move anyone to be more careful behind the wheel of a car. But to paint a word picture of your frightening experience, using the full range of multisensory phraseology, will etch the event upon the consciousness of the listeners. For instance, here is the way one class member developed an Example step that points up vividly the need for great caution on wintry roads:

I was driving north on Highway 41 in Indiana one morning just before Christmas, in 1949. In the car were my wife and two children. For several hours we had been creeping along on a sheet of mirror-like ice; the slightest touch on the steering wheel sent the rear of my Ford into a sickening slide. Few drivers got out of line or attempted to pass, and the hours seemed to creep as slowly as the cars.

Then we came to an open stretch where the ice was melted by the sun and I stepped on the accelerator to make up for lost time. Other cars did the same. Everybody suddenly seemed in a hurry to get to Chicago first. The children began to sing in the backseat as the tension of danger subsided.

The road suddenly went uphill and into a wooded area. As the speeding car reached the top I saw, too late, that the northern slope of the hill, still untouched by the sun's rays, was like a smooth river of ice. I had a fleeting glance of two wildly careening cars in front of us and then we went into a skid. Over the shoulder we went, hopelessly out of control, and landed in a snowbank, still upright; but the car that had been following us went into a skid, too, and crashed into the side of our car, smashing in the doors and showering us with glass.

The abundance of detail in this example made it easy for the audience to project themselves into the picture. After all, your purpose is to make your audience see what you saw, hear what you heard, feel what you felt. The only way you can possibly achieve this effect is to use an abundance of concrete details. As was pointed out in Chapter Four, the task of preparation of a talk is a task of reconstructing the answers to the questions Who? When? Where? How? and Why? You must stimulate the visual imagination of your listeners by painting word pictures.

RELIVE YOUR EXPERIENCE AS YOU RELATE IT

In addition to using picturesque details, the speaker should relive the experience he is describing. Here is where speaking approaches its sister field of acting. All great speakers have a sense of the dramatic, but this is not a rare quality, to be found only in the eloquent. Most children have a plentiful supply of it. Many persons of our acquaintance are gifted with a sense of timing, facial expression, mimicry, or pantomime that is a part, at least, of this priceless ability to dramatize. Most of us have some skill along these lines, and with a little effort and practice we can develop more of it.

The more action and excitement you can put into the retelling of your incident, the more it will make an impression on your listeners. No matter how rich in detail a talk may be, it will lack punch if the speaker does not give it with all the fervor of re-creation. Are you describing a fire? Give us the feeling of excitement that ran through the crowd as the firemen battled the blaze. Are you telling us about an argument with your neighbor? Relive it; dramatize it. Are you relating your final struggles in the water as panic swept over you? Make your audience feel the desperation of those awful moments in your life. For one of the purposes of the example is to make your talk memorable. Your listener will remember your talk and what you want them to do only if the example sticks in their minds. We recall George Washington's honesty because of the cherry tree incident popularized in the Weems biography. The New Testament is a rich storehouse of principles of ethical conduct reinforced by examples full of human interest—for instance, the story of the Good Samaritan.

In addition to making your talk more easily remembered, the incident-example makes your talk more interesting, more convincing, and easier to understand. Your experience of what life has taught you is freshly perceived by the audience: they are in a sense, predetermined to respond to what you want them to do. This brings us right to the doorstep of the second phase of the Magic Formula.

SECOND
State Your Point, What You Want The Audience To Do

The Example step of your talk to get action has consumed more than three-quarters of your time. Assume you are talking for two minutes. You have about twenty seconds in which to hammer home the desired action you wish the audience to take and the benefit they can expect as a result of doing what you ask. The need for detail is over. The time for forthright, direct assertion has come. It is the reverse of the newspaper technique. Instead of giving the headline first, you give the news story and then you headline it with your Point or appeal for action. This step is governed by three rules:

MAKE THE POINT BRIEF AND SPECIFIC

Be precise in telling the audience exactly what you want them to do. People will do only what they clearly understand. It is essential to ask yourself just exactly what it is you want the audience to do now that they have been disposed to action by your example. It is a good idea to write the point out as you would a telegram, trying to reduce the number of words and to make your language as clear and explicit as possible. Don't say: "Help the patients in our local orphanage." That's too general. Say instead: "Sign up tonight to meet next Sunday to take twenty-five children on a picnic." It is important to ask for an overt action, one that can be seen, rather than mental actions, which are too vague. For instance, "Think of your grandparents now and then," is too general to be acted upon. Say instead: "Make a point of visiting your grandparents this weekend." A statement such as, "Be patriotic," should be converted into "Cast your vote next Tuesday."

MAKE THE POINT EASY FOR LISTENERS TO DO

No matter what the issue is, controversial or otherwise, it is the speaker's responsibility to word his point, the request for action, in such a way that it will be easy for his listeners to understand and to do. One of the best ways to do this is to be specific. If you want your listeners to improve their ability to remember names, don't say: "Start now to improve your memory of names." That is so general it is difficult to do. Say instead; "Repeat the name of the next stranger you meet five times within five minutes after you meet him."

Speakers who give detailed action points are more apt to be successful in motivating their audiences than those who rest upon generalities. To say: "Sign the get well card in the back of the room" is far better than to urge your listeners to send a card or write a letter to a hospitalized fellow class member.

The question whether to state the point negatively or positively should be answered by looking at it from the listeners' point of view. Not all negatively phrased points are ineffective. When they epitomize an avoidance attitude they are probably more convincing to listeners than a positively stated appeal. Don't be a bulb-snatcher was an avoidance phrase employed with great effect some years ago in an advertising campaign designed to sell electric light bulbs.

STATE THE POINT WITH FORCE AND CONVICTION

The Point is the entire theme of your talk. You should give it, therefore, with forcefulness and conviction. As a headline stands out in block letters, your request for action should be emphasized by vocal animation and directness. You are about to make your last impression on the audience. Make it in such a way that the audience feels the sincerity of your appeal for action. There should be no uncertainty or diffidence about the way you ask for the order. This persuasiveness of manner should carry over to your last words, in which you give the third step of the Magic Formula.

THIRD

Give The Reason Or Benefit The Audience May Expect

Here again, brevity and economy are necessary. In the Reason step you hold out the incentive or reward the listeners may expect if they do what you have asked in the Point.

BE SURE THE REASON IS RELEVANT TO THE EXAMPLE

Much has been written about motivation in public speaking. It is a vast subject and a useful one for anyone engaged in persuading others to act. In the short talk to get action, on which we are centering our attention in this chapter, all you can hope to do is highlight the benefit in a sentence or two and then sit down. It is most important, however, that you focus upon the benefit that was brought out in the Example step. If you tell of your experience in saving money by buying a used car, and urge your listeners to buy a secondhand car, you must emphasize in your reason that they, too, may enjoy the economical advantages of buying secondhand. You should not deviate from the example by giving as your reason the fact that some used cars have better styling than the latest models.

BE SURE TO STRESS ONE REASON AND ONE ONLY

Most salesmen can give a half-dozen reasons why you should buy their product, and it is quite possible that you can give several reasons to back up your Point and all of them may be relevant to the Example you used. But again it is best to choose one outstanding reason or benefit and rest your case on it Your final words to the audience should be as clear-cut as the message on an advertisement in a national magazine. If you study these ads upon which so much talent has been expended, you will develop skill in handling the point and reason of your talk. No ad attempts to sell more than one product or one idea at a time. Very few ads in the big circulation magazines use more than one reason why you should buy. The same company may change its motivational appeal from one medium to another, from television to newspapers, for instance, but rarely will the same company make different appeals in one ad, whether vocal or visual.

If you study the ads you see in magazines and newspapers and on television and analyze their content you will be amazed at how often the Magic Formula is used to persuade people to buy. You will become aware of the ribbon of relevancy which binds the whole ad or commercial together into a unified package.

There are other ways of building up an example, for instance, by using exhibits, giving a demonstration, quoting authorities, making comparisons, and citing statistics. These will be explained more at length in Chapter Thirteen, where the longer talk to persuade will be discussed. In this chapter, the formula has been restricted to the personal incident type of example because, in the short talk to get action, it is by far the easiest and most interesting, dramatic, and persuasive method a speaker can use.

No one ever complains about a speech being too short!

—Ira Hayes

~

Your purpose is to make your audience see what you saw, hear what you heard, feel what you felt. Relevant detail, couched in concrete, colorful language, is the best way to recreate the incident as it happened and to picture it for the audience.

—Dale Carnegie

12

The Talk To Inform

Probably you often have heard speakers like one who once made a United States Senate investigating committee squirm with annoyance. He was a high-ranking government official, but he did not know any better than to talk on and on, vaguely, without ever making his meaning clear. He was pointless and obscure, and the committees confusion mounted by the moment. Finally one of its members, Samuel James Ervin, Jr., speaking as the senior Senator from North Carolina, got a chance to say a few words—and they were telling ones.

He said the official reminded him of a husband he knew back home. The husband notified his lawyer he wanted to divorce his wife, although he conceded she was beautiful, a fine cook, and a model mother.

"They why do you want to divorce her?" his lawyer asked.

"Because she talks all the time," the husband replied.

"What does she talk about?"

"That's the trouble," the husband answered, "she never says!

This is the trouble, too, with many speakers, both women and men. Their listeners don't know what such speakers are talking about. They never say. They never make their meaning clear.

In Chapter Seven, you received a formula for making short talks to get action from your listeners. Now, I am going to give you methods to help make your meaning clear when you set out to inform, and not motivate, your listeners.

We make informative talks many times every day: giving directions or instructions, making explanations and reports. Of all the types of talks given every week to audiences everywhere, the talk to inform is second only to the talk to persuade or get action. The ability to speak clearly precedes the ability to move others to action. Owen D. Young, one of America's top industrialists, emphasizes the need for clear expression in today's world:

As one enlarges his ability to get others to understand him, he opens up to that extent his opportunity for usefulness. Certainly in our society, where it is necessary for men even in the simplest matters to co-operate with each other, it is necessary for them first of all to understand each other. Language is the principal conveyor of understanding, and so we must learn to use it, not crudely but discriminately.

In this chapter are some suggestions to help you see language so clearly and discriminately that your audience will have no difficulty understanding you. "Everything that can be thought at all," said Ludwig Wittgenstein, "can be thought clearly. Everything that can be said, can be said clearly."

~

FIRST

Restrict Your Subject To Fit The Time At Your Disposal

In one of his talks to teachers, Professor William James pauses to remark that one can make only one point in a lecture, and the lecture he referred to lasted an hour. Yet I recently heard a speaker, who was limited by a stop watch to three minutes, begin by saying that he wanted to call our attention to eleven points. Sixteen and a half seconds to each phase of his subject! Seems incredible, doesn't it, that an intelligent man should attempt anything so manifestly absurd? True, this is an extreme case but the tendency to err in that fashion, if not to that degree, handicaps almost every novice. He is like a Cook's guide who shows Paris to the tourist in one day. It can be done, just as one can walk through the American Museum of Natural History in thirty minutes. But neither clearness nor enjoyment results. Many a talk fails to be clear because the speaker seems intent upon establishing a world's record for ground coveted in the allotted time. He leaps from one point to another with the swiftness and agility of a mountain goat

If, for example, yon are to speak on Labor Unions, do not attempt to tell us in three or six minutes why they came into existence, the methods they employ, the good they have accomplished, the evil they have wrought, and how to solve industrial disputes. No, no; if you strive to do that, no one will have a very clear conception of what you have said. It will be all confused, a blur, too sketchy, too much of a mere outline.

Wouldn't it be the part of wisdom to take one phase, and one phase only, of labor unions, and cover that adequately and illustrate it? It would. That kind of talk leaves a single impression. It is lucid, easy to listen to, easy to remember.

When I went to call one morning on a company president whom I know, I found a strange name on his door. The personnel director, an old friend of mine, told me why.

"His name caught up with him," my friend said.

"His name?" I repeated. "He was one of the Joneses who control the company, wasn't he?"

"I mean his nickname," my friend said. "It was 'Where-Is-He-Now?' Everyone called him 'Where-Is He-Now' Jones. He didn't last long. The family put a cousin in his place. He never took the pains to know what this business is all about. He'd put in a good long day, all right, but doing what? Popping in here, popping in there, all over the place, all the time. Just sort of covering ground. He thought it was more important for him to see that a shipping clerk turned out an electric light or that a stenographer picked up a paper clip than it was for him to study a big sales campaign. He wasn't in his office much. That's why we called him 'Where-Is-He-Now.'"

"Where-Is-He-Now" Jones reminds me of many speakers who could do much better than they do. They don't do better because they won't discipline themselves. They are the ones who, like Mr. Jones, try to cover too much ground. Haven't you heard them? And in the midst of a talk, haven't you wondered, "Where is he now?"

Even some experienced speakers are guilty of this fault. Perhaps the fact that they are capable in many other ways blinds them to the danger in dispersed effort. You need not be like them. Hold fast to your main theme. If you are to make yourself clear, your hearers must always be able to say, "I understand him. I know where he is now!"

SECOND

Arrange Your Ideas In Sequence

Almost all subjects can be developed by using a logical sequence based on time, space, or special topics. In the time sequence, for instance, you might consider your subject under the three categories of past, present, and future, or you might begin at a certain date and move backward or forward from that date. All process talks, for example, should begin at the raw-material stage and move through the various manufacturing steps that produce the finished product. How much detail you bring in will, of course, be governed by the time you have.

In the space sequence, you arrange your ideas according to some central point and go outward from there or you cover the material directionally, north, south, east, and west. If you were to describe the city of Washington, D. C., you might take your listeners to the top of the Capitol building and indicate the points of interest in each direction. If you are describing a jet engine or an automobile, for example, you might best discuss it by breaking it down into its component parts.

Some subjects have a built-in sequence. If you set out to explain the structure of the United States Government, you will do well to follow this inherent organizational pattern and discuss it according to the legislative, executive, and judicial branches.

THIRD
Enumerate Your Points As You Make Them

One of the simplest ways to keep a talk shipshape in the minds of your listeners is to mention plainly as you go along that you are taking up first one point and then another.

"My first point is this:...." You can be as blunt as that. When you've discussed the point, you can say frankly that you are going to the second one. You can keep on that way to the end.

Dr. Ralph J. Bunche, when assistant secretary-general of the United Nations, began an important talk sponsored by the City Club of Rochester, New York, in this straightforward manner:

"I have chosen to speak tonight on the topic 'The Challenge of Human Relations,' for two reasons," he said. He went on at once to add, "In the first place...." He continued soon, "In the second place...." Throughout the talk, he was careful to make clear to his audience that he was leading it, point by point, to his conclusion:

"We must never lose faith in man's potential power for good."

The same method was given an effective twist when the economist, Paul H. Douglas, spoke to a congressional joint committee struggling with means to stimulate business when it once was lagging in this country. He spoke both as a tax expert and as Senator from Illinois.

"My theme," he began, "is this: The quickest and most effective way to act is by means of a tax cut for lower and middle income groups—that is, those groups which tend to spend almost all their income."

"Specifically...," he went on.

"Further...," he continued.

"In addition...," he continued.

"There are three principal reasons: First...Second... Third...

"In summation, what we need is an immediate tax cut for low and middle income groups in order to increase demand and purchasing power."

FOURTH

Compare The Strange With The Familiar

Sometimes you will find yourself floundering in a vain attempt to explain your meaning. It's something quite clear to you but requiring involved explanation if your listeners are to be clear about it too. What to do? Compare it with something your listeners do understand; say one thing is like the other, the strange like the familiar.

Suppose you are discussing one of chemistry's contributions to industry—a catalyst. It is a substance that causes changes to occur in other substances without changing itself. That's fairly simple. But isn't this better? It is like a little boy in a schoolyard, tripping, punching, upsetting, poking all the other children there, and never being touched by a blow from anyone else.

Some missionaries once had to face this problem of putting strange statements into familiar terms when they translated the Bible into the dialect of a tribe living in equatorial Africa. Should they translate literally? They realized that if they did, the words at times would be meaningless to the natives.

They came, for example, to the lines: "Though your sins be as scarlet, they shall be white as snow." Should they translate this literally? The natives didn't know snow from jungle moss. But they had often climbed coconut trees and had shaken down nuts for lunch. The missionaries likened the unknown to the known. They changed the lines to read:

"Though your sins be as scarlet, they shall be white as the meat of a coconut."

Under the circumstances, it would be hard to improve on that, wouldn't it?

TURN A FACT INTO A PICTURE

How far away is the moon? The sun? The nearest other star? Scientists are apt to answer space-travel questions with a lot of mathematics. But science lecturers and writers know this is no way to make a fact clear to an average audience. They turn the figures into pictures.

The famous scientist Sir James Jeans was particularly interested in mankind's yearnings to explore the universe. As a scientific expert, he knew the mathematics involved, and he also knew that he would be most effective in writing or speaking if he dropped in a figure only here and there.

Our sun (a star) and the planets around us are so near that we do not realize how far away other objects whirling in space are, he pointed out in his book, *The Universe Around Us*. "Even the nearest star (Proxima Centauri) is 25,000,000,000,000 miles away," he said. Then, to make this figure more vivid, he explained that if one were to take off from the earth at the speed of light—186,000 miles a second—it would take him four and a quarter years to reach Proxima Centauri.

In this way, he made the vast distances in space seem more real than did another speaker whom I once heard describe such a simple thing as distances in Alaska. He said Alaska's area was 590,804 square miles, and dropped the attempt to show its size right there.

Does this give you any kind of picture of the size of the 49th State? It didn't give me one. To visualize its bigness, I had to wait until I learned from another source that its area more than equals the combined areas of Vermont, New Hampshire, Maine, Massachusetts, Rhode Island, Connecticut, New York, New Jersey, Pennsylvania, Delaware, Maryland, West Virginia, North Carolina, South Carolina, Georgia, Florida, Tennessee, and Mississippi. Now the 590,804 square miles take on a new meaning, don't they? You realize that in Alaska there's plenty of room to move around.

Some years ago a member of one of our classes described the fearful toll of fatal accidents on our highways by this appalling picture: "You are driving across the country from New York to Los Angeles. Instead of highway markers, imagine coffins standing upright in the earth, each containing a victim of last year's slaughter on the roads. As you speed along your car passes one of these gruesome markers every five seconds, for they are spaced twelve to a mile from one end of the country to the other!"

I never take a ride in a car very far before that picture comes back to me with startling realism.

Why is that so? Because ear impressions are hard to retain. They roll away like sleet striking the smooth bark of a beech tree. But eye impressions? I saw, a few years ago, a cannon ball embedded in an old house standing on the banks of the Danube—a cannon ball that Napoleon's artillery had fired at the battle of Ulm. Visual impressions are like that cannon ball; they come with a terrific impact. They embed themselves. They stick. They tend to drive out all opposing suggestions as Bonaparte drove away the Austrians.

AVOID TECHNICAL TERMS

If you belong to a profession the work of which is technical—if you are a lawyer, a physician, an engineer, or are in a highly specialized line of business— be doubly careful, when you talk to outsiders, to express yourself in plain terms and to give necessary details.

Be doubly careful, for, as a part of my professional duties, I have listened to hundreds of speeches that failed right at this point, and failed woefully. The speakers appeared totally unconscious of the general public's widespread and profound ignorance regarding their particular specialties. So what happened? They rambled on and on, uttering thoughts, using phrases that fitted into their experience and were instantly and continuously meaningful to them; but to the uninitiated, they were about as clear as the Missouri

River after the June rains have fallen on the newly plowed cornfields of Iowa and Kansas.

What should such a speaker do? He ought to read and heed the following advice from the facile pen of former Senator Beveridge of Indiana:

It is a good practice to pick out the least intelligent-looking person in the audience and strive to make that person interested in your argument. This can be done only by lucid statements of fact and clear reasoning. An even better method is to center your talk on some small boy or girl present with parents.

Say to yourself—say out loud to your audience, if you like—that you will try to be so plain that the child will understand and remember your explanation of the question discussed, and after the meeting be able to tell what you have said.

A physician in one of our classes remarked in a talk that "diaphragmatic breathing is a distinct aid to the peristaltic action of the intestines and a boon to health." He was about to dismiss that phase of his talk with that one sentence and to rush on to something else. The instructor stopped him, and asked for a show of hands of those who had a clear conception of how diaphragmatic breathing differs from other kinds of breathing, why it is especially beneficial to physical well-being, and what peristaltic action is. The result of the vote surprised the doctor; so he went back, explained, enlarged in this fashion:

> The diaphragm is a thin muscle forming the floor of the chest at the base of the lungs and the roof of the abdominal cavity. When inactive and during chest breathing, it is arched like an inverted washbowl.
>
> In abdominal breathing every breath forces this muscular arch down until it becomes nearly flat and you can feel your stomach muscles pressing against your belt. This downward pressure of the diaphragm massages and stimulates the organs of the upper part of the abdominal cavity—the stomach, the liver, the pancreas, the spleen, the solar plexus.
>
> When you breathe out again, your stomach and your intestines will be forced up against the diaphragm and will be given another massage. This massaging helps the process of elimination.
>
> A vast amount of ill health originates in the intestines. Most indigestion, constipation, and autointoxication would disappear if our stomachs and intestines were properly exercised through deep diaphragmatic breathing.

It is always best to go from the simple to the complex in giving explanations of any kind. For example, suppose you were trying to explain to a group of housewives why refrigerators must be defrosted. This would be the wrong way to go about it:

> The principle of refrigeration is based on the fact that the evaporator pulls heat from the inner portion of the refrigerator. As the heat is pulled out, the accompanying humidity clings to the evaporator, piling up into a thickness which insulates the

> evaporator and necessitates more frequent turning on of the motor to compensate for the thickening frost.

Notice how much easier it is to understand if the speaker starts with what the housewives are familiar with:

> You know where you freeze meat in your refrigerator. Well, you know, too, how the frost gathers on that freezer. Every day the frost gets thicker and thicker until the freezer must be defrosted to keep the refrigerator in good working order. You see, frost around the freezer is really like a blanket covering you in bed or like rock wool between the walls insulating your house. Now the thicker the frost gets, the harder it is for the freezer to pull the warm air out of the rest of the refrigerator and keep the refrigerator cold. The refrigerator motor then must work more often and longer to keep the box cold. But with an automatic defroster on your refrigerator, the frost never gets a chance to build up thickly. Consequently, the motor works less often and for shorter periods.

Aristotle gave some good advice on the subject: "Think as wise men do, but speak as the common people do." If you must use a technical term, don't use it until you have explained it so everybody in the audience knows what it means. This is especially true of your keystone words, the ones you use over and over.

I once heard a stockbroker speak to a group of women who wanted to learn fundamentals of banking and investment. He used simple language and he put them at ease in a conversational way. He made everything clear except his foundation words, which were strange to them. He spoke of the "clearing house," "puts and calls," "refunding mortgages," and "short sales and long sales." What could have been a fascinating discussion became a puzzle because he did not realize his listeners were unfamiliar with the words that were part and parcel of his trade.

There is no reason to avoid a keystone word which you know will not be understood. Just explain it as soon as you use it. Never fail to do this; the dictionary is all yours.

Do you want to say something about singing commercials? Or about impulse buying? About liberal arts courses, or cost accounting? About government subsidies, or automobiles that pass on the wrong side? Would you like to advocate a permissive attitude toward children, or the LIFO system of valuing inventories? Merely make sure that your listeners accept your keystone words in these specialized fields in the same sense in which you accept them.

FIFTH

Use Visual Aids

The nerves that lead from the eye to the brain are many times larger than those leading from the ear; and science tells us that we give twenty-five times as much attention to eye suggestions as we do to ear suggestions.

"One seeing," says an old Japanese proverb, "is better than a hundred times telling about."

So, if you wish to be clear, picture your points, visualize your ideas. That was the plan of John H. Patterson, founder of the National Cash Register Company. He wrote an article for *System Magazine,* outlining the methods he used in speaking to his workmen and his sales forces:

> I hold that one cannot rely on speech alone to make himself understood or to gain and hold attention. A dramatic supplement is needed. It is better to supplement whenever possible with pictures which show the right and the wrong way: diagrams are more convincing than mere words, and pictures are more convincing than diagrams. The ideal presentation of a subject is one in which every subdivision is pictured and in which the words are used only to connect them. I early found that in dealing with men, a picture was worth more than anything I could say.

If you use a chart or diagram, be sure it is large enough to see, and don't overdo a good thing. A long succession of charts is usually boring. If you make the diagram as you go along, be careful to sketch roughly and swiftly on the blackboard or flip chart. Listeners are not interested in great art work. Use abbreviations; write largely and legibly; keep talking as you draw or write; and keep turning back to your audience.

When you use exhibits, follow these suggestions and you will be assured of the rapt attention of your audience.

1. Keep the exhibit out of sight until you are ready to use it.
2. Use exhibits large enough to be seen from the very last row. Certainly your audience can't learn from any exhibit unless they see it.

3. Never pass an exhibit around among your listeners while you are speaking. Why invite competition?
4. When you show an exhibit, hold it up where your listeners can see it.
5. Remember, one exhibit that moves is worth ten that don't. Demonstrate if practicable.
6. Don't stare at the exhibit as you talk—you are trying to communicate with the audience, not with the exhibit.
7. When you have finished with the exhibit, get it out of sight if practicable.
8. If the exhibit you are going to use lends itself to "mystery treatment," have it placed on a table which will be at your side as you speak. Have it covered. As you talk, make references to it that will arouse curiosity—but don't tell what it is. Then, when you are ready to unveil it, you have aroused curiosity, suspense, and real interest.

Visual materials are becoming more and more prominent as devices to promote clarity. There is no better way to insure that your audience will understand what you have to say than to go before them prepared to show as well as to tell them what you have in mind.

Two American presidents, both masters of the spoken word, have indicated that the ability to be clear is the result of training and discipline. As Lincoln said, we must have a passion for clarity. He told Dr. Gulliver, the President of Knox College, how he developed this "passion" in early life:

> Among my earliest recollections I remember how, when a mere child, I used to get irritated when anybody talked to me in a way I could not understand. I don't think I ever got angry at anything else in my life. But that always disturbed my temper, and has ever since. I can remember going to my little bedroom, after hearing the neighbors talk of an evening with my father, and spending no small part of the night walking up and down and trying to make out the exact meaning of some of their, to me, dark sayings. I could not sleep, though I often tried to, when I got on such a hunt after an idea, until I had repeated it over and over, until I had put it in language plain enough as I thought for any boy I knew to comprehend. This was a kind of passion with me, and it has since stuck by me.

The other distinguished president, Woodrow Wilson, wrote some words of advice that strike the right note to end this chapter on making your meaning clear:

> My father was a man of great intellectual energy. My best training came from him. He was intolerant of vagueness, and from the time I began to write until his death in 1903, when he was eighty-one years old, I carried everything I wrote to him. He would make me read it aloud, which was always painful to me. Every now and then, he would stop me. "What do you mean by that?" I would tell him, and, of course, in doing so would express myself more simply than I had on paper. "Why didn't you say so?" he would go

on. "Don't shoot at your meaning with birdshot and hit the whole countryside; shoot with a rifle at the thing you have to say."

He who wants to persuade should put his trust not in the right argument, but in the right word. The power of sound has always been greater than the power of sense.

—Joseph Conrad

~

Applause is a receipt, not a bill.

—Dale Carnegie

13

The Talk To Convince

There was once a small group of men and women who found themselves in the path of a hurricane. Not a real hurricane, but the next thing to it. In short, a hurricane of a man named Maurice Goldblatt. Here is how one of that group described it:

> We were sitting around a luncheon table in Chicago. We knew this man was reputed to be a powerful speaker. We watched him intently as he stood up to speak.
>
> He began quietly—a spruce, pleasant man of middle age—thanking us for inviting him. He wanted to talk about something serious, he said, and he hoped we would forgive him if he disturbed us.
>
> Then, like a whirlwind, he struck. He leaned forward and his eyes transfixed us. He didn't raise his voice, but it seemed to me that it crashed like a gong.
>
> "Look around you," he said. "Look at one another.
>
> Do you know how many of you sitting now in this room are going to die of cancer? One in four of all of you who are over forty-five. One in four!"

He paused, and his face lightened. "That's a plain, harsh fact, but it needn't be for long," he said. "Something can be done about it. This something is progress in the treatment of cancer and in the search for its cause."

He looked at us gravely, his gaze moving around the table. "Do you want to help toward this progress?" he asked.

Could there have been an answer except "Yes!" in the minds of any of us then? "Yes!" I thought, and I found later that so did the others.

In less than a minute, Maurice Goldblatt had won us. He had drawn us personally into his subject. He had us on his side, in the campaign he was waging for a humanitarian cause.

Getting a favorable reaction is every speaker's objective any time, anywhere. As it happened, Mr. Goldblatt had a dramatically good reason for wanting to get one from us. He and his brother, Nathan, starting with little more than nothing, had built up a department store chain doing a business of more than $ 100,000,000 a year. Fabulous success had come to them after long, hard years, and then Nathan, ill only a short time, had died of cancer. After that, Maurice Goldblatt saw to it that the Goldblatt Foundation gave the first million dollars to the University of Chicago's cancer research program, and he gave his own time—retiring from business—to the work of interesting the public in the fight against cancer.

These facts, together with Maurice Goldblatt's personality, won us. Sincerity, earnestness, enthusiasm—a blazing determination to give himself to us for a few minutes, just as he was giving himself year in and out to a great cause—all of these factors swept us up into a feeling of agreement with the speaker, a friendliness for him, a willingness to be interested and moved.

FIRST

Win Confidence By Deserving It

Quintilian described the orator as "a good man skilled in speaking." He was talking about sincerity and character. Nothing said in this book, nor anything which will be said, can take the place of this essential attribute of speaking effectiveness. Pierpont Morgan said that character was the best way to obtain credit; it is also the best way to win the confidence of the audience.

"The sincerity with which a man speaks," said Alexander Woolcott, "imparts to his voice a color of truth no perjurer can feign."

Especially when the purpose of our talk is to convince, it is necessary to set forth our own ideas with the inner glow that comes from sincere conviction. We must first be convinced before we attempt to convince others.

SECOND

Get A Yes-Response

Walter Dill Scott, former president of Northwestern University, said that "every idea, concept, or conclusion which enters the mind is held as true unless hindered by some contradictory idea." That boils down to keeping the audience yes-minded. My good friend Professor Harry Overstreet brilliantly examined the psychological background of this concept in a lecture at the New School for Social Research in New York City:

> The skillful speaker gets at the outset a number of yes-responses. He has thereby set the psychological processes of his listeners moving in the affirmative direction. It is like the movement of a billiard ball. Propel it in one direction, and it takes some force to deflect it, far more force to send it back in the opposite direction.
>
> The psychological patterns here are quite clear.
>
> When a person says "No" and really means it, he is doing far more than saying a word of two letters. His entire organism—glandular, nervous, muscular—gathers itself together into a condition of rejection. There is, usually in minute but sometimes in observable degree, a physical withdrawal, or readiness for withdrawal. The whole neuromuscular system, in short, sets itself on guard against acceptance. Where, on the contrary, a person says "Yes," none of the withdrawing activities takes place. The organism is in a forward-moving, accepting, open attitude. Hence the more "Yesses" we can, at the very outset, induce, the more likely we are to succeed in capturing the attention for our ultimate proposal.
>
> It is a very simple technique—this yes-response. And yet how much neglected! It often seems as if people get a sense of their own importance by antagonizing at the outset. The radical comes into a conference with his conservative brethren; and

> immediately he must make them furious! What, as a matter of fact, is the good of it? If he simply does it in order to get some pleasure out of it for himself, he may be pardoned. But if he expects to achieve something, he is only psychologically stupid.
>
> Get a student to say "No" at the beginning, or a customer, child, husband, or wife, and it takes the wisdom and patience of angels to transform that bristling negative into an affirmative.

How is one going to get these desirable "yes-responses" at the very outset? Fairly simple. "My way of opening and winning an argument," confided Lincoln, "is to first find a common ground of agreement." Lincoln found it even when he was discussing the highly inflammable subject of slavery. "For the first half hour," declared *The Mirror,* a neutral paper reporting one of his talks, "his opponents would agree with every word he uttered. From that point he began to lead them off, little by little, until it seemed as if he had got them all into his fold."

Is it not evident that the speaker who argues with his audience is merely arousing their stubbornness, putting them on the defensive, making it well-nigh impossible for them to change their minds? Is it wise to start by saying, "I am going to prove so and so"? Aren't your listeners liable to accept that as a challenge and remark silently, "Let's see you do it"?

Is it not much more advantageous to begin by stressing something that you and all of your listeners believe, and then to raise some pertinent question that everyone would like to have answered? Then take your audience with you in an earnest search for the answer. While on that search, present the facts as you see them so clearly that they will be led to accept your conclusions as their own. They will have much more faith in some truth that they have discovered for themselves. "The best argument is that which seems merely an explanation."

In every controversy, no matter how wide and bitter the differences, there is always some common ground of agreement on which a speaker can invite everyone to meet. To illustrate: On February 3, 1960, the prime minister of Great Britain, Harold Macmillan, addressed both houses of the Parliament of the Union of South Africa. He had to present the United Kingdom's non-racial viewpoint before the legislature body at a time when apartheid was the prevailing policy. Did he begin his talk with this essential difference in outlook? No. He began by stressing the great economic progress made by South Africa, the significant contributions made by South Africa to the world. Then, with skill and tact he brought up the questions of differing viewpoints. Even here, he indicated that he was well aware that these differences were based on sincere conviction. His whole talk was a masterly statement reminding one of Lincoln's gentle but firm utterances in the years before Fort Sumter. "As a fellow member of the Commonwealth," said the Prime Minister, "it is our earnest desire to give South Africa our support and encouragement, but I hope you won't mind my saying frankly that there are some aspects of your policies which make it impossible for us to do this without being false to our deep convictions about the political destinies of free men to which in our own territories we are trying to give effect. I think we ought as friends to face together, without seeking to apportion credit or blame, the fact that in the world of today this difference of outlook lies between us." No matter how determined one was to differ with a speaker, a statement like that would tend to convince you of the speaker's fair-mindedness.

What would have been the result had Prime Minister Macmillan set out immediately to emphasize the difference in policy rather than the common ground of agreement? Professor James Harvey Robinson's enlightening book, *The Mind in the Making*, gives the psychological answer to that question:

> We sometimes find ourselves changing our minds without any resistance or heavy emotion, but if we are told we are wrong we resent the imputation and harden our hearts. We are incredibly heedless in the formation of our beliefs, but find ourselves filled with an illicit passion for them when anyone proposes to rob us of their companionship. It is obviously not the ideas themselves that are dear to us, but our self-esteem which is threatened... The little word *my* is the most important one in human affairs, and properly to reckon with it is the beginning of wisdom. It has the same force whether it is *my* dinner, *my* dog, and *my* house, or *my* faith, *my* country and *my* God. We not only resent the imputation that our watch is wrong, or our car shabby, but that our conception of the canals of Mars, of the pronunciation of "Epictetus," of the medicinal value of salicine, or of the date of Sargon I, are subject to revision... We like to continue to believe what we have been accustomed to accept as true, and the resentment aroused when doubt is cast upon any of our assumptions leads us to seek every manner of excuse for clinging to it. The result is that

most of our so-called reasoning consists in finding arguments for going on believing as we already do.

THIRD

Speak With Contagious Enthusiasm

Contradicting ideas are much less likely to arise in the listener's mind when the speaker presents his ideas with feeling and contagious enthusiasm. I say "contagious," for enthusiasm is just that. It thrusts aside all negative and opposing ideas. When your aim is to convince, remember it is more productive to stir emotions than to arouse thoughts. Feelings are more powerful than cold ideas. To arouse feelings one must be intensely in earnest. Regardless of the petty phrases a man may concoct, regardless of the illustrations he may assemble, regardless of the harmony of his voice and the grace of his gestures, if he does not speak sincerely, these are hollow and glittering trappings. If you would impress an audience, be impressed yourself. Your spirit, shining through your eyes, radiating through your voice, and proclaiming itself through your manner, will communicate itself to your audience.

Every time you speak, and especially when your avowed purpose is to convince, what you do determines the attitude of your listeners. If you are lukewarm, so will they be; if you are flippant and antagonistic, so will they be. "When the congregation falls asleep," wrote Henry Ward Beecher, "there is only one thing to do; provide the usher with a sharp stick and have him prod the preacher."

I was once one of three judges called on to award the Curtis medal at Columbia University. There were half a dozen undergraduates, all of them elaborately trained, all of them eager to acquit themselves well. But—with only a single exception—what they were striving for was to win the medal. They had little or no desire to convince.

They had chosen their topics because these topics permitted oratorical development. They had no deep personal interest in the arguments they were making. And their successive talks were merely exercises in the art of delivery.

The exception was a Zulu Prince. He had selected as his theme "The Contribution of Africa to Modern Civilization." He put intense feeling into every word he uttered. His talk was no mere exercise; it was a living thing, born of conviction and enthusiasm. He spoke as the representative of his people, of his continent; with wisdom, high character, and good will, he brought us a message of his people's hopes and a plea for our understanding.

We gave him the medal although he was possibly no more accomplished in addressing a large group than two or three of his competitors. What we judges recognized was that his talk had the true fire of sincerity; it was ablaze with truth. Beside it, the other talks were only flickering gas-logs.

The Prince had learned in his own way in a distant land that you can't project your personality in a talk to others by using reason alone: you have to reveal to them how deeply you yourself believe in what you say.

FOURTH

Show Respect And Affection For Your Audience

"The human personality demands love and it also demands respect," Dr. Norman Vincent Peale said as a prelude to speaking of a professional comedian. "Every human being has an inner sense of worth, of importance, of dignity. Wound that and you have lost that person forever. So when you love and respect a person you build him up and, accordingly, he loves and esteems you.

"At one time I was on a program with an entertainer. I did not know the man well, but since that meeting I read that he was having difficulty, and I think I know why.

"I had been sitting beside him quietly for I was about to speak. 'You aren't nervous, are you?' he asked

"'Why, yes,' I replied. 'I always get a little nervous before I stand up before an audience. I have a profound respect for an audience and the responsibility makes me a bit nervous. Don't you get nervous?'

"'No,' he said, 'Why should I? Audiences fall for anything. They are a lot of dopes.'

"'I don't agree with you,' I said. They are your sovereign judges. I have great respect for audiences.'"

When he read about this man's waning popularity Dr. Peale was sure the reason lay in an attitude that antagonized others instead of winning them.

What an object lesson for all of us who want to impart something to other people!

FIFTH

Begin In A Friendly Way

An athetist once challenged William Paley to disprove his contention that there was no Supreme Being. Very quietly Paley took out his watch, opened the case, and said: "If I were to tell you that those levers and wheels and springs made themselves and fitted themselves together and started running on their owrn account, wouldn't you question my intelligence? Of course, you would. But look up at the stars. Every one of them has its perfect appointed course and motion—the earth and planets around the sun, and the whole group pitching along at more than a million miles a day. Each star is another sun with its own group of worlds, rushing on through space like our own solar system. Yet there are no collisions, no disturbance, no confusion. All quiet, efficient, and controlled. Is it easier to believe that they just happened or that someone made them so?"

Suppose he had retorted to his antagonist at the outset: "No God? Don't be a silly ass. You don't know what you are talking about." What would have happened? Doubtlessly a verbal joust—a wordy war would have ensued, as futile as it was fiery. The atheist would have risen with an unholy zeal upon him to fight for his opinions with all the fury of a wildcat. Why? Because, as Professor Overstreet has pointed out, they were *his* opinions, and his precious, indispensable self-esteem would have been threatened; his pride would have been at stake.

Since pride is such a fundamentally explosive characteristic of human nature, wouldn't it be the part of wisdom to get a man's pride working for us, instead of against us? How? By showing, as Paley did, that the thing we propose is very similar to something that our opponent already believes. That renders it easier for him to accept than to reject your proposal. That prevents contradictory and opposing ideas from arising in the mind to vitiate what we have said.

Paley showed delicate appreciation of how the human mind functions. Most men, however, lack this subtle ability to enter the citadel of a man's beliefs arm in arm with the owner. They erroneously imagine that in order to take the citadel, they must storm it, batter it down by a frontal attack. What happens? The moment hostilities commence, the drawbridge is lifted, the great gates are slammed and bolted, the mailed archers draw their long bows—the battle of words and wounds is on. Such frays always end in a draw; neither has convinced the other of anything.

This more sensible method I am advocating is not new. It was used long ago by Saint Paul. He employed it in that famous address of his to the Athenians on Mars Hill— employed it with an adroitness and finesse that compels our admiration across nineteen centuries. He was a man of finished education; and, after his conversion to Christianity, his eloquence made him its leading advocate. One day he arrived at Athens—the post-Pericles Athens, an Athens that had passed the summit of its glory and was now on the decline. The Bible says of it at this period; "All the Athenians and strangers which were there spent their time in nothing else but either to tell or to hear some new thing."

No radios, no cables, no news dispatches; those Athenians must have been hard put in those days to scratch up something fresh every afternoon. Then Paul came. Here was something new. They crowded about him, amused, curious, interested. Taking him to the Aeropagus, they said: "May we know what this new doctrine, whereof thou speakest, is? For thou bringest certain strange things to our ears: we would know therefore what these things mean."

In other words, they invited a speech; and, nothing loath, Paul agreed. In fact, that was what he had come for. He probably stood up on a block or stone, and, being a bit nervous, as all good speakers are at the very outset, he may have given his hands a dry wash, and have cleared his throat before he began.

However, he did not altogether approve of the way they had worded their invitation; "New doctrines... strange things." That was poison. He must eradicate those ideas. They were fertile ground for the propagating of contradictory and clashing opinions. He did not wish to present his faith as something strange and alien. He wanted to tie it up to, liken it to. something they already believed. That would smother dissenting suggestions. But how? He thought a moment; hit upon a brilliant plan; he began his immortal address: "Ye men of Athens, I perceive that in all things ye are very superstitious."

Some translations read, "Ye are very religious." I think that is better, more accurate. They worshipped many gods; they were very religious. They were proud of it. He complimented them, pleased them. They began to warm toward him. One of the rules of the art of effective speaking is to support a statement by an illustration. He does just that:

"For, as I passed by, and beheld your devotions, I found an altar with this inscription, TO THE UNKNOWN GOD."

That proves, you see, that they were very religious. They were so afraid of slighting one of the deities that they had put up an altar to the unknown God, a sort of blanket insurance policy to provide against all unconscious slights and unintentional oversights. Paul, by mentioning this specific altar, indicated that he was not dealing in flattery; he showed that his remark was a genuine appreciation born of observation.

Now, here comes the consummate rightness of this opening; "Whom therefore ye ignorantly worship, Him declare I unto you."

"New doctrine...strange things?" Not a bit of it. He was there merely to explain a few truths about a God they were already worshipping without being conscious of it. Likening the things they did not believe, you see, to something they already passionately accepted—such was his superb technique.

He pronounced his doctrine of salvation and resurrection, quoted a few words from one of their own Greek poets; and he was done. Some of his listeners mocked, but others said, "We will hear thee again on this matter."

Our problem in making a talk to convince or impress others is just this: to plant the idea in their minds and to keep contradicting and opposing ideas from arising. He who is skilled in doing that has power in speaking and influencing others. Here is precisely where the rules in my book *How to Win Friends and Influence People* will be helpful.

Almost every day of your life you are talking to people who differ from you on some subject under discussion. Aren't you constantly trying to win people to your way of thinking, at home, in the office, in social situations of all kinds? Is there room for improvement in your methods? How do you begin? By showing Lincoln's tact and Macmillan's? If so, you are a person of rare diplomacy and extraordinary discretion. It is well to remember Woodrow Wilson's words, "If you come to me and say, 'Let us sit down and take counsel together, and, if we differ from one another, understand why it is that we differ from one another, just what the points at issue are,' we will presently find that we are not so far apart after all, that the points on which we differ are few and the points on which we agree are many, and that if we only have the patience and the candor and the desire to get together, we will get together."

The success of your presentation will be judged not by the knowledge you send but by what the listener receives.

—Lilly Walters

~

You have it easily in your power to increase the sum total of this world's happiness now. How? By giving a few words of sincere appreciation to someone who is lonely or discouraged. Perhaps you will forget tomorrow the kind words you say today, but the recipient may cherish them over a lifetime.

—Dale Carnegie

14

Impromptu Talks

Not long ago a group of business leaders and government officials met at the dedication of a pharmaceutical corporation's new laboratory. One after another, half a dozen subordinates to the research director arose and told of the fascinating work being done by chemists and biologists. They were developing new vaccines against communicable diseases, new antibiotics to fight viruses, new tranquilizers to ease tension. Their results, first with animals and then with human beings, were dramatic.

"This is marvelous," an official said to the research director. "Your men are really magicians. But why aren't you up there, speaking, too?"

"I can talk to my feet—not to an audience," the research director said gloomily.

A little later, the chairman took him by surprise.

"We haven't heard from our director of research," he said. "He doesn't like to give a formal speech. But I'm going to ask him to say a few words to us."

It was pitiful. The director stood up and managed no more than a couple of sentences. He apologized for not speaking at length, and that was the gist of his contribution.

There he was, a brilliant man in his field, and he seemed as awkward and confused as a man could be. This was not necessary. He could have learned to speak impromptu on his feet. I have never seen a serious and determined member of our classes who couldn't learn this. At the start, it takes what this research director hadn't given it—a resolute and brave rejection of one's defeatist attitude. Then, perhaps for quite a while, it takes an unwavering will to do the job no matter how hard it may be.

"I get along all right if I've prepared my talk and practiced it," you may say. "But I'm at a loss for words if I'm asked to talk when I don't expect it."

The ability to assemble one's thoughts and to speak on the spur of the moment is even more important, in some ways, than the ability to speak only after lengthy and laborious preparation. The demands of modern business and the current casualness with which modern oral communication is carried on make it imperative to be able to mobilize our thoughts quickly and verbalize fluently. Many of the decisions that affect industry and government today are made, not by one man, but around the conference table. The individual still has his say, but what he has to say has to be forcefully stated in the forum of group opinion. This is where the ability to speak impromptu comes alive and produces results.

FIRST
Practice Impromptu Speaking

Anyone of normal intelligence who possesses a fair portion of self-control can make an acceptable, often a brilliant, impromptu talk—which simply means "talking off the cuff." There are several ways you can improve your ability to express yourself fluently when called upon suddenly to say a few words. One method is to use a device that some famous movie actors used.

Years ago Douglas Fairbanks wrote an article for *American Magazine* in which he described a game of wits he, Charlie Chaplin, and Mary Pickford played almost every night for two years. It was more than a game. It was practice in that most difficult of all speaking arts—thinking on one's feet. As Fairbanks wrote, the "game" went like this:

Each of us would write a subject on a slip of paper. Then we folded the slips and shook them up. One would draw. Immediately he would have to stand and talk for sixty seconds on that subject. We never used the same subject twice. One night I had to talk on "lampshades." Just try it if you think it is easy. I got through somehow.

But the point is all three of us have sharpened up since we began the game. We know a lot more about a variety of miscellaneous subjects. But, far better than that, we are learning to assemble our knowledge and thoughts on any topic at a moment's notice. We are learning how to think on our feet.

Several times during my course the class members are asked to talk impromptu. Long experience has taught me that this kind of practice does two things: (1) it proves to the people in the class that they can think on their feet, and (2) this experience makes them much more secure and confident when they are giving their prepared talks. They realize that, if the worst should happen and they experience a blackout while giving their prepared material, they still can talk intelligently on an impromptu basis until they get back on the track again.

So, at one time or another, the class member hears, "Tonight each of you will be given a different subject on which to talk. You won't know what it is until you stand up to speak. Good luck!"

What happens? An accountant finds he is called on to speak about advertising. An advertising salesman has to talk on kindergartens. A schoolteacher's topic may be banking, and a banker's topic may be school teaching. A clerk may be assigned to talk on production, and a production expert may be asked to discuss transportation.

Do they hang their heads, and give up? Never! They don't pretend to be authorities. They work the subjects around to fit their knowledge of something familiar to them. In their first efforts, they may not give a fine talk. But they *do* get up; they *do* talk. For some it is easy; for some it is hard, but they don't give up; they all find that they can do far better than they'd thought they would. This is thrilling to them. They see that they can develop an ability which they didn't believe they had.

I believe that if they can do this, anybody can do it—with willpower and confidence—and that the more often one tries to do it, the easier it will be.

Another method we use to train people to speak on their feet is the linkage technique of impromptu speaking. It is a stimulating feature of one of our class sessions. One class member is told to begin a story in the most fantastic terms he can invent. For instance he might say, "The other day I was piloting my helicopter when I noticed a swarm of flying saucers approaching. I started to descend. But a little man in the nearest saucer started to open fire. I..."

At this point a bell sounds indicating the end of this speaker's time, and the next class member in line must continue the story. By the time everyone in the class has contributed his share, the action may end along the canals of Mars or in the halls of Congress.

This method of developing skill in speaking without preparation is admirable as a training device. The more such practice a person gets the better he will be qualified to meet the real situations that may arise when he has to speak "for keeps in his business and social life.

SECOND

Be Mentally Ready To Speak Impromptu

When you are called on to speak without preparation usually you are expected to make some remarks about a subject upon which you can speak with authority. The problem here is to face up to the situation of talking and to decide what exactly you want to cover in the short time at your disposal. One of the best ways to become adept at this is to prepare yourself mentally for these situations. When you are at a meeting keep asking yourself what you would say now if you were called upon. What aspect of your subject would be most appropriate to cover at this time? How would you phrase your approval or rejection of the proposals now being put forth on the floor?

So the first bit of advice I offer is this: condition yourself mentally to speak impromptu on all occasions.

This requires thinking on your part, and thinking is the hardest thing in the world to do. But I am certain that no man ever made a reputation as an impromptu speaker who did not prepare himself by devoting hours of analysis to every public situation in which he was a participant. Just as an airline pilot readies himself to act with cool precision in an emergency by continually posing to himself problems that could arise at any moment, the man who shines as an impromptu speaker prepares himself by making countless talks that are never given. Such talks really are not "impromptu"; they are talks with general preparation.

Because your subject is known, your problem is one of organization to fit the time and the occasion. As an impromptu speaker you will naturally speak for only a short time. Decide what aspect of your topic would fit the situation. Don't apologize because you are unprepared. This is the expected thing. Launch into your topic as soon as possible, if not immediately, and please, I beg you, follow this advice.

THIRD

Get Into An Example Immediately

Why? For three reasons: (1) You will free yourself at once of the necessity to think hard about your next sentence, for experiences are easily recounted even in an impromptu situation. (2) You will get into the swing of speaking, and your first-moment jitters will fly away, giving you the opportunity to warm up to your subject matter. (3) You will enlist the attention of your audience at once. As pointed out in Chapter Seven, the incident- example is a sure-fire method of capturing attention immediately.

An audience absorbed in the human interest aspect of your example will give you reassurance when you need it most—during the first few moments of speaking. Communication is a two-way process; the speaker who captures attention is immediately aware of it. As he notes the receptive forces and feels the glow of expectancy, like an electric current, play over the heads of his audience, he is challenged to go on, to do his best, to respond. The rapport thus established between speaker and audience is the key to all successful speaking—

without it true communication is impossible. That is why I urge you to begin with an example, especially when you are called on to say a few words.

FOURTH
Speak With Animation And Force

As has been said several times before in this book, if you speak with energy and forcefulness, your external animation will have a beneficial effect upon your mental processes. Have you ever watched a man in a conversational group who suddenly begins to gesture as he speaks? Soon he is talking fluently, sometimes brilliantly, and he begins to attract a group of eager listeners. The relation of physical activity to the mind is a close one. We use the same words to describe manual and mental operations; for instance, we say "we grasp an idea," or "we clutch at a thought." Once we get the body charged up and animated, as William James pointed out, we very soon will get the mind functioning at a rapid pace. So my advice to you is to throw yourself with abandon into your talk and you will help to insure your success as an impromptu speaker.

FIFTH
Use The Principle Of The Here And Now

The time will come when someone will tap you on the shoulder and say "How about a few words?" Or it might come without warning at all. You are relaxed and enjoying the remarks of the master of ceremonies when suddenly you realize he is talking about you. Everybody turns in your direction and before you know it you are introduced as the next speaker.

In this kind of situation your mind is apt to shoot off, like Stephen Leacock's famous but befuddled horseman, who got on his horse "and made off in all directions." Now, if ever, is the time to remain calm. You can get a breather as you address the chairman. Then it is best to stay close to the meeting in the remarks you make. Audiences are interested in themselves and what they are doing. There are three sources therefore from which you can draw ideas for an impromptu speech.

First is the audience itself. Remember this, I pray you, for easy speaking. Talk about your listeners, who they are and what they are doing, especially what specific good they perform to the community or for humanity. Use a specific example.

The *second* is the occasion. Surely you can dwell on the circumstances that brought the meeting about. Is it an anniversary, a testimonial, an annual meeting, a political or patriotic occasion?

Lastly, if you have been an attentive listener, you might indicate your pleasure in something specific another speaker said before you and amplify that. The most successful impromptu talks are those that are really impromptu. They express things that the speaker feels in his heart about the audience and the occasion. They fit the situation like hand in glove. They are tailor-made for this occasion, and this occasion alone. Therein lies their success: they flower out of the moment and then, like rare-blossoming roses, they fade from the scene. But the pleasure enjoyed by your audience lives on, and sooner than you think you begin to be looked upon as an impromptu speaker.

SIXTH
Don't Talk Impromptu—Give An Impromptu Talk

There is a difference as implied in the statement above. It is not enough just to ramble on and string together a series of disconnected nothings on a flimsy thread of inconsequence. You must keep your ideas logically grouped around a central thought which might well be the point you want to get across. Your examples will cohere to this central idea. And again, if you speak with enthusiasm, you will find that what you say off the cuff has a vitality and punch that your prepared talks do not have.

You can become a competent impromptu speaker if you take to heart some of the suggestions made in this chapter. You can practice along lines of the classroom techniques explained in the early part of this chapter.

At a meeting you can do a little preliminary planning and you can keep yourself aware of the possibility of being called upon at any moment If you think you may be asked to contribute your comments or suggestions, pay careful attention to the other speakers. Try to be ready to condense your ideas into a few words. When the time comes, say what you have in mind as plainly as you can. Your views have been sought. Give them briefly, and sit down.

Norman Bel Geddes, the architect and industrial designer, used to say that he couldn't put his thoughts into words unless he was on his feet. Pacing up and down his office, as he talked to associates about complex plans for building or exhibit, he was at his best. He had to learn how to speak when sitting down, and of course he did.

With most of us, it's the other way around; we have to learn to speak standing up, and of course we can. The chief secret lies in making a start—giving one short talk—and then making another start, and another, and another.

We will find that each successive talk comes more easily. Each talk will be better than its predecessors. We will realize in the end speaking impromptu to a group is merely an extension of the same thing we do when we speak impromptu to friends in our living room.

It usually takes me more than three weeks to prepare a good impromptu speech.

—Mark Twain

~

When dealing with people, remember you are not dealing with creatures of logic, but creatures of emotion.

—Dale Carnegie

Develop
SELF-CONFIDENCE,
Improve
PUBLIC
SPEAKING

1

Increase Courage And Self-Confidence

Courage is one step ahead of fear.

—Coleman Young

More than eighteen thousand businesspersons, since 1912, have been members of the various public speaking courses conducted by me. Most of them have, at my request, written stating why they had enrolled for this training and what they hoped to obtain from it. Naturally, the phraseology varied, but the central desire in these letters, the basic want in the vast majority remained surprisingly the same: "When I am called upon to stand up and speak," man after man wrote, "I become so self-conscious, so frightened, that I can't think clearly, can't concentrate, can't remember what I had intended to say. I want to gain self-confidence, poise, and the ability to think on my feet. I want to get my thoughts together in logical order and I want to be able to say clearly and convincingly before a business group or audience." Thousands of their confessions sounded about like that. Years ago, a gentleman here called D.W. Ghent joined my public speaking course in Philadelphia. Shortly after the opening session, he invited me to lunch with him in the

Manufacturers' Club. He was a man of middle age and had always led an active life, was head of his own manufacturing establishment, a leader in church work and civic activities. While we were having lunch that day, he leaned across the table and said: "I have been asked many times to talk before various gatherings but I have never been able to do so. I get so fussed, my mind becomes an utter blank: so I have side-stepped it all my life. But I am chairman now of a board of college trustees. I must preside at their meetings. Do you think it will be possible for me to learn to speak at this late date in my life?"

"Do I *think*, Mr. Ghent?" I replied. "It is *not* a question of my *thinking*. I *know you can*, and I *know you will* if you will only practice and follow the directions and instructions."

After he had completed his training, we lost touch with each other for awhile. In 1921, we met and lunched together again at the Manufacturers' Club. We sat in the same corner and occupied the same table that we had had on the first occasion. Reminding him of our former conversation, I asked him if I had been too sanguine then. He took a little red-backed notebook out of his pocket and showed me a list of talks and dates for which he was booked. "And the ability to make these," he confessed, "the pleasure I get in doing it, the additional service I can render to the community—these are among the most gratifying things in my life."

The International Conference for the Limitation of Armaments had been held in Washington shortly before that. When it was known that Lloyd George was planning to attend it, the Baptists of Philadelphia cabled, inviting him to speak at a great mass meeting to be held in their city. Lloyd George cabled back that if he came to Washington he would accept their invitation. And Mr. Ghent informed me that he himself had been chosen, from among all the Baptists of that city, to introduce England's premier to the audience.

And this was the man who had sat at that same table less than three years before and solemnly asked me if I thought he would ever be able to talk in public!

Was the rapidity with which he forged ahead in his speaking ability unusual? Not at all. There have been hundreds of similar cases. For example—to quote one more specific instance—years ago, a Brooklyn physician, whom we will call Dr. Curtis, spent the winter in Florida near the training grounds of the Giants. Being an enthusiastic baseball fan, he often went to see them practice. In time, he became quite friendly with the team, and was invited to attend a banquet given in their honour.

After the coffee and nuts were served, several prominent guests were called upon to "say a few words". Suddenly, with the abruptness and unexpectedness of an explosion, he heard the toast-master remark: "We have a physician with us tonight, and I am going to ask Dr. Curtis to talk on a baseball player's health."

Was he prepared? Of course. He had had the best preparation in the world: he had been studying hygiene and practicing medicine for almost a third of a century. He could have sat in his chair and talked about this subject all night to the man seated on his right or left. But to get up and say the same things to even a small audience—that was another matter. That was a paralyzing matter. His heart doubled its pace and skipped beats at the very contemplation of it. He had never made a public speech in his life, and every thought that he had had now took wings.

What was he to do? The audience was applauding. Everyone was looking at him. He shook his head. But that served only to heighten the applause, to increase the demand. The cries of "Dr. Curtis! Speech! Speech!" grew louder and more insistent.

He was in positive misery. He knew that if he got up he would fail, that he would be unable to utter half a dozen sentences. So he arose and, without saying a word, turned his back on his friends and walked silently out of the room, a deeply embarrassed and humiliated man.

Small wonder that one of the first things he did after getting back to Brooklyn was to come to the Central Y.M.C.A. and enrol in the course in Public Speaking. He didn't propose to be put to the blush and be stricken dumb a second time.

He was the kind of student that delights an instructor: he was in dead earnest. He wanted to be able to talk, and there was no half-heartedness about his desires. He prepared his talks thoroughly, he practiced them with a will, and he never missed a single session of the course.

He did precisely what such a student always does: he progressed at a rate that surprised him, that surpassed his fondest hopes. After the first few sessions his nervousness subsided, and his confidence mounted higher and higher. In two months he had become the star speaker of the group. He was soon accepting invitations to speak elsewhere; he now loved the feel and exhilaration of it, the distinction and the additional friends it brought him.

The gaining of self-confidence and courage and the ability to think calmly and clearly while talking to a group is not one-tenth as difficult as most men imagine. It is not a gift bestowed by Providence on only a few rarely endowed individuals. It is like the ability to play golf. Any man can develop his own latent capacity if he has sufficient desire to do so.

Is there the faintest shadow of a reason why you should not be able to think as well in a perpendicular position before an audience as you can when sitting down? Surely, you know there is not. In fact, you ought to think better when facing a group of men. Their presence ought to stir you and lift you. A great many speakers will tell you that the presence of an audience is a stimulus, an inspiration, that drives their brains to function more clearly, more keenly. At such times, thoughts, facts, ideas, that they did not know they possessed, drift smoking by, as Henry Ward Beecher said, and they have but to reach out and lay their hands hot upon them. They ought to be your experience. It probably will be if you practice and persevere.

Of this much, however, you may be absolutely sure: training and practice will wear away your audience-fright and give you self-confidence and an abiding courage.

Do not imagine that your case is unusually difficult. Even those who afterwards became the most eloquent representatives of their generation were, at the outset of their careers, afflicted by this blinding fear and self-consciousness.

Mark Twain, the first time he stood up to lecture, felt as if his mouth were filled with cotton and his pulse were speeding for some prize cup.

The late Jean Jaurès, the most powerful political speaker that France produced during his generation, sat, for a year, tongue-tied in the Chamber of Deputies before he could summon up the courage to make his initial speech.

John Bright, the illustrious Englishman who, during the civil war, defended in England the cause of union and emancipation, made his maiden speech before a group of countryfolk gathered in a school building. He was so frightened on the way to the place, so fearful that he would fail, that he implored his companion to start applause to bolster him up whenever he showed signs of giving way to his nervousness.

Charles Stewart Parnell, the great Irish leader, at the outset of his speaking career, was so nervous, according to the testimony of his brother, that he frequently clenched his fists until his nails sank into his flesh and his palms bled.

Disraeli admitted that he would rather have led a cavalry charge than have faced the House of Commons for the first time. His opening speech there was a ghastly failure. So was Sheridan's.

In fact, so many of the famous speakers of England have made poor showings at first that there is now a feeling in Parliament that it is rather an inauspicious omen for a young man's initial talk to be a decided success. So take heart.

After watching the careers and aiding somewhat in the development of so many speakers, the author is always glad when a student has, at the outset, a certain amount of flutter and nervous agitation.

There is a certain responsibility in making a talk, even if it is to only two dozen men in a business conference—a certain strain, a certain shock, a certain excitement. The speaker ought to be keyed up like a thoroughbred straining at the bit. The immortal Cicero said, two thousand years ago, that all public speaking of real merit was characterized by nervousness.

Speakers often experience this same feeling even when they are talking over the radio. "Microphone fright", it is called. When Charlie Chaplin went "on the air", he had his speech all written out. Surely he was used to audiences. He toured America back in 1912 with a vaudeville sketch entitled "A Night in a Music Hall". Before that he was on the legitimate stage in England. Yet, when he went into the padded room and faced the microphone, he had a feeling in the stomach not unlike the sensation one gets when he crosses the Atlantic during a stormy February.

James Kirkwood, a famous motion picture actor and director, had a similar experience. He used to be a star on the speaking stage, but when he came out of the sending room after addressing the invisible audience, he was mopping perspiration from his brow. "An opening night on Broadway," he confessed, "is nothing in comparison to that."

Some men, no matter how often they speak, always experience this self-consciousness just before they commence, but in a few seconds after they have got on their feet, it disappears.

Even Lincoln felt shy for the few opening moments. In a few moments he gained composure and warmth and earnestness, and his real speech began.

Your experience may be similar to his.

In order to get the most out of this training, and to get it with rapidity and dispatch, four things are essential:

FIRST

Start With A Strong And Persistent Desire

This is of far more importance than you probably realize. If your instructor could look into your mind and heart now and ascertain the depth of your desires, he could foretell, almost with certainty, the swiftness of the progress you will make. If your desire is pale and flabby, your achievements will also take on that hue and consistency. But, if you go after this subject with persistence, and with the energy of a bulldog after a cat, nothing underneath the Milky Way will defeat you.

Therefore, arouse your enthusiasm for this study. Enumerate its benefits. Think of what additional self-confidence and the ability to talk more convincingly in business will mean to you. Think of what it may mean to you socially, of the friends it will bring, of the increase of your personal influence, of the leadership it will give you. And it will give you leadership more rapidly than almost any other activity you can think of or imagine.

It is an attainment that almost every person of education longs for. After Andrew Carnegie's death there was found, among his papers, a plan for his life drawn up when he was thirty-three years of age. He then felt that in two more years he could so arrange his business as to have an annual income of fifty thousand dollars; so he proposed to retire at thirty-five, go to Oxford and get a thorough education, and *"pay special attention to speaking in public."* Think of the glow of satisfaction and pleasure that will accrue from the exercise of this new power. The author has travelled round over no small part of this terrestrial ball, and has had many and varied experiences, but for downright, and lasting inward satisfaction, he knows of few things that will compare to standing before an audience and making men think your thoughts after you. It will give you a sense of strength, a feeling of power. It will appeal to your pride of personal accomplishment. It will set you off from and raise you above your fellowmen. There is magic in it and a never-to-be-forgotten thrill. "Two minutes before I begin," a speaker confessed, "I would rather be whipped than start, but two minutes before I finish, I would rather be shot than stop."

In every course, some men grow faint-hearted and fall by the wayside, so you should keep thinking of what this course will mean to you until your desire is white hot. You should start this programme with an enthusiasm that will carry you through every session, triumphant to the end. Tell your friends that you have joined this course. Set aside one certain night of the week for the reading of these lessons and the preparation of your talks. In short, make it as easy as possible to go ahead. Make it as difficult as possible to retreat.

When Julius Caesar sailed over the channel from Gaul and landed with his legions on what is now England, what did he do to insure the success of his arms? A very clever thing: he halted his soldiers on the chalk cliffs of Dover, and, looking down over the waves two hundred feet below, they saw red tongues of fire consume every ship in which they had crossed. In the enemy's country, with the last link with the Continent gone, the last means of retreating burned, there was but one thing left for them to do: to advance, to conquer. That is precisely what they did.

Such was the spirit of the immortal Caesar. Why not make it yours, too, in this war to exterminate your foolish fear of audiences.

SECOND

Act Confidently

To develop courage when you are facing an audience, act as if you already have it. Of course, unless you are prepared, all the acting in the world will avail but little. But granted that you know what you are going to talk about, step out briskly and take a deep breath. In fact, breathe deeply for thirty seconds before you ever face your audience. The increased supply of oxygen will buoy you up and give you courage. The great tenor, Jean de Reszke, used to say that when you had your breath so you "could sit on it", nervousness vanished.

When a youth of the Peuhl tribe in Central Africa attains manhood and wishes to take unto himself a wife, he is compelled to undergo the ceremony of flagellation. The women of the tribe foregather, singing and clapping their hands to the rhythm of tom-toms. The candidate strides forth stripped naked to the waist. Suddenly a man armed with a cruel whip sets upon the lad, beating his bare skin, lashing him, flogging him like a fiend. Welts appear; often the skin is cut; blood flows; scars are made that last a lifetime. During this scourging, a venerable judge of the tribe crouches at the feet of the victim to see if he moves or exhibits the slightest evidence of pain. To pass the test successfully the tortured aspirant must not only endure the ordeal, but, as he endures it, he must sing a paean of praise.

In every age, in every clime, men have always admired courage; so, no matter how your heart may be pounding inside, stride forth bravely, stop, stand still like the scourged youth of Central Africa, and like him, act as if you loved it.

Draw yourself up to your full height and look your audience straight in the eyes, and begin to talk as confidently as if every one of them owed you money. Imagine that they do. Imagine that they have assembled there to bet you for an extension of credit. The psychological effect on you will be beneficial.

Do not nervously button and unbutton your coat, and fumble with your hands. If you must make nervous movements, place your hands behind your back and twist your fingers there where no one can see the performance—or wiggle your toes.

As a general rule, it is bad for a speaker to hide behind furniture, but it may give you a little courage the first few times to stand behind a table or chair and to grip them tightly—or hold a coin firmly in the palm of your hand.

How did Theodore Roosevelt develop his characteristic courage and self-reliance? Was he endowed by nature with a venturesome and daring spirit? Not at all. "Having been a rather sickly and awkward boy," he confesses in his *Autobiography*, "I was, as a young man, at first both nervous and distrustful of my own prowess. I had to train myself painfully and laboriously not merely as regards my body but as regards my soul and spirit."

Fortunately, he has told us how he achieved the transformation: "When a boy," he writes, "I read a passage in one of Marryat's books which always impressed me. In this passage the captain of some small British man-of-war is explaining to the hero how to acquire the quality of fearlessness. He says that at the outset almost every man is frightened when he goes into action, but that the course to follow is for the man to keep such a grip on himself that he can act just as if he were not frightened. After this is kept up long enough, it changes from pretence to reality, and the man does in very fact become fearless by sheer dint of practicing fearlessness when he does not feel it. (I am using my own language, not Marryat's.)

"This was the theory upon which I went. There were all kinds of things of which I was afraid at first, ranging from grizzly bears to mean horses and gun-fighters, but by acting as if I was not afraid I gradually ceased to be afraid. Most men can have the same experience if they choose."

So take the offensive against your fears. Go out to meet them, battle them, conquer them by sheer boldness at every opportunity.

Have a message, and then think of yourself as a courier boy instructed to deliver it. We pay slight attention to the boy. It is the courier that we want. The message—that is the thing. Keep your mind on it. Keep your heart in it. Know it like the back of your hand. Believe it feelingly. Then talk as if you were determined to say it. Do that, and the chances are ten to one that you will soon be master of the occasion and master of yourself.

THIRD

Know Thoroughly What You Are Going To Talk About

Unless a man has thought out and planned his talk and knows what he is going to say, he can't feel very comfortable when he faces his auditors. He is like the blind leading the blind. Under such circumstances, your speaker ought to be self-conscious, ought to feel repentant, ought to be ashamed of his negligence.

"I was elected to the Legislature in the autumn of 1881," Theodore Roosevelt wrote in his *Autobiography*, "and found myself the youngest man in that body. Like all young men and inexperienced members, I had considerable difficulty in teaching myself to speak. I profited much by the advice of a hard-headed old countryman—who was unconsciously paraphrasing the Duke of Wellington, who was himself doubtless paraphrasing somebody else. The advice ran: 'Don't speak until you are sure you have something to say, and know just what it is; then say it, and sit down.'"

This "hard-headed old countryman" ought to have told Roosevelt of another aid in overcoming nervousness. He ought to have added: "It will help you to throw off your embarrassment if you can find something to do before an audience—if you can exhibit something, write a word on the blackboard, or point out a spot on the map, or move a table or throw open a window, or shift some books and papers—any physical action with a purpose behind it may help you to feel more at home."

True, it is not always easy to find an excuse for doing such things, but there is the suggestion. Use it if you can, but use it the first few times only. A baby does not cling to chairs after it learns to walk.

FOURTH

Practice! Practice! Practice!

The last point we have to make here is emphatically the most important. Even though you forget everything you have read so far, do remember this: the first way, the last way, the never-failing way to develop self-confidence in speaking is—to speak. Really the whole matter finally simmers down to but one essential: practice, practice, practice. That is the *sine qua non* of it all, "the without which not".

"Any beginner," warned Roosevelt, "is apt to have 'buck fever'. 'Buck fever' means a state of intense nervous excitement which may be entirely divorced from timidity. It may affect a man the first time he has to speak to a large audience just as it may affect him the first time he sees a buck-deer or goes into battle. What such a man needs is not courage, but nerve control and cool-headedness. This he can get only by actual practice. He must, by custom and repeated exercise of self-mastery, get his nerves thoroughly under control. This is largely a matter of habit, in the sense of repeated effort and repeated exercise of willpower. If the man has the right stuff in him, he will grow stronger and stronger with each exercise of it."

So, persevere. Don't remain away from any session of the course because the business duties of the week have rendered it impossible for you to prepare something. Prepared or unprepared, come. Let the instructor, the class, suggest a topic for you after you have come before them.

You want to get rid of your audience fear? Let us see what causes it.

Fear is the result of a lack of confidence and what causes that? It is the result of not knowing what you can really do. And not knowing what you can do is caused by a lack of experience. When you get a record of successful experience behind you, your fears will vanish; they will melt like night mists under the glare of a July sun.

One thing is certain: the accepted way to learn to swim is to plunge into the water. You have been reading this book long enough. Let us toss it aside now, and get busy with the real work at hand.

Choose your subject, preferably one on which you have some knowledge, and construct a three-minute talk. Practice the talk by yourself a number ot times. Then give it, if possible, to the group for whom it is intended, or before your class, putting into the effort all your force and power.

It is never easy to keep reaching for dreams. Strength and courage can sometimes be lonely friends, but those who reach, walk in stardust.

—Anonymous

~

Healing takes courage, and we all have courage, even if we have to dig a little to find it.

—Tori Amos

2

How To Open A Talk

You have to care. And that care has to come from your soul. Public speaking is the art of having everybody thinking you are talking to them.

—Dennis Van Gerven

I once asked Dr. Lynn Harold Hough, formerly president of Northwestern University, what was the most important fact that his long experience as a speaker had taught him. After pondering for a minute, he replied, "To get an arresting opening, something that will seize the attention immediately." He plans in advance almost the precise words of both his opening and closing. John Bright did the same thing. Gladstone did it. Webster did it. Lincoln did it. Practically every speaker with common sense and experience does it.

But does the beginner? Seldom. Planning takes time, requires thought, demands willpower. Cerebration is a painful process. Thomas Edison had this quotation from Sir Joshua Reynolds nailed on the walls of his plants: "There is no expedient to which a man will not resort to avoid the real labour of thinking."

The tyro usually trusts to the inspiration of the moment with the consequence that he finds:

"Beset with pitfall and with gin,
The road he is to wander in."

The late Lord Northcliffe, who fought his way up from a meagre weekly salary to being the richest and most influential newspaper owner in the British Empire, said that these five words from Pascal had done more to help him succeed than anything else he had ever read:

"To foresee is to rule."

That is also a most excellent motto to have on your desk when you are planning your talk. Foresee how you are going to begin when the mind is fresh to grasp every word you utter. Foresee what impression you are going to leave last—when nothing else follows to obliterate it.

Ever since the days of Aristotle, books on this subject have divided the speech into three sections: the introduction, the body, the conclusion. Until comparatively recently, the introduction often was, and could really afford to be, as leisurely as a cart ride. The speaker then was both a bringer of news and an entertainer. A hundred years ago he often filled the niche in the community that is usurped today by the newspaper, the radio, the telephone, the movie theatre.

But conditions have altered amazingly. The world has been made over. Inventions have speeded up life more in the last hundred years than they had formerly in all the ages since Belshazzar and Nebuchadnezzar. Automobiles, aeroplanes, radio; we are moving with increasing speed. And the speaker must fall in line with the impatient tempo of the times. If you are going to use an introduction, believe me, it ought to be short as a billboard advertisement. This is about the temper of the average modern audience: "Got anything to say? All right, let's have it quickly and with very little trimmings. No oratory! Give us the facts quickly and sit down."

When Woodrow Wilson addressed Congress on such a momentous question as an ultimatum on submarine warfare, he announced his topic and centred the audience's attention on the subject with just twenty-three words:

"A situation has arisen in the foreign relations of the country of which it is my plain duty to inform you very frankly."

The salesmanager for the National Cash Register Company opened one of his talks to his men in this fashion. Only three sentences in this introduction; and they are all easy to listen to, they all have vigour and drive: "You men who get the orders are the chaps who are supposed to keep the smoke coming out of the factory chimney. The volume of smoke emitted from our chimney during the past two summer months hasn't been large enough to darken the landscape to any great extent. Now that the dog days are over and the business-revival season has begun, we are addressing to you a short, sharp request on this subject: We want more smoke."

But do inexperienced speakers usually achieve such commendable swiftness and succinctness in their openings? Strict veracity compels us to record that they do not. The majority of untrained and unskilled speakers will begin in one of two ways—both of which are bad. Let us discuss them forthwith.

THE PITFALLS OF OPENING WITH A SO-CALLED HUMOROUS STORY

For some lamentable reason, the novice often feels that he ought to be funny as a speaker. He may, by nature, mind you, be as solemn as the encyclopaedia, utterly devoid of the lighter touch, yet the moment he stands up to talk he imagines he feels, or ought to feel, the spirit of Mark Twain descending upon him. So he is inclined to open with a humorous story, especially if the occasion is an after-dinner affair. What happens? The chances are twenty to one that the narration, the manner of this hardware merchant newly-turned reconteur, is as heavy as the dictionary. The chances are his stories don't "click". In the immortal language of the immortal Hamlet, they prove "weary, stale, flat and unprofitable".

If an entertainer were to misfire a few times like that before a vaudeville audience that had paid for their seats, they would "boo" and shout "give him the bird". But the average group listening to a speaker is very sympathetic; so, out of sheer charity, they will do their best to manufacture a few chuckles while, deep in their hearts, they pity the would-be humorous speaker for his failure! They themselves feel uncomfortable. Haven't you, my dear reader, witnessed this kind of fiasco time after time? The writer has. In all the difficult realm of speech-making, what is more difficult, more rare, than the ability to make an audience laugh? Humour is a hair-trigger affair; it is so much a matter of individuality, of personality. You are either born with the predilection for being humorous or you are not—much as you are born with or without brown eyes. Not much can be done about either.

Remember, it is seldom the story that is funny of, by, and in itself. It is the way it is told that makes it a success. Ninety-nine men out of a hundred will fail woefully with the identical stories that made Mark Twain famous. Read the stories that Lincoln repeated in the taverns of the Eighth Judicial District of Illinois, stories that men drove miles to hear, stories that men sat up all night to hear, stories that, according to an eye witness, sometimes caused the natives to "whoop and roll off their chairs". Read those stories aloud to your family and see if you conjure up a smile. Here is one Lincoln used to tell with roaring success. Why not try it? Privately, please—not before an audience. A late traveller, trying to reach home over the muddy roads of the Illinois prairies, was overtaken by a storm. The night was black as ink, the rain descended as if some dam in the heavens had broken, thunder rent the angry clouds like the explosion of dynamite. Chain lightning showed trees falling around. The roar of it was very nearly deafening. Finally a crash more terrific, more terrible than any the helpless man had ever heard in his life, brought him to his knees. He was not given to praying usually, but "Oh, Lord," he gasped, "if it is all the same to you, please give us a little more light and a little less noise."

You may be one of those fortunately endowed individuals who has the rare gift of humour. If so, by all means, cultivate it. You will be thrice welcome wherever you speak. But if your talent lies in other directions, it is folly—and it ought to be high treason—for you to attempt to wear the mantle of Chauncey M. Depew.

Were you to study his speeches, and Lincoln's, and Job Hedges', you would probably be surprised at the few stories they told, especially in their openings. Edwin James Cattell confided to me that he had never told a funny story for the mere sake of humour. It had to be relevant, had to illustrate a point. Humour ought to be merely the frosting on the cake, merely the chocolate between the layers, not the cake itself Strickland Gillilan, the best humorous lecturer, makes it a rule never to tell a story during the first three minutes of his talk. If he finds that practice advisable, I wonder if you and I would not also.

Must the opening then be heavy-footed, elephantine and excessively solemn? Not at all. Tickle our risibilities, if you can, by some local reference, something about the occasion or the remarks of some other speaker. Observe some incongruity. Exaggerate it. That brand of humour is forty times more likely to succeed than stale jokes about Pat and Mike, or a mother-in-law, or a goat.

Perhaps the easiest way to create merriment is to tell a joke on yourself. Depict yourself in some ridiculous and embarrassing situation. That gets down to the very essence of much humour. The Eskimos laugh even at a chap who has broken his leg. The Chinese chuckle over the dog that has fallen out of a second storey window and killed himself. We are a bit more sympathetic than that, but don't we smile at the fellow chasing his hat, or slipping on a banana skin?

Almost anyone can make an audience laugh by grouping incongruous ideas or qualities as, for example, the statement of a newspaper writer that he "hated children, tripe, and Democrats".

Note how cleverly Rudyard Kipling raised laughs in this opening to one of his talks in England. He is retailing here, not manufactured anecdotes, but some of his own experiences and playfully stressing their incongruities:

> My Lords, Ladies and Gentlemen: When I was a young man in India I used to report criminal cases for the newspaper that employed me. It was interesting work because it introduced me to forgers and embezzlers and murderers and enterprising sportsmen of that kind. (Laughter.) Sometimes, after

> I had reported their trials, I used to visit my friends in jail when they were doing their sentences. (Laughter.) I remember one man who got off with a life sentence for murder. He was a clever, smoothspeaking chap, and he told me what he called the story of his life. He said: "Take it from me that when a man gets crooked, one thing leads to another until he finds himself in such a position that he has to put somebody out of the way to get straight again." (Laughter.) Well, that exactly describes the present position of the Cabinet. (Laughter and cheers.)

This is the way William Howard Taft managed a bit of humour at the annual banquet of the superintendents of the Metropolitan Life Insurance Company. The beautiful part of it is this: he is humorous and pays his audience a gracious compliment at the same time:

> Mr. President and Gentlemen of the Metropolitan Life Insurance Company,
>
> I was out in my old home about nine months ago, and I heard an after-dinner speech there by a gentleman who had some trepidation in making it; and he said he had consulted a friend of his, who had had a great deal of experience in making after-dinner speeches, which friend advised him that the best kind of audience to address, as an after-dinner speaker, was an audience intelligent and well- educated but half-tight. (Laughter and applause.) Now, all I can say is that this audience is one of the best audiences I ever saw for an after-dinner speaker. Something has made up for the absence of that element that the remark implied (applause), and I must think

it is the spirit of the Metropolitan Life Insurance Company. (Prolonged applause.)

DON'T BE APOLOGETIC

The second egregious blunder that the beginner is wont to make in his opening, is this: he apologizes. "I am no speaker... I am not prepared to talk I have nothing to say....'

Don't! Don't! The opening words of a poem by Kipling are: "There's no use in going further." That is precisely the way an audience feels when a speaker opens in that fashion.

Anyway, if you are not prepared, some of us will discover it without your assistance. Others will not. Why call their attention to it? Why insult your audience by suggesting that you did not think them worth preparing for, that just any old thing you happened to have on the fire would be good enough to serve them? No. No. We don't want to hear your apologies. We are there to be informed and interested, to be *interested,* remember that.

The moment you come before the audience, you have our attention naturally, inevitably It is not difficult to get it for the first five seconds, but it is difficult to hold it for the next five minutes. If you once lose it, it will be doubly difficult to win it back. So begin with something interesting in your very first sentence. Not the second. Not the third. The first! F-I-R-S-T. First!

"How?" you ask. Rather a large order, I admit. And in attempting to harvest the material to fill it, we must tread our way down devious and dubious paths, for so much depends upon you, upon your audience, your subject, your material, the occasion, and so on. However, we hope that the tentative suggestions discussed and illustrated in the remainder of this chapter will yield something usable and of value.

CURIOSITY WINS OVER THE CAT

Here is an opening used by Mr. Howell Healy in a talk given before a session of this course. Do you like it? Does it get your interest immediately?

Eighty-two years ago, and just about this time of year, there was published in London a little volume, a story, which was destined to become immortal. Many people have called it "the greatest little book in the world". When it first appeared, friends meeting one another in the Strand or Pall Mall, asked the question, "Have you read it?" The answer invariably was: "Yes, God bless him, I have."

> The day it was published a thousand copies were sold. Within a fortnight, the demand had consumed fifteen thousand. Since then it has run into countless editions, and has been translated into every language under heaven. A few years ago, J.P. Morgan purchased the original manuscript for a fabulous sum; it now reposes among his other priceless treasures in that magnificent art gallery which he called his library.
>
> What is this world-famous book? Dickens' *A Christmas Carol*....

Do you consider that a successful opening? Did it hold your attention, heighten your interest as it progressed? Why? Was it not because it aroused your curiosity, held you in suspense?

Curiosity! Who is not susceptible to it?

I have seen birds in the woods fly about by the hour watching me out of sheer curiosity. I know a hunter in the high Alps who lures chamois by throwing a bedsheet around him and crawling about and arousing their curiosity. Dogs have curiosity, and so have kittens, and all manner of animals including the well-known *genus homo.*

So arouse your audience's curiosity with your first sentence, and you have their interested attention.

The writer used to begin his lecture on Colonel Thomas Lawrence's adventures in Arabia in this fashion:

"Lloyd George says that he regards Colonel Lawrence as one of the most romantic and picturesque characters of modern times."

That opening had two advantages. In the first place, a quotation from an eminent man always has a lot of attention value. Second, it aroused curiosity: "Why romantic?" was the natural question, and "why picturesque?" "I never heard about him before.... What did he do?"

Lowell Thomas began his lecture on Colonel Thomas Lawrence with this statement:

"I was going down Christian Street in Jerusalem one day when I met a man clad in the gorgeous robes of an oriental potentate; and, at his side, hung the curved gold sword worn only by the descendants of the prophet Mohammed. But this man had none of the appearances of an Arab. He had blue eyes; and the Arabs' eyes are always black or brown."

That piques your curiosity, doesn't it? You want to hear more. Who was he? Why was he posing as an Arab? What did he do? What became of him?

The student who opened his talk with this question: "Do you know that slavery exists in seventeen nations of the world today?" not only aroused curiosity, but in addition, he shocked his auditors. "Slavery? Today? Seventeen countries? Seems incredible. What nations? Where are they?"

One can often arouse curiosity by beginning with an effect, and making people anxious to hear the cause. For example, one student began with this striking statement: "A member of one of our state legislatures recently stood up in his legislative assembly and proposed the passage of a law prohibiting tadpoles from becoming frogs within two miles of any school house."

You smile. Is the speaker joking? How absurd. Was that actually done? Yes. The speaker went on to explain:

> Every man who aspires to speak in public ought to study the technique that magazine writers employ to hook the reader's interest immediately. You can learn far more from them about how to open a speech than you can by studying collections of printed speeches.

WHY NOT BEGIN WITH A STORY

Harold Bell Wright has admitted in an interview that his novels have brought him more than a hundred thousand dollars a year. Booth Tarkington and Robert W Chambers earned similar amounts. For seventeen years Doubleday Page and Company had one large press, which did nothing in all that time but turn out a ceaseless flood of the novels by the late Gene Stratton Porter. Over seventeen million copies of her books were sold, and they brought her more than three million dollars in royalties. Do people like to hear stories? Those figures sound like it, don't they?

We especially like to hear a man relate narratives from his own experience. The late Russell E. Conwell delivered his lecture, "Acres of Diamonds", over six thousand times, and received millions for it.

Here are opening sentences taken from two stories that appeared in a single issue of *The Saturday Evening Post:*

1. "The sharp crack of a revolver punctuated the silence."
2. "An incident, trivial in itself but not at all trivial in its possible consequences, occurred at the Montview Hotel, Denver, during the first week of July. It so aroused the curiosity of Goebel, the resident manager, that he referred it to Steve Faraday, owner of the Montview and half a dozen other Faraday hotels, when Steve made his regular visit a few days later on his midsummer swing of inspection."

Note that those openings have action. They start something. They arouse your curiosity. You want to read on, you want to know more, you want to find out what it is all about.

Even the unpracticed beginner can usually manage a successful opening if he employs the story technique and arouses our curiosity.

BEGIN WITH A SPECIFIC ILLUSTRATION

It is difficult, it is arduous, for the average audience to follow abstract statements very long. Illustrations are easier to listen to, far easier. Then why not start with one?

It is hard to get men to do that. I know. I have tried. They feel somehow that they must first make a few general statements. Not at all. Open with your illustration, arouse the interest, then follow with your general remarks.

What technique was employed to open this chapter you are now reading?

USE AN EXHIBIT

Perhaps the easiest way in the world to gain attention is to hold up something for people to look at. Even savages and halfwits, and babes in the cradle and monkeys in a zoo and dogs on the street will give heed to that kind of stimulus. It can be used sometimes with effectiveness before the most dignified audience. For example, Mr. S.S. Ellis opened one of his talks by holding a coin between his thumb and forefinger, and high above his shoulder. Naturally everyone looked. Then he inquired: "Has anyone here ever found a coin like this on the pavement? It announces that the fortunate finder will be given a lot free in such and such an estate development. He has but to call and present this coin..." Mr. Ellis then proceeded condemn the misleading and unethical practices involved.

ASK A QUESTION

Mr. Ellis' opening has another commendable feature. It begins by asking a question, by getting the audience thinking with the speaker, cooperating with him. Note that the *Saturday Evening Post* article on gangsters opens with two questions in the first three sentences: "Are gangsters really organized?... How?" The use of this question-key is really one of the simplest, surest ways to unlock the minds of your audience and let yourself in. When other tools prove useless, you can always fall back on it.

WHY NOT OPEN WITH A QUESTION FROM SOME FAMOUS MAN?

The words of a prominent man always have attention power; so a suitable quotation is one of the very best ways of launching a harangue. Do you like the following opening of a discussion on business success?

"The world bestows its big prizes both in honours and money for but one thing," says Elbert Hubbard. "And that is initiative. And what is initiative? I'll tell you: it is doing the right thing without being told."

As a starter, that has several commendable features. The initial sentence arouses curiosity; it carries us forward, we want to hear more. If the speaker pauses skillfully after the words, "Elbert Hubbard," it arouses suspense. "What does the world bestow its big prizes for?" we ask. Quick. Tell us. We may not agree with you, but give us your opinion anyway.... The second sentence leads up right into the heart of the subject. The third sentence, a question, invites the audience to get in on the discussion, to think, to do a little something. And how audiences like to do things. They love it! The fourth sentence defines initiative.... After this opening, the speaker led off with a human interest story illustrating that quality. As far as construction is concerned, Moody might have rated the stock of that talk *Aaa*.

TIE YOUR TOPIC UP TO THE VITAL INTERESTS OF YOUR HEARERS

Begin on some note that goes straight to the selfish interests of the audience. That is one of the best of all possible ways to start. It is sure to get attention. We are mightily interested in the things that touch us significantly, momentously.

That is only common sense, isn't it? Yet the use of it is very uncommon. For example, recently I heard a speaker begin a talk on the necessity of periodic health examinations. How did he open? By telling the history of the Life Extension

Institute, how it was organized and the service it was rendering. Absurd! Our hearers have not the foggiest, not the remotest interest in how some company somewhere was formed, but they are stupendously and eternally interested in themselves.

Why not recognize that fundamental fact? Why not show how that company is of vital concern to them? Why not begin something like this? "Do you know how long you are expected to live according to life insurance tables? Your expectancy of life, as insurance statisticians phrase it, is two-thirds of the time between your present age and eighty. For example, if you are thirty-five now, the difference between your present age and eighty is forty-five; you can expect to live two-thirds of that amount, or another thirty years.... Is that enough? No, no, we are all passionately eager for more. Yet those tables are based upon millions of records. May you and I, then, hope to beat them? Yes, with proper precaution, we may, but the very first step is to have a thorough physical examination."

Then, if we explain in detail why the periodic health examination is necessary, the hearer might be interested in some company formed to render that service. But to begin talking about the company in an impersonal way. It is disastrous! Deadly!

Take another example: During the last season, I heard a student begin a talk on the prime urgency of conserving our forests. He opened like this: "We ought to be proud of our national resources...." From that sentence, he went on to show that we were wasting our timber at a shameless and indefensible pace. But the opening was bad, too general, too vague. He did not make his subject seem vital to us. There was a printer in that audience. The destruction of our forests will mean something very real to his business. There was a banker; it is going to affect him for it will affect our general prosperity...and so on. Why not begin, then, by saying: "The subject I am going to speak about affects your business, Mr. Appleby, and yours, Mr. Saul. In fact, it will, in some measure, affect the price of the food we eat and the rent that we pay. It touches the welfare and prosperity of us all."

Is that exaggerating the importance of conserving our forests? No, I think not. It is only obeying Elbert Hubbards injunction to "paint the picture large and put the matter in a way that compels attention".

THE ATTENTION POWER OF SHOCKING FACTS

"A good magazine article," said S.S. McClure, the founder of the periodical bearing his name, "is a series of shocks."

They jar us out of our daydreams, they seize, they demand attention. Here are some illustrations: Mr. N.D. Ballantine began his address on *The Marvels of Radio* with this statement: "Do you realize that the sound of a fly walking across a pane of glass here can be broadcasted by radio and made to roar away off in Central Africa like the falls of Niagara?"

Mr. Harry G. Jones, President of Harry G. Jones Company, began his talk on the *Criminal Situation* with these words: "'The administration of our criminal law,' declared William Howard Taft, then Chief Justice of the Supreme Court of the United States, 'is a disgrace to civilization.'"

That has the double advantage of being not only a shocking opening, but the shocking statement is quoted from an authority on jurisprudence.

Mr. Paul Gibbons, former President of the Optimist Club, opened an address on *crime* with these arresting statements: "The American people are the worst criminals in the world. Astounding as that assertion is, it is true. Cleveland, Ohio, has six times as many murders as all London. It has one hundred and seventy times as many robberies, according to its population, as has London. More people are robbed every year, or assaulted with intent to rob, in Cleveland than in all England, Scotland and Wales combined. More people are murdered every year in St. Louis than in all England and Wales. There are more murders in New York City than in all France or Germany or Italy or the British Isles. The sad truth of the matter is that the criminal is not punished. If you commit a murder, there is less than one chance in a hundred that you will ever be executed for it. You, as a peaceful citizen, are ten times as liable to die from cancer as you would be to be hanged if you shot a man."

That opening was successful, for Mr. Gibbons put the requisite power and earnestness behind his words. They lived. They breathed. However, I have heard other students begin their talks on the crime situation with somewhat similar illustrations; yet their openings were mediocre. Why? Words. Words. Words. Their technique of construction was flawless, but their spirit was nil. Their manner vitiated and emaciated all they said.

THE VALUE OF THE SEEMINGLY CASUAL OPENING

How do you like the following opening, and why? Mary E. Richmond is addressing the anual meeting of the League of Women Voters in the days before legislation against child marriages: Yesterday, as the train passed through a city not far away from here, I was reminded of a marriage that took place there a few years ago. Because many other marriages in this state have been just as hasty and disastrous as this one, I am going to begin what I have to say today with some of the details of this individual instance.

> It was on December 12th that a high school girl of fifteen in that city met for the first time a junior in a nearby college who had just attained his majority. On December 15th, only three days later, they procured a marriage licence by swearing that the girl was eighteen and was therefore free from the necessity of procuring parental consent. Leaving the city clerk's office with their licence, they applied at once to a priest (the girl was a Catholic), but very properly he refused to marry them. In some way, perhaps through this priest, the child's mother received news of the attempted marriage. Before she could find her daughter, however, a justice of the peace had united the pair. The bridegroom then took his bride to a hotel where they spent two days and two nights, at the end of which time he abandoned her and never lived with her again.

Personally, I like that opening very much. The very first sentence is good. It forecasts an interesting reminiscence. We want to hear the details. We settle down to listen to a human interest story. In addition to that, it seems very natural. It does not smack of the study, it is not formal, it does not smell of the lamp. "Yesterday, as the train passed through a city not far from here, I was reminded of a marriage that took place there a few years ago." Sounds natural, spontaneous, human. Sounds like one person relating an interesting story to another. An audience likes that. But it is very liable to shy at something too elaborate, something that reeks of preparation with malice aforethought. We want the art that conceals art.

> *I've always been good at public speaking, but I never really enjoyed it. Then I started to really enjoy it, and that's made all the difference.*
>
> —Mimi Kennedy

~

> *Before anything else, preparation is the key to success.*
>
> —Alexander Graham Bell

3

How To Close A Talk

Good speech: A beginning and a conclusion placed not too far apart.

—Anonymous

Would you like to know in what parts of your speech you are most likely to reveal your inexperience or your expertness, your inaptitude or your finesse? I'll tell you: in the opening and the closing. There is an old saying in the theatre, referring, of course, to actors, that goes like this: "By their entrances and their exits shall ye know them." The beginning and the ending: They are the hardest things in almost any activity to manage adroitly. For example, at a social function aren't the most trying feats the graceful entrance and the graceful leave-taking? In a business interview, aren't the most difficult tasks the winning approach and the successful close?

The close is really the most strategic point in a speech; what one says last, the final words left ringing in the ears when one ceases—these are likely to be remembered longest. Beginners, however, seldom appreciate the importance of this coign of vantage. Their endings often leave much to be desired.

What are their most common errors? Let us discuss a few and search for remedies.

First, there is the man who finishes with: "That is about all I have to say on the matter; so I guess I shall stop." That is not an ending. That is a mistake. That reeks of the amateur.

That is almost unpardonable. If that is all you have to say, why not round off your talk, and promptly take your seat and stop without talking about stopping. Do that, and the inference that that is all you have to say may, with safety and good taste, be left to the discernment of the audience.

Then there is the speaker who says all he has to say, but he does not know how to stop. I believe it was Josh Billings who advised people to take the bull by the tail instead of the horns, since it would be easier to let go. This speaker has the bull by the frontal extremities, and wants to part company with him, but try as hard as he will, he can't get near a friendly fence or tree. So he finally thrashes about in a circle, covering the same ground, repeating himself, leaving a bad impression.

The remedy? An ending has to be planned some time, doesn't it? Is it the part of wisdom to try to do it after you are facing an audience, while you are under the strain and stress of talking, while your mind must be intent on what you are saying? Or does common sense suggest the advisability of doing it quietly, calmly, beforehand?

Even such accomplished speakers as Webster, Bright, Gladstone, with their admirable command of the English language, felt it necessary to write down and all but memorize the exact words of their closings.

The beginner, if he follows in their footsteps, will seldom have cause to regret it. He ought to know very definitely with what ideas he is going to close. He ought to rehearse the ending several times, using not necessarily the same phraseology during each repetition, but putting the thoughts definitely into words.

An extemporaneous talk, during the process of delivery, sometimes has to be altered very materially; has to be cut and slashed to meet unforeseen developments, to harmonize with the reactions of one's hearers; so it is really wise to have two or three closings planned. If one does not fit, another may.

Some speakers never get to the end at all. Along in the middle of their journey, they begin to sputter and misfire like an engine when the petrol supply is about exhausted; after a few desperate lunges, they come to a complete standstill, a breakdown. They need, of course, better preparation, more practice—more petrol in the tank.

Many novices stop too abruptly. Their method of closing lacks smoothness, lacks finish. Properly speaking, they have no close; they merely cease suddenly, jerkily. The effect is unpleasant, amateurish. It is as if a friend in a social conversation were to break off brusquely and dart out of the room without a graceful leave-taking.

No less a speaker than Lincoln made that mistake in the original draft of his first inaugural. That speech was delivered at a tense time. The black storm clouds of dissension and hatred were already milling overhead. A few weeks later, the cyclone of blood and destruction burst upon the nation. Lincoln, addressing his closing words to the people of the South, had intended to end in this fashion:

> In your hands, my dissatisfied fellow-countrymen, and not in mine, is the momentous issue of the Civil War. The government will not assail you. You

> can have no conflict without being yourselves the aggressors. You have no oath registered in heaven to destroy the government, while I have a most solemn one to preserve, protect and defend it. You can forbear the assault upon it. I cannot shrink from the defence of it. With you and not with me is the solemn question of "Shall it be peace or a sword?"

He submitted his speech to Secretary Seward. Seward quite appropriately pointed out that the ending was too blunt, too abrupt, too provocative. So Seward himself tried his hand at a closing; in fact, he wrote two. Lincoln accepted one of them and used it, with slight modifications, in place of the last three sentences of the close he had originally prepared. The result was that his First Inaugural Address now lost its provocative abruptness and rose to a climax of friendliness, of sheer beauty and poetical eloquence:

> I am loath to close. We are not enemies but friends. We must not be enemies. Though passion may have strained, it must not break our bonds of affection. The mystic chords of memory, stretching from every battlefield and patriot's grave to every living heart and hearthstone all over this broad land, will swell the chorus of the Union when again touched, as surely they will be, by the better angel of our nature.

How can a beginner develop the proper *feeling* for the close of an address? By mechanical rules?

No. Like culture, it is too delicate for that. It must be a matter of sensing, almost of intuition. Unless a speaker can *feel* when it is done harmoniously, adroitly, how can he himself hope to do it?

However, this *feeling* can be cultivated; this expertness can be developed somewhat, by studying the ways in which accomplished speakers have achieved it. Here is an illustration, the close of an address by the then Prince of Wales before the Empire Club of Toronto:

> I am afraid, gentlemen, that I have departed from my reserve, and talked about myself a good deal too much. But I wanted to tell you, as the largest audience that I have been privileged to address in Canada, what I feel about my position and the responsibility which it entails. I can only assure you that I shall always endeavour to live up to that great responsibility and to be worthy of your trust.

A blind man listening to that talk would *feel* that it was ended. It isn't left dangling in the air like a loose rope. It isn't left ragged and jagged. It is rounded off, it is finished.

The famous Dr. Harry Emerson Fosdick spoke in the Geneva Cathedral of St. Pierre the Sunday after the opening of the sixth assembly of the League of Nations. He chose for his text: "All they that take the sword shall perish with the sword." Note the beautiful and lofty and powerful way in which he brought his sermon to a close:

> We cannot reconcile Jesus Christ and war—that is the essence of the matter. That is the challenge which today should stir the conscience of Christendom. War is the most colossal and ruinous social sin that afflicts mankind; it is utterly and irremediably unchristian; in its total method and effect it means everything that Jesus did not mean and it means nothing that he did mean; it is a more blatant denial

> of every Christian doctrine about God and man than all the theoretical atheists on earth ever could devise. It would be worthwhile, would it not, to see the Christian Church claim as her own this greatest moral issue of our time, to see her lift once more as in our fathers' days, a clear standard against the paganism of this present world and, refusing to hold her conscience at the beck and call of belligerent states, put the kingdom of God above nationalism and call the world to peace? That would not be the denial of patriotism but its apotheosis.
>
> Here today, as an American, under this high and hospitable roof, I cannot speak for my government, but both as an American and as a Christian I do speak for millions of my fellow citizens in wishing your great work, in which we believe, for which we pray, our absence from which we painfully regret, the eminent success which it deserves. We work in many ways for the same end—a world organized for peace. Never was an end better worth working for. The alternative is the most appalling catastrophe mankind has ever faced. Like gravitation in the physical realm, the law of the Lord in the moral realm bends for no man and no nation: "All they that take the sword shall perish with the sword."

But this collection of speech endings would not be complete without the majestic tones, the organ-like melody of the close of Lincoln's Second Inaugural. The late Earl Curzon of Keddleston, Chancellor of Oxford University, declared that this selection was "among the glories and treasures of mankind...the purest gold of human eloquence, nay, of eloquence almost divine":

> Fondly do we hope, fervently do we pray, that this mighty scourge of war may speedily pass away. Yet if God wills that it continue until all the wealth piled by the bondsman's two hundred and fifty years of unrequited toil shall be sunk, and until every drop of blood drawn with the lash shall be paid by another drawn with the sword, as was said three thousand years ago, so still it must be said that 'the judgments of the Lord are true and righteous altogether'.
>
> With malice toward none; with charity for all; with firmness in the right, as God gives us to see the right, let us strive on to finish the work we are in; to bind up the nation's wounds; to care for him who shall have borne the battle, and for his widow and his orphan—to do all which may achieve and cherish a just and lasting peace among ourselves, and with all nations.

You have just read, my dear reader, what is, in my opinion, the most beautiful speech ending ever delivered by the lips of mortal man.... Do you agree with my estimate? Where, in all the range of speech literature, will you find more humanity, more sheer loveliness, more sympathy?

"Noble as was the Gettysburg Address," says William E. Barton in *Life of Abraham Lincoln,* "this rises to a still higher level of nobility.... It is the greatest of the addresses of Abraham Lincoln and registers his intellectual and spiritual power at their highest altitude."

"This was like a sacred poem," wrote Carl Schurz. "No American President had ever spoken words like these to the American people. America had never had a president who had found such words in the depths of his heart." But you are not going to deliver immortal pronouncements as President in Washington or as Prime Minister in Ottawa or Melbourne. Your problem, perhaps, will be how to close a simple talk before a group of businessmen. How shall you set about it? Let us search a bit. Let us see if we cannot uncover some fertile suggestions.

SUMMARIZE YOUR POINTS

Even in a short talk of three to five minutes, a speaker is very apt to cover so much ground that at the close the listeners are a little hazy about all his main points. However, few speakers realize that. They are misled into assuming that because these points are crystal clear in their own minds, they must be equally lucid to their hearers. Not at all. The speaker has been pondering over his ideas for some time. But his points are all new to the audience; they are flung at the audience like a handful of shot. Some may stick, but the most are liable to roll off in confusion. The hearers are liable, like Iago, to "remember a mass of things but nothing distinctly".

Some anonymous Irish politician is reported to have given this recipe for making a speech: "First, tell them that you are going to tell them, then tell them, then tell them that you have told them." Not bad, you know. In fact, it is often highly advisable to "tell them that you have told them". Briefly, of course, speedily—a mere outline, a summary.

Here is a good example. The speaker is a student of Mr. Bills' class in Public Speaking. He is also a traffic manager for railways:

> In short, gentlemen, our own backdoor yard experience with this block device, the experience in its use in the East, in the West, in the North—the

> sound operating principles underlying its operation, the actual demonstration in the money saved in one year in wreck prevention, move me most earnestly and unequivocally to recommend its immediate installation on our Southern branch.

You see what he has done? You can see it and feel it without having heard the rest of the talk. He has summed up in a few sentences, in sixty-two words, practically all the points he has made in the entire talk.

Don't you feel that a summary like that helps? If so, make that technique your own.

APPEAL FOR ACTION

The closing just quoted is an excellent illustration of the appeal-for-action ending. The speaker wanted something done: a block device installed on the Southern branch of his road. He based his appeal for it on the money it would save, on the wrecks it would prevent. The speaker wanted action, and he got it. This was not a mere practice talk. It was delivered before the board of directors of a certain railway, and it secured the installation of the block device for which it asked.

A TERSE, SINCERE COMPLIMENT

> The great state of Pennsylvania should lead the way in hastening the coming of the new day. Pennsylvania, the great producer of iron and steel, mother of the greatest railroad company in the world, third among our agricultural states—Pennsylvania is the keystone of our business arch. Never was the prospect before her greater, never was her opportunity for leadership more brilliant.

With these words, Charles Schwab closed his address before the Pennsylvania Society of New York. He left his hearers pleased, happy, optimistic. That is an admirable way to finish; but, in order to be effective, it must be sincere. No gross flattery. No extravagances. This kind of closing, if it does not ring true, will ring false, very false. And like a false coin, people will have none of it.

A HUMOROUS CLOSE

"Always leave them laughing," said George Cohan, "when you say goodbye." If you have the ability to do it, and the material, fine! But how? That, as Hamlet said, is the question. Each man must do it in his own individual way.

One would hardly expect Lloyd George to leave a gathering of Methodists laughing when he was talking to them on the ultra-solemn subject of John Wesley's Tomb, but note how cleverly he managed it. Note, also, how smoothly and beautifully the talk is rounded off:

> I am glad you have taken in hand the repair of his tomb. It should be honoured. He was a man who had a special abhorrence of any absence of neatness or cleanliness. He it was, I think, who said, "Let no one ever see a ragged Methodist." It is due to him that you never can see one. (Laughter.) It is a double unkindness to leave his tomb ragged. You remember what he said to a Derbyshire girl who ran to the door as he was passing and cried, "God bless you, Mr. Wesley". "Young woman," he answered, "your blessing would be of more value if your face and apron were cleaner." (Laughter.) That was his feeling about untidiness. Do not leave his grave untidy. If

> he passed along, that would hurt him more than anything. Do look after that. It is a memorable and sacred shrine. It is your trust. (Cheers.)

CLOSING WITH A POETICAL QUOTATION

Of all methods of ending, none are more acceptable, when well done, than humour or poetry. In fact, if you can get the proper verse of poetry for your closing, it is almost ideal. It will give the desired flavour. It will give dignity. It will give individuality. It will give beauty.

Rotarian Sir Harry Lauder closed his address to the Rotarian delegates at the Edinburgh convention in this fashion:

> And when you get back home, some of you send me a postcard. I will send you one if you do not send me one. You will easily know it is from me because there will be no stamp on it. (Laughter.) But I will have some writing on it, and the writing will be this:
>
> "Seasons may come and seasons may go,
> Everything withers in due course, you know,
> But there is one thing still blooms as fresh as the dew,
> That is the love and affection I still have for you."

That little verse fits Harry Lauder's personality, and no doubt it fitted the whole tenor of his talk. Therefore, it was excellent for him. Had some formal and restrained Rotarian used it at the end of a solemn talk, it might have been so out of key as to be almost ridiculous. The longer I teach public speaking, the more clearly I see, the more vividly I feel, that it is impossible to give general rules that will serve on all occasions. So much depends upon the subject, the time, the place, and the man. Everyone must, as Saint Paul said, "work out his own salvation."

I was a guest recently at a farewell dinner given in honour of the departure of a certain professional man from New York City. A dozen speakers stood up in turn, eulogizing their departing friend, wishing him success in his new field of activity. A dozen talks, and only one ended in an unforgettable manner. That was one that closed with a poetical quotation. The speaker, with emotion in his voice, turned directly to the departing guest, crying: "And now, goodbye. Good luck. I wish you every good wish that you can wish yourself."

I touch my heart as the Easterns do:
May the peace of Allah abide with you.
Wherever you come, wherever you go,
May the beautiful palms of Allah grow.
Through days of labour and nights of rest,
May the love of Allah make you blest.
I touch my heart as the Easterns do:
May the peace of Allah abide with you.

Mr. J.A. Abbott, Vice-President of the L.A.D. Motors Corporation of Brooklyn, spoke to the employees of his organization on the subject of Loyalty and Cooperation. He closed his address with this ringing verse from Kipling's *Second Jungle Book:*

Now this is the Law of the Jungle—as old and as true as the sky;
And the Wolf that shall keep it may prosper, but the Wolf that shall break it must die.
As the creeper that girdles the tree-trunk, the Law runneth forward and back—
For the strength of the Pack is the Wolf, and the strength of the Wolf is the Pack.

If you will go to the public library in your town and tell the librarian that you are preparing a talk on a certain subject and that you wish a poetical quotation to express this idea or that, she may be able to help you find something suitable in some reference volume such as Bartlett's book of quotations.

THE POWER OF A BIBLICAL QUOTATION

If you can quote a passage from Holy Writ to back up your speech, you are fortunate. A choice Biblical quotation often has a profound effect. The well-known financier, Frank Vanderlip, used this method in ending his address on the Allied Debts to the United States:

> If we insist to the letter upon our claim, our claim will in all probability never be met. If we insist upon it selfishly, we realize in hatreds but not in cash. If we are generous, and wisely generous, those claims can all be paid, and the good we do with them will mean more to us materially than anything we would conceivably be parting with. "For whosoever will save his life shall lose it, but whosoever shall lose his life for my sake and the Gospel's, the same shall save it."

THE CLIMAX

The climax is a popular way of ending. It is often difficult to manage and is not an ending for all speakers nor for all subjects. But when well done, it is excellent. It works up to a crest, a peak, getting stronger sentence by sentence.

Lincoln used the climax in preparing his notes for a lecture on Niagara Falls. Note how each comparison is stronger than the preceding, how he gets a cumulative effect by comparing its age to Columbus, Christ, Moses, Adam, and so on:

It calls up the indefinite past. When Columbus first sought this continent—when Christ suffered on the cross—when Moses led Israel through the Red Sea—nay, even when Adam first came from the hands of his Maker; then, as now, Niagara was roaring here. The eyes of that species of extinct giants whose bones fill the mounds of America have gazed on Niagara, as ours do now. Contemporary with the first race of men, and older than the first man, Niagara is as strong and fresh today as ten thousand years ago. The Mammoth and Mastodon, so long dead that fragments of their monstrous bones alone testify that they ever lived, have gazed on Niagara—in that long, long time never still for a moment, never dried, never frozen, never slept, never rested.

Wendell Phillips employed this selfsame technique in his address on Toussaint L'Ouverture. The close of it is quoted below. This selection is often cited in books on public speaking. It has vigour, vitality. It is interesting even though it is a bit too ornate for this practical age. This speech was written more than half a century ago. Amusing, isn't it, to note how woefully wrong were Wendell Phillips' prognostications concerning the historical significance of John Brown and Toussaint L'Ouverture "fifty years hence when truth gets a hearing"? It is as hard evidently to guess history as it is to foretell next year's stock market or the price of lard.

> I would call him Napoleon, but Napoleon made his way to empire over broken oaths and through a sea of blood. This man never broke his word. "No Retaliation" was his great motto and the rule of his

> life; and the last words uttered to his son in France were these: "My boy, you will one day go back to Santo Domingo; forget that France murdered your father." I would call him Cromwell, but Cromwell was only a soldier, and the state he founded went down with him into his grave. I would call him Washington, but the great Virginian held slaves. This man risked his empire rather than permit the slave-trade in the humblest village of his dominions.
>
> You think me a fanatic tonight, for you read history, not with your eyes, but with your prejudices. But fifty years hence, when Truth gets a hearing, the Muse of History will put Phocion for the Greek, and Brutus for the Roman, Hampden for England, Lafayette for France, choose Washington as the bright, consummate flower of our earlier civilization, and John Brown the ripe fruit of our noonday, then, dipping her pen in the sunlight, will write in the clear blue, above them all, the name of the soldier, the statesman, the martyr, Toussaint L'Ouverture.

WHEN THE TOE TOUCHES

Hunt, search, experiment until you get a good ending and a good beginning. Then get them close together.

The speaker who does not cut his talk to fit in with the prevailing mood of this hurried, rapid age will be unwelcome and, sometimes, positively disliked.

No less a saint than Saul of Tarsus sinned in this respect. He preached until a chap in the audience, "a young man named Eutychus", went to sleep and fell out of a window and all but broke his neck. Even then he may not have stopped talking. Who knows? I remember a speaker, a doctor, standing up one night at a University Club. It had been a long banquet. Many speakers had already talked. It was two o' clock in the morning when his turn came. Had he been endowed with tact and fine feeling and discretion, he would have said half a dozen sentences and let us go home. But did he? No, not he. He launched into a forty-five minute tirade against vivisection. Long before he was halfway through his audience were wishing that he, like Eutychus, would fall out of a window and break something, anything, to silence him.

Mr. Lorimer, the editor of the *Saturday Evening Post,* told me that he always stopped a series of articles in the *Post* when they were at the height of their popularity, and people were clamouring for more. Why stop then? Why then of all times?

"Because," said Mr. Lorimer—and he ought to know—"the point of satiation is reached very soon after that peak of popularity."

The same wisdom will apply, and ought to be applied, to speaking. Stop while the audience is still eager to have you go on.

The greatest speech Christ ever delivered, the Sermon on the Mount, can be repeated in five minutes. Lincoln's Gettysburg address has only ten sentences. One can read the whole story of creation in Genesis in less time than it takes to peruse a murder story in the morning paper.... Be brief! Be brief!

Dr. Johnson, Archdeacon of Nyasa, has written a book about the primitive peoples of Africa. He has lived among them, observed them, for forty-nine years. He relates that when a speaker talks too long at a village gathering or the Gwang-wara, the audience silences him with shouts of "Imetosha! Imerosha!"—"Enough! Enough!"

Another tribe is said to permit a speaker to hold forth only so long as he can stand on one foot. When the toe of the lifted member touches the ground, *finito*. He has come to an end.

And the average white audience, even though they are more polite, more restrained, dislike long speeches as much as do those African negroes.

So be warned by their lot,
Which I know *you* will not,
And learn about speaking from them.

The conclusion, too, has definite work to perform. It rounds out the talk; it holds the audience's earnest attention for a brief moment on the speech as a whole.

—George Rowland Collins

~

Life is the art of drawing sufficient conclusions from insufficient premises.

—Samuel Butler

4

Self-Confidence Through Preparation

One important key to success is self-confidence. An important key to self-confidence is preparation.

—Arthur Ashe

It has been my professional duty as well as pleasure to listen to and criticize approximately six thousand speeches a year each season since 1912. These were made, not by college students, but by mature business and professional men. If that experience has engraved on my mind any one thing more deeply than another, surely it is this: the urgent necessity of preparing a talk before one starts to make it and of having something clear and definite to say, something that has impressed one, something that won't stay unsaid. Aren't you unconsciously drawn to the speaker who, you feel, has a real message in his head and heart that he zealously desires to communicate to your head and heart? That is half the secret of speaking.

When a speaker is in that kind of mental and emotional state he will discover a significant fact: namely, that his talk will almost make itself. Its yoke will be easy, its burden will be light. A well-prepared speech is already nine-tenths delivered.

The primary reason why most men take this course, is to acquire confidence and courage and self-reliance. And the one fatal mistake many make is neglecting to prepare their talks. How can they even hope to subdue the cohorts of fear, the cavalry of nervousness, when they go into the battle with wet powder and blank shells, or with no ammunition at all? Under the circumstances, small wonder that they are not exactly at home before an audience. "I believe," said Lincoln in the White House, "that I shall never be old enough to speak without embarrassment when I have nothing to say."

If you want confidence, why not do the things necessary to bring it about?

Why don't those enrolled in this course prepare their talks more carefully? Why? Some don't clearly understand what preparation is nor how to go about it wisely; others plead a lack of time. So we shall discuss these problems rather fully—and we trust lucidly and profitably—in this chapter.

THE RIGHT WAY TO PREPARE

What is preparation? Reading a book? That is one kind, but not the best. Reading may help but if one attempts to lift a lot of "canned" thoughts out of a book and to give them out immediately as his own, the whole performance will be lacking in something. The audience may not know precisely what is lacking, but they will not warm to the speaker.

To illustrate, some time ago I conducted a course in public speaking for the senior officers of banks. Naturally, the members of such a group, having many demands upon their time, frequently found it difficult to prepare adequately or to do what they conceived of as preparing. All their lives they had been thinking their own individual thoughts, nurturing their own personal convictions, seeing things from their own distinctive angles, living their own original experiences. So, in that fashion they had spent forty years storing up material for speeches. But it was hard for some of them to realize that. They could not see the forest for "the murmuring pines and the hemlocks".

This group met Friday evenings from five to seven. One Friday, a certain gentleman connected with a bank— for our purposes here, we shall designate him as Mr. Jackson—found four-thirty had arrived, and, what was he to talk about? He walked out of his office, bought a copy of a magazine at a news stand and, in the subway coming down to the bank where the class met, he read an article entitled, "You Have Only Ten Years To Succeed". He read it not because he was interested in the article especially, but because he must speak on something, on anything, to fill his quota of time.

An hour later, he stood up and attempted to talk convincingly and interestingly on the contents of this article.

What was the result, the inevitable result?

He had not digested, had not assimilated what he was trying to say. "Trying to say"—that expresses it precisely. He was *trying*. There was no real message in him seeking for an outlet, and his whole manner and tone revealed it unmistakably How could he expect the audience to be any more impressed than he himself was? He kept referring to the article saying the author said so and so. There was a surfeit of the magazine in it, but regrettably little of Mr. Jackson.

So I addressed him somewhat in this fashion: "Mr. Jackson, we are not interested in this shadowy personality who wrote that article. He is not here. We can't see him. But we are interested in you and your ideas. Tell us what you think, personally, not what somebody else said. Put more of Mr. Jackson in this. Why not take this same subject for next week? Why not read this article again, and ask yourself whether you agree with the author or not? If you do, think out his suggestions and illustrate them with observations from your own experience. If you don't agree with him, say so and tell us why. Let this article be merely the starting point from which you launch your own speech."

Mr. Jackson accepted the suggestion, reread the article and concluded that he did not agree with the author at all. He did not sit down in the subway and try to prepare this next speech to order. He let it grow. It was a child of his own brain, and it developed and expanded and took on stature just as his physical children had done. And like his daughters, this other child grew day and night when he was least conscious of it. One thought was suggested to him while reading some item in the newspaper, another illustration swam into his mind unexpectedly when he was discussing the subject with a friend. The thing deepened and heightened, lengthened and thickened, as he thought over it during the odd moments of the week.

The next time Mr. Jackson spoke on this subject, he had something that was his ore that he dug out of his own mine, currency coined in his own mint. And he spoke all the better because he was disagreeing with the author of the article. There is no spur to rouse one like a little opposition.

What an incredible contrast between these two speeches by the same man, in the same fortnight, on the same subject. What a colossal difference the right kind of preparation makes!

Let us cite another illustration of how to do it and how not to do it. A gentleman, whom we shall call Mr. Flynn, was a student of this course. One afternoon he devoted his talk to eulogizing his home tour. He had hastily and superficially gleaned his facts from a tourist booklet. They sounded like it—dry, disconnected, undigested. He had not thought over his subject adequately. It had not elicited his enthusiasm. He did not feel what he was saying deeply enough to make it worthwhile expressing. The whole affair was flat and flavourless and unprofitable.

A fortnight later something happened that touched Mr. Flynn to the core: a thief stole his motorcar out of a public garage. He rushed to the police and offered rewards, but it was all in vain. The police admitted that it was well nigh impossible for them to cope with the crime situation; yet, only a week previously, they had found time to walk about the street, chalk in hand, and fine Mr. Flynn because he had parked his car fifteen minutes at a kerb. These "chalk cops", who were so busy annoying respectable citizens that they could not catch criminals, aroused his ire. He was indignant. He had something now to say, not something that he had got out of a book, but something that was leaping hot out of his own life and experience. Here was something that was part and parcel of the real man—something that had aroused his feelings and convictions. In his speech eulogizing the city, he had laboriously pulled out sentence by sentence, but now he had but to stand on his feet and open his mouth, and his condemnation of the police welled up and boiled forth like Vesuvius in action. A speech like that is almost foolproof. It can hardly fail. It was experience plus reflection.

WHAT IS MEANT BY PREPARATION

Does the preparation of a speech mean the getting together of some faultless phrases written down or memorized? No. Does it mean the assembling of a few casual thoughts that really convey very little to you personally? Not at all. It means the assembling of *your* thoughts, *your* ideas, *your* convictions, *your* urges. And you have such thoughts, such urges. You have them every day of your waking life. They even swarm through your dreams. Your whole existence has been filled with feelings and experiences. These things are lying deep in your subconscious mind as thick as pebbles on the seashore. Preparation means thinking, brooding, recalling, selecting the ones that appeal to you most, polishing them, working them into a pattern, a mosaic of your own. That doesn't sound like such a difficult programme, does it? It isn't. It just requires a little concentration and thinking to a purpose.

THE SAGE ADVICE OF DEAN BROWN OF YALE

A few years ago the Yale Divinity School celebrated the one hundredth anniversary of its founding. On that occasion, the Dean, Dr. Charles Reynold Brown, delivered a series of lectures on the Art of Preaching. These are now published in book form under that name by the Macmillan Company, New York. Dr. Brown has been preparing addresses himself weekly for a third of a century, and also training others to prepare and deliver; so he was in a position to dispense some sage advice on the subject, advice that will hold good regardless of whether the speaker is a man of the cloth preparing a discourse on the Ninety-first Psalm, or a shoe manufacturer preparing a speech on Labour Unions. So I am taking the liberty of quoting Dr. Brown here:

> Brood over your text and your topic. Brood over them until they become mellow and responsive. You will hatch out of them a whole flock of promising ideas as you cause the tiny germs of life there contained to expand and develop....

It will be all the better if this process can go on for a long time and not be postponed until Saturday afternoon when you are actually making your final preparation for Sunday. If a minister can hold a certain truth in his mind for a month, for six months perhaps, for a year it may be before he preaches on it he will find new ideas perpetually sprouting out of it, until it shows an abundant growth. He may meditate on it as he walks the streets, or as he spends some hours on a train, when his eyes are too tired to read.

He may indeed brood upon it in the night-time. It is better for the minister not to take his church or his sermon to bed with him habitually—a pulpit is a splendid thing to preach from, but it is not a good bedfellow. Yet, for all that, I have sometimes got out of bed in the middle of the night to put down the thoughts which came to me, for fear I might forget them before morning....

When you are actually engaged in assembling the material for a particular sermon, write down everything that comes to you bearing upon that text and topic. Write down what you saw in the text when you first chose it. Write down all the associated ideas which now occur to you....

Put all these ideas of yours down in writing, just a few words, enough to fix the idea, and keep your mind reaching for more all the time as if it were never to see another book as long as it lived. This is the way to train the mind in productiveness. You will by this method keep your own mental processes fresh, original, creative....

Put down all of those ideas which you have brought to the birth yourself, unaided. They are more precious for your mental unfolding than rubies and diamonds and fine gold. Put them down, preferably on scraps of paper, backs of old letters, fragments of envelopes, waste paper, anything which comes to your hand. This is much better in every way than to use nice, long, clean sheets of foolscap. It is not a mere matter of economy—you will find it easier to arrange and organize these loose bits when you come to set your material in order.

Keep on putting down all the ideas which come to your mind, thinking hard all the while. You need not hurry this process. It is one of the most important mental transactions in which you will be privileged to engage. It is this method which causes the mind to grow in real productive power....

You will find that the sermons you enjoy preaching the most and the ones which actually accomplish the most good in the lives of your people will be those sermons which you take most largely out of your own interiors. They are bone of your bone, flesh of your flesh, the children of your own mental labour, the output of your own creative energy. The sermons which are garbled and compiled will always have a kind of second-hand, warmed-over flavour about them. The sermons which live and move and enter into the temple, walking and leaping and praising God, the sermons which enter into the hearts of men causing them to mount up with wings like eagles and to walk in the way of duty and not faint—these real sermons are the ones which are actually born from the vital energies of the man who utters them.

HOW LINCOLN PREPARED HIS SPEECHES

How did Lincoln prepare his speeches? Fortunately, we know the facts and, as you read here of his method, you will observe that Dean Brown, in his lecture, commended several of the procedures that Lincoln had employed three-quarters of a century previously. One of Lincoln's most famous addresses was that in which he declared with prophetic vision: "A house divided against itself cannot stand.' I believe this government cannot endure, permanently, half-slave and half-free." This speech was thought out as he went about his usual work, as he ate his meals, as he walked the street, as he sat in his barn milking his cow, as he made his daily trip to the butcher shop and grocery, an old grey shawl over his shoulders, his market basket over his arm, his little son at his side, chattering and questioning, growing peeved, and jerking at the long bony fingers in a vain effort to make his father talk to him. But Lincoln stalked on, absorbed in his own reflections, thinking of his speech, apparently unconscious of the boy's existence.

From time to time during this brooding and hatching process, he jotted down notes, fragments, sentences here and there on stray envelopes, scraps of paper, bits torn from paper sacks—anything that was near. These he stowed away in the top of his hat and carried them there until he was ready to sit down and arrange them in order, and to write and revise the whole thing, and to shape it up for delivery and publication.

In the joint debates of 1858, Senator Douglas delivered the same speech wherever he went; but Lincoln kept studying and contemplating and reflecting until he found it easier, he said, to make a new speech each day than to repeat an old one. The subject was for ever widening and enlarging in his mind.

A short time before he moved into the White House, he took a copy of the Constitution and three speeches, and with only these for reference, he locked himself in a dingy, dusty back room over a store in Springfield; and there, away from all intrusion and interruption, he wrote out his inaugural address.

How did Lincoln prepare his Gettysburg address? Unfortunately, false reports have been circulated about it. The true story, however, is fascinating. Let us have it:

When the commission in charge of the Gettysburg cemetery decided to arrange for a formal dedication, they invited Edward Everett to deliver the speech. He had been a Boston minister, President of Harvard, Governor of Massachusetts, United States Senator, Minister to England, Secretary of State, and was generally considered to be America's most capable speaker. The date first set for the dedication ceremonies was October 23, 1863. Mr. Everett very wisely declared that it would be impossible for him to prepare adequately on such short notice. So the dedication was postponed until November 19, nearly a month, to give him time to prepare. The last three days of that period he spent in Gettysburg, going over the battlefield, familiarizing himself with all that had taken place there. That period of brooding and thinking was most excellent preparation. It made the battle real to him.

Invitations to be present were despatched to all the members of Congress, to the President and his cabinet. Most of these declined; the committee was surprised when Lincoln agreed to come. Should they ask him to speak? They had not intended to do so. Objections were raised. He would not have time to prepare. Besides, even if he did have time, had he the ability? True, he could handle himself well in a debate on slavery; but no one had ever heard him deliver a dedicatory address. This was a grave and solemn occasion. They ought not to take any chances. Should they ask him to speak? They wondered, wondered.... But they would have wondered a thousand times more had they been able to look into the future and to see that this man, whose ability they were questioning, was to deliver on that occasion what is very generally accepted now as one of the most enduring addresses ever delivered by the lips of mortal man.

Finally, a fortnight before the event, they sent Lincoln a belated invitation to make "a few appropriate remarks". Yes, that is the way they worded it; "a few appropriate remarks". Think of writing that to the President of the United States!

Lincoln immediately set about preparing. He wrote to Edward Everett, secured a copy of the address that that classic scholar was to deliver and, a day or two later, going to a photographer's gallery to pose for his photograph, Lincoln took Everett's manuscript with him and read it during the spare time that he had at the studio. He thought over his talk for days, thought over it while walking back and forth between the White House and the War Office, thought over it while he stretched out on a leather couch in the War Office waiting for the late telegraphic reports. He wrote a rough draft of it on a piece of foolscap paper, and carried it about in the top of his tall silk hat. Ceaselessly he was brooding over it, ceaselessly it was taking shape. The Sunday before it was delivered he said to Noah Brooks: "It is not exactly written. It is not finished anyway. I have written it over two or three times, and I shall have to give it another lick before I am satisfied."

He arrived in Gettysburg the night before the dedication. The little town was filled to overflowing. Its usual population of thirteen hundred had suddenly swelled to fifteen thousand. The pavements became clogged, impassable, men and women took to the dirt streets. Half a dozen bands were playing; crowds were singing "John Brown's Body". People foregathered before the home of Mr. Wills where Lincoln was being entertained. They serenaded him; they demanded a speech. Lincoln responded with a few words which conveyed with more clearness than tact, perhaps, that he was unwilling to speak until the morrow. The facts are that he was spending the latter part of that evening giving his speech "another lick". He even went to an adjoining house where Secretary Seward was staying and read the speech aloud to him for his criticism. After breakfast the next morning, he continued "to give it another lick", working on it until a rap came at the door informing him that it was time for him to take his place in the procession. "Colonel Carr, who rode just behind the President, stated that when the procession started, the President sat erect on his horse, and looked the part of the commander-in-chief of the army; but, as the procession moved on, his body leaned forward, his arms hung limp, and his head was bowed. He seemed absorbed in thought."

We can only guess that even then he was going over his little speech of ten immortal sentences, giving it "another lick".

Some of Lincoln's speeches, in which he had only a superficial interest, were unquestioned failures, but he was possessed of extraordinary power when he spoke of slavery and the union. Why? Because he thought ceaselessly on these problems and felt deeply. A companion who shared a room with him one night in an Illinois tavern woke up next morning at daylight to find Lincoln sitting up in bed, staring at the wall, and his first words were: "This government cannot endure permanently, half-slave and half-free."

How did Christ prepare His addresses? He withdrew from the crowd. He thought. He brooded. He pondered. He went out alone into the wilderness and meditated and fasted for forty days and forty nights. "From that time on," records Saint Matthew, "Jesus began to preach." Shortly after that, He delivered one of the world's most celebrated speeches: the Sermon on the Mount.

"That is all very interesting," you may protest, "but I have no desire to become an immortal orator. I merely want to make a few simple talks in business occasionally."

True, and we realize your wants fully. This course is for the specific purpose of helping you and other businessmen like you to do just that. But, unpretending as the talks of yours may prove to be, you can profit by and utilize in some measure the methods of the famous speakers of the past.

HOW TO PREPARE YOUR TALK

What topics ought you to speak on during the sessions of this course? Anything that interests you. If possible, choose your own topics; you will be more fortunate still if your topic chooses you. However, you will often have topics suggested for you by your instructor.

Don't make the almost universal mistake of trying to cover too much ground in a brief talk. Just take one or two angles of a subject and attempt to cover them adequately. You will be fortunate if you can do that in the short speeches that are necessitated by the time schedule of this course.

Determine your subject a week in advance so that you will have time to think it over in odd moments. Think it over for seven days; dream over it for seven nights. Think of it the last thing when you retire. Think of it the next morning while you are shaving, while you are bathing, while you are riding downtown, while you are waiting for lifts, for lunch, for appointments. Discuss it with your friends. Make it a topic of conversation.

Ask yourself all possible questions concerning it. If, for example, you are to speak on divorce, ask yourself what causes divorce, what are the effects economically, socially. How can the evil be remedied? Should divorce be made impossible? More difficult? Easier?

Suppose you were going to talk on why you enrolled for this course. You ought then to ask yourself such questions as these: What are my troubles? What do I hope to get out of this instruction? Have I ever made a public talk? If so, when? Where? What happened? Why do I think this training is valuable for a businessman? Do I know men who are forging ahead commercially largely because of their self-confidence, their presence, their ability to talk convincingly? Do I know others who will probably never achieve a gratifying measure of success because they lack these positive assets? Be specific. Tell the stories of these men without mentioning their names.

If you stand up and think clearly and keep going for two or three minutes, that is all that will be expected of you during your first few talks. A topic, such as why you enrolled for this course, is very easy; that is obvious. If you will spend a little time selecting and arranging your material on that topic, you will be almost sure to remember it, for you will be speaking of your own observations, your own desires, your own experiences.

On the other hand, let us suppose that you have decided to speak on your business or profession. How shall you set about preparing such a talk? You already have a wealth of material on that subject. Your problem, then, will be to select and arrange it. Do not attempt to tell us all about it in three minutes. It can't be done. The attempt will be too sketchy, too fragmentary. Take one and only one phase of your topic: expand and enlarge that. For example, why not tell us how you came to be in your particular business or profession? Was it a result of accident or choice? Relate your early struggles, your defeats, your hopes, your triumphs. Give us a human interest narrative, a real-life picture based on first-hand experiences. The truthful, inside story of almost any man's life—if told modestly and without offending egotism—is most entertaining. It is almost sure-fire speech material.

Or take another angle of your business: What are its troubles? What advice would you give to a young man entering it?

Or tell us about the people with whom you come in contact—the honest and dishonest onces. Tell us of your problems with labour, your problems with your customers. What has your business taught you about the most interesting topic in the world: human nature? If you speak about the technical side of your business, about things, your talk may very easily prove uninteresting to others. But people, personalities—one can hardly go wrong with that kind of material.

Above all else, don't make your talk an abstract preachment. That will bore us. Make your talk a regular layer cake of illustrations and general statements. Think of concrete cases you have observed, and of the fundamental truths which you believe those specific instances illustrate. You will also discover that these concrete cases are far easier to remember than abstractions; they are far easier to talk about. They will also aid and brighten your delivery.

Some men, in speaking of their businesses, commit the unforgivable error of talking only of the features that interest them. Shouldn't the speaker try to ascertain what will entertain not himself but his hearers? Shouldn't he try to appeal to their selfish interests? If, for example, he sells fire insurance, shouldn't he tell them how to prevent fires on their own property? If he is a banker, shouldn't he give them advice on finance or investments?

While preparing, study your audience. Think of their wants, their wishes. That is sometimes half the battle.

In preparing some topics, it is very advisable—if time permits—to do some reading, to discover what others have thought, what others have said on the same subject. But don't read until you have first thought yourself dry. That is important—very. Then go to the public library and lay your needs before the librarian. Tell her you are preparing a speech on such and such a topic. Ask her frankly for help. If you are not in the habit of doing research work, you will probably be surprised at the aids she can put at your disposal; perhaps a special volume on your very topic, outlines and briefs for debate, giving the principal arguments on both sides of the public questions of the day, the *Reader's Guide to Periodical Literature* listing the magazine articles that have appeared on various topics since the beginning of the century, the *Daily Mail Almanac*, the Encyclopaedias, and dozens of reference books. They are tools in your workshop. Use them.

THE SECRET OF RESERVE POWER

A speech ought to be prepared somewhat in a lavish and discriminating spirit. Assemble a hundred thoughts, and discard ninety.

Collect more material, more information, than there is any possibility of employing. Get it for the additional confidence it will give you, for the sureness of touch. Get it for the effect it will have on your mind and heart and whole manner of speaking. This is a basic, important factor of preparation; yet it is constantly ignored by speakers, both in public and private.

"I have drilled hundreds of salesmen, canvassers, and demonstrators," says Arthur Dunn, "and the principal weakness which I have discovered in most of them has been their failure to realize the importance of knowing everything possible about their products and getting such knowledge before they start to sell.

> Many salesmen have come to my office and after getting a description of the article and a line of sales talk have been eager to get right out and try to sell. Many of these salesmen have not lasted a week and a large number have not lasted forty-eight hours. In educating and drilling canvassers and salesmen in the sale of a food specialty, I have endeavoured to make food experts of them. I have compelled them to study food charts issued by the Department of Agriculture, which show in food the amount of water, the amount of protein, the amount of carbohydrates, the amount of fat, and ash. I have had them study the elements which make up the products which they are to sell. I have had them go to school for several days and then pass examinations. I have had them sell the product to other salesmen. I have offered prizes for the best sales talks.
>
> I have often found salesmen who get impatient at the preliminary time required for the study of

their articles. They have said, "I will never have time to tell all of this to a retail grocer. He is too busy. If I talk protein and carbohydrates, he won't listen and, if he does listen, he won't know what I am talking about." My reply has been, "You don't get all of this knowledge for the benefit of your customer, but for the benefit of yourself. If you know your product from A to Z you will have a feeling about it that is difficult to describe. You will be so positively charged, so fortified, so strengthened in your own mental attitude that you will be both irresistible and unconquerable."

Miss Ida M. Tarbell, the well-known historian of the Standard Oil Company, told the writer that years ago, when she was in Paris, Mr. S.S. McClure, the founder of *McClure's Magazine*, cabled her to write a short article about the Atlantic Cable. She went to London, interviewed the European manager of the principal cable, and obtained sufficient data for her assignment. But she did not stop there. She wanted a reserve supply of facts, so she studied all manner of cables on display in the British Museum, she read books on the history of the cable and even went to manufacturing concerns on the edge of London and saw cables in the process of construction.

Why did she collect ten times as much information as she could possibly use? She did it because she felt it would give her reserve power; because she realized that the things she knew and did not express would lend force and colour to the little she did express.

Edwin James Cattell has spoken to approximately thirty million people, yet he confided to me recently that if he did not, on the way home, kick himself for the good things he had left out of his talk, he felt that the performance must have been a failure. Why? Because he knew from long experience that the talks of distinct merit are those in which there abounds a reserve of material, a plethora, a profusion of it—far more than the speaker has time to use.

"What!" you object. "Does this author imagine that I can find time for all this? I would like him to know that I have a business to conduct and a wife and two children and a couple of Airedale dogs to support...I can't be running to museums and looking at cables and reading books and sitting up in bed at daylight mumbling my speeches."

My dear sir, we know all about your case, and sympathetic allowance has been made for it. The assigned topics will be questions on which you have already done considerable thinking. Sometimes you will not be asked to plan any kind of a speech in advance, but you will be given an easy topic for impromptu speaking after you face your audience. This will afford you most useful practice in thinking on your feet—the sort of thing that you may be forced to do in business discussions.

Some of the men who join this course are only slightly interested in learning to prepare talks in advance. They want to be able to think on their feet and to join in discussions that come up at various business meetings. Such students sometimes prefer to come to the class, listen, and then take their cue from some of the preceding speakers. A limited amount of this may be advisable, but don't overdo it. Follow the suggestions given in this chapter. They will give you the ease and freedom you are seeking and also the ability to prepare talks effectively.

If you procrastinate until you have leisure to prepare and plan your talk, the leisure will probably never be found.

However, it is easy to do the habitual, the accustomed thing, isn't it? So why not set aside one specific evening a week, from eight to ten o'clock, to be devoted to nothing but this task? That is the sure way, the systematic way. Why not try it?

> *There is only one security, and when you've lost that security, you've lost everything you've got. And that is the security of confidence in yourself; to be, to create, to make any position you want to make for yourself. And when you lose that confidence, you've lost the only security you can have.... Self-confidence is self-determinism. One's belief in one's ability to determine his own course. As long as one has that, he's got the universe in his pocket. And when he hasn't got that, not all the pearls in China nor all the grain and corn in Iowa can give him security, because that's the only security there is.*
>
> —L. Ron Hubbard

5

How Famous Speakers Prepared Their Addresses

Luck is what happens when preparation meets opportunity.

—Seneca

I was present once at a luncheon of a Rotary Club when the principal speaker was a prominent government official. The high position that he occupied gave him prestige, and we were looking forward with pleasure to hearing him. He had promised to tell us about the activities of his own department, and it was one in which almost every businessman was interested.

He knew his subject thoroughly, knew far more about it than he could possibly use, but he had not planned his speech. He had not selected his material. He had not arranged it in orderly fashion. Nevertheless, with a courage born of inexperience, he plunged heedlessly, blindly, into his speech. He did not know where he was going, but he was on his way.

His mind was, in short, a mere hodgepodge, and so was the mental feast he served us. He brought on the ice cream first, and then placed the soup before us. Fish and nuts came next. And, on top of that, there was something that seemed to be a mixture of soup and ice cream and good red herring. I have never, anywhere or at any time, seen a speaker more utterly confused.

He had been trying to talk impromptu, but, in desperation now, he drew a bundle of notes out of his pocket, confessing that his secretary had compiled them for him—and no one questioned the veracity of his assertion. The notes themselves evidently had no more order than a van full of scrap iron. He fumbled through them nervously, glancing from one page to another, trying to orient himself, trying to find a way out of the wilderness, and he attempted to talk as he did so. It was impossible. He apologized and, calling for water, took a drink with a trembling hand, uttered a few more scattering sentences, repeated himself, dug into his notes again... Minute by minute he grew more helpless, more lost, more bewildered, more embarrassed. Nervous perspiration stood out on his forehead, and his handkerchief shook as he wiped it away. We in the audience sat watching the fiasco, our sympathies stirred, our feelings harrowed. We suffered positive and vicarious embarrassment. But with more doggedness than discretion, the speaker continued, floundering, studying his notes, apologizing and drinking. Everyone except him felt that the spectacle was rapidly approaching total disaster, and it was a relief to us all when he sat down and ceased his death struggles. It was one of the most uncomfortable audiences I have ever been in, and he was the most ashamed and humiliated speaker I have ever seen. He had made his talk as Rousseau said a love letter should be written: he had begun without knowing what he was going to say, and he had finished without knowing what he had uttered.

The moral of the tale is just this: "When a man's knowledge is not in order," said Herbert Spencer, "the more of it he has, the greater will be his confusion of thought."

No sane man would start to build a house without some sort of plan, but why will he begin to deliver a speech without the vaguest kind of outline or programme?

A speech is a voyage with a purpose, and it must be charted. The man who starts nowhere, generally gets there.

I wish that I could paint this saying of Napoleon in flaming letters of red, a foot high over every doorway on the globe where students of public speaking foregather: "The art of war is a science in which nothing succeeds which has not been calculated and thought out."

That is just as true of speaking as of shooting. But do speakers realize it, or, if they do, do they always act on it? They do not. Most emphatically they do not. Many a talk has just a trifle more plan and arrangement than a bowl of Irish stew.

What is the best and most effective arrangement for a given set of ideas? No one can say until he has studied them. It is always a new problem, an eternal question that every speaker must ask and answer himself again and again. No infallible rules can be given, but we can, at any rate, illustrate briefly here with a concrete case just what we mean by orderly arrangements.

HOW A PRIZE WINNING SPEECH WAS CONSTRUCTED

Here is a speech that was delivered by a student of this course before the Thirteenth Annual Convention of the American National Association of Real Estate Boards. It won first prize in competition with twenty-seven other speeches on various cities. This speech, well constructed, full of facts stated clearly, vividly, interestingly. It has spirit. It marches. It will merit reading and study.

Mr. Chairman and Friends:

144 years ago, this great nation, the United States of America, was born in my City of Philadelphia, and so it is quite natural that a city having such a historical record should have that strong an American spirit that has not only made it the greatest industrial centre in this country, but also one of the largest and most beautiful cities in the whole world.

Philadelphia has a population close to two millions of people, and our city has an area that is equal to the combined size of Milwaukee and Boston, Paris and Berlin, and out of our 130 square miles of territory we have given up nearly 8,000 acres of our best land for beautiful parks, squares and boulevards, so that our people would have the proper places for recreation and pleasure, and the right kind of environment that belongs to every decent American.

Philadelphia, friends, is not only a large, clean and beautiful city, but it is also known everywhere as the great workshop of the world, and the reason it is called the workshop of the world is because we have a vast army ot over 400,000 people employed in 9,200 industrial establishments that turn out one hundred thousand dollars' worth of useful commodities every ten minutes of the working day, and, according to a well-known statistician, there is no city in this country that equals Philadelphia in the production of woollen goods, leather goods, knit goods, textiles, felt hats, hardware, tools, storage batteries, steel ships and a great many other things. We build a railroad locomotive every two hours day and night, and more than one-half the people in this great country ride in street cars made in the City of Philadelphia. We manufacture a thousand cigars every minute, and last year, in our 115 hosiery mills, we made two pairs of stockings for every man, woman and child in this country. We make more carpets and rugs than all of Great Britain and Ireland combined, and, in fact, our total commercial and industrial business is so stupendous that our bank clearings last year, amounting to thirty-seven billions of dollars, would have paid for every Liberty Bond in the entire country.

But, friends, while we are very proud of our wonderful industrial progress, and while we are also very proud of being one of the largest medical, art and educational centres in this country, yet, we feel a still greater pride in the fact that we have more individual homes in the City of Philadelphia than there are in any other city in the whole world. In Philadelphia we have 397,000 separate homes, and if these homes were placed on twenty-five-foot lots, side by side, in one single row, that row would reach all the way from Philadelphia clear through to this Convention Hall, at Kansas City, and then on to Denver, a distance of 1,881 miles.

But, what I want to call your special attention to, is the significance of the fact, that tens of thousands of these homes are owned and occupied by the working people of our city, and when a man owns

> the ground upon which he stands and the roof over his head, there is no argument ever presented that would infect that man with those imported diseases, known as Socialism and Communism.
>
> Philadelphia is not a fertile soil for anarchy, because our homes, our educational institutions, and our gigantic industry have been produced by that true American spirit that was born in our city, and is a heritage from our forefathers. Philadelphia is the mother city of this great country, and the very fountainhead of American liberty. It is the city where the first American flag was made; it is the city where the first Congress of the United States met; it is the city where the Declaration of Independence was signed; it is the city where that best loved relic in America, the Liberty Bell, has inspired tens of thousands of our men, women and children, so that we believe we have a sacred mission, which is not to worship the golden calf, but to spread the American spirit, and to keep the fires of freedom burning, so that with God's permission, the Government of Washington, Lincoln and Roosevelt may be an inspiration to all humanity.

In the first place, this speech has a beginning and an ending. That is a rare virtue, my dear reader, more rare than you may be inclined to think. It starts somewhere. It goes there straight as wild geese on the wing. It doesn't dawdle. It loses no time.

It has freshness, individuality. The speaker opens by saying something about his city that the other speakers could not possibly say about theirs: he points out that his city is the birthplace of the entire nation.

He states that it is one of the largest and most beautiful cities in the world. But that claim is general, trite; standing by itself, it would not impress anyone very much. The speaker knew that, so he helped his audience visualize the magnitude of Philadelphia by stating it "has an area equal to the combined size of Milwaukee, Boston, Paris and Berlin." That is definite, concrete. It is interesting. It is surprising. It makes a mark. It drives home the idea better than a whole page of statistics would have done.

Next he declares that Philadelphia is "known everywhere as the great workshop of the world". Sounds exaggerated, doesn't it? Like propaganda. Had he proceeded immediately to the next point no one would have been convinced. But he doesn't. He pauses to enumerate the products in which Philadelphia leads the world: "woollen goods, leather goods, knit goods, textiles, felt hats, hardware, tools, storage batteries, steel ships." Doesn't sound so much like propaganda now, does it? Philadelphia "builds a railroad locomotive every two hours day and night, and more than one-half the people in this great country ride in street cars made in the city of Philadelphia".

"Well, I never knew that," we muse. "Perhaps I rode downtown yesterday in one of those street cars. I'll look tomorrow and see where my town buys its cars."

"A thousand cigars every minute...two pairs of stockings for every man, woman and child in this country."

We are still more impressed..."Maybe my favourite cigar is made in Philadelphia...and these socks I have on..."

What does the speaker do next? Jump back to the subject of the size of Philadelphia that he covered first and give us some fact that he forgot then? No, not at all. He sticks to a point until he finishes it, has done with it, and need never return to it again. For that we are duly grateful, Mr. Speaker. For what is more confusing and muddling than to have a speaker darting from one tiling to another and back again as erratic as a bat in "the twilight? Yet many a speaker does just that. Instead of covering his points in order, 1, 2, 3, 4, 5, he covers them as a football captain calls out signals—27, 34, 19, 2. No, he is worse than that. He covers them like this—27, 34, 27, 19, 2, 34, 19.

But this speaker, however, steams straight ahead on schedule time, never idling, never turning back, swerving neither to the right nor left, like one of those locomotives he has been talking about.

But he makes now the weakest point of his entire speech: Philadelphia, he declares, is "one of the largest medical, art and educational centres in this country". He merely announces that, then speeds on to something else—only twelve words to animate that fact, to make it vivid, to engrave it on the memory. Only twelve words lost, submerged, in a sentence containing a total of sixty- five. It doesn't work. Of course not. The human mind does not operate like a string of steel traps. He devotes so little time to this point, is so general, so vague, seems so unimpressed himself, that the effect on the hearer is almost nil. What should he have done? He realized that he could establish this point with the selfsame technique that he just employed to establish the fact that Philadelphia is the workshop of the world. He knew that. He also knew that he would have a stopwatch held on him during the contest, that he would have five minutes, not a second more; so he had to slur over this point or slight others.

There are "more individual homes in the city of Philadelphia than there are in any other city in the world". How does he make this phase of his topic impressive and convincing? First, he gives the number: 397,000. Second, he visualizes the number: "If these homes were placed on twenty-five foot lots, side by side, in one single row, that row would reach all the way from Philadelphia clear through this Convention Flail at Kansas City, and then on to Denver, a distance of 1,881 miles."

His audience probably forgot the number he gave before he had finished the sentence. But forget that picture? That would have been well, not impossible.

So much for cold material facts. But they are not the stuff out of which eloquence is fashioned. This speaker aspired to build up to a climax, to touch the heart, to stir the feelings. So now on the home stretch, he deals with emotional material. He tells what the ownership of those homes means to the spirit of the city. He denounced "those imported diseases, known as Socialism and Communism... anarchy". He eulogizes Philadelphia as "the very fountainhead of American liberty". Liberty! A magic word, a word full of feeling, a sentiment for which millions have laid down their lives. That phrase in itself is good, but it is a thousand times better when he backs it up with concrete references to historic events and documents, dear, sacred, to the hearts of his hearers.... "It is the city where the first American Flag was made; it is the city where the first Congress of the United States met; it is the city where the Declaration of Independence was signed...Liberty Bell...a sacred mission... to spread the American spirit...to keep the fires of freedom burning, so that with God's permission, the Government of Washington, Lincoln and Roosevelt may be an inspiration to all humanity." That is a real climax!

So much for the composition of this talk. But admirable as it is from the standpoint of construction, this speech could have come to grief, could easily have been brought to naught, had it been expressed in a calm manner devoid of all spirit and vitality. But the speaker delivered it as he composed it; with a feeling and enthusiasm born of the deepest sincerity. Small wonder that it won first prize, that it was awarded the Chicago Cup.

THE WAY DOCTOR CONWELL PLANNED HIS SPEECHES

There are not, as I have already said, any infallible rules that will solve the question of the best arrangement. There are no designs or schemes or charts that will fit all or even a majority of speeches; yet here are a few speech plans that will prove usable in some instances. The late Dr. Russell H. Conwell, the author of the famous *Acres of Diamonds*—once informed me that he had built many of his innumerable speeches on this outline:

1. State your facts.
2. Argue from them.
3. Appeal for action.

Many students of this course have found this plan very helpful and stimulating.

1. Show something that is wrong.
2. Show how to remedy it.
3. Ask for cooperation.

Or to put it in another way:

1. Here is a situation that ought to be remedied.
2. We ought to do so and so about the matter.

3. You ought to help for these reasons.

Yet another speech plan could be:

1. Secure interested attention.
2. Win confidence.
3. State your facts; educate people regarding the merits of your proposition.
4. Appeal to the motives that make men act.

SECRETS OF GREAT SPEAKERS

Woodrow Wilson

"I begin," said Woodrow Wilson when asked to explain his methods, "with a list of the topics I want to cover, *arranging them in my mind in their natural relations*—that is, I fit the bones of the thing together; then I write it out in shorthand. I have always been accustomed to writing in shorthand, finding it a great saver of time. This done, I copy it on my own typewriter, changing phrases, correcting sentences, and adding material as I go along."

Theodore Roosevelt

Theodore Roosevelt prepared his talks in the characteristic Rooseveltian manner: he dug all the facts, reviewed them, appraised them, determined their findings, arrived at his conclusions, arrived with a feeling of certainty that was unshakable.

Then, with a pad of notes before him, he started dictating and he dictated his speech very rapidly so that it would have spontaneity and the spirit of life. Then, he went over this typewritten copy, revised it, inserted, deleted, filled it with pencil marks, and then dictated it all over again. "I never won anything," said he, "without hard labour and the exercise of my best judgment and careful planning and working long in advance."

Often he called in critics to listen to him as he dictated or read his speech to them. He refused to debate with them the wisdom of what he had said. His mind was already made up on that point, and made up irrevocably. He wanted to be told, not what to say, but how to say it. Again and again he went over his typewritten copies, cutting, correcting, improving. That was the speech that the newspapers printed. Of course, he did not memorize it. He spoke extemporaneously. So the talk he actually delivered often differed somewhat from the published and polished one. But the task of dictating and revising was excellent preparation. It made him familiar with his material, with the order of his points. It gave him a smoothness and, sureness and polish that he could hardly have obtained in any other fashion.

Sir Oliver Lodge

Sir Oliver Lodge told me that dictating his talks— dictating them rapidly and with substance, dictating them just as if he were actually talking to an audience—he had discovered to be an excellent means of preparation and practice.

Many of the students of this course have found it illuminating to dictate their talks to the dictaphone, and then to listen to themselves. Illuminating? Yes, and sometimes disillusioning and chastening also, I fear. It is a most wholesome exercise. I recommend it.

This practice of actually writing out what you are going to say will force you to think. It will clarify your ideas. It will hook them in your memory. It will reduce your mental wandering to a minimum. It will improve your diction.

Benjamin Franklin

Benjamin Franklin tells in his *Autobiography* how he improved his diction, how he developed readiness in using words and how he taught himself method in arranging his thoughts. This story of his life is a literary classic and, unlike most classics, it is easy to read and is thoroughly enjoyable. It is almost a model of plain, straightforward English. Every businessman can peruse it with pleasure and profit. I think you will like the selection I refer to; here it is:

> About this time I met with an odd volume of the *Spectator.* It was the third. I had never before seen any of them. I bought it, read it over and over and was much delighted with it. I thought the writing excellent, and wished, if possible, to imitate it. With this view I took some of the papers, and, making short hints of the sentiment in each sentence laid them by a few days, and then, without looking at the book, try'd to complete the papers again, by expressing each hinted sentiment at length, and as fully as it had been expressed before, in any suitable words that should come to hand. Then I compared my *Spectator* with the original, discovered some of my faults and corrected them. But I found a stock of words, and a readiness in recollecting and using them, which I thought I should have acquired before that time if I had gone on making verses; since the continual occasion for words of the same import, but of different length, to suit the measure, or of different sounds for the rhyme, would

> have laid me under a constant necessity of searching for variety, and also have tended to fix that variety in my mind, and make me master of it. Therefore I took some of the tales and turned them back again. I also sometimes jumbled my collections of hints into confusion, and after some weeks endeavoured to reduce them into the best order, before I began to form the full sentences and complete the paper. *This was to teach me method in the arrangement of thoughts.* By comparing my work afterwards with the original, I discovered many faults and amended them; but I sometimes had the pleasure of fancying that, in certain particulars of small import, I had been lucky enough to improve the method of the language, and this encouraged me to think I might possibly in time come to be a tolerable English writer, of which I was extremely ambitious.

PLAY PATIENCE WITH YOUR NOTES

Make notes. Having got your various ideas and illustrations down on scraps of paper, play patience with them—toss them into series of related piles. These main piles ought to represent, approximately, the main points of your talk. Subdivide them into smaller lots. Throw out the chaff until there is nothing but number one wheat left—and even some of the wheat will probably have to be put aside and not used. No man, if he works right, is ever able to use but a percentage of the material he gathers.

One ought never to cease this process of revision until the speech has been made—even then he is very likely to think of points and improvements and refinements that ought to have been made.

A good speaker usually finds when he finishes that there have been four versions of his speech: the one that he prepared, the one that he delivered, the one that the newspapers said that he delivered, and the one that he wishes, on his way home, that he had delivered.

TO USE OR NOT TO USE NOTES

Although he was an excellent impromptu speaker, Lincoln, after he reached the White House, never made any address, not even an informal talk to his cabinet, until he had carefully put it all down in writing beforehand. Of course, he was obliged to read his inaugural addresses. The exact phraseology of historical state papers of that character is too important to be left to extemporizing. But, before in Illinois, Lincoln never used even notes in his speaking. "They always tend to tire and confuse the listener," he said.

And who of us, pray, would contradict him? Don't notes destroy about 50 per cent of your interest in a talk? Don't they prevent, or at least render difficult, a very precious contact and intimacy that ought to exist between the speaker and the audience? Don't they create an air of artificiality? Don't they restrain an audience from feeling that the speaker has the confidence and reserve power that he ought to have?

Make notes, I repeat, during the preparation—elaborate ones, profuse ones. You may wish to refer to them when you are practicing your talk alone. You may possibly feel more comfortable if you have them stored away in your pocket when you are facing an audience; but, like the hammer and saw and axe in a train, they should be emergency tools, only for use in the case of a smash-up, a total wreck, and threatening death and disaster.

If you must use notes, make them extremely brief and write them in large letters on an ample sheet of paper. Then arrive early at the place where you are to speak and hide your notes behind some books on a table. Glance at them when you must, but endeavour to screen your weakness from the audience. John Bright used to secrete his notes in his big hat lying on the table before him.

However, in spite of all that has been said there may be times when it is the part of wisdom to use notes. For example, some men during their first few talks, are so nervous and self-conscious that they are utterly unable to remember their prepared speeches. The result? They shoot off at a tangent, they forget the material they had so carefully rehearsed, they drift off the high road and flounder about in a morass. Why should not such men hold a few very condensed notes in their hands during their maiden efforts? A child clutches the furniture when it is first attempting to walk, but it does not continue it very long.

DO NOT MEMORIZE WORD FOR WORD

Don't read, and don't attempt to memorize your talk word for word. That consumes time, and courts disaster. Yet, in spite of this warning, some of the men reading these lines will try it; if they do, when they stand up to speak they will be thinking of what? Of their messages? No, they will be attempting to recall their exact phraseology. They will be thinking backward, not forward, reversing the usual processes of the human mind. The whole exhibition will be stiff and cold and colourless and inhuman. Do not, I beg of you, waste hours and energy in such futility.

When you have an important business interview, do you sit down and memorize verbatim what you are going to say?

Do you? Of course not. You reflect until you get your main ideas clearly in mind. You may make a few notes and consult some records. You say to yourself, "I shall bring out this point and that. I am going to say that a certain thing ought to be done for these reasons..." Then you enumerate the reasons to yourself and illustrate them with concrete cases. Isn't that the way you prepare for a business interview? Why not use the same common sense method in preparing a talk?

REHEARSE

Two thousand years ago, Horace wrote:

> Seek not for words, seek only fact and thought,
> And crowding in will come the words unsought.

After you have your ideas firmly in mind, then rehearse your talk from beginning to end. Do it silently, mentally, as you walk the street, as you wait for cars and lifts. Get off in a room by yourself and go over it aloud, gesturing, saying it with life and energy. As you practice, imagine there is a real audience before you. Imagine it so strongly that when there is one, it will seem like an old experience. That is the reason why so many criminals are able to go to the scaffold with such bravado; they have already done it so many thousand times in their imagination that they have lost fear of it. When the actual execution does take place, it seems like something that they have gone through very often before.

WHY THE FARMERS THOUGHT LINCOLN AWFULLY LAZY

If you practice your talks in this fashion, you will be faithfully following the examples of many famous speakers.

Lloyd George, when he was a member of a debating society in his hometown in Wales, often strolled along the country lanes, talking and gesturing to the trees and fence posts.

Lincoln, in his younger days, often walked a round trip of thirty or forty miles to hear a famous speaker like Breckenridge. He came home from these scenes so stirred, so determined to be a speaker that he gathered the other hired workers about him in the fields and, mounting a stump, he made speeches and told them stories. His employers grew angry, declaring that this country Cicero was "awfully lazy" that his jokes and his oratory were ruining the rest of the workers.

Asquith gained his first facility by becoming an active worker in the Union Debating Society in Oxford. Later he organized one of his own. Woodrow Wilson learned to speak in a debating society. So did Henry Ward Beecher. So did the mighty Burke.

Study the careers of famous speakers and you will find one fact that is true of them all: *they practiced.* THEY PRACTICED. And the men who make the most rapid progress in this course are those who practice most.

No time for all this? Then do what Joseph Choate used to do. He bought a newspaper of a morning and buried his head in it as he rode to work so no one would bother him. Then, instead of reading the ephemeral scandal and gossip of the day, he thought out and planned his talks.

Chauncey M. Depew led a fairly active life as a railroad president and a United States Senator. Yet, during it all, he made speeches almost every night. "I did not let them interfere with my business," he says. "They were all prepared after I had arrived home from my office late in the afternoon."

We all have three hours a day that we can do with as we please. That was all Darwin had to work with, as he had poor health. Three hours out of twenty-four, wisely used, made him famous.

Theodore Roosevelt, when he was in the White House, often had an entire afternoon given over to a series of five-minute interviews. Yet he kept a book by his side to utilize even the few spare seconds that came between his engagements.

If you are very busy and pushed for time, read Arnold Bennett's *How To Live On Twenty-Four Hours a Day*. Rip out a hundred pages, put them in your hip pocket, read then during your spare seconds. I got through the book in two days in that fashion. It will show you how to save time, how to get more out of the day.

You must have relaxation and a change from your regular work. That is what the practicing of your talks ought to be. If possible, arrange with the other men in this course to meet together an additional night each week for rehearsal. If you cannot do that, play the game of extemporaneous speaking in your own home with your own family.

HOW DOUGLAS FAIRBANKS AND CHARLIE CHAPLIN ENTERTAINED THEMSELVES

It is common knowledge that Douglas Fairbanks and Charlie Chaplin have incomes permitting them to enjoy a little recreation; yet, with all their wealth and fame, they were able to find no greater entertainment, no more enjoyable way of spending their evenings, than by practicing extemporaneous speaking.

Here is their story as Douglas Fairbanks told it in the *American Magazine* a few years ago:

One evening we were fooling and I pretended to introduce Charlie Chaplin at a dinner. He had to rise and make a speech to fit the introduction. And out of that developed a game that we have been playing almost every night for two years. We three (Mary Pickford, Fairbanks, and Chaplin) each write a subject on a slip of paper and fold the slips and shake them up. Each of us draws. No matter what the word is, each of us has to rise and talk for sixty seconds on that word. We never use the same word again. That's what keeps the stunt new. And we use all kinds of words. I remember one evening when two of the words were 'Faith' and 'Lampshades'. 'Lampshades' fell to me, and I had one of the hardest times I ever had, talking for sixty seconds on 'Lampshades'. Just try if you think it is easy. You start out bravely: "Lampshades have two uses. They modify and soften the glare of light, and they are decorative." Then you are through unless you know a lot more about lampshades than I do. I got through somehow. But the point is how all three of us have sharpened up since we began that game. We know a lot more about a variety of miscellaneous subjects. But, far better than that, we are learning to assemble our knowledge and thoughts on any topic at a moment's notice and to give it out briefly. We are learning to think on our feet. I say "we are learning", because we are still at this game. We haven't tired of it in almost two years, which means that it is still making us grow.

Before a speaker faces his audience, he should write a letter to a friend and say: 7 am to make an address on a subject, and I want to make these points. 'He should then enumerate the things he is going to speak about in their correct order. If he finds that he has nothing to say in his letter, he had better write to the committee that invited him and say that the probable death of his grandmother will possibly prevent his being present on the occasion.

—Dr. Edward Everett Hale

~

Luck is what happens when preparation meets opportunity.

—Seneca

6

Essential Elements Of Successful Speaking

Life is not easy for any of us. But what of that? We must have perseverance and above all confidence in ourselves. We must believe that we are gified for something, and that this thing, at whatever cost, must be attained.

—Marie Curie

Sir Ernest died while steaming southward on the good ship *Quest* to explore the Antarctic. The first thing that attracted one's eyes on going aboard the *Quest* were these lines of Kipling engraved on a brass plate:

If you can dream and not make dreams your master;
If you can think and not make thoughts your aim;
If you can meet with triumph and disaster;
And treat those two imposters just the same;
If you can force your heart, and nerve, and sinew
To serve your turn long after they are gone;
And so hold on when there is nothing in you
Except the will which says to them, "Hold on!"
If you can fill the unforgiving minute
With sixty seconds' worth of distance run,

Yours is the earth and everything that's in it,
And, what is more, you'll be a man, my son.

"The spirit of the *Quest*," Shackleton called those verses and, truly, they are the proper spirit with which a man should start out to reach the South Pole or to gain confidence in public speaking.

But that is not the spirit, I regret to add, in which all men begin the study of public speaking. Years ago, when I first engaged in educational work, I was astounded to learn how large a percentage of students who enrolled in night schools of all sorts grew weary and fainted by the wayside before their goals were attained. The number is both lamentable and amazing. It is a sad commentary on human nature.

This is the sixth lesson of this course, and I know from experience that some of the men who are reading these lines are already growing disheartened because they have not, in six short weeks, conquered their fear of audiences, and gained self-confidence. What a pity, for "how poor are they that have not patience. What wound did ever heal but by degrees?"

THE NECESSITY OF PERSISTENCE

When we start to learn any new thing, like French, or golf, or public speaking, we never advance steadily. We do not improve gradually. We do it by sudden jerks, by abrupt starts. Then we remain stationary a time, or we may even slip back and lose some of the ground we have previously gained. These periods of stagnation, or retrogression, are well known by all psychologists; and they have been named "plateaus in the curve of learning". Students of public speaking will sometimes be stalled for weeks on one of these plateaus. Work as hard as they may, they cannot get off it. The weak ones give up in despair. Those with grit persist, and they find that suddenly, overnight, without their knowing how or why it has happened, they have made great progress. They have lifted from the plateau like an aeroplane. Abruptly they have found the knack of the thing. Abruptly they have acquired naturalness, force and confidence in their speaking.

You may always, as we have noted elsewhere in these pages, experience some fleeting fear, some shock, some nervous anxiety the first few moments you face an audience. John Bright felt it to the end of his busy career; so did Gladstone; so did Bishop Wilberforce; so did a score of other eminent speakers. Even the greatest of the musicians have felt it in spite of their innumerable public appearances. Paderewski always fidgeted nervously with his cuffs immediately before he sat down at the piano. Nordica felt her heart racing. So did Sembrich. So did Emma Eames. But it vanished quickly, all of this audience fear, like a mist in the August sunshine.

Their experience will be yours. If you will but persevere, you will soon eradicate everything but this initial fear; and that will be initial fear, and nothing more. After the first few sentences, you will have control of yourself. You will be speaking with positive pleasure.

DON'T GIVE UP

One time a young man who aspired to study law, wrote to Lincoln for advice, and Lincoln replied: "If you are resolutely determined to make a lawyer of yourself, the thing is more than half done already...Always bear in mind that your own resolution to succeed is more important than any other one thing."

Lincoln knew. He had gone through it all. He had never, in his entire life, had more than a total of one year's schooling.

And books? Lincoln once said he had walked and borrowed every book within fifty miles of his home. A log fire was usually kept going all night in the cabin. Sometimes he read by the light of that fire. There were cracks between the logs, and Lincoln often kept a book sticking in a crack. As soon as it was light enough to read in the morning, he rolled over on his bed of leaves, rubbed his eyes, pulled out the book and began devouring it.

He walked twenty and thirty miles to hear a speaker and, returning home, he practiced his talks everywhere—in the fields, in the woods, before the crowds gathered at Jones' grocery at Gentryville. He joined literary and debating societies in New Salem and Springfield, and practiced speaking on the topics of the day much as you are doing now as a member of this course.

A sense of inferiority always troubled him. In the presence of women he was shy and dumb. When he courted Mary Todd he used to sit in the parlour, bashful and silent, unable to find words, listening while she did the talking. Yet that was the man who, by practice and home study, made himself- into the speaker who debated with the accomplished orator, Senator Douglas. That was the man who, at Gettysburg, and again in his second inaugural address, rose to heights of eloquence that have rarely been attained in all the annals of mankind.

Small wonder that, in view of his own terrific handicaps and pitiful struggle, he wrote: "If you are resolutely determined to make a lawyer of yourself, the thing is more than half done already."

There is an excellent picture of Abraham Lincoln in the President's office. "Often when I had some matter to decide," said Theodore Roosevelt, "something involved and difficult to dispose of, something where there were conflicting rights and interests, I would look up at Lincoln, try to imagine him in *my* place, try to figure out what he would do in the same circumstances. It may sound odd to you, but, frankly, it seemed to make my troubles easier of solution."

Why not try Roosevelt's plan? Why not, if you are discouraged and feeling like giving up the fight to make a speaker of yourself, why not pull out of your pocket one of the five dollar notes that bear a likeness of Lincoln, and ask yourself what he would do under the circumstances. You know what he would do. You know what he did do. After he had been beaten by Stephen A. Douglas in the race for the US Senate, he admonished his followers not to "give up after one nor one hundred defeats".

THE CERTAINTY OF REWARD

How I wish I could get you to prop this book open on your breakfast table every morning for a week until you had memorized these words from Professor William James, the famous psychologist:

> Let no youth have any anxiety about the upshot of his education, whatever the line of it may be. If he keeps faithfully busy each hour of the working day, he may safely leave the final result to itself. He can, with perfect certainty, count on waking up some fine morning to find himself one of the competent ones of his generation, in whatever pursuit he may have singled out.

And now, with the renowned Professor James to fall back upon, I shall go so far as to say that if you pursue this course faithfully and with enthusiasm, and keep right on practicing intelligently, you may confidently hope to wake up one fine morning and find yourself one of the competent speakers of your city or community.

Regardless of how fantastic that may sound to you now, *it is true as a general principle*. Exceptions, of course, there are. A man with an inferior mentality and personality, and with nothing to talk about, is not going to develop into a local Daniel Webster, but, *within reason*, the assertion is correct.

The entire question of your success as a speaker hinges upon only two things—your native ability, and the depth and strength of your desires.

I have known and carefully watched thousands of men trying to gain self-confidence and the ability to talk in public. Those that succeeded were, in only a few instances, men of unusual brilliance. For the most part, they were the ordinary run of businessmen that you will find in your own hometown. But they kept on. Smarter men sometimes got discouraged or too deeply immersed in money making, and they did not get very far, but the ordinary individual with grit and singleness of purpose—at the end of the chapter, he was at the top.

That is only human and natural. Don't you see the same thing occurring all the time in commerce and the professions? Rockefeller said some time ago that the first essential for success in business was patience. It is likewise one of the first essentials for success in this course.

Marshal Foch led to victory by far the greatest army the world has ever seen, and he declared that he had only one virtue: never despairing.

When the French had retreated to the Marne in 1914, General Joffre instructed the generals under him, in charge of two million men, to stop retreating and begin an offensive.

This new battle, one of the most decisive in the world's history, had raged for two days when General Foch, in command of Joffre's centre, sent him one of the most impressive messages in military records: "My centre gives way. My right recedes. The situation is excellent. I shall attack."

That attack saved Paris.

So, my dear speaker, when the fight seems hardest and most hopeless, when your centre gives way and your right recedes, "the situation is excellent". Attack! Attack! Attack, and you will save the best part of your manhood—your courage and faith.

CLIMBING THE "WILDER KAISER"

A few summers ago, I started out to scale a peak in the Austrian Alps called the Wilder Kaiser. Baedeker said that the ascent was difficult, and a guide was essential for amateur climbers. We, a friend and I, had none, and we were certainly amateurs, so a third party asked us if we thought we were going to succeed. "Of course," we replied.

"What makes you think so?" he inquired.

"Others have done it without guides," I said, "so I know it is within reason, and *I never undertake anything thinking defeat.*"

As an Alpinist, I am the merest, bungling novice, but that is the proper psychology for anything from essaying public speaking to an assault on Mount Everest.

Think success in this course. See yourself in your imagination talking in public with perfect self-control.

It is easily in your power to do this. Believe that you will succeed. Believe it firmly and you will then do what is necessary to bring success about.

The most valuable thing that most members acquire from a course in public speaking is an increased confidence in themselves, an additional faith in their ability to achieve. And other than that, what is more important for one's success in almost any undertaking?

THE WILL TO WIN

Here is a bit of sage advice from Elbert Hubbard that I cannot refrain from quoting. If the average man would only apply and live the wisdom contained in it, he would be happier, more prosperous:

> Whenever you go out of doors, draw the chin in, carry the crown of the head high and fill the lungs to the utmost; drink in the sunshine, greet your friends with a smile and put soul into every handclasp. Do not fear being misunderstood and do not waste a minute thinking about your enemies. Try to fix firmly in your mind what you would like to do, and then, without veering off direction, you will move straight to the goal. Keep your mind on the great and splendid things you would like to do, and then, as the days go gliding by, you will find yourself unconsciously seizing upon the opportunities that are required for the fulfilment of your desire, just as the coral insect takes from the running tide the elements it needs. Picture in your mind the able, earnest, useful person you desire to be, and the thought you hold is hourly transforming you into that particular individual... Thought is supreme. Preserve a right mental attitude—the attitude of courage, frankness and good cheer. To think rightly is to create. All things come through desire and every sincere prayer is answered. We become like that on which our hearts are fixed. Carry your chin

in and the crown of your head high. We are gods in the chrysalis.

Napoleon, Wellington, Lee, Grant, Foch—all great military leaders have recognized that an army's will to win and its confidence in its ability to win, do more than any other one thing to determine its success.

"Ninety thousand conquered men," says Marshal Foch, "retire before ninety thousand conquering men only because they have had enough, because they no longer believe in victory, because they are demoralized—at the end of their moral resistance."

In other words, the ninety thousand retiring men are not really whipped physically, but they are conquered because they are whipped mentally, because they have lost their courage and confidence. There is no hope for an army like that. There is no hope for a man like that.

Chaplain Frazier, the ranking chaplain of the US Navy, interviewed those who wished to enlist for the chaplaincy service during the World War. When asked what qualities were essential for the success of a navy chaplain, he replied with four Gs: "Grace, gumption, grit, and *guts*."

Those are also the requisites for success in speaking. Take them as your motto. Take this Robert Service poem as your battle song:

When you're lost in the wild, and you're scared as a child,
And death looks you bang in the eye.
And you're sore as a boil, it's according to Hoyle
To cock your revolver and...die.
But the code of a man, says: "Fight all you can," And self-dissolution is barred.
In hunger and woe, oh, it's easy to blow...

It's the hell-served-for-breakfast that's hard.

You're sick of the game! "Well, now, that's a shame." You're young and you're brave and you're bright. "You've had a raw deal!" I know—but don't squeal. Buck up, do your damnedest, and fight.

It's the plugging away that will win you the day,
So don't be a piker, old pard!
Just draw on your grit: it's so easy to quit:
It's the keeping-your-chin-up that's hard.
It's easy to cry that you're beaten—and die.
It's easy to crawfish and crawl;
But to fight and to fight when hope's out of sight,
Why, that's the best game of them all!
And though you come out of each gruelling bout
All broken and beaten and scarred,
Just have one more try—it's dead easy to die,
It's the keeping-on-living that's hard.

I never allow myself to become discouraged under any circumstances.... The three great essentials to achieve anything worthwhile are, first, hard work; second, stick-to-itiveness, third, common sense.

—Thomas A. Edison

~

Permanence, perseverance and persistence in spite of all obstacles, discouragement, and impossibilities: It is this, that in all things distinguishes the strong soul from the weak.

—Thomas Carlyle

7

The Improvement Of Memory

Memory...is the diary that we all carry about with us.

—Oscar Wilde

"The average man," says the noted psychologist, Professor Carl Seashore, "does not use above 10 per cent of his actual inherited capacity for memory. He wastes the 90 per cent in violating the natural laws of remembering."

Are you one of these average men? If so, you are struggling under a handicap both socially and commercially; consequently, you will be interested in, and profit by reading and rereading this chapter. It describes and explains these natural laws of remembering and shows how to use them in business as well as in speaking.

These "natural laws of remembering" are very simple. There are only three. Every so-called "memory system" has been founded upon them. Briefly, they are *impression*, *repetition*, and *association*.

The first mandate of memory is: get a deep, vivid and lasting *impression* of the thing you wish to retain. And to do that, you must concentrate. Theodore Roosevelt's remarkable memory impressed everyone he met. And no little amount of his extraordinary facility was due to this: his impressions were scratched on steel, not written in water. He had, by persistence and practice, trained himself to concentrate under the most adverse conditions. In 1912, during the Bull Moose Convention in Chicago, his headquarters were in the Congress Hotel. Crowds surged through the street below, crying, waving banners, shouting, "We want Teddy! We want Teddy!" The roar of the throng, the music of bands, the coming and going of politicians, the hurried conferences, the consultations—would have driven the ordinary individual to distraction, but Roosevelt sat in an easy chair in his room, oblivious to it all, reading Herodotus, the Greek historian. On his trip through the Brazilian wilderness, as soon as he reached the camping ground in the evening, he found a dry spot under some huge tree, got out a camp stool and his copy of Gibbon's *Decline and Fall of the Roman Empire*, and, at once, he was so immersed in the book that he was oblivious to the rain, to the noise and activity of the camp, to the sounds of the tropical forest. Small wonder that the man remembered what he read.

Five minutes of vivid, energetic concentration will produce greater results than days of mooning about in a mental haze. "One intense hour," wrote Henry Ward Beecher, "will do more than dreamy years." "If there is any one thing that I have learned which is more important than anything else," says Eugene Grace, president of the Bethlehem Steel Company, "and which I practice every day under any and all circumstances, it is *concentration of the particular job I have at hand.*"

This is one of the secrets of power, especially memory power.

POWER OF OBSERVATION

Thomas Edison found that 27 of his assistants had used, every day for six months, a certain path which led from his lamp factory to the main works at Menlo Park, New Jersey. A cherry tree grew along that path, and yet not one of these 27 men had, when questioned, ever been conscious of that tree's existence.

"The average person's brain," observes Mr. Edison with heat and energy, "does not observe a thousandth part of what the eye observes. It is almost incredible how poor our powers of observation—genuine observation—are."

Introduce the average man to two or three of your friends and, the chances are that two minutes afterwards he cannot recall the name of a single one of them. And why? Because he never paid sufficient attention to them in the first place; he never accurately observed them. He will likely tell you he has a poor memory. No, he has a poor observation. He would not condemn a camera because it failed to take pictures in a fog, but he expects his mind to retain impressions that are hazy and foggy to a degree. Of course, it can't be done.

The late Mr. Pulitzer, who made the *New York World*, had three words placed over the desk of every man in his editorial offices:

Accuracy

ACCURACY

ACCURACY

That is what we want. Hear the man's name precisely. Insist on it. Ask him to repeat it. Inquire how it is spelled. He will be flattered by your interest and you will be able to remember his name because you have concentrated on it. You have got a clear accurate impression.

THE "BLAB SCHOOL"

Lincoln, in his youth, attended a country school where the floor was made out of split logs: greased pages, torn from the copybooks and pasted over the windows, served instead of glass to let in the light. Only one copy of the textbook existed, and the teacher read from it aloud. The pupils repeated the lesson after him, all of them talking at once. It made a constant uproar, and the neighbours called it the "blab school".

At the "blab school", Lincoln formed a habit that clung to him all his life: he forever after read aloud everything he wished to remember. Each morning, as soon as he reached his law office in Springfield, he spread himself out on the couch, hooked one long, ungainly leg over a neighbouring chair, and read the newspaper audibly. "He annoyed me," said his partner, "almost beyond endurance. I once asked him why he read in this fashion. This was his explanation: 'When I read aloud, two senses catch the idea: first, I see what I read; second, I hear it, and therefore I can remember it better.'"

His memory was extraordinarily retentive. "My mind," he said, "is like a piece of steel—very hard to scratch anything on it, but almost impossible, after you get it there, to rub it out."

Appealing to two of the senses was the method he used to do the scratching. Go thou, and do likewise....

The ideal thing would be not only to see and hear the thing to be remembered, but to touch it, and smell it, and taste it.

But, above all else, see it. We are visual minded. Eye impressions stick. We can often remember a man's face, even though we cannot recall his name. The nerves that lead from the eye to the brain are twenty times as large as those leading from the ear to the brain. The Chinese have a proverb that says "One time seeing is worth a thousand times hearing".

Write down the name, the telephone number, the speech outline you want to remember. Look at it. Close your eyes. Visualize it in flaming letters of fire.

HOW MARK TWAIN LEARNED TO SPEAK WITHOUT NOTES

The discovery of how to use his visual memory enabled Mark Twain to discard the notes that had hampered his speeches for years. Here is his story as he told it:

> Dates are hard to remember because they consist of figures: figures are monotonously unstriking in appearance, and they don't take hold; they form no pictures, and so they give the eye no chance to take hold. Pictures can make dates stick. They can make nearly anything stick—particularly if you make the picture yourself. Indeed, that is the great point— make the picture yourself. I know about this from experience. Thirty years ago I was delivering a memorized lecture every night, and every night I had to help myself with a page of notes to keep from getting myself mixed. The notes consisted of beginnings of sentences, and were eleven in number, and they ran something like this:
>
> In that region the weather—
> At that time it was a custom—
> But in California one never heard—
>
> Eleven of them. They initialled the brief of the lecture and protected me against skipping. But they

all looked about alike on the page; they formed no picture; I had them by heart, but I could never with certainty remember the order of their succession; therefore, I always had to keep those notes by me and look at them every little while. Once I mislaid them; you will not be able to imagine the terrors of that evening. I now saw that I must invent some other protection. So I got ten of the initial letters by heart in their proper order—I, A, B, and so on—and I went on the platform the next night with these marked in ink on my ten finger nails. But it didn't answer. I kept track of the fingers for a while, then I lost it, and after that I was never quite sure which finger I had used last. I couldn't lick off a letter after using it, for while they would have made success certain, it would also have provoked too much curiosity. There was curiosity enough without that. To the audience I seemed more interested in my finger nails than I was in my subject; one or two persons asked afterward what was the matter with my hands.

It was then that the idea of pictures occurred to me! Then my troubles passed away. In two minutes I made six pictures with my pen, and they did the work of the eleven catch-sentences and did it perfectly. I threw the pictures away as soon as they were made, for I was sure I could shut my eyes and see them any time. That was a quarter of a century ago; the lecture vanished out of my head more than twenty years ago, but I could rewrite it from the pictures—for they remain.

I recently had occasion to deliver a talk on memory. I wanted to use, very largely, the material in this chapter. I memorized the points by pictures. I visualized Roosevelt reading history while the crowds were yelling and bands playing outside his window. I saw Thomas Edison looking at a cherry tree. I pictured Lincoln reading a newspaper aloud. I imagined Mark Twain licking ink off his finger nails as he faced an audience.

How did I remember the order of the pictures? By one, two, three, and four? No, that would have been too difficult. I turned these numbers into pictures, and combined the pictures of the numbers with the pictures of the points. To illustrate: number *one* sounds like *run,* so I made a racehorse stand for *one.* I pictured Roosevelt in his room, reading astride a racehorse. For *two,* I chose a word that sounds like two—*zoo.* I had the cherry tree that Thomas Edison was looking at standing in the bear cage at the zoo. For *three,* I pictured an object that sounds like *three*—tree. I had Lincoln sprawled out in the top of a tree, reading aloud to his partner. For *four* I imagined a picture that sounds like four—*door.* Mark Twain stood at an open door, leaning against the jamb, licking the ink off his fingernails as he talked to the audience.

I realize full well that many men who read this will think that such a method verges on the ridiculous. It does. That is one reason why it works. It is comparatively easy to remember the bizarre and ridiculous. Had I tried to remember the order of my points by numbers only, I might easily have forgotten, but by the system I have just described, it was almost impossible to forget. When I wished to recall my third point, I had but to ask myself what was in the top of the tree. Instantly I saw Lincoln.

I have, very largely for my own convenience, turned the numbers from one to twenty into pictures, choosing pictures that sound like the numbers. I have set them down here. If you will spend half an hour memorizing these picture—numerals you will then be able, after having a list of twenty objects called to you but once, to repeat them in their exact order and to skip about at random announcing which object was called to you eighth, which fourteenth, which third, and so on.

Here are the picture numbers. Try the test. You will find it decidedly amusing.

1. Run—visualize a race horse.
2. Zoo—see the bear cage in the zoo.
3. Tree—picture the third object called to you as lying in the top of a tree.
4. Door—or wild boar. Take any object or animal that sounds like four.
5. Beehive.
6. Sick—see a Red Cross nurse.
7. Heaven—a street paved with gold, and angels playing on harps.
8. Gate.
9. Wine—the bottle has fallen over on the table, and the wine is streaming out and pouring down on something below. Put action into the pictures. It helps to make them stick.
10. Den of wild animals in a rocky cave in the deep woods.
11. A football eleven, rushing madly across the field. I picture them carrying aloft the object that I wish to recall as number eleven.
12. Shelve—see someone shoving something back on a shelf.
13. Hurting—see the blood spurting out of a wound and reddening the thirteenth object.

14. Courting—a couple are sitting on something and making love.
15. Lifting—a strong man, a regular John L. Sullivan, is lifting something high above his head.
16. Licking—a fist fight.
17. Leavening—a housewife is kneading dough, and into the dough she kneads the seventeenth object.
18. Waiting—a woman is standing at a forked path in the deep woods for someone.
19. Pining—a woman is weeping. See her tears falling on the nineteenth thing you wish to recall.
20. Horn of Plenty—a goat's horn overflowing with flowers and fruit and corn.

If you wish to try the test, spend a few minutes memorizing these picture-numbers. If you prefer, make pictures of your own. For ten, think of *wren* or fountain *pen* or *hen* or *sen-sen*—anything that sounds like ten. Suppose that the tenth object recalled to you a windmill. See the hen sitting on the windmill, or see it pumping ink to fill the fountain pen. Then, when you are asked what was the tenth object called, do not think of ten at all, but merely ask yourself where was the hen sitting. You may not think it will work, but try it. You can soon astound people, with what they will consider to be an extraordinary capacity for remembering. You will find it entertaining if nothing else.

MEMORIZING A BOOK AS LONG AS THE NEW TESTAMENT

One of the largest universities in the world is the El Hazar at Cairo. It is a Mohammedan institution with twenty-one thousand students. The entrance examination requires every applicant to repeat the Koran from memory.

The Koran is about as long as the New Testament, and three days are required to recite it!

The Chinese students, or "study boys" as they are called, have to memorize some of the religious and classical books of China.

How are these Arab and Chinese students—many of them men of mediocre ability—able to perform these apparently prodigious feats of memory?

By *repetition*, the second "natural law of remembering". You can memorize an almost endless amount of material if you will repeat it often enough. Go over the knowledge you want to remember. Use it. Apply it. Employ the new word in your conversation. Call the stranger by his name if you want to remember it. Talk over in conversation the points you want to make in your public address. The knowledge that is used tends to stick.

THE KIND OF REPETITION THAT COUNTS

But the mere blind, mechanical going over a thing by rote is not enough. Intelligent repetition, repetition done in accordance with certain well-established traits of the mind—that is what we must have. For example, Professor Ebbinghaus gave his students a long list of nonsense syllables to memorize, such as "deyux", "qoli", and so on.

He found that these students memorized as many of these syllables by thirty-eight repetitions, distributed over a period of three days, as they did by sixty-eight repetitions done at a single sitting. Other psychological tests have repeatedly shown similar results.

This is a very significant discovery about the working of our memories. It means that we know now that the man who sits down and repeats a thing over and over until he finally fastens it in his memory, is using twice as much time and energy as is necessary to achieve the same results when the repeating process is done at judicious intervals.

This peculiarity of the mind—if we can call it such—can be explained by two factors:

First, during the intervals between repetitions, our subconscious minds are busy making the associations more secure. As Professor William James sagely remarks: "We learn to swim during the winter and to skate during the summer."

Second, the mind, coming to the task at intervals, is not fatigued by the strain of an unbroken application. Sir Richard Burton, the translator of the *Arabian Nights*, spoke twenty-seven languages like a native: yet he confessed that he never studied or practiced any language for more than fifteen minutes at a time, "for, after that, the brain lost its freshness."

Surely, now, in the face of these facts, no man who prides himself on his common sense, will delay the preparation of a talk until the night before it is to be given. If he does, his memory will, of necessity, be working at only one-half its possible efficiency.

Here is a very helpful discovery about the way in which we forget. Psychological experiments have repeatedly shown that of the new material we have learned, we forget more during the first eight hours than during the next thirty days. An amazing ratio! So, immediately before you go into a business conference, immediately before you make a speech, look over your data, think over your facts, refresh your memory.

Lincoln knew the value of such a practice, and employed it. The scholarly Edward Everett preceded him at the programme of speech-making at Gettysburg. When he saw that Everett was approaching the close of his long, formal oration, Lincoln "grew visibly nervous, as he always did when another man was speaking and he was to follow. Hastily adjusting his spectacles, he took his manuscript from his pocket and read it silently to himself to refresh his memory.

PROFESSOR WILLIAM JAMES EXPLAINS THE SECRET OF A GOOD MEMORY

So much for the first two laws of remembering. The third one, *association*, however, is the indispensable element in recalling. In fact, it is the explanation of memory itself. "Our mind is," as Professor James has sagely observed,

> essentially an associating machine Suppose I am silent for a moment, and then say in commanding accents: 'Remember! Recollect!' Does your faculty of memory obey the order, and reproduce any definite image from your past? Certainly not. It stands staring into vacancy, and asking, 'What kind of thing do you wish me to remember?' It needs, in short, a cue. But, if I say, remember the date of your birth, or remember what you had for breakfast, or remember the succession of notes in the musical scale, then your faculty of memory immediately produces the required result: the *cue* determines its vast set of potentialities toward a particular point. And if you now look to see how this happens, you immediately perceive that the *cue* is something contiguously associated with the thing recalled. The words, 'date of my birth,' have an ingrained association with a particular number, month, and year; the words, 'breakfast this morning,' cut off all other lines of recall except those which lead to coffee and bacon and eggs; the words, 'musical scale,' are inveterate mental neighbours

of do, re, mi, fa, sol, la, etc. The laws of association govern, in fact, all the trains of our thinking which are not interrupted by sensations breaking on us from without. Whatever appears in the mind must be *introduced*, and, when introduced, it is as the associate of something already there. This is as true of what you are recollecting as it is of everything else you think of.... An educated memory depends upon an organized system of associations, and its goodness depends on two of their peculiarities: first, on the persistency of the associations; and, second, on their number.... The 'secret of a good memory' is thus the secret of forming diverse and multiple associations with every fact we care to retain. But this forming of associations with a fact—what is it but thinking about the fact as much as possible? Briefly, then, of two men with the same outward experiences, *the one who thinks over his experiences most*, and weaves them into the most systematic relations with each other, will be the one with the best memory.

HOW TO LINK YOUR FACTS TOGETHER

Very good, but how are we to set about weaving our facts into systematic relations with each other? The answer is: by finding their meaning, by thinking them over. For example, if you will ask and answer these questions about any new fact, that process will help to weave it into a systematic relation with other facts.

(a) Why is this so?
(b) How is this so?

(c) When is it so?
(d) Where is it so?
(e) Who said it is so?

If it is a stranger's name, for example, and it is a common one, we can perhaps tie it to some business friend who bears the same name. On the other hand, if it unusual, we can take occasion to say so. This often leads the stranger to talk about his name. For example: while writing this chapter, I was introduced to a Mrs. Soter. I requested her to spell the name and remarked upon its unusualness. "Yes," she replied, "it is very uncommon. It is a Greek word meaning 'the Saviour.'" Then she told me about her husband's people who had come from Athens and of the high positions they had held in the government there. I have found it quite easy to get people to talk about their names, and it always helps me to remember them.

Observe the stranger's looks sharply. Note the colour of his eyes and his hair, and look closely at his features. Note how he is dressed. Listen to his manner of talking. Get a clear, keen, vivid impression of his looks and personality, and associate these with his name. The next time these sharp impressions return to your mind, they will help bring the name with them.

Haven't you had the experience, when meeting a man for the second or third time, to discover that although you could remember his business or profession, you could not recall his name? The reason is this: a man's business is something definite and concrete. It has a meaning. It will adhere like a court plaster while his meaningless name will roll away like hail falling on a steep roof. Consequently, to make sure of your ability to recall a man's name, fashion a phrase about it that will tie it up to his business. There can be no doubt whatever about the efficacy of this method. For example, twenty men, strangers to one another, recently met in an Athletic Club to study this course. Each man was asked to rise, announce his name and business. A phrase was then manufactured to connect the two; and, within a few minutes, each person present could repeat the name of every other individual in the room. Even to the end of the course, neither the names nor businesses were forgotten, for they were linked together. They adhered.

Here are the first ten names, in alphabetical order, from that group, and here are the crude phrases that were used to tie the names to the businesses:

Mr. G.P. Albrecht (sand business)—"Sand makes all bright."

Mr. George A. Ansley (real estate)—"To sell real estate, advertise in *Ansley's Magazine*."

Mr. G.W Bayliss (asphalt)—"Use asphalt and pay less."

Mr. H.M. Biddle (woollen cloth)—"Mr. Biddle piddles about the wool business."

Mr. Gideon Boericke (mining)—"Boericke bores quickly for mines."

Mr. Thomas J. Devery (printing)—"Every man needs Devery's printing."

Mr. O.W Doolittle (automobiles)—"Do little and you won't succeed in selling cars."

Mr. Thomas Fischer (coal)—"He fishes for coal orders."

Mr. Frank H. Goldey (lumber)—"There is gold in the lumber business."

Mr. J.H. Hancock (*Saturday Evening Post*)—"Sign your John Hancock to a subscription plan for the *Saturday Evening Post!*"

HOW TO REMEMBER DATES

Dates can best be retained by connecting them with important dates already firmly established in the mind. Isn't it far more difficult, for example, for an American to remember that the Suez Canal was opened in 1869 than to remember that the first ship passed through it four years after the close of the Civil War? If an American tried to remember that the first settlement in Australia was made in 1788, the date is likely to drop out of his mind like a loose bolt out of a car; it is far more likely to stick if he thinks of it in connection with July 4, 1776, and remembers that it occurred twelve years after the Declaration of Independence. That is like screwing a nut on the loose bolt. It holds.

It is well to bear this principle in mind when you are selecting a telephone number. For example, the writer's phone number, during the last war, was 1776. No one had difficulty in remembering it. If you can secure from the phone company some such number as 1492, 1861, 1865, 1914, 1918, your friends will not have to consult the directory. They might forget that your phone number was 1492, if you gave them the information in a colourless fashion, but would it stick in their minds if you said, "You can easily remember my phone number; 1492, the year Columbus discovered America."

The Australians, New Zealanders, and Canadians who are reading these lines would, of course, substitute for 1776, 1861, 1865 significant dates in their own history.

What is the best way to memorize the following dates?

(a) 1564—Birth of Shakespeare.
(b) 1607—The first English settlement in America was made in Jamestown.

(c) 1819—The birth of Queen Victoria.
(d) 1807—The birth of Robert E. Lee.
(e) 1789—The Bastille was destroyed.

You would doubtlessly find it tiresome to memorize, by sheer mechanical repetition, the names of the thirteen original states in the order in which they entered the Union. But tie them together with a story and the memorizing can be done with a fraction of the time and trying. Read the following paragraph just once. Concentrate. When you have finished, see if you cannot name the thirteen states in their correct order:

> One Saturday afternoon, a young lady from Delaware bought a ticket over the Pennsylvania railroad for a little outing. She packed a New Jersey sweater in her suitcase, and visited a friend, Georgia, in Connecticut. The next morning the hostess and her visitor attended Mass in a church on Mary's land. Then they took the South car-line home, and dined on a new ham, which had been roasted by Virginia, the coloured cook, from New York. After dinner they took the North car line and rode to the island.

HOW TO REMEMBER THE POINTS OF YOUR TALK

There are only two ways by which we can possibly think of a thing: first, by means of an *outside stimulus;* second, by *association* with something already in the mind. Applied to speeches, that means just this: first, you can recall your points by the aid of some outside stimulus such as notes—

but who likes to see a speaker use notes? Second, you can remember your points by associating them with something already in the mind. They should be arranged in such a logical order that the first one leads inevitably to the second, and the second to the third as naturally as the door of one room leads into another.

That sounds simple, but it may not prove so for the beginner whose thinking powers are rendered *hors de combat with* fear. There is, however, a method of tying your points together that is easy, rapid, and all but foolproof. I refer to the use of a nonsense sentence. To illustrate: suppose you wish to discuss a veritable jumble of ideas, unassociated and hence hard to remember, such as, for example, *cow, cigar, Napoleon, house, religion*. Let us see if we cannot weld those ideas like the links of a chain by means of this absurd sentence: "The cow smoked a cigar and hooked Napoleon, and the house burned down with religion."

Now, will you please cover the above sentence with your hand while you answer these questions? What is the third point in that talk, the fifth, fourth, second, first?

Does the method work? It does! And the members of this course are urged to use it.

Any group of ideas can be linked together in some such fashion, and the more ridiculous the sentence used for the linking, the easier it will be to recall.

WHAT TO DO IN CASE OF A COMPLETE BREAKDOWN

Let us suppose that, in spite of all his preparation and precaution, a speaker, in the middle of his talk, suddenly finds his mind a blank—suddenly finds himself staring at his hearers completely balked, unable to go on—a terrifying situation. His pride rebels at sitting down in confusion and defeat—he feels that he might be able to think of his next point, of some point, if he had only ten, fifteen seconds of grace, but even fifteen seconds of frantic silence before an audience would be little less than disastrous. What is to be done? When a certain well-known US Senator recently found himself in this situation he asked his audience if he were speaking loudly enough, if he could be heard distinctly in the back of the room. He knew that he was. He was not seeking information. He was seeking time. And in that momentary pause, he rasped his thought and proceeded.

But perhaps the best life-saver in such a mental hurricane is this: use the last word, or phrase, or idea in your last sentence for the beginning of a new sentence. This will make an endless chain that, like Tennyson's brook and, I regret to say, with as little purpose as Tennyson's brook, will run on forever. Let us see how it works in practice. Let us imagine that a speaker, talking on Business Success, finds himself in a blind mental alley after having said: "The average employee does not get ahead because he takes so little real interest in his work, displays so little initiative."

"*Initiative.*" Start a sentence with "*initiative.*" You will probably have no idea of what you are going to say or how you are going to end the sentence, but, nevertheless, begin. Even a poor showing is more to be desired than utter defeat.

"Initiative means originality, doing a thing on your own, without eternally waiting to be told."

That is not a scintillating observation. It won't make speech history. But isn't it better than an agonizing silence? Our last phrase was what?—"waiting to be told." All right, let us start a new sentence with that idea.

"The constant telling and guiding and driving of employees who refuse to do any original thinking is one of the most exasperating things imaginable."

Well, we got through that one. Let us plunge again. This time we must say something about imagination: "Imagination—that is what is needed. Vision. 'Where there is no vision,' Solomon said, 'the people perish.'"

We did two that time without a hitch. Let us take heart and continue:

"The number of employees who perish each year in the battle of business is really lamentable. I say lamentable, because with just a little more loyalty, a little more ambition, a little more enthusiasm, these same men and women might have lifted themselves over the line of demarcation between success and failure. Yet the failure in business never admits that this is the case."

And so on while the speaker is saying these platitudes off the top of his mind, he should, at the same time, be thinking hard of the next point in his planned speech, of the thing he had originally intended to say.

This endless chain method of talking will, if continued very long, trap the speaker into discussing plum pudding or the price of canary birds. However, it is a splendid first aid to the injured mind broken down temporarily through forgetfulness: and, as such, it has been the means of resuscitating many a gasping and dying speech.

WE CANNOT IMPROVE OUR MEMORIES FOR ALL CLASSES OF THINGS

I have pointed out in this chapter how we may improve our *methods* of getting vivid impressions, of repeating and of tying our facts together. But memory is so essentially a matter of association that "there can be", as Professor James points out, "no improvement of the general or elementary faculty of memory; there can only be improvement of our memory for special systems of associated things."

By memorizing, for instance, a quotation a day from Shakespeare, we may improve our memory for literary quotations to a surprising degree. Each additional quotation will find many friends in the mind to tie to. But the memorizing of everything from Hamlet to Romeo will not necessarily aid one in retaining facts about the cotton market or the Bessemer process for desiliconizing pig iron.

Let us repeat; if we apply and use the principles discussed in this chapter, we will improve our *manner* and *efficiency* for memorizing anything, but, if we do not apply these principles, then the memorizing of ten million facts about football will not help us in the slightest in memorizing facts about the stock market. Such unrelated data cannot be tied together. "Our mind is essentially an associating machine."

Memory is the greatest of artists, and effaces from your mind what is unnecessary.

—Maurice Baring

~

It is safe to say that the businessman's most immediate need is a serviceable memory.

—E.B. Gowin

8

The Secret Of Good Delivery

Instructions for making a speech: be sincere, be brief, be seated.

—Franklin D. Roosevelt

Shortly after the close of the last war, I met two brothers in London, Sir Ross and Sir Keith Smith. They had just made the first aeroplane flight from London to Australia, had won the fifty thousand dollar prize offered by the Australian government, had created a sensation throughout the British Empire, and had been knighted by the King.

Captain Hurley, a well-known scenic photographer, had flown with them over a part of their trip, taking motion pictures; so I helped them prepare an illustrated travel talk of their flight and trained them in the delivery of it. They gave it twice daily for four months in Philharmonic Hall, London, one speaking in the afternoon and the other at night.

They had had identically the same experience, had sat side by side as they flew halfway around the world, and they delivered the same talk almost word for word. Yet, somehow it didn't sound like the same talk at all.

There is something besides the mere words in a talk which counts. It is the flavour with which they are delivered. "It is not so much what you say as how you say it."

I once sat beside a young woman at a public concert who was reading, as Paderewski played them, the notes of a Mazurka by Chopin. She was mystified. She couldn't understand. His fingers were touching precisely the same notes that hers had touched when she had played it; yet her rendition had been commonplace, and his was inspired, a thing of surpassing beauty, a performance that held the audience enthralled. It was not the mere notes that he touched, it was the way he touched them, a feeling, an artistry, a personality that he put into the touching that made all the difference between mediocrity and genius.

The same thing holds true when one is touching words. There is an old saying in the English Parliament that everything depends upon the manner in which one speaks and not upon the matter. Quintilian said that long ago when England was one of the outlying colonies of Rome.

Like most old sayings, it needs to be taken *cum grano salis,* but good delivery will make very thin matter go a very long way. I have often noticed in college contests that it is not always the speaker with the best material who wins. Rather, it is the speaker who can talk so well that his material sounds best.

"Three things matter in a speech," Lord Morley once observed with gay cynicism, "who says it, how he says it, and what he says—and, of the three, the last matters the least." An exaggeration? Yes, but scratch the surface of it and you will find the truth shining through.

Edmund Burke wrote speeches so excellent in logic and reasoning and composition that they are today studied as classic models of oration in half the colleges of the land; yet Burke, as a speaker, was a notorious failure. He didn't have the ability to deliver his gems, to make them interesting and forceful; so he was called "the dinner bell" of the House of Commons. When he arose to talk, the other members coughed and shuffled and went out in droves.

You can throw a steel-jacketed bullet at a man with all your might, and you cannot make even a dent in his clothing. But put powder behind a tallow candle and you can shoot it through a pine board. Many a tallow-candle speech with powder makes, I regret to say, more of an impression than a steel-jacketed talk with no force behind it.

Look well, therefore, to your delivery.

THE ART OF DELIVERY

What does a department store do when it "delivers" the article you have bought? Does the driver just toss the package into the backyard and let it go at that? Is merely getting a thing out of one's own hands the same as getting it delivered? The messenger boy with a telegram delivers the "wire" into the direct possession of the person for whom it is intended. But do all speakers?

Let me give you an illustration that is typical of the fashion in which thousands of men talk. I happened on one occasion to be stopping in Murren, a summer resort in the Swiss Alps. I was living at a hotel operated by a London company, and they usually sent out from England a couple of lecturers each week to talk to the guests. One of them was a well-known English novelist. Her topic was "The Future of the Novel". She admitted that she had not selected the subject herself; and the long and short of it was that she had nothing to say about it that she really cared enough about saying to make it worthwhile expressing. She had hurriedly made some rambling notes, and she stood before the audience ignoring her hearers, not even looking at them, staring sometimes over their heads, sometimes at her notes, sometimes at the floor. She called off her words into the primeval void with a faraway look in her eyes and a faraway ring in her voice.

That kind of performance isn't delivering a talk at all. It is a soliloquy. It has no sense of communication. And that is the first essential of good talking: *a sense ofcommunication.* The audience must feel that there is a message being delivered straight from the mind and heart of the speaker to their minds and their hearts. The kind of talk I have just described might just as well have been spoken out in the sandy, waterless wastes of the Gobi desert. In fact, it sounded as if it were being delivered in some such spot rather than to a group of living human beings.

This matter of delivering a talk is, at the same time, a very simple and a very intricate process. It is also a very much misunderstood and abused one.

THE SECRET OF GOOD DELIVERY

An enormous amount of nonsense and twaddle has been written about delivery. It has been shrouded in rules and rites and made mysterious. Old-fashioned "elocution", that abomination in the sight of God and man, has often made it ridiculous.

The businessman, going to the library or bookshop, has found volumes on "oratory" that were utterly useless. In spite of progress in other directions, in almost every state in the Union today, schoolboys are still being forced to recite the ornate "oratory" of Webster and Ingersoll—a thing that is as much out of style and as far removed from the spirit of this age as the hats worn by Mrs. Ingersoll and Mrs. Webster would be if they were resurrected today.

An entirely new school of speaking has sprung up since the Civil War. In keeping with the spirit of the times, it is as modern as the *Saturday Evening Post,* direct as a telegram, businesslike as an automobile advertisement. The verbal fireworks that were once the vogue would no longer be tolerated by an audience in this year of grace.

A modern audience, regardless of whether it is fifteen people at a business conference or a thousand people under a tent, wants the speaker to talk just as directly as he would in a chat, and in the same general manner that he would employ in speaking to one of them in conversation.

In the same *manner,* but not with the same amount of force. If he tries that, he will hardly be heard. In order to appear natural he has to use much more energy in talking to forty people than he does in talking to one; just as a statue on top of a building has to be of heroic size in order to make it appear of lifelike proportions to an observer on the ground.

At the close of Mark Twain's lecture in a Nevada mining camp, an old prospector approached him and inquired: "Be them your natural tones of eloquence?"

That is what the audience wants: "your natural tones of eloquence", enlarged a bit.

Speak to the Chamber of Commerce just as you would to John Henry Smith. What is a meeting of the Chamber of Commerce, after all, but a mere collection of John Henry Smiths? Won't the same methods that are successful with those men individually be successful with them collectively?

I have just described the delivery of a certain novelist. In the same ballroom in which she had spoken, I had the pleasure, a few nights later, of hearing Sir Oliver Lodge. His subject was "Atoms and Worlds". He had devoted to it more than half a century of thought and study and experiment and investigation. He had something that was essentially a part of his heart and mind and life, something that he wanted very much to say. He forgot—and I, for one, thanked God that he did forget—that he was trying to make a speech. That was the least of his worries. He was concerned only with telling the audience about atoms, telling us accurately and lucidly and feelingly. He was earnestly trying to get us to see what he saw and to feel what he felt.

And what was the result? He delivered a remarkable talk. It had both charm and power. It made a deep impression. He was a speaker of unusual ability. Yet I am sure he didn't regard himself in that light. I am sure that few people who heard him ever think of him as a public speaker at all.

If you, my dear reader, speak in public so that people hearing you will suspect that you have had training in public speaking, you will not be a credit to your instructor. He desires you to speak with such intensified and exalted naturalness that your auditors will never dream that you have been trained. A good window does not call attention to itself. It merely lets in the light. A good speaker is like that. He is so natural that his hearers never notice his manner of speaking; they are conscious only of his matter.

STEPHEN A. DOUGLAS VS. ABRAHAM LINCOLN

> "All Fords are exactly alike," their maker used to say, but no two men are just alike. Every new life is a new thing under the sun; there has never been anything just like it before, and never will be again. A young man ought to get that idea about himself; he should

look for the single spark of individuality that makes him different from other folks, and develop that for all he is worth. Society and schools may try to iron it out of him; their tendency is to put us all in the same mould, but I say don't let that spark be lost; it's your only real claim to importance.

All that is doubly true of public speaking. There is no other human being in the world like you. Hundreds of millions of people have two eyes and a nose and a mouth, but none of them look precisely like you; and none of them have exactly your traits and methods and cast of mind. Few of them will talk and express themselves just as you do when you are speaking naturally. In other words, you have an individuality. As a speaker, it is your most precious possession. Cling to it. Cherish it. Develop it. It is the spark that will put force and sincerity into your speaking. "It is your only real claim to importance."

Sir Oliver Lodge spoke differently from other men, because he himself was different. The man's manner of speaking is as essentially a part of his own individuality as are his beard and bald head. If he had tried to imitate Lloyd George, he would have been false, he would have failed.

The most famous debates ever held in America took place in 1858 in the prairie towns of Illinois between Senator Stephen A. Douglas and Abraham Lincoln. Lincoln was tall and awkward. Douglas was short and graceful. These men were as unlike in their characters and mentality and personalities and dispositions as they were in their physiques.

Douglas was the cultured man of the world. Lincoln was the rail splitter who went to the front door in his sock feet to receive company. Douglas' gestures were graceful. Lincoln's were ungainly. Douglas was utterly destitute of humour. Lincoln was one of the greatest storytellers who ever lived. Douglas seldom used a simile. Lincoln constantly argued by analogy and illustration. Douglas was haughty and overbearing. Lincoln was humble and forgiving. Douglas thought in quick flashes. Lincoln's mental processes were much slower. Douglas spoke with the impetuous rush of a whirlwind. Lincoln was quieter and deeper and more deliberate.

Both of these men, unlike as they were, were able speakers because they had the courage and good sense to be themselves. If either had tried to imitate the other, he would have failed miserably. But each one, by using to the utmost his own peculiar talents, made himself individual and powerful. *Go thou and do likewise.*

That is an easy direction to give. But is it an easy one to follow? Most emphatically it is not. As Marshal Foch said of the art of war: "It is simple enough in its conception, but unfortunately complicated in its execution."

It takes practice to be natural before an audience. Actors know that. When you were a little boy, four years old, you probably could, had you but tried, have mounted a platform and "recited" naturally to an audience. But when you are twenty-and-four, or forty-and-four, what will happen if you mount a platform and start to speak? Will you retain that unconscious naturalness that you possessed at four? You may, but it is dollars to doughnuts that you will become stiff and stilted and mechanical, and draw back into your shell like a snapping turtle.

The problem of teaching or of training men in delivery is not one of superimposing additional characteristics; it is largely one of removing impediments, of freeing men, of getting them to speak with the same naturalness that they would display if someone were to knock them down.

Hundreds of times I have stopped speakers in the midst of their talks and implored them to "talk like a human being". Hundreds of nights I have come home mentally fatigued and nervously exhausted from trying to drill and force men to talk naturally. No, believe me, it is not so easy as it sounds.

And the only way under high Heaven by which you can get the knack of this enlarged naturalness is by practice. And, as you practice, if you find yourself talking in a stilted manner, pause and say sharply to yourself mentally: "Here! What is wrong? Wake up. Be human." Then pick out some man in the audience, some man in the back, the dullest looking chap you can find, and talk to him. Forget there is anyone else present at all. *Converse* with him. Imagine that he has asked you a question and that you are answering it. If he were to stand up and talk to you, and you were to talk back to him, that process would immediately and inevitably make your talking more conversational, more natural, more direct. So, imagine that that is precisely what is taking place.

You may go so far as to actually ask questions and answer them. For example, in the midst of your talk, you may say, "and you ask what proof have I for this assertion? I have adequate proof and here it is..." Then proceed to answer the imaginary question. That sort of thing can be done very naturally. It will break up the monotony of one's delivery; it will make it direct and pleasant and conversational.

Sincerity and enthusiasm and high earnestness will help you too. When a man is under the influence of his feelings, his real self comes to the surface. The bars are down. The heat of his emotions has burned all barriers away. He acts spontaneously. He talks spontaneously. He is natural.

So, in the end, even this matter of delivery comes back to the thing which has already been emphasized repeatedly in these pages: namely, put your heart in your talks.

"I shall never forget," said Dean Brown in his lectures on Preaching before the Yale Divinity School, the description given by a friend of mine of a service which he once attended in the city of London. The preacher was George MacDonald. He read for the Scripture lesson that morning the eleventh chapter of Hebrews. When the time came for the sermon, he said: "You have all heard about these men of faith. I shall not try to tell you what faith is. There are theological professors who could do that much better than I could do it. I am here to help you believe."

Then followed such a simple, heartfelt and majestic manifestation of the man's own faith in those unseen realities which are eternal, as to beget faith in the minds and hearts of all his hearers. *His heart was in his work, and his delivery was effective because it rested back upon the genuine beauty of his own inner life.*

"His heart was in his work." That is the secret. Yet I know that advice like this is not popular. It seems vague. It sounds indefinite. The average student wants foolproof rules. Something definite. Something he can put his hands on. Rules as precise as the directions for operating a car.

That is what he wants. That is what I would like to give him. It would be easy for him. It would be easy for me. There are such rules, and there is only one little thing wrong with them: they don't work. They take all the naturalness and spontaneity and life and juice out of a man's speaking. I know. In my younger days I wasted a great deal of energy trying them. They won't appear in these pages, for, as Josh Billings observed in one of his lighter moments: "There ain't no use in knowin' so many things that ain't so."

FEATURES OF NATURAL SPEAKING

We are going to discuss here some of the features of natural speaking in order to make them more clear, more vivid. I have hesitated about doing it, for someone is almost sure to say: "Ah, I see, just force myself to do these things and I'll be all right." No, you won't. *Force* yourself to do them and you will be all wooden and all mechanical.

You used most of these principles yesterday in your conversation, used them as unconsciously as you digested your dinner last night. That is the way to use them. It is the *only* way. And it will come, as far as public speaking is concerned, as we have already said, only by practice.

First: Stress Important Words, Subordinate Unimportant Ones

In conversation, we hit one syllable in a word, and hit it hard, and hurry over the others like a pay car passing a string of hoboes. For example, MassaCHUsetts, afFLICtion, atTRACtiveness, enVIRonment. We do almost the same thing with a sentence. We make one or two important words tower up like a skyscraper.

This is not a strange or unusual process I am describing. Listen. You can hear it going on about you all the time. You yourself did it a hundred, maybe a thousand, times yesterday. You will doubtless do it a hundred times tomorrow.

Here is an example. Read the following quotation, striking the works in big type hard. Run over the others quickly. What is the effect?

"I have SUCCEEDED in whatever I have undertaken, because I have WILLED it. I have NEVER HESITATED which has given me an ADVANTAGE over the rest of mankind."—Napoleon.

This is not the only way to read these lines. Another speaker would do it differently perhaps. There are no ironclad rules for emphasis. It all depends.

Read these selections aloud in an earnest manner, trying to make the ideas clear and convincing. Don't you find yourself stressing the big, important words and hurrying over the others?

> If you think you are beaten, you are.
> If you think you dare not, you don't.
> If you'd like to win, but think you can't,
> It's almost a cinch you won't.
> Life's battles don't always go To the stronger or faster man;
> But soon or late the man who wins Is the one who thinks he can.
>
> —Anonymous

Second: Change Your Pitch

The pitch of our voices in conversation flows up and down the scale from high to low and back again, never resting, but always shifting like the face of the sea. Why? No one knows, and no one cares. The effect is pleasing, and it is the way of nature. We never had to learn to do this: it came to us as children, unsought and unaware, but let us stand up and face an audience, and the chances are our voices will become as dull and flat and monotonous as the alkali deserts.

When you find yourself talking in a monotonous pitch—and usually it will be a high one—just pause for a second and say to yourself: "I am speaking like a wooden Indian. *Talk* to these people. Be human. Be natural."

Will that kind of lecture to yourself help you any? A little, perhaps. The pause itself will help you. You have to work out your own salvation by practice.

You can make any phrase or word that you choose stand out like a green bay-tree by either suddenly lowering or raising your pitch on it. Dr. Cadman, the famous Congregational minister, often did it. So does Sir Oliver Lodge. So did Bryan. So did Roosevelt. So does almost every speaker of note.

In the following quotations, try saying the italicized words in a much lower pitch than you use for the rest of the sentence. What is the effect?

> *I have but one merit, that of never despairing.*
>
> —Marshal Foch

~

> *I have lived eighty-six years. I have watched men climb up to success, hundreds of them, and of all the elements that are important for success, the most important is faith.*
>
> —Cardinal Gibbons

Third: Vary Your Rate of Speaking

When a little child talks, or when we talk in ordinary conversation, we *constantly change our rate of speaking.* It is pleasing. It is natural. It is unconscious. It is emphatic. It is, in fact, one of the very best of all possible ways to make an idea stand out prominently.

Walter B. Stevens, in his *Reporters Lincoln,* issued by the Missouri Historical Society, tells us that this was one of Lincoln's favourite methods of driving a point home:

> He would speak several words, with great rapidity, come to the word or phrase he wished to emphasize, and let his voice linger and bear hard on that, and then he would rush to the end of his sentence like lightning.... He would devote as much time to the word or two he wished to emphasize as he did to half a dozen less important words following it.

Such a method invariably arrests attention. To illustrate: I have often quoted in a public talk the following statement by Cardinal Gibbons. I wanted to emphasize the idea of courage; so I lingered on these italicized words, drew them out and spoke as if I myself were impressed with them—and I was. Will you please read the selection aloud, trying the same method and note the results.

"A short time before his death, Cardinal Gibbons said: I have lived *eighty-six years*. I have watched men *climb* up to *success, hundreds* of them, and of all the elements that are *important* for success, the *most important* is *faith. No great thing comes to any man unless he has courage.*"

Try this: say "thirty million dollars" quickly and with an air of triviality so that it sounds like a very small sum. Now, say "thirty thousand dollars": say it slowly, say it feelingly, say it as if you were tremendously impressed with the hugeness of the amount. Haven't you now made the thirty thousand sound larger than the thirty million?

Fourth: Pause Before and After Important Ideas

Lincoln often paused in his speaking. When he had come to a big idea that he wished to impress deeply on the minds of his hearers, he bent forward, looked directly into their eyes for a moment and said nothing at all. This sudden silence had the same effect as a sudden noise: it attracted notice. It made everyone attentive, alert, awake to what was coming next. For example, when his famous debates with Douglas were drawing to a close, when all the indications pointed to his defeat, he became depressed, his old habitual melancholy stealing over him at times, and imparting to his words a touching pathos. In one of his concluding speeches, he suddenly "*stopped and stood silent for a moment,* looking round upon the throng of half-indifferent, half-friendly faces before him, with those deep-sunken weary eyes that always seemed full of unshed tears. Folding his hands, as if they too were tired of the helpless fight, he said, in his peculiar monotone: 'My friends, it makes little difference, very little difference, whether Judge Douglas or myself is elected to the United States Senate, but the great issue which we have submitted to you today is far above and beyond any personal interests or the political fortunes of any man. And my friends,' here he paused again, and the audience were intent on every word, 'that issue will live and breathe and burn when the poor, feeble, stammering tongues of Judge Douglas and myself are silent in the grave.'"

"These simple words," relates one of his biographers, "and the manner in which they were spoken, touched every heart to the core."

Lincoln also paused after the phrase he wanted to emphasize. He added to their force by keeping silent while the meaning sank in and effected its mission.

Sir Oliver Lodge paused frequently in his speaking, both before and after important ideas; paused as often as three or four times in one sentence, but he did it naturally and unconsciously. No man, unless he were analyzing Sir Olivers methods, would have noticed it.

"By your silence," says Kipling, "ye shall speak." Nowhere is silence more golden than when it is judiciously used in talking.

It is a powerful tool, too important to be ignored, yet it is usually neglected by the beginning speaker. In the following excerpt from Holman's *Ginger Talks,* I have marked the places where a speaker might profitably pause. I do not say that these are the *only* places where one ought to pause, or even the best places. I say only that it is *one* way of doing it. Where to pause is not a matter of hard and fast rules. It is a matter of meaning and temperament and feeling. You might pause one place in a speech today, and in another place in the same speech tomorrow.

Read this selection aloud without pausing; then read it again, making the pauses I have indicated. What is the effect of the pauses?

> "Selling goods is a battle," (pause and let the idea of *battle* soak in) "and only fighters can win in it." (Pause and let that point soak in.) "We may not like these conditions, but we didn't have the making of them and we can't alter them." (Pause.) "Take your courage with you when you enter the selling game." (Pause.) "If you don't," (pause and lengthen out suspense for a second) "you'll strike out every time you come to bat, and score nothing higher than a string of goose eggs." (Pause). "The fellow who knocks the cover off the ball or lifts it over the fence is always the chap who steps up to the plate" (pause and increase the suspense as to what you are going to say about this extraordinary player) "with grim determination in his heart."

A speaker may follow the directions I have set down in this lesson and still have a hundred faults. He may talk in public just as he does in conversation and consequently, he may speak with an unpleasant voice and make grammatical errors and be awkward and offensive and do a score of unpleasant things. A man's natural method of every day talking may need a vast number of improvements. Perfect your natural method of talking in conversation, and then carry that method to the platform.

The mastery of forceful speech is one of the noblest purposes to which a man can address himself.

—Newell Dwight Hillis

~

Perhaps there is no more important component of character than steadfast resolution. The boy who is going to make a great man, or is going to count in any way in after-life, must make up his mind not merely to overcome a thousand obstacles, but to win in spite of a thousand repulses and defeats.

—Theodore Roosevelt

9

Platform Presence And Personality

Let the counsel of thine own heart stand, for no man is more faithful unto thee than it. It is sometimes wont to show thee more than seven watchmen who sit above a high tower.

—Rudyard Kipling

The Carnegie Institute of Technology at one time gave intelligence tests to one hundred prominent businessmen. The tests were similar to those used in the army during the war, and the results led the institute to declare that personality contributes more to business success than does superior intelligence.

That is a very significant pronouncement: very significant for the businessman, very significant for the educator, very significant for the professional man, very significant for the speaker.

Personality—with the exception of preparation—is probably the most important factor in public address. "In eloquent speaking," declared Elbert Hubbard, "it is manner that wins, not words." Rather it is manner plus ideas. But personality is a vague and elusive thing, defying analysis like the perfume of the violet. It is the whole combination of the man, the physical, the spiritual, the mental; his traits, his predilections, his tendencies, his temperament, his cast of mind, his vigour, his experience, his training, his life. It is as complex as Einstein's Theory of Relativity, almost as little understood.

A man's personality is very largely the result of his inheritances. It is largely determined before birth. True, his later environment has something to do with it. But, all in all, it is an extremely difficult factor to alter or improve. Yet we can, by taking thought, strengthen it to some extent and make it more forceful, more attractive. At any rate, we can strive to get the utmost possible out of this strange thing that nature has given us. The subject is of vast importance to every one of us. The possibilities for improvement, limited as they are, are still large enough to warrant a discussion and investigation.

If you wish to make the most of your individuality, go before your audience rested. A tired man is not magnetic nor attractive. Don't make the all-too-common error of putting off your preparation and your planning until the very last moment, and then working at a furious pace, trying to make up for lost time. If you do, you are bound to store up bodily poisons and brain fatigues that will prove terrific drags, holding you down, sapping your vitality, weakening both your brain and your nerves.

If you must make an important talk to a committee meeting at four, do not, if you can well avoid it, come back to the office after lunch. Go home, if possible, have a light lunch and the refreshment of a siesta. Rest—that is what you need—physical and mental and nervous.

When you have to make an important talk, beware of your hunger. Eat as sparingly as a saint. On Sunday afternoons, Henry Ward Beecher used to have biscuits and milk at five, and nothing after that.

"When I am singing in the evening," said Madame Melba, "I do not dine but have a very light repast at five o'clock, consisting of either fish, chicken, or sweetbread, with a baked apple and a glass of water. I always find myself very hungry for supper when I get home from the opera or concert."

How wisely Melba and Beecher acted, I never realized until after I became a professional speaker myself and tried to deliver a two-hour talk each evening having consumed a hearty meal.

Experience taught me that I couldn't enjoy a *filet de sole aux pommes nature* and follow that by a beef-steak and fried potatoes and salad and vegetables and a sweet, and then stand up an hour afterwards and do either myself or my subject or my body justice. The blood that ought to have been in my brain was down in my stomach wrestling with that steak and potatoes. Paderewski was right: he said when he ate what he wanted to eat before a concert, the animal in him got uppermost, that it even got into his fingertips and clogged and dulled his playing.

WHAT MAKES A GOOD SPEAKER

Do nothing to dull your energy. It is magnetic. Vitality, aliveness, enthusiasm: they are among the first qualities I have always sought for in employing speakers and instructors of speaking. People cluster around the energetic speaker, the human dynamo of energy, like wild geese around a field of autumn wheat.

I have often seen this illustrated by the open air speakers in Hyde Park, London. A spot near Marble Arch entrance is a rendezvous for speakers of every creed and colour. On a Sunday afternoon, one can take his choice and listen to a Catholic explaining the doctrine of the infallibility of the Pope, to a Socialist propounding the economic gospel of Karl Marx, to an Indian explaining why it is right and proper for a Mohammedan to have four wives, and so on. Hundreds crowd about one speaker, while his neighbour has only a handful. Why? Is the topic always an adequate explanation of the disparity between the drawing powers of different speakers? No. More often the explanation is to be found in the speaker himself: he is more interested and, consequently, interesting. He talks with more life and spirit. He radiates vitality and animation; they always challenge attention.

THE IMPORTANCE OF GROOMING

An inquiry was sent to a large group of people by a psychologist and university president, asking them the impression clothes made on them. All but unanimously, they testified that when they were well groomed and faultlessly and immaculately attired, the knowledge of it, the feeling of it, had an effect which, while it was difficult to explain, was still very definite, very real. It gave them more confidence, brought them increased faith in themselves, and heightened their self-respect. They declared that when they had the look of success they found it easier to think success, to achieve success. Such is the effect of clothes on the wearer himself.

What effect do they have on an audience? I have noticed time and again that if a speaker has baggy trousers, shapeless coat and footwear, fountain pen and pencils peeping out of his breast pocket, a newspaper or a pipe and tin of tobacco bulging out the sides of his garment—I have noticed that an audience has as little respect for that man as he has for his own appearance. Aren't they very likely to assume that his mind is as sloppy as his unkempt hair and unpolished shoes?

BEING IN THE SPOTLIGHT

When General Lee came to Appomattox Court House to surrender his army, he was immaculately attired in a new uniform and, at his side, hung a sword of extraordinary value. Grant was coatless, swordless, and was wearing the shirt and trousers of a private. "I must have contrasted very strangely," he wrote in his *Memoirs*, "with a man so handsomely dressed, six feet high, and of faultless form." The fact that he had not been appropriately attired for this historic occasion came to be one of the real regrets of Grant's life.

The Department of Agriculture has several hundred stands of bees on its experimental farm. Each hive has a large magnifying glass built into it, and the interior can be flooded with electric light by pressing a button; so, any moment, night or day, these bees are liable to be subject to the minutest scrutiny. A speaker is like that; he is under the magnifying glass, he is in the spotlight, all eyes are upon him. The smallest disharmony in his personal appearance now looms up like a mountain from the plains.

"HE WHO CANNOT SMILE OUGHT NOT TO KEEP A SHOP"

A number of years ago, I was writing the life story of a certain banker for a magazine. I asked one of his friends to explain the reason for his success. No small amount of it, he said, was due to the man's winning smile. At first thought, that may sound like exaggeration but I believe it is really true. Other men, scores of them, hundreds of them, may have had more experience and as good financial judgment, but he had an additional asset they didn't possess—he had a most agreeable personality. And a warm, welcoming smile was one of the striking features of it. It gained one's confidence immediately. It secured one's goodwill instantly. We all want to see a man like that succeed, and it is a real pleasure to give him our patronage.

"He who cannot smile," says a Chinese proverb, "ought not to keep a shop." And isn't a smile just as welcome before an audience as behind a counter? I am thinking now of a particular student who attended a course in public speaking conducted by a Chamber of Commerce. He always came out before the audience with an air that said he liked to be there, that he loved the job that was before him. He always smiled and acted as if he were glad to see us, and so immediately and inevitably his hearers warmed towards him and welcomed him.

But I have seen speakers—students of this course, I regret to admit—who walked out before the other members in a cold, perfunctory manner as if they had a disagreeable task to perform, and that, when it was over, they would thank God. We in the audience were soon feeling the same way. These attitudes are contagious.

SEAT YOUR AUDIENCE TOGETHER

As a public lecturer, I have frequently spoken to a small audience scattered through a large hall in the afternoon, and to a large audience packed into the same hall at night. The evening audience has laughed heartily at the same things that brought only a smile to the faces of the afternoon group; the evening crowd has applauded generously at the very places where the afternoon gathering was utterly unresponsive. Why?

For one thing, the elderly women and the children that are likely to come in the afternoon cannot be expected to be as demonstrative as the more vigorous and discriminating evening crowd, but that is only a partial explanation.

The fact is that no audience will be easily moved when it is scattered. Nothing so dampens enthusiasm as wide, open spaces and empty chairs between the listeners. Henry Ward Beecher said in his *Lectures on Preaching*,

> People often say, "Do you not think it is much more inspiring to speak to a large audience than a small one?" No, I say. I can speak just as well to twelve persons as to a thousand, provided those twelve are crowded around me and close together, so that they can touch each other. But even a thousand people with four feet of space between every two of them, would be just the same as an empty room.... Crowd your audience together and you will set them off with half the effort.

A man in a large audience tends to lose his individuality. He becomes a member of the crowd and is swayed far more easily than he would be as a single individual. He will laugh at and applaud things that would leave him unmoved if he were only one of half a dozen people listening to you.

It is far easier to get people to act as a body than to act singly. Men going into battle, for example, invariably want to do the most dangerous and reckless thing in the world—they want to huddle together. During the Late War, German soldiers were known to go into battle at times with their arms locked about one another.

Crowds! Crowds! Crowds! They are a curious phenomenon. All great popular movements and reforms have been carried forward by the aid of the crowd mentality. An interesting book on this subject is Everett Dean Martin's *The Behaviour of Crowds.*

If we are going to talk to a small group, we should choose a small room. Better to pack the aisles of a small place than to have people scattered through the lonely, deadening spaces of a large hall.

If your hearers are scattered, ask them to move down front and be seated near you. Insist on this, before you start speaking.

Unless the audience is a fairly large one, and there is a real reason, a necessity, for the speaker standing on a platform, don't do so. Get down on the same level with them. Stand near them. Break up all formality. Get an intimate contact. Make the thing conversational.

OPEN THE WINDOWS

Keep the air fresh. In the well-known process of public speaking, oxygen is just as essential as the larynx, pharynx and human epiglottis. All the eloquence of Cicero, and all the feminine pulchritude in Ziegfeld's Follies, could hardly keep an audience awake in a room poisoned with bad air. So, when I am one of a number of speakers, before beginning, I almost always ask the audience to stand up and rest for two minutes while the windows are thrown open.

For fourteen years Major James B. Pond travelled all over the United States and Canada as manager for Henry Ward Beecher when that famous preacher was at his flood tide as a popular lecturer. Before the audience assembled, Pond always visited the hall or church or theatre where Beecher was to appear, and rigorously inspected the lighting, seating, temperature and ventilation. Pond had been a blustering, roaring old army officer and he loved to exercise authority; so if the place was too warm or the air was dead and he could not get the windows open, he hurled books through them, smashing and shattering the glass. He believed with Spurgeon that "the next best thing to the Grace of God for a preacher is oxygen".

LET LIGHT SHINE ON YOUR FACE

Unless you are demonstrating spiritualism before a group of people, flood the room, if possible, with lights. It is as easy to domesticate a quail as to develop enthusiasm in a half-lighted room gloomy as the inside of a thermos bottle.

Read David Belasco's articles on stage production, and you will discover that the average speaker does not have the foggiest shadow of the ghost of an idea of the tremendous importance of proper lighting.

Let the light strike your face. People want to see you. The subtle changes that ought to play across your features are a part, and a very real part, of the process of self-expression. Sometimes they mean more than your words. If you stand directly under a light, your face may be dimmed by a shadow; if you stand directly in front of a light, it is sure to be. Would it not, then, be the part of wisdom to select, before you arise to speak, the spot that will give you the most advantageous illumination?

NO TRUMPERY ON THE PLATFORM

And do not hide behind a table. People want to look at the whole man. They will even lean out in the aisles to see all of him.

Some well-meaning soul is pretty sure to give you a table and a water pitcher and a glass; but if your throat becomes dry, a pinch of salt or a taste of lemon will start the saliva again better than Niagara.

You do not want the water nor the pitcher. Neither do you want all the other useless and ugly impedimenta that clutter up the average platform.

The sales rooms of the various automobile makers are beautiful, orderly, pleasing to the eye. The Paris offices of the large perfumers and jewellers are artistically and luxuriously appointed. Why? It is good business. One has more respect, more confidence, more admiration for a concern housed like that.

For the same reason, a speaker ought to have a pleasing background. The ideal arrangement, to my way of thinking, would be no furniture at all. Nothing behind the speaker to attract attention or at either side of him—nothing but a curtain of dark blue velvet.

But what does he usually have behind him? Maps and signs and tables, perhaps a lot of dusty chairs, some piled on top of the others. And what is the result? A cheap, slovenly, disorderly atmosphere. So clear all the trumpery away.

"The most important thing in public speaking," said Henry Ward Beecher, "is the man."

So let the man stand out like the snow-clad top of the Jungfrau towering against the blue skies of Switzerland.

NO GUESTS ON THE PLATFORM

I was once in London, Ontario, when the Prime Minister of Canada was speaking. Presently the janitor, armed with a long pole, started to ventilate the room, moving about from window to window. What happened? The audience, almost to a man, ignored the speaker for a little while and stared at the janitor as intently as if he had been performing some miracle.

An audience cannot resist—or, what comes to the same thing, it *will not* resist—the temptation to look at moving objects. If a speaker will only remember that truth, he can save himself some trouble and needless annoyance.

First, he can refrain from twiddling his thumbs, playing with his clothes and making little nervous movements that detract from him. I remember seeing a New York audience watch a well-known speaker's hands for half an hour while he spoke and played with the covering of a pulpit at the same time.

Second, the speaker should arrange, if possible, to have the audience seated so they won't have their attention distracted by seeing the latecomers enter.

Third, he should have no guests on the platform. A few years ago Raymond Robins delivered a series of talks. I along with a number of others, was invited to sit on the platform with him. I declined on the ground that it was unfair to the speaker. I noted the first night how many of these guests shifted about and put one leg over the other and back again, and so on; and every time one of them moved, the audience looked away from the speaker to the guest. I called Mr. Robins' attention to this the next day; and during the remainder of his evenings with us, he very wisely occupied the platform alone.

David Belasco did not permit the use of red flowers on the stage because they attract too much attention. Then why should a speaker permit a restless human being to sit facing the audience while he talks? He shouldn't. And, if he is wise, he won't.

THE ART OF SITTING DOWN

Isn't it well for the speaker himself not to sit facing the audience before he begins? Isn't it better to arrive as a fresh exhibit than an old one?

But, if we *must* sit, let us be careful of *how* we sit. You have seen men look round to find a chair with the modified movements of a foxhound lying down for the night. They turned round and when they did locate a chair, they doubled up and flopped down into it with all the self-control of a sack of sand.

A man who knows how to sit feels the chair strike the back of his legs, and, with his body easily erect from head to hips, he *sinks* into it with his body under perfect control.

POISE

We just said, a few pages previously, not to play with your clothes because it attracted attention. There is another reason also. It gives an impression of weakness, a lack of self-control. Every movement that does not add to your presence detracts from it. There are no neutral movements. None. So stand still and control yourself physically and that will give you an impression of mental control, of poise.

After you have risen to address your audience, do not be in a hurry to begin. That is the hallmark of the amateur. Take a deep breath. Look over your audience for a moment, and, if there is a noise or disturbance, pause until it quiets down.

Hold your chest high. But why wait until you get before an audience to do this? Why not do it daily in private? Then you will do it unconsciously in public.

"Not one man in ten," says Luther H. Gulick in his book *The Efficient Light,* "carries himself so as to look his best.... Keep the neck pressed against the collar." Here is a daily exercise he recommends: "Inhale slowly and as strongly as possible. At the same time press the neck back firmly against the collar. Now hold it there hard. There is no harm in doing this in an exaggerated way. The object is to "straighten out that part of the back which is directly between the shoulders. This deepens the chest."

And what shall you do with your hands? Forget them. If they fall naturally to your sides, that is ideal. If they feel like a bunch of bananas to you, do not be deluded into imagining that anyone else is paying the slightest attention to them or has the slighest interest in them.

They will look best hanging relaxed at your sides. They will attract the minimum of attention there. Not even the hypercritical can criticize that position. Besides, they will be unhampered and free to flow naturally into gestures when the urge makes itself felt.

But suppose that you are very nervous and that you find putting them behind your back or shoving them into your pockets helps to relieve your self-consciousness—what should you do? Use your common sense. I have heard a number of celebrated speakers of this generation.

Many, if not most, put their hands into their pockets occasionally while speaking. Bryan did it. Chauncey M. Depew did it. Teddy Roosevelt did it. Even so fastidious a dandy as Disraeli sometimes succumbed to this temptation. But the sky did not fall and, according to the weather reports, if my memory serves me right, the sun came up on time as usual the next morning. If a man has something to say worthwhile, and says it with contagious conviction, surely it will matter little what he does with his hands and feet. If his head is full and heart stirred, these secondary details will very largely take care of themselves. After all, the stupendously important thing in making a talk is the psychological aspect of it, not the position of the hands and feet.

ABSURD ANTICS TAUGHT IN THE NAME OF GESTURE

And this brings us very naturally to the much-abused question of gesture. My first lesson in public speaking was given by the president of a college in the Middle West. This lesson, as I remember it, was chiefly concerned with gesturing; it was not only useless but misleading and positively harmful. I was taught to let my arm hang loosely at my side palm facing the rear, fingers half closed and thumb touching my leg. I was drilled to bring the arm up in a graceful curve, to make, a classical swing with the wrist and then to unfold the forefinger first, the second finger next, and the little finger last. When the whole aesthetic and ornamental movement had been executed, the arm was then to retrace the same graceful and unnatural curve and rest again by the side of the leg. The whole performance was wooden and affected. There was nothing sensible or honest about it. I was drilled to act as no man in his right mind ever acted anywhere.

There was no attempt whatever to get me to put my own individuality into my movements; no attempt to spur me on to feeling like gesturing; no endeavour to get the flow and blood of life in the process, and make it natural and unconscious and inevitable; no urging me to let go, to be spontaneous, to break through my shell of reserve, to talk and act like a human being. No, the whole regrettable performance was as mechanical as a typewriter, as lifeless as a last year's bird nest, as ridiculous as a Punch and Judy show.

That was in 1902. It seems incredible that such absurd antics could have been taught in the twentieth century, but they are still going on. Only a few years ago a whole book about gesturing was published by a professor teaching in one of the large colleges of the East—a whole book trying to make automatons out of men, telling them which gesture to make on this sentence, which to make on that, which to make with one hand, which with both, which to make high, which to make medium, which to make low, how to hold this finger and how to hold that. I have seen twenty men at a time standing before a class, all reading the same ornate oratorical selections from such a book, all making precisely the same gestures on precisely the same words, and all making themselves precisely ridiculous. Artificial, time-killing, mechanical, injurious—it has brought this whole subject into disrepute with many men. The dean of a large college in Massachusetts recently said that his institution had no course in public speaking because he had never seen one that was practical, one that taught men to speak sensibly. My sympathy was all with the dean.

Nine-tenths of the stuff that has been written on gestures has been a waste and worse than a waste of good white paper and good black ink. Any gesture out of a book is very likely to look like it. The place to get it is out of yourself, out of your heart out of your mind, out of your own interest in the subject, out of your own desire to make someone else see as you see, out of your own impulses. The only gestures that are worth one, two, three, are those that are born on the spur of the instant. An ounce of spontaneity is worth a ton of rules.

Gesture is not a thing to be put on at will like a dinner jacket. It is merely an outward expression of inward condition just as are kisses and colic and laughter and sea sickness.

And a man's gestures, like his toothbrush, should be very personal things. And, as all men are different, their gestures will be individual if they will only act naturally.

No two men should be drilled to gesture in precisely the same fashion. In the last chapter, I discussed the difference between Lincoln and Douglas as speakers. Imagine trying to make the long, awkward, slow-thinking Lincoln gesture in the same fashion as did the rapidly-talking, impetuous and polished Douglas. It would be ridiculous.

"Lincoln," according to his biographer and law partner, Herndon, "did nor gesticulate as much with his hands as with his head. He used the latter frequently, throwing it with vim this way and that. This movement was a significant one when he sought to enforce his statement. It sometimes came with a quick jerk, as if throwing off electric sparks into combustible material. He never sawed the air or rent space into tatters and rags as some orators do. He never acted for stage effect.

As he moved along in his speech, he became freer and less uneasy in his movements; to that extent he was graceful. He had a perfect naturalness, a strong individuality, and to that extent he was dignified. He despised glitter, show, set forms, and shams.... There was a world of meaning and emphasis in the long, bony finger of his right hand as he dotted the ideas on the minds of his hearers. Sometimes, to express joy or pleasure, he would raise both hands at an angle of about fifty degrees, the palms upward, as if desirous of embracing the spirit of that which he loved. If the sentiment was one of detestation—denunciation of slavery, for example—both arms, thrown upward and fists clenched, swept through the air, and he expressed an execration that was truly sublime. This was one of his most effective gestures, and signified most vividly a fixed determination to drag down the object of his hatred and trample it in the dust. He always stood squarely on his feet, toe even with toe; that is, he never put one foot before the other. He neither touched nor leaned on anything for support. He made but few changes in his positions and attitudes. He never ranted, never walked backward and forward on the platform. To ease his arms, he frequently caught hold, with his left hand of the lapel of his coat, keeping his thumb upright and leaving his right hand free to gesticulate." St. Gaudens caught him in just that attitude in the statue facing Westminster Abbey.

Such was Lincoln's method. Theodore Roosevelt was more vigorous, fiery, active, his whole face alive with feeling, his fist clenched, his entire body an instrument of expression. Bryan often used the outstretched hand with open palm. Gladstone often struck a table or his open palm with his fist, or stamped his foot with a resounding thud on the floor. Lord Rosebery used to raise his right arm and bring it down with a bold sweep that had tremendous force. Ah, but there was force first in the speaker's thoughts and convictions; that was what made the gesture strong and spontaneous.

Spontaneity... life... they are the *summum bonum* of action. Burke was angular and exceedingly awkward in his gestures. Pitt sawed the air with his arms "like a clumsy clown". Sir Henry Irving was handicapped by a lame leg and decidedly odd movements. Lord Macaulay's actions on the platform were ungainly. So were Grattan's. So were Parnell's. "The answer then appears to be," said the late Lord Curzon at Cambridge University, in an address on Parliamentary Eloquence, "that great public speakers make their own gestures, and that while a great orator is doubtless aided by a handsome exterior and graceful action, it does not matter very much if he happens to be ugly and awkward."

Some years ago, I heard the famous Gypsy Smith preach. I was enthralled by the eloquence of this man who has led so many thousands to Christ. He used gestures—lots of them—and was no more conscious of them than of the air he breathed. Such is the ideal way.

And such is the way you, my dear reader, will find yourself making gestures if you will but practice and apply the principles already enunciated in this course. I can't give you any rules for gesturing, for everything depends upon the temperament of the speaker, upon his preparation, his enthusiasm, his personality, the subject, the audience, the occasion.

SOME SUGGESTIONS

Here are, however, a few limited suggestions that may prove useful. Do not repeat one gesture until it becomes monotonous. Do not make short, jerky movements from the elbow. The movements from the shoulder look better on the platform. Do not end your gestures too quickly. If you are using the index finger to drive home your thought, do not be afraid to hold that gesture through an entire sentence. The failure to do this is a very common error and a serious one. It distorts your emphasis, making small things unimportant, and truly important points seem trivial by comparison.

When you are doing real speaking before a real audience, make only the gestures that come natural. But while you are practicing before the members of this course, *force* yourself, if necessary, to use gestures. Force yourself to do it and the doing of it will so awaken and stimulate you that your gestures will soon be coming unsought.

Shut your book. You can't learn gestures from a printed page. Your own impulses, as you are speaking, are more to be trusted, more valuable than anything any instructor can possibly tell you.

If you forget all else we have said about gesture and delivery, remember this: if a man is so wrapped up in what he has to say, if he is so eager to get his message across that he forgets himself and talks and acts spontaneously, then his gestures and his delivery, unstudied though they may be, are very likely to be almost above criticism. If you doubt this, walk up to a man and knock him down. You will probably discover that, when he regains his feet, the talk he delivers will be well nigh flawless as a gem of eloquence.

Here are the best eleven words I have ever read on the subject of delivery:

> Fill up the barrel.
> Knock out the bung.
> Let nature caper.

> *Action is eloquence, and the eyes of the ignorant are more learned than their ears.*
>
> —Shakespeare

~

> *There is often as much eloquence in the tone of the voice, in the eyes, and in the air of a speaker as in his choice of words.*
>
> —La Rochefoucauld

10

How To Make Your Meaning Clear

Be brief, be pointed, let your matter stand lucid in order, solid and at hand; spend not your words on trifles but condense; strike with the mass of thought, not drops of sense; press to the close with vigor, once begun, and leave, (how hard the task!) leave off, when done.

—Joseph Story

A famous English bishop, during the last war, spoke to some unlettered negro troops. They were on their way to the trenches; but a very small percentage of them had any adequate idea why they were being sent. I know; I questioned them. Yet the Lord Bishop talked to these negroes about "international amity" and "Servia's right to a place in the sun". Why, the half of those negroes did not know whether Servia was a town or a disease. He might as well, as far as results were concerned, have delivered a sonorous eulogy on the Nebular Hypothesis. However, not a single trooper left the hall while he was speaking: the military police with revolvers were stationed at every exit to prevent that consummation.

I do not wish to belittle the bishop. He is every inch a scholar, and before a body of collegiate men he would probably have been powerful, but he failed with these negroes, and he failed utterly: he did not know his audience, and he evidently knew neither the precise purpose of his talk nor how to accomplish it.

What do we mean by the purpose of an address? Just this: every talk, regardless of whether the speaker realizes it or not, has one of four major goals. What are they?

1. To make something clear.
2. To impress and convince.
3. To get action.
4. To entertain.

Let us illustrate these by a series of concrete examples.

Lincoln, who was always more or less interested in mechanics, once invented and patented a device for lifting stranded boats off sand bars and other obstructions. He worked in a mechanic's shop near his law office, making a model of his apparatus. Although the device finally came to naught, he was decidedly enthusiastic over its possibilities. When friends came to his office to view the model, he took no end of pains to explain it. The main purpose of those explanations was clearness.

When he delivered his immortal oration at Gettysburg, when he gave his first and second inaugural addresses, when Henry Clay died and Lincoln delivered an eulogy on his life—on all these occasions, Lincoln's main purpose was impressiveness and conviction. He had to be clear, of course, because he could be convincing; but, in these instances, clearness was not his major consideration.

In his talks to juries, he tried to win favorable decisions. In his political talks, he tried to win votes. His purpose, then, was *action*.

Two years before he was elected President, Lincoln prepared a lecture on Inventions. His purpose was entertainment. At least, that should have been his goal, but he was evidently not very successful in attaining it. His career as a popular lecturer was, in fact, a distinct disappointment. In one town, not a person came to hear him.

But he did succeed and he succeeded famously in the other speeches of his that I have referred to. And why? Because, in those instances, he knew his goal, and he knew how to achieve it. He knew where he wanted to go and how to get there. And because so many speakers don't know just that, they often flounder and come to grief.

For example: I once saw a United States Congressman hooted, hissed and forced to leave the stage of the old New York Hippodrome, because he had—unconsciously, no doubt, but nevertheless, unwisely—chosen clearness as his goal. It was during the last war. He talked to his audience about how the United States was preparing. The crowd did not want to be instructed. They wanted to be entertained. They listened to him patiently, politely, for ten minutes, a quarter of an hour, hoping the performance would come to a rapid end. But it didn't. He rambled on and on; patience snapped and the audience would not stand for more. Someone began to cheer ironically. Others took it up. In a moment, a thousand people were whistling and shouting. The speaker, obtuse and incapable as he was of sensing the temper of his audience, had the bad taste to continue. That aroused them. A battle was on. Their impatience mounted to ire. They were determined to silence him. Louder and louder grew their storm of protest. Finally, the roar of it, the anger of it drowned his words—he could not have been heard twenty feet away. So he was forced to give up, acknowledge defeat, and retire in humiliation.

Profit by his example. Know your goal. Choose it wisely before you set out to prepare your talk. Know how to reach it. Then set about it, doing it skilfully and with science.

All this requires knowledge, special and technical instruction. The remainder of this chapter will show you how to make your talks clear.

USE COMPARISONS TO PROMOTE CLEARNESS

As to clearness: do not underestimate the importance of it nor the difficulty. I recently heard a certain Irish poet give an evening of readings from his own poems. Not 10 per cent of the audience, half the time, knew what he was talking about. Many talkers, both in public and private, are a lot like that.

When I discussed the essentials of public speaking with Sir Oliver Lodge, a man who has been lecturing to university classes and to the public for forty years, he emphasized most of all the importance, first, of knowledge and preparation, and second, of "taking good pains to be clear".

The great General Von Moltke, at the outbreak of the Franco-Prussian War, said to his officers: "Remember, gentlemen, that any order that *can* be misunderstood, *will bc* misunderstood."

Napoleon recognized the same danger. His most emphatic and oft-reiterated instruction to his secretaries was: "Be clear! Be clear!"

When the disciples asked Christ why He taught the public by parables, He answered, "Because they seeing, see not: and hearing, hear not; neither do they understand."

And when you talk on a subject strange to your hearer or hearers, can you hope that they will understand you any more readily than people understood the Master?

Hardly. So what can we do about it? What did He do when confronted by a similar situation? Solved it in the most simple and natural manner imaginable: described the things people did not know by likening them to things they did know. The kingdom of Heaven...what would it be like? How could those untutored peasants of Palestine know? So Christ described it in terms of objects and actions with which they were already familiar:

> The kingdom of Heaven is like unto leaven, which a woman took, and hid in three measures of meal, till the whole was leavened.
>
> Again, the kingdom of Heaven is like unto a merchantman seeking goodly pearls...
>
> Again, the kingdom of Heaven is like unto a net that was cast into the sea....

That was lucid; they could understand that. The housewives in the audience were using leaven every week; the fishermen were casting their nets into the sea daily; the merchants were dealing in pearls.

And how did David make clear the watchfulness and loving kindness of Jehovah?

"The Lord is my shepherd, I shall not want. He maketh me to lie down in green pastures, He leadeth me beside the still waters...."

Green grazing grounds in that almost barren country... still waters where the sheep could drink—those pastoral people could understand that.

Here is a rather striking and half-amusing example of the use of this principle: some missionaries were translating the *Bible* into the dialect of a tribe near equatorial Africa. They progressed to the verse: "Though your sins be as scarlet, they shall be white as snow." How were they to translate that? Literally? Meaningless. Absurd. The natives had never scooped snow off the pathway on a February morning. They did not even have a word for snow. They could not have told the difference between snow and coal tar, but they had climbed coconut trees many times and shaken down a few nuts for lunch; so the missionaries likened the unknown to the known, and changed the verse to read: "Though your sins be as scarlet, they shall be as white as the meat of a coconut." Under the circumstances, it would be hard to improve on that, wouldn't it?

At a Teachers' College, I once heard a lecturer on Alaska who failed, in many places, to be either clear or interesting because, unlike those African missionaries, he neglected to talk in terms of what his audience knew. He told us, for example, that Alaska had a gross area of 590,804 square miles, and a population of 64,356.

Half a million square miles—what does that mean to the average man? Precious little. He is not used to thinking in terms of square miles. They conjure up no mental picture. Suppose the speaker had said that the coastline of Alaska and its islands is longer than the distance around the globe, and that its area more than equals the combined areas of Vermont, New Hampshire, Maine, Massachusetts, Rhode Island, Connecticut, New York, New Jersey, Pennsylvania, Delaware, Maryland, West Virginia, North Carolina, South Carolina, Georgia, Florida, Mississippi and Tennessee. Would not that give everyone a fairly clear conception of the area of Alaska?

He said the population was 64,356. The chances are that not one person in ten remembered the census figures for five minutes—or even one minute. Why? Because the rapid saying of "sixty-four thousand, three hundred and fifty-six" does not make a very clear impression. It leaves only a loose, insecure impression, like words written on the sand of the seashore. The next wave of attention quite obliterates them. Would it not have been better to have stated the census in terms of something with which they were very familiar? Better still, why not talk about Alaska in terms of the very town where you are speaking?

In the following illustrations, which are clearer: (a) or (b)?

(a) Our nearest star is thirty-five trillion miles away.

(b) A train going at the rate of a mile a minute would reach our nearest star in forty-eight million years; if a song were sung there and the sound could travel here it would be three million eight hundred thousand years before we could hear it. A spider's thread reaching to it would weigh five hundred tons.

(a) St. Peter's, the biggest church in the world, is 232 yards long, and 364 feet wide.

(b) It is about the size of two buildings like the capital at Washington piled on top of one another.

Sir Oliver Lodge happily uses this method when explaining the size and nature of atoms to a popular audience. I heard him tell a European audience that there were as many atoms in a drop of water as there were drops of water in the Mediterranean Sea; and many of his hearers had spent over a week sailing from Gibraltar to the Suez Canal. To bring the matter still closer home, he said there were as many atoms in one drop of water as there were blades of grass on the earth.

Richard Harding Davis told a New York audience that the Mosque of St. Sophia was "about as big as the auditorium of the Fifth Avenue theatre". He said Brindisi "looks like Long Island City when you come into it from the rear."

Use this principle henceforth in your talks. If you are describing the Great Pyramid, first tell your hearers it is 451 feet, then tell them how high that is in terms of some building they see every day. Tell how many city blocks the base would cover. Don't speak about so many thousand gallons of this or so many hundred thousand barrels of that without also telling how many rooms the size of the one you are speaking in could be filled with that much liquid. Instead of saying twenty feet high, why not say one and a half times as high as this ceiling? Instead of talking about distance in terms of rods or miles, is it not clearer to say as far as from here to some station, or to such and such a street?

AVOID TECHNICAL TERMS

If you belong to a profession the work of which is technical—if you are a lawyer, a physician, an engineer, or are in a highly specialized line of business—be doubly careful when you talk to outsiders, to express yourself in plain terms and to give necessary details.

I say be doubly careful for, as a part of my professional duties, I have listened to hundreds of speeches that failed right at this point and tailed woefully. The speakers appeared totally unconscious of the general public's widespread and profound ignorance regarding their particular specialties. So what happened? They rambled on and on, uttering thoughts, using phrases that fitted into their experience and were instantly and continuously meaningful to them; but to the uninitiated, they were about as clear as a river after the rains have fallen on the newly-ploughed cornfields along its banks.

What should such a speaker do? He ought to read and heed the following advice from the facile pen of ex-Senator Beveridge:

> It is a good practice to pick out the least intelligent looking person in the audience and strive to make that person interested in your argument. This can be done only by lucid statement of fact and clear reasoning. An even better method is to centre your talk on some small boy or girl present with parents.
>
> Say to yourself—say out loud to your audience, if you like—that you will try to be so plain that the child will understand and remember your explanation of the question discussed, and after the meeting be able to tell what you have said.

THE SECRET OF LINCOLN'S CLEARNESS

Lincoln had a deep and abiding affection for putting a proposition so that it would be instantly clear to everyone. In his first message to Congress, he used the phrase "sugar-coated". Mr. Defrees, the public printer, being Lincoln's personal friend, suggested to him that although the phrase might be all right for a stump speech in Illinois, it was not dignified enough for a historical state paper. "Well, Defrees," Lincoln replied, "if you think the time will ever come when the people will not understand what "sugar-coated" means, I'll alter it; otherwise, I think I'll let it go."

He once explained to Dr. Gulliver, the President of Knox College, how he developed his "passion" for plain language, as he phrased it:

> Among my earliest recollections I remember how, when a mere child, I used to get irritated

> when anybody talked to me in a way I could not understand. I don't think I ever got angry at anything else in my life. But that always disturbed my temper, and has ever since. I can remember going to my little bedroom, after hearing the neighbours talk of an evening with my father, and spending no small part of the night walking up and down and trying to make out the exact meaning of some of their, to me, dark sayings. I could not sleep, though I often tried to, when I got on such a hunt after an idea, until I had caught it, and when I thought I had got it I was not satisfied until I had repeated it over and over, until I had put it in language plain enough as I thought for any boy I knew to comprehend. This was a kind of passion with me, and it has since stuck by me.

A passion? Yes, it must have amounted to that, for Mentor Graham, the schoolmaster of New Salem, testified: "I have known Lincoln to study for hours the best way of three to express an idea."

An all too common reason why men fail to be intelligible is this: the thing they wish to express is not clear even to themselves. Hazy impressions! Indistinct, vague ideas! The result? Their minds work no better in a mental fog than a camera does in a physical fog. They need to be as disturbed over obscurity and ambiguity as Lincoln was. They need to use his methods.

APPEAL TO THE SENSE OF SIGHT

The nerves that lead from the eye to the brain are many times larger than those leading from the ear; and science tells us that we give twenty-five times as much attention to eye suggestions as we do to ear suggestions.

"One seeing," says an old Japanese proverb, "is better than a hundred times telling about."

So, if you wish to be clear, picture your points, visualize your ideas. That was the plan of the late John H. Patterson, President of the well-known National Cash Register Company. He wrote an article for *System Magazine*, outlining the methods he used in speaking to his workmen and his sales forces:

> I hold that one cannot rely on speech alone to make himself understood or to gain and hold attention. A dramatic supplement is needed. It is better to supplement whenever possible with pictures which show the right and the wrong way; diagrams are more convincing than mere words, and pictures are more convincing than diagrams. The ideal presentation of a subject is one in which every subdivision is pictured and in which the words are used only to connect them. I early found that in dealing with men, a picture was worth more than anything I could say.
>
> Little grotesque drawings are wonderfully effective...I have a whole system of cartooning or "chart talks". A circle with a dollar mark means a piece of money, a bag marked with a dollar is a lot of money. Many good effects can be had with moon faces. Draw a circle, put in a few dashes for the eyes, nose, mouth, and ears. Twisting these lines gives the expressions. The out-of-date man has the corner of his mouth down; the chipper, up-to-date fellow has the curves up. The drawings are homely, but the most effective cartoonists are not the men who make the prettiest pictures; the thing is to express the idea and the contrast.

> The big bag and the little bag of money, side by side, are the natural heads for the right way as opposed to the wrong way; the one brings much money, the other little money. If you sketch these rapidly as you talk, there is no danger of people's letting their minds wander; they are bound to look at what you are doing and thus to go with you through the successive stages to the point you want to make. And again, the funny figures put people in good humour.
>
> I used to employ an artist to hang around in the shops with me and quietly make sketches of things that were not being done right. Then the sketches were made into drawings and I called the men together and showed them exactly what they were doing. When I heard of the stereopticon I immediately bought one and projected the drawings on the screen, which, of course, made them even more effective than on paper. Then came the moving picture. I think that I had one of the first machines ever made and now we have a big department with many motion picture films and more than 60,000 coloured stereopticon slides.

Not every subject or occasion, of course, lends itself to exhibits and drawings; but let us use them when we can. They attract attention, stimulate interest and often make our meaning doubly clear.

ROCKEFELLER RAKING OFF THE COINS

Mr. Rockefeller also used the columns of *System Magazine* to tell how he appealed to the sense of sight to make clear the financial situation of the Colorado Fuel and Iron Company:

> I found that they (the employees of the Colorado Fuel and Iron Co.) imagined the Rockefellers had been drawing immense profits from their interests in Colorado; no end of people had told them so. I explained the exact situation to them. I showed them that during the fourteen years in which we had been connected with the Colorado Fuel and Iron Co., it had never paid one cent in dividends upon the common stock.
>
> At one of our meetings, I gave a practical illustration of the finances of the company. I put a number of coins on the table. I swept off a portion which represented their wages—for the first claim upon the company is the payroll. Then I took away more coins to represent the salaries of the officers, and then the remaining coins to represent the fees of the directors. There were no coins left for the stockholders. And when I asked: "Men, is it fair, in this corporation where we are all partners, that three of the partners should get all the earnings, be they large or small— all of them—and the fourth nothing?"
>
> After the illustration, one of the men made a speech for higher wages. I asked him, "Is it fair for you to want more wages when one of the partners gets nothing?" He admitted that it did not look like a square deal; I heard no more about increasing the wages.

Make your eye appeals definite and specific. Paint mental pictures that stand out as sharp and clear as a stag's horn silhouetted against the setting sun. For example, the word "dog" calls up a more or less definite picture of such an animal—perhaps a cocker spaniel, a Scotch terrier, a St. Bernard, or a Pomeranian. Notice how much more distinct an image springs into your mind when I say "bulldog"—the term is less inclusive. Doesn't "a brindle bulldog" call up a still more explicit picture? Is it not more vivid to say "a black Shetland pony" than to talk of "a horse"? Doesn't "a white bantam rooster with a broken leg" give a much more definite and sharp picture than merely the word "fowl"?

RESTATE YOUR IMPORTANT IDEAS IN DIFFERENT WORDS

Napoleon declared repetition to be the only serious principle of rhetoric. He knew that because an idea which was clear to him was not always proof that it was instantly grasped by others. He knew that it takes time to comprehend new ideas, that the mind must be kept focussed on them. In short, he knew they must be repeated. Not in exactly the same language. People will rebel at that, and rightly so. But if the repetition is couched in fresh phraseology, if it is varied, your hearers will never regard it as repetition at all.

Let us take a specific example. The late Mr. Bryan said: "You cannot make people understand a subject, unless you understand that subject yourself. The more clearly you have a subject in mind, the more clearly can you present that subject to the minds of others."

The last sentence here is merely a restatement of the idea contained in the first, but when these sentences are spoken, the mind does not have time to see that it is repetition. It only *feels* that the subject has been made more clear.

I seldom teach a single session of this course without hearing one or perhaps half a dozen talks that would have been more clear, more impressive, had the speaker but employed this principle of restatement. It is almost entirely ignored by the beginner. And what a pity!

USE GENERAL ILLUSTRATIONS AND SPECIFIC INSTANCES

One of the surest and easiest ways to make your points clear is to follow them with general illustrations and concrete cases. What is the difference between the two? One, as the term implies, is general; the other, specific.

Let us illustrate the difference between them and the uses of each with a concrete example. Suppose we take the statement: "There are professional men and women who earn astonishingly large incomes."

Is that statement very clear? Have you a clearcut idea of what the speaker really means? No, and the speaker himself cannot be sure of what such an assertion will call up in the minds of others. It may cause the country doctor to think of a family doctor in a small city with an income of five thousand. It may cause a successful mining engineer to think in terms of the men in his profession who make a hundred thousand a year. The statement, as it stands, is entirely too vague and loose. It needs to be tightened. A few illuminating details ought to be given to indicate what professions the speaker refers to and what he means by "astonishingly large".

"There are lawyers, prize-fighters, song-writers, novelists, playwrights, painters, actors and singers who make more than the President of the United States." Now, hasn't one a much clearer idea of what the speaker meant? However, he has not individualized. He has used general illustrations, not specific instances. He has said "singers", not Rosa Ponselle, Kirsten Flagstad, or Lily Pons.

So the statement is still more or less vague. We cannot call up concrete cases to illustrate it. Should not the speaker do it for us? Would he not be clearer if he employed specific examples—as is done in the following paragraph:

> The great trial lawyers Samuel Untermeyer and Max Steuer earn as much as one million dollars a year. Jack Dempsey's annual income has been known to be as high as a half-million dollars. Joe Louis, the young, uneducated negro pugilist, while still in his twenties, has earned more than a half-million dollars. Irving Berlin's rag-time music is reported to have brought him a half million dollars yearly. Sidney Kingsley has made ten thousand dollars a week royalty on his plays. H.G. Wells has admitted, in his autobiography, that his pen has brought him three million dollars. Diego Rivera has earned, from his paintings, more than half a million dollars in a year. Katherine Cornell has repeatedly refused five thousand dollars a week to go into pictures. Lawrence Tibbet and Grace Moore are reported to have an annual income of a quarter-million dollars.

Now, has not one an extremely plain and vivid idea of exactly and precisely what the speaker wanted to convey?

Be concrete. Be definite. Be specific. This quality of definiteness not only makes for clearness but for impressiveness and conviction and interest also.

DO NOT EMULATE THE MOUNTAIN GOAT

Professor William James, in one of his talks to teachers, pauses to remark that one can make only one point in a lecture, and the lecture he referred to lasted an hour. Yet I recently heard a speaker, who was limited by a stopwatch to three minutes, begin by saying that he wanted to call our attention to eleven points. Sixteen and a half seconds to each phase of his subject! Seems incredible, doesn't it, that an intelligent man should attempt anything so manifestly absurd. True, I am quoting an extreme case, but the tendency to err in that fashion, if not to that degree, handicaps almost every novice. He is like a Cook's guide who shows Paris to the tourist in one day. It can be done, just as one can walk through the Museum of Natural History in thirty minutes. But neither clearness nor enjoyment results. Many a talk fails to be clear because the speaker seems intent upon establishing a world's record for ground covered in the allotted time. He leaps from one point to another with the swiftness and agility of a mountain goat.

The talks in this course must, owing to the pressure of time, be short; so cut your cloth accordingly. If, for example, you are to speak on Labour Unions, do not attempt to tell us in three or six minutes why they came into existence, the methods they employ, the good they have accomplished, the evil they have wrought, and how to solve industrial disputes. No, no; if you strive to do that, no one will have a very clear conception of what you have said. It will be all confused, a blur, too sketchy, too much of a mere outline.

Wouldn't it be the part of wisdom to take one phase and one phase only of labour unions, and cover that adequately and illustrate it? It would. That kind of speech leaves a single impression. It is lucid, easy to listen to, easy to remember.

However, if you must cover several phases of your topic, it is often advisable to summarize briefly at the end. Let us see how that suggestion operates. Here is a summary of this lesson. Does the reading of it help to make the message we have been presenting more lucid, more comprehensible?

One picture is worth ten thousand words.

—Chinese Proverb

~

Clarity of mind means clarity of passion, too; this is why a great and clear mind loves ardently and sees distinctly what he loves.

—Blaise Pascal

11

Improving Your Diction

Be impeccable with your word. Speak with integrity. Say only what you mean. Avoid using the word to speak against yourself or to gossip about others. Use the power of your word in the direction of truth and love.

—Don Miguel Ruiz

A short time ago an Englishman, without employment and without financial reserves, was walking the streets seeking a position. He entered the office of Mr. Paul Gibbons, a well-known businessman, and asked for an interview. Mr. Gibbons looked at the stranger distrustfully. His appearance was emphatically against him. His clothes were shabby and threadbare, and over all of him were written large unmistakable signs of financial distress. Half out of curiosity, half out of pity, Mr. Gibbons granted the interview. At first, he had intended to listen for only a moment, but the moments grew into minutes, and the minutes mounted into an hour; and the conversation still continued. It ended by Mr. Gibbons telephoning Mr. Roland Taylor, the manager of a well-known firm of stockbrokers; and Mr. Taylor, one of the leading financiers of that city, invited this stranger to lunch and secured for him a desirable position. How was this man, with the air and outward appearance of failure, able to effect such a prized connection within so short a time?

The secret can be divulged in a single phrase: his command of the English language. He was, in reality, an Oxford man who had come to town on a business mission which had ended in disaster, leaving him stranded, without funds and without friends. But he spoke his mother tongue with such precision and beauty that his listeners soon forgot his rusty shoes, his frayed coat, his unshaven face. His diction became an immediate passport into the best business circles.

This man's story is somewhat extraordinary, but it illustrates a broad and fundamental truth, namely, that we are judged each day by our speech. Our words reveal our refinements; they tell the discerning listener of the company we have kept; they are the hallmarks of education and culture.

We have only four contacts with the world, you and I. We are evaluated and classified by four things: by what we do, by how we look, by what we say, and by how we say it. Yet many a man blunders through a long life time, after he leaves school, without any conscious effort to enrich his stock of words, to master their shades of meaning, to speak with precision and distinction. He comes habitually to use the overworked and exhausted phrases of the office and street. Small wonder that his talk lacks distinction and individuality. Small wonder that he often violates the accepted traditions of pronunciation, and that he sometimes transgresses the very canons of English grammar itself. I have heard even college graduates say "ain't", and "he don't", and "between you and I". And if men with academic degrees gracing their names commit such errors, what can we expect of those whose education has been cut short by the pressure of economic necessity?

Years ago, I stood one afternoon day-dreaming in the Colosseum at Rome. A stranger approached me, an English colonial. He introduced himself, and began talking of his experiences in the Eternal City. He had not spoken three minutes until he had said "you was", and "I done". That morning, when he arose, he had polished his shoes and put on spotless linen in order to maintain his own self-respect and to win the respect of those with whom he came in contact, but he had made no attempt whatever to polish his phrases and to speak spotless sentences. He would have been ashamed, for example, of not raising his hat to a woman when he spoke, but he was not ashamed—no, he was not even conscious—of violating the usages of grammar, of offending the ears of discriminating auditors. By his own words, he stood revealed and placed and classified. His woeful use of the English language proclaimed to the world continually and unmistakably that he was not a person of culture.

Dr. Charles W. Eliot, after he had been President of Harvard for a third of a century, declared: "I recognize but one mental acquisition as a necessary part of the education of a lady or gentleman, namely, an accurate and refined use of the mother tongue." This is a significant pronouncement. Ponder over it.

But how, you ask, are we to become intimate with words, to speak them with beauty and accuracy? Fortunately, there is no mystery about the means to be employed, no legerdemain. The method is an open secret. Lincoln used it with amazing success. No other American ever wove words into such comely patterns, or produced with prose such matchless music: "with malice towards none, with charity for all." Was Lincoln, whose father was a shiftless, illiterate carpenter and whose mother was a woman of no extraordinary attainments—was he endowed by nature with this gift for words? There is no evidence to support such an assumption. When he was elected to Congress, he described his education in the official records at Washington, with one adjective: "defective". He had attended school less than twelve months in his entire life. And who had been his mentors? Zachariah Birney and Caleb Hazel in the forests of Kentucky, Azel Dorsey and Andrew Crawford along Pigeon Creek in Indiana—itinerant pedagogues, all of them, drifting from one pioneer settlement to another, eking out an existence wherever a few scholars could be found who were willing to exchange hams and maize and wheat for the three R's. Lincoln had meagre assistance, little of uplift or inspiration from them and little, too, from his daily environment.

The farmers and merchants, the lawyers and litigants with whom he associated in the Eighth Judicial District of Illinois, possessed no magic with words. But Lincoln did not—and this is the significant fact to remember— Lincoln did not squander all his time with his mental equals and inferiors. He made boon companions out of the elite minds, the singers, the poets of the ages. He could repeat from memory whole pages of Burns and Byron and Browning. He wrote a lecture on Burns. He had one copy of Byron's poems for his office and another for his home. The office copy had been used so much that it fell open, whenever it was lifted, to *Don Juan*. Even when he was in the White House and the tragic burdens of the Civil War were sapping his strength and etching deep furrows in his face, he often found time to take a copy of Hood's poems to bed. Sometimes he awoke in the middle of the night and, opening the book, he chanced upon verses that especially stirred or pleased him. Getting up, clad only in his night-shirt and slippers, he stole through the halls until he found his secretary and read to him poem after poem. In the White House, he found time to repeat long, memorized passages from Shakespeare, to criticize the actor's reading of them, to give his own individual interpretation. "I have gone over some of Shakespeare's plays," he wrote to Hackett, the actor, "perhaps as frequently as any unprofessional reader. *Lear, Richard III, Henry VIII, Hamlet,* and especially *Macbeth.* I think nothing equals *Macbeth.* It is wonderful!"

Lincoln was devoted to verse. Not only did he memorize and repeat it, both in private and public, but he even essayed to write it. He read one of his long poems at his sister's wedding. Later, in middle life, he filled a notebook with his original compositions, but he was so shy about these creations that he never permitted even his closest friends to read them.

"This self-educated man," writes Robinson in his book *Lincoln as a Man of Letters,* "clothed his mind with the materials ot genuine culture. Call it genius or talent, the process of his attainment was that described by Professor Emerton in speaking of the education of Erasmus: 'He was no longer at school, but was simply educating himself by the only pedagogical method which ever yet produced any results anywhere, namely, by the method of his own tireless energy in continuous study and practice.'"

This awkward pioneer, who used to shuck Indian corn and butcher hogs for thirty-one cents a day on the Pigeon Creek farms of Indiana, delivered, at Gettysburg, one of the most beautiful addresses ever spoken by mortal man. One hundred and seventy thousand men fought there. Seven thousand were killed. Yet Charles Sumner said, shortly after Lincoln's death, that Lincoln's address would live when the memory of the battle was lost, and that the battle would one day be remembered largely because of the speech. Who will doubt the correctness of this prophecy? Isn't it, even in this generation, beginning to be fulfilled? Do you not, even now, think of the speech as much as of the fighting when you hear the name "Gettysburg"?

Edward Everett spoke for two hours at Gettysburg; all that he said has long since been forgotten. Lincoln spoke for less than two minutes: a photographer attempted to take his picture while delivering the speech, but Lincoln had finished before the primitive camera could be set up and focused.

Lincoln's address has been cast in imperishable bronze and placed in a library at Oxford as an example of what can be done with the English language. It ought to be memorized by every student of public speaking.

> Four score and seven years ago our fathers brought forth on this continent a new nation, conceived in liberty, and dedicated to the proposition that all men are created equal. Now we are engaged in a great civil war testing whether that nation, or any nation so conceived and so dedicated can long endure. We are met on a great battlefield of that war. We have come to dedicate a portion of that field as a final resting place for those who here gave their lives so that that nation might live. It is altogether fitting and proper that we should do this. But in a larger sense we cannot dedicate, we cannot consecrate, we cannot hallow this ground. The brave men, living and dead, who struggled here, have consecrated it, far above our

> poor power to add or detract. The world will little note, nor long remember, what we say here, but it can never forget what they did here. It is for us, the living, rather to be dedicated here to the unfinished work which they who fought here have thus far so nobly advanced. It is rather for us to be here dedicated to the great task remaining before us, that from these honoured dead we take increased devotion to that cause for which they gave the last full measure of devotion; that we here highly resolve that these dead shall not have died in vain; that this nation, under God, shall have a new birth of freedom; and that government of the people, by the people, for the people, shall not perish from the earth.

It is commonly supposed that Lincoln originated the immortal phrase which closed this address; but did he? Herndon, his law partner, had given Lincoln, several years previously, a copy of Theodore Parker's addresses. Lincoln read and underscored in this book the words "Democracy is direct self-government, over all the people, by all the people, and for all the people". Theodore Parker may have borrowed his phraseology from Webster who had said, four years earlier, in his famous reply to Hayne: "The people's government, made for the people, made by the people, and answerable to the people." Webster may have borrowed his phraseology from President James Monroe who had given voice to the same idea a third of a century earlier. And to whom was James Monroe indebted? Five hundred years before Monroe was born, Wyclif had said, in the preface to the translation of the Scriptures, that "this Bible is for the government of the people, by the people, and for the people".

And long before Wycliffe lived, more than 400 years before the birth of Christ, Cleon, in an address to the men of Athens, spoke of a ruler "of the people, by the people, and for the people". And from what ancient source Cleon drew his inspiration, is a matter lost in the fog and night of antiquity.

How little there is that is new! How much even the great speakers owe to their reading and to their association with books!

Books! There is the secret! He who would enrich and enlarge his stock of words must soak and tan his mind constantly in the vats of literature. "The only lamentation that I always feel in the presence of a library", said John Bright, "is that life is too short and I have no hope of a full enjoyment of the ample repast spread before me". Bright left school at fifteen, and went to work in a cotton mill, and he never had the chance of schooling again. Yet he became one of the most brilliant speakers of the generation, famous for his superb command of the English language. He read and studied and copied in notebooks and committed to memory long passages from the poetry of Byron and Milton, and Wordsworth, and Shakespeare and Shelley. He went through *Paradise Lost* each year to enrich his stock of words.

Charles James Fox read Shakespeare aloud to improve his style. Gladstone called his study a "Temple of Peace", and in it he kept 15,000 books. He was helped most, he confessed, by reading the works of St. Augustine, Bishop Butler, Dante, Aristotle, and Homer. *The Iliad* and *The Odyssey* enthralled him. He wrote six books on Homeric poetry and Homeric times.

The younger Pitt's practice was to look over a page or two of Greek or Latin and then to translate the passage into his own language. He did this daily for ten years, and "he acquired an almost unrivalled power of putting his thoughts, without pre-meditation, into words well selected and well arranged."

Demosthenes copied Thucydides' history eight times in his own handwriting in order that he might acquire the majestic and impressive phraseology of that famous historian. The result? Two thousand years later, in order to improve his style, Woodrow Wilson studied the works of Demosthenes. Mr. Asquith found his best training in reading the works of Bishop Berkeley,

Tennyson studied the Bible daily. Tolstoy read and reread the Gospels until he knew long passages by memory. Ruskin's mother forced him by steady, daily toil to memorize long chapters of the Bible and to read the entire Book through aloud each year, "every syllable, hard names and all, from Genesis to the Apocalypse." To that discipline and study Ruskin attributed his taste and style in literature.

R.L.S. are said to be the best-loved initials in the English language. Robert Louis Stevenson was essentially a writer's writer. How did he develop the charming style that made him famous? Fortunately, he has told us the story himself.

> Whenever I read a book or a passage that particularly pleased me, in which a thing was said or an effect rendered with propriety, in which there was either some conspicuous force or some happy distinction in the style, I must sit down at once and set myself to ape that quality. I was unsuccessful, and I knew it; and tried again, and was again unsuccessful, and always unsuccessful; but at least in these vain bouts I got some practice in rhythm, in harmony, in construction, and coordination of parts.

> I have thus played the sedulous ape to Hazlitt, to Lamb, to Wordsworth, to Sir Thomas Browne, to Defoe, to Hawthorne, to Montaigne.
>
> That, like it or not, is the way to learn to write; whether I have profited or not, that is the way. It was the way Keats learned, and there never was a finer temperament for literature than Keats'.
>
> It is the great point of these imitations that there still shines beyond the student's reach, his inimitable model. Let him try as he please, he is still sure of failure; and it is an old and very true saying that failure is the only high road to success.

Enough of names and specific stories. The secret is out. Lincoln wrote it to a young man eager to become a successful lawyer: "It is only to get the books and to read and study them carefully. Work, work, work is the main thing."

What books? Begin with Arnold Bennett's *How to Live on Twenty-four Hours a Day*. This book will be as stimulating as a cold bath. It will tell you a lot about that most interesting of all subjects—yourself. It will reveal to you how much time you are wasting each day, how to stop the wastage, and how to utilize what you salvage. The entire book has only 103 pages. You can get through it easily in a week. Tear out twenty pages each morning, put them in your hip pocket. Then offer up upon the altar of the morning newspaper only ten minutes instead of the customary twenty or thirty minutes.

"I have given up newspapers in exchange for Tacitus and Thucydides, for Newton and Euclid," wrote Thomas Jefferson, "and I find myself much the happier." Don't you believe that you, by following Jefferson's example at least to the extent of cutting your newspaper reading in half, would find yourself happier and wiser as the weeks go by? Aren't you, at any rate, willing to try it for a month, and to devote the time you have thus salvaged to the more enduring value of a good book? Why not read the pages you are to carry with you while waiting for lifts, for buses, for food, for appointments?

After you have read those twenty pages, replace them in the book, tear out another twenty. When you have consumed them all, put a rubber band around the covers to hold the loose pages in place. Isn't it better far to have a book butchered and mutilated in that fashion, with its message in your head, than to have it reposing unbruised and unread upon the shelves of your library?

After you have finished *How to Live on Twenty-four Hours a Day,* you may be interested in another book by the same author. Try *The Human Machine.* This book will enable you to handle people more tactfully. It will develop your poise and self-possession. These books are recommended here not only for what they say, but for the way they say it, for the enriching and refining effect they are sure to have upon your vocabulary.

Some other books that will be helpful are suggested: *The Octopus* and *The Pit* by Frank Norris are two of the best American novels ever written. The first deals with turmoils and human tragedies occurring in the wheat fields of California; the second portrays the battles of the bears and bulls on the Chicago Board of Trade. *Tess of the D' Urbervilles* by Thomas Hardy is one of the most beautiful tales ever written. *A Man's Value to Society* by Newell Dwight Hillis and Professor William James' *Talks to Teachers* are two books well worth reading. *Ariel, A Life of Shelley,* by Andre Maurois, Byron's *Childe Harolds Pilgrimage* and Robert Louis Stevenson s *Travels with a Donkey* should also be on your list.

Make Ralph Waldo Emerson your daily companion. Command him to give you first his famous essay on Self-Reliance. Let him whisper into your ear marching sentences like these:

> Speak your latent conviction, and it shall be the universal sense; for always the inmost becomes the outmost—and our first thought is rendered back to us by the trumpets of the Last Judgment. Familiar as the voice of the mind is to each, the highest merit we ascribe to Moses, Plato, and Milton, is that they set at naught books and traditions, and spoke not what men said but what they thought. A man should learn to detect and watch that gleam of light which flashes across his mind from within, more than the lustre of the firmament of bards and sages. Yet he dismisses without notice his thought, because it is his. In every work of genius we recognize our own rejected thoughts: they come back to us with a certain alienated majesty. Great works of art have no more affecting lesson for us than this. They teach us to abide by our spontaneous impression with good-humoured inflexibility then most when the whole cry of voice is on the other side. Else, tomorrow a stranger will say with masterly good sense precisely what we have thought and felt all the time, and we shall be forced to take with shame our own opinion from another.
>
> There is a time in every man's education when he arrives at the conviction that envy is ignorance; that imitation is suicide; that he must take himself for better, for worse, as his portion; that though the

> wide universe is full of good, no kernel of nourishing corn can come to him but through his toil bestowed on that plot of ground which is given to him to till. The power which resides in him is new in nature, and none but he knows what that is which he can do, nor does he know until he has tried.

But we have really left the best authors to the last. What are they? When Sir Henry Irving was asked to furnish a list of what he regarded as the hundred best books, he replied: "Before a hundred books, commend me to the study of two—the Bible and Shakespeare." Sir Henry was right. Drink from these two great fountain sources of English literature. Drink long and often. Toss your evening newspaper aside and say, "Shakespeare, come here and talk to me tonight of Romeo and his Juliet, of Macbeth and his ambition."

If you do these things, what will be your reward? Gradually, unconsciously but inevitably, your diction will begin to take on added beauty and refinement. Gradually, you will begin to reflect somewhat the glory and beauty and majesty of your companions. "Tell me what you read," observed Goethe, "and I will tell you what you are." This reading programme that I have suggested will require little but willpower, little but a more careful husbanding of time.... You can purchase pocket copies of Emerson's essays and Shakespeare's plays for a few pence each.

THE SECRET OF MARK TWAIN'S WAY WITH WORDS

How did Mark Twain develop his delightful facility with words? As a young man, he travelled all the way from Missouri to Nevada by the ponderously slow and really painful stage coach. Food—and sometimes even water—had to be carried for both passengers and horses. Extra weight might have meant the difference between safety and disaster; baggage was charged for by the ounce, and yet Mark Twain carried with him a Webster's Unabridged Dictionary over mountain passes, across scorched deserts, and through a land infested with bandits and Indians. He wanted to make himself master of words, and with his characteristic courage and common sense, he set about doing the things necessary to bring that mastery about.

Both William Pitt and his father, Lord Chatham, studied the dictionary twice, every page, every word of it. Browning pored over it daily, finding in it entertainment as well as instruction. Lincoln "would sit in the twilight", records his biographers, Nicolay and Hay, "and read a dictionary as long as he could see". These are not exceptional instances. Every writer and speaker of distinction has done the same.

Woodrow Wilson was superbly skilful with the English language. Some of his writings—parts of his Declaration of War against Germany—will undoubtedly take a place in literature. Here is his own story of how he learned to marshal words:

> My father never allowed any member of his household to use an incorrect expression. Any slip on the part of one of the children was at once corrected; any unfamiliar word was immediately explained; each of us was encouraged to find a use for it in our conversation so as to fix it in our memories.

A speaker who is often complimented upon the firm texture of his sentences and the simple beauty of his language, during the course of a conversation recently, lifted the embargo on the secret of his power to choose true and incisive words. Each time he discovers an unfamiliar word in conversation or reading matter, he notes it in his memorandum book. Then, just prior to retiring at night, he consults his dictionary and makes the word his own. If he has gathered no material in this fashion during the day, he studies a page or two of Fernald's *Synonyms, Antonyms and Prepositions,* noting the exact meaning of the words which he would ordinarily interchange as perfect synonyms. A new word a day—that is his motto. This means in the course of a year three hundred and sixty-five additional tools for expression. These new words are stored away in a small pocket notebook, and their meanings reviewed at odd moments during the day. He has found that a word becomes a permanent acquisition to his vocabulary when he has used it three times.

ROMANTIC STORIES BEHIND THE WORDS YOU USE

Use a dictionary not only to ascertain the meaning of the word, but also to find its derivation. Its history, its origin is usually set down in brackets after the definition. Do not imagine for a moment that the words you speak each day are only dull, listless sounds. They are reeking with colour, they are alive with romance. You cannot, for example, say so prosaic a thing as, "Telephone the grocer for sugar", without using words that we have borrowed from many different languages and civilizations. *Telephone* is made from two Greek words, *tele,* meaning far, and *phone,* meaning sound. *Grocer* comes from an old French word, *grossier,* and the French came from the Latin, *grossarius;* it literally means one who sells by the wholesale or gross. We got our word *sugar* from the French; the French borrowed it from the Spanish;

the Spanish lifted it from the Arabic; the Arabic took it from the Persian; and the Persian word *shaker* was derived from the Sanskrit *carkara,* meaning candy.

You may work for or own a *company*. *Company* is derived from an old French word meaning *companion*; and *companion* is literally *com,* with, and *panis,* bread. Your *companion* is one with whom you have bread. A *company* is really an association of people who are trying to make their bread together. Your *salary* literally means your *salt* money. The Roman soldiers drew a certain allowance for salt, and one day some wag spoke of his entire income as his *salarium,* and created a bit of slang which has long since become respectable English. You are holding in your hand a *book*. It literally means *beech,* for a long time ago the Anglo-Saxons scratched their words on *beech* trees and on tablets of *beech* wood. A *dollar* literally means *valley*. *Dollars* were first coined in St. Joachim's *Thaler* or *dale* or *valley* in the sixteenth century.

The words *janitor* and *January* have both come down from the name of an Etruscan blacksmith who lived in Rome and made a specialty of locks and bolts for doors. When he died, he was deified as a pagan god, and was represented as having two faces, so that he could look both ways at the same time, and was associated with the opening and closing of doors. So the month that stood at the close of one year and the opening of another was called *January,* or the month of *Janus*. So when we talk of *January* or a *janitor,* a keeper of doors, we are honouring the name of a blacksmith who lived a thousand years before the birth of Christ and who had a wife by the name of Jane.

The seventh month, *July,* was named after Julius Caesar; so the Emperor Augustus, not to be outdone, called the next month *August*. But the eighth month had only thirty days at that time, and Augustus did not propose to have the month named after him any shorter than a month named after Julius; so he took one day away from February and added it to August, and the marks of this vainglorious theft are evident on the calendar hanging in your home today. Truly, you will find the history of words fascinating.

Please look up in a large dictionary the derivation of these words: atlas, boycott, cereal, colossal, concord, curfew, education, finance, lunatic, panic, palace, pecuniary, sandwich, tantalize. Get the stories behind them. It will make them doubly colourful, doubly interesting. You will use them, then, with added zest and pleasure.

REWRITING ONE SENTENCE A HUNDRED AND FOUR TIMES

Strive to say precisely what you mean, to express the most delicate nuances of thought. That is not always easy—not even for experienced writers. Fanny Hurst told me that she sometimes rewrote her sentences from fifty to a hundred times. Only a few days prior to the conversation she said she had rewritten one sentence one hundred and four times by actual count. Yet she was so accomplished a writer that the magazines were paying her four hundred pounds a story. Mabel Herbert Urner confided to me that she sometimes spent an entire afternoon eliminating only one or two sentences from a short story that was to be syndicated through the newspapers.

Gouverneur Morris has told how Richard Harding Davis laboured incessantly for just the right word:

> Every phrase in his fiction was, of all the myriad phrases he could think of, the fittest in his relentless

> judgment to survive. Phrases, paragraphs, pages, whole stories even, were written over and over again. He worked upon a principle of elimination. If he wished to describe an automobile turning in at a gate, he made first a long and elaborate description from which there was omitted no detail, which the most observant pair of eyes in Christendom has ever noted with reference to just such a turning. Thereupon he would begin a process of omitting one by one those details which he had been at such pains to recall; and after each omission he would ask himself, 'Does the picture remain?' If it did not, he restored the detail which he had just omitted, and experimented with the sacrifice of some other, and so on, and so on, until after Herculean labour there remained for the reader one of those swiftly flashed ice-clear pictures (complete in every detail) with which his tales and romances are so delightfully and continuously adorned.

Most students of this course have neither time nor disposition to search as diligently for words as the author just described. These instances are cited to show you the importance successful writers attach to proper diction and expression, in the hope that it may encourage students to take an increased interest in the use of English. It is, of course, not practical for a speaker to hesitate in a sentence and *tih-uh* about, hunting for the word which will exactly express the shade of meaning he desires to convey, but he should practice preciseness of expression in his daily intercourse until it comes unconsciously. He should, but does he? He does not.

Milton is reported to have employed eight thousand words, and Shakespeare fifteen thousand. A standard dictionary contains fifty thousand less than half a million; but the average man, according to popular estimates, gets along with approximately two thousand. He has some verbs, enough connectives to stick them together, a handful of nouns, and a few overworked adjectives. He is too lazy, mentally, or too absorbed in business, to train for precision and exactness. The result? Let me give you an illustration. I once spent a few unforgettable days on the rim of the Grand Canyon of Colorado. In the course of an afternoon, I heard a lady apply the same adjective to a Chow dog, an orchestral selection, a man's disposition, and the Grand Canyon itself. They were all "beautiful".

What should she have said? Here are the synonyms that Roget lists for *beautiful*. Which adjectives do you think she should have employed?

Adjective: *beautiful*, beauteous, handsome, pretty, lovely, graceful, elegant, exquisite, delicate, dainty.

Comely, fair, goodly, bonny good-looking, well- favoured, well-informed, well-proportioned, shapely, symmetrical, harmonious.

Bright, bright-eyed, rosy-cheeked, rosy, ruddy, blooming, in full bloom.

Trim, trig, tidy, neat, spruce, smart, jaunty, dapper. *Brilliant*, shining, sparkling, radiant, splendid, resplendent, dazzling, glowing, glossy, sleek, rich, gorgeous, superb, magnificent, grand, fine.

Artistic, aesthetic, picturesque, pictorial, enchanting, attractive, becoming, ornamental.

Perfect, unspotted, spotless, immaculate, undeformed, undefaced.

Passable, presentable, tolerable, not amiss

The synonyms just quoted have been taken from Roget's *Treasury of Words.* It is an abridged edition of Roger's *Thesaurus.* What a help this book is! Personally, I never write without having it at my elbow. I find occasion to use it ten times as often as I use the dictionary.

What years of toil Roget consecrated to its making; yet it will come and sit on your desk and serve you a lifetime for the price of an inexpensive necktie. It is not a book to be stored away on a library shelf. It is a tool to be used constantly. Use it when writing out and polishing the diction of your talks. Use it in dictating your letters and your business reports. Use it daily, and it will double and treble your power with words.

SHUN WORN-OUT PHRASES

Strive not only to be exact, but to be fresh and original. Have the courage to say the thing as you see it, for "the God of things as they are". For example, shortly after the flood, some original mind first used the comparison, "cool as a cucumber". It was extraordinarily good then because it was extraordinarily fresh. Even as late as Belshazzar's famous feast, it may still have retained enough of its pristine vigour to warrant its use in an after-dinner speech. But what man who prides himself on his originality would be guilty of repeating it at this somewhat late date?

Here are a dozen similes to express coldness. Aren't they just as effective as the hackneyed "cucumber" comparison, and far fresher and more acceptable?

Cold as a frog.

Cold as a hot-water bag in the morning.

Cold as a ramrod.

Cold as a tomb.

Cold as Greenland's icy mountains.

Cold as clay—*Coleridge*

Cold as a turtle—Richard Cumberland

Cauld as the drifting snow—*Allan Cunningham*

Cold as salt—-James Huneker

Cold as an earthworm—*Maurice Maeterlinck*

Cold as dawn.

Cold as rain in autumn.

While the mood is upon you, think now of similes of your own to convey the idea of coldness. Have the courage to be distinctive. Write them here:

Cold as ....

Cold as ....

Cold as ....

Cold as ....

Cold as ....

I once asked Kathleen Norris, who is reputed to be the highest paid writer of magazine serial fiction, how style could be developed. "By reading classics of prose and poetry," she replied, "and by critically eliminating stock phrases, and hackneyed expressions from your work."

A magazine editor once told me that when he found two or three hackneyed expressions in a story submitted for publication, he returned it to the author without wasting time reading it; for, he added, one who has no originality of expression will exhibit little originality of thought.

Ten people tuho speak make more noise than ten thousand who are silent.

—Napoleon Bonaparte

~

Soak yourself fill of the world's best literature so that you will have words, strong words, clear words, for your speaking.

—Dr. Lynn Harold Hough

12

How To Interest Your Audience

I believe in anything that will engage the audience and make the story more effective.

—J.J. Abrams

If you were invited to dine at the home of a rich man in certain sections of China, it would be proper to toss chicken bones and olive seeds over your shoulder on to the floor. You pay your host a compliment when you do that. You show that you realize that he is wealthy, that he has plenty of servants to tidy up after the meal. And he likes it.

You can be reckless with the remains of your sumptuous meal in a rich man's home, but in some parts of China the poorer people must save even the water they bathe in. To heat water costs so much that they must buy it at a hot-water shop. After they have bathed in it, they can take it back and sell it secondhand to the shopkeeper from whom they purchased it. When the second customer has soiled it, the water still retains a market value, although the price has softened a bit.

Have you found these facts about Chinese life interesting? If so, do you know why? Because those are very unusual aspects of very usual things. They are strange truths about such commonplace events as dining out and bathing.

That is what interests us—something new about the old.

Let us take another illustration. This page you are reading now, this sheet of paper you are looking at—it is very ordinary, isn't it? You have seen countless thousands of such pages. It seems dull and insipid now; but if I tell you a strange fact about it, you are almost sure to be interested. Let us see! This page seems like solid matter as you look at it now. But, in reality, it is more like a cobweb than solid matter. The physicist knows it is composed of atoms. And how small is an atom? There are as many atoms in one drop of water as there are drops of water in the Mediterranean Sea, that there are as many atoms in one drop of water as there are blades of grass in all the world. And the atoms that make this paper are composed of what? Still smaller things called electrons and protons. These electrons are all rotating around the central proton of the atom, as far from it, relatively speaking, as the moon is from the earth. And they are swinging through their orbits, these electrons of this tiny universe, at the inconceivable speed ot approximately ten thousand miles a second. So the electrons that compose this sheet of paper you are holding have moved since you began reading this very sentence, a distance equal to that which stretches between New York and Tokyo...

And only two minutes ago you may have thought this piece of paper was still and dull and dead; but, in reality, it is one of God's mysteries. It is a veritable cyclone of energy.

If you are interested in it now, it is because you have learned a new and strange fact about it. There lies one of the secrets of interesting people. That is a significant truth, one that we ought to profit by in our every day intercourse.

The entirely new is not interesting; the entirely old has no attractiveness for us. We want to be told something new about the old. You cannot, for example, interest a farmer with a description of the Cathedral at Bourges, or the Mona Lisa. They are too new to him. There is no tie-up to his old interests. But you can interest him by relating the fact that farmers in Holland till land below the level of the sea and dig ditches to act as fences and build bridges to serve as gates. Your farmer will listen open-mouthed while you tell him that Dutch farmers keep the cows, during the winter, under the same roof that houses the family, and sometimes the cows look out through lace curtains at driving snows. He knows about cows and fences—new slants, you see, on old things. "Lace curtains! For a cow!" he'll exclaim. "I'll be jiggered!" And he will retail that story to his friends.

Here is a talk delivered by a student of this course. As you read it, see if it interests you. If it does, do you know why?

HOW SULPHURIC ACID AFFECTS YOU

> Most liquids are measured by the pint, quart, gallon or barrel. We ordinarily speak of quarts of wine, gallons of milk, and barrels of molasses. When a new oil gusher is discovered, we speak of its output as so many barrels per day. There is one liquid, however, that is manufactured and consumed in such large quantities that the unit of measurement employed is the ton. This liquid is sulphuric acid.
>
> It touches you in your daily life in a score of ways. If it were not for sulphuric acid, your car would stop, and you would go back to "old Dobbin" and the buggy, for it is used extensively in the refining of parafine and petrol. The electric lights that illuminate your office,

that shine upon your dinner table, that show you the way to bed at night, would not be possible without it.

When you get up in the morning and turn on the water for your bath, you use a nickel-plated tap, which requires sulphuric acid in its manufacture. It was required also in the finishing of your enamelled tub. The soap you use has possibly been made from greases or oils that have been treated with the acid... Your towel has made its acquaintance before you made the acquaintance of your towel. The bristles in your hairbrush have required it, and your celluloid comb could not have been produced without it. Your razor, no doubt, has been pickled in it after annealing.

You put on your underwear; you button up your outer garments. The bleacher, the manufacturer of dyes and the dyer himself used it. The button-maker possibly found the acid necessary to complete your buttons. The tanner used sulphuric acid in making the leather for your shoes, and it serves us again when we wish to polish them.

You come down to breakfast. The cup and saucer, if they be other than plain white, could not have come into being without it. It is used to produce the gilt and other ornamental colourings. Your spoon, knife and fork have seen a bath of sulphuric acid, if they be silver-plated.

The wheat of which your bread or rolls are made has possibly been grown by the use of a phosphate fertilizer, whose manufacture rests upon this acid.

And so on through the whole day, its work affects you at every turn. Go where you will, you cannot escape its influence. We can neither go to

> war without it nor live in peace without it. So it hardly seems possible that this acid, so essential to mankind, should be totally unfamiliar to the average man... But such is the case.

THE THREE MOST INTERESTING THINGS IN THE WORLD

What would you say they are—the three most interesting subjects in the world? Sex, property and religion. By the first we can create life, by the second we maintain it, by the third we hope to continue it in the world to come.

But it is *our* sex, *our* property, *our* religion that interests us. Our interests swarm about our own egos.

We are not interested in a talk on How to Make Wills in Peru; but we may be interested in a talk entitled "How to Make Our Wills". We are not interested—except, perhaps, out of curiosity—in the religion of the Hindoo; but we are vitally interested in a religion that insures *us* unending happiness in the world to come.

When the late Lord Northcliffe was asked what interests people, he answered with one word—and that word was "themselves". Northcliffe ought to have known for he was the wealthiest newspaper owner in Great Britain.

Do you want to know what kind of person you are? Ah, now we are on an interesting topic. We are talking about *you*. Here is a way for *you* to hold the mirror up to your real self, and see *you* as *you* really are. Watch your reveries. What do we mean by reveries? Let Professor James Harvey Robinson answer. We are quoting from *The Mind in the Making*.

> We all appear to ourselves to be thinking all the time during our waking hours, and most of us are aware

> that we go on thinking while we are asleep, even more foolishly than when awake. When uninterrupted by some practical issue we are engaged in what is known as a *reverie*. This is our spontaneous and favourite kind of thinking. We allow our ideas to take their own course and this course is determined by our hopes and tears, our spontaneous desires, their fulfilment or frustration, by our likes and dislikes, our loves and hates and resentments. *There is nothing else anything like so interesting to ourselves as ourselves.* All thought that is not more or less laboriously controlled and directed will inevitably circle about the beloved ego. It is amusing and pathetic to observe this tendency in ourselves and in others. We learn politely and generously to overlook this truth, but if we dare to think of it, it blazes forth like the noontide sun.
>
> Our reveries form the chief index of our fundamental character. They are a reflection of our nature as modified by often hidden and forgotten experiences...The reverie doubtless influences all our speculations in its persistent tendency to self-magnification and self-justification, which are its chief preoccupations.

So remember that the people you are to talk to spend most of their time when they are not concerned with the problems of business, in thinking about and justifying and glorifying themselves. Remember that the average man will be more concerned about the cook leaving than about Italy paying her debts. He will be more wrought up over a dull razor blade than over a revolution in South America. His own toothache will distress him more than an earthquake in

Asia destroying half a million lives. He would rather listen to you say some nice thing about him than hear you discuss the ten greatest men in history.

HOW TO BE A GOOD CONVERSATIONALIST

The reason so many people are poor conversationalists is because they talk about only the things that interests them. That may be deadly boring to others. Reverse the process. Lead the other person into calking about *his* interests, *his* business, *his* golf score, *his* success—or, if it is a mother, *her* children. Do that and listen intently and you will give pleasure; consequently you will be considered a good conversationalist—even though you have done very little of the talking.

Mr. Harold Dwight recently made an extraordinarily successful speech at a banquet which marked the final session of a public speaking course. He talked about each man in turn around the entire table, told how he had talked when the course started, how he had improved; recalled the talks various members had made, the subjects they had discussed; he mimicked some of them, exaggerated their peculiarities, had everyone laughing, had everyone pleased. With such material, he could not possibly have failed. It was absolutely ideal. No other topic under the blue dome of Heaven would have so interested that group. Mr. Dwight knew how to handle human nature.

AN IDEA THAT WON TWO MILLION READERS

A few years ago, the *American Magazine* enjoyed an amazing growth. Its sudden leap in circulation became one of the sensations of the publishing world. The secret? The secret was the late John M. Siddall and his ideas. When I first met Siddall he had charge of the Interesting People Department of that periodical. I had written a few articles for him; and one day he sat down and talked to me for a long time.

"People are selfish," he said. "They are interested chiefly in themselves. They are not very much concerned about whether the government should own the railroads; but they do want to know how to get ahead, how to draw more salary, how to keep healthy. If I were editor of this magazine," he went on,

> I would tell them how to take care of their teeth, how to take baths, how to keep cool in summer, how to get a position, how to handle employees, how to buy homes, how to remember, how to avoid grammatical errors, and so on. People are always interested in human stories, so I would have some rich man tell how he made a million. I would get prominent bankers and presidents of various corporations to tell the stories of how they battled their ways up from the ranks to power and wealth.

Shortly after that, Siddall was made editor. The magazine then had a small circulation, and was comparatively a failure. Siddall did just what he said he would do. The response? It was overwhelming. The circulation figures climbed up to two hundred thousand, three, four, half a million Here was something the public wanted. Soon a million people a month were buying it, then a million and a half, finally two millions. It did not stop there, but continued to grow for many years. Siddall appealed to the selfish interests of his readers.

HOW DR. CONWELL INTERESTED MILLIONS OF HEARERS

What was the secret of the world's most popular lecture, "Acres of Diamonds"? Just the thing we have been talking about.

John M. Siddall discussed this lecture in the conversation I have just referred to, and I think its enormous success had something to do with determining the policy of his magazine.

It tells people how they can get ahead, how they can make more out of themselves in their present environment.

It was never a static lecture. Dr. Conwell made it personal to each town where he spoke. That was of immense importance. The local references made it appear fresh and new. They made that town, that audience, seem important. Here is his own story of how he did it:

> I visit a town or city, and try to arrive there early enough to see the postmaster, the barber, the keeper of the hotel, the principal of the schools, and the ministers of some of the churches, and then go into some of the factories and stores, and talk with the people, and get into sympathy with the local conditions of that town or city and see what has been their history, what opportunities they had, and what they had failed to do—and every town fails to do something—and then go to the lecture and talk to those people about the subjects which apply to their locality. Acres of Diamonds—the idea—has continuously been precisely the same. The idea is that in this country, every man has the opportunity to make more of himself than he does in his own environment, with his own skill, with his own energy, and with his own friends.

THE KIND OF SPEECH MATERIAL THAT ALWAYS HOLDS ATTENTION

You may possibly bore people if you talk about things and ideas, but you can hardly fail to hold their attention when you talk about people. Tomorrow there will be millions of conversations floating over fences in the backyards, over tea tables and dinner tables—and what will be the predominating note in most of them? Personalities. He said this. Mrs. So-and-so did that. I saw her doing this, that and the other. He is making a fortune, and so on.

I have addressed many gatherings of school children, and I soon learned by experience that in order to keep them interested I had to tell them stories about people. As soon as I became general and dealt with abstract ideas, Johnny became restless and wriggled in his seat, Tommy made a face at someone, Billy threw something across the aisle.

True, these were audiences of children; but the intelligence tests used in the army during the last war revealed the startling fact that 49 per cent of the people in the United States have a mental age of about thirteen. So one can hardly go wrong in making a generous use of human interest stories. Our magazines that are read by millions are filled with them.

I once asked a group of businessmen in Paris to talk on How to Succeed. Most of them praised the homely virtues, preached at, lectured to, and bored their hearers. (Incidentally, I recently heard one of the most prominent businessmen make this identical mistake in a radio talk on this identical topic.)

So I halted this class, and said something like this:

> We don't want to be lectured to. No one enjoys that. Remember you must be entertaining or we will pay no attention whatever to what you are saying. Also remember that one of the most interesting things in the world is sublimated, glorified gossip. So tell us the stories of two men you have known. Tell

why one succeeded and why the other failed. We will gladly listen to that, remember it and possibly profit by it. It will also, by the way, be far easier for you to deliver than are these wordy, abstract preachments.

There was a certain member of that course who invariably found it difficult to interest either himself or his audience. This night, however, he seized the human story suggestion, and told us of two of his classmates in college. One of them had been so conservative that he had bought shirts at the different stores in town, and made charts showing which ones laundered best, wore longest and gave the most service for the money invested. His mind was always on pennies; yet, when he graduated—from an engineering college—he had such a high opinion of his own importance that he was not willing to begin at the bottom and work his way up, as the other graduates were doing. Even when the third annual reunion of the class came, he was still making laundry charts of his shirts, while waiting for some extraordinarily good thing to come his way. It never came. A quarter of a century has passed since then, and this man, dissatisfied and soured, still bolds a minor position.

The speaker then contrasted with this failure the story of one of his classmates who had surpassed all expectations. This particular chap was a good mixer. Everyone liked him. Although he was ambitious to do big things later, he started as a draughtsman. But he was always on the lookout for opportunity. Plans were then being made for an exposition. He knew engineering talent would be needed there, so he resigned from his position and moved to the town of the exhibition. Through his agreeable personality, he soon won the friendship of a man with considerable influence. The two formed a partnership, and engaged immediately in the contracting business. They did considerable work for the telephone company, and this man was finally taken over by that concern at a large salary. Today he is a multimillionaire, one of the principal owners of Western Union.

We have recorded here only the bare outline of what the speaker told. He made his talk interesting and illuminating with a score of amusing and human details. He talked on and on—this man who could not ordinarily find material for a three minute speech—and he was surprised beyond words to learn when he stopped that he had held the floor on this occasion for half an hour. The speech had been so interesting that it seemed short to everyone. It was this student's first real triumph.

Almost every student can profit by this incident. The average speech would be far more appealing if it were rich and replete with human interest stories. The speaker ought to attempt to make only a few points and to illustrate them with concrete cases. Such a method of speech building can hardly fail to get and hold attention.

If possible, these stories ought to tell of struggles, of things fought for and victories won. All of us are tremendously interested in fights and combats. There is an old saying that all the world loves a lover. It doesn't. What all the world loves is a scrap. It wants to see two lovers struggling for the hand of one woman. As an illustration of this fact, read almost any novel, magazine story, or go to see almost any film drama. When all the obstacles are removed and the reputed hero rakes the so-called heroine in his arms, the audience begins reaching for their hats and coats. Five minutes later the sweeping women are gossiping over their broom handles.

Almost all magazine fiction is based on this formula. Make the reader like the hero or heroine. Make him or her long for something intensely. Make that something seem impossible to get. Show how the hero or heroine fights and gets it.

The story of how a man battled in business or profession against discouraging odds and won is always inspiring, always interesting. A magazine editor once told me that the real, inside story of any person's life is entertaining. If one has struggled and fought—and who hasn't—his story, if correctly told, will appeal. There can be no doubt of that.

BE CONCRETE

The writer once had in the same course in public speaking, a Doctor of Philosophy and a rough-and-ready fellow who had spent his youth thirty years ago in the British Navy. The polished scholar was a university professor; his classmate from the seven seas was the proprietor of a small side street moving-van establishment. Strange to say, the moving-van man's talks during the course would have held a popular audience far better than the talks of the college professor. Why? The college man spoke in beautiful English, with a demeanor of culture and refinement, and with logic and clearness; but his talks lacked one essential, *concreteness*. They were too vague, too general. On the other hand, the van owner possessed hardly enough power of cerebration to generalize. When he talked he got right down to business immediately. He was definite; he was concrete. That quality, coupled with his virility and his fresh phraseology, made his talks very entertaining.

I have cited this instance, not because it is typical either of college men or moving-van proprietors, but because it illustrates the interest-getting power that accrues to the man—regardless of education—who has the happy habit of being concrete and definite in his speaking.

This principle is so important that we are going to use several illustrations to try to lodge it firmly in your mind. We hope you will never forget it, never neglect it.

Is it, for example, more interesting to state that Martin Luther, as a boy, was "stubborn and intractable", or is it better to say that he confessed that his teachers had flogged him as olten as "fifteen times in a forenoon"?

Words like "stubborn and intractable" have very little attention value. But isn't it easy to listen to the flogging count?

The old method of writing a biography was to deal in a lot of generalities which Aristotle called, and rightly called, "The refuge of weak minds." The new method is to deal with concrete facts that speak for themselves. The old-fashioned biographer said that John Doe was born of "poor but honest parents". The new method would say that John Doe's father couldn't afford a pair of overshoes, so when the snow came, he had to tie gunny sacking around his shoes to keep his feet dry and warm; but, in spite of his poverty, he never watered the milk and he never traded a horse with the heaves as a sound animal. That shows that his parents were "poor but honest", doesn't it? And doesn't it do it in a way that is far more interesting than the "poor but honest" method?

If this method works for modern biographers it will work also for modern speakers.

Let us take one more illustration. Suppose you wished to state that the potential horse power wasted at Niagara every day was appalling. Suppose you said just that, and then added, that if it were utilized and the resulting profits turned to purchasing the necessities of life, crowds could be clothed and fed. Would that be the way to make it interesting and entertaining? No—No. Isn't this far better? We are quoting from Edwin E. Slosson in the *Daily Science News Bulletin*:

> We are told that there are some millions of people in poverty and poorly nourished in this country, yet here at Niagara is wasted the equivalent of 250,000 loaves of bread an hour. We may see with our mind's eye 600,000 nice fresh eggs dropping over the precipice every hour and making a gigantic omelette in the whirlpool. If calico were continuously pouring from the looms in a stream 4,000 feet wide like Niagara River, it would represent the same destruction of property. If a Carnegie Library were held under the spout it would be filled with good books in an hour or two. Or we can imagine a big department store floating down from Lake Erie every day and smashing its varied contents on the rocks 160 feet below. That would be an exceedingly interesting and diverting spectacle, quite as attractive to the crowd as the present, and no more expensive to maintain. Yet some people might object to that on the ground of extravagance who now object to the utilization of the power of the falling water.

PICTURE-BUILDING WORDS

In this process of interest-getting, there is one aid, one technique, that is of the highest importance; yet it is all but ignored. The average speaker does not seem to be aware of its existence. He has probably never consciously thought about it at all. I refer to the process of using words that create pictures. The speaker who is easy to listen to is the one who sets images floating before your eyes. The one who employs foggy, commonplace, colourless symbols sets the audience to nodding.

Pictures. Pictures. Pictures. They are as free as the air you breathe. Sprinkle them through your talks, your conversation, and you will be more entertaining, more influential.

To illustrate, let us take the excerpt just quoted from the *Daily Science Neios Bulletin* regarding Niagara. Look at the picture words. They leap up and go scampering away in every sentence, as thick as rabbits in Australia: "250,000 loaves of bread, 600,000 eggs dropping over the precipice, gigantic omelette in the whirlpool, calico pouring from the looms in a stream 4,000 feet wide, Carnegie library held under the spout, books, a big department store floating, smashing, rocks below, falling water."

It would be almost as difficult to ignore such a talk or article as it would be to pay not the slightest attention to the scenes from a film unwinding on the silver screen of the motion picture theatre.

Picture-building phrases swarm through the pages of the *Bible* and through Shakespeare like bees around a cider mill. For example, a commonplace writer would have said that a certain thing would be superfluous, like trying to improve the perfect. How did Shakespeare express the same thought? With a picture phrase that is immortal: "To gild refined gold, to paint the lily, to throw perfume on the violet."

Did you ever pause to observe that the proverbs that are passed on from generation to generation are almost all visual sayings? "A bird in the hand is worth two in the bush." "It never rains but it pours." "You can lead a horse to water but you can't make him drink," And you will find the same picture element in almost all the similes that have lived for centuries and grown hoary with too much use: "Sly as a fox." "Dead as a door nail." "Flat as a pancake." "Hard as a rock."

Lincoln continually talked in visual terminology. When he became annoyed with the long, complicated, red-tape reports that came to his desk in the White House, he objected to them, not with a colourless phraseology, but with a picture phrase that it is almost impossible to forget. "When I send a man to buy a horse," said he, "I don't want to be told how many hairs the horse has in his tail. I wish only to know his points."

THE INTEREST-GETTING VALUE OF CONTRASTS

Listen to the following condemnation of Charles I by Macaulay.

Note that Macaulay not only uses pictures, but he also employs balanced sentences. Violent contrasts almost always hold our interests; violent contrasts are the very brick and mortar of this paragraph:

> We charge him with having broken his coronation oath, and we are told that he kept his marriage vow! We accuse him of having given up his people to the merciless inflictions of the most hot-headed of prelates, and the defence is that he took his little son on his knee and kissed him! We censure him for having violated the articles of the Petition of Right, after having, for good and valuable consideration, promised to observe them, and we are informed that he was accustomed to hear prayers at six o'clock in the morning! It is to such considerations as these, together with his Vandyke dress, his handsome face

and his peaked beard, that he owes, we verily believe, most of his popularity with the present generation.

INTEREST IS CONTAGIOUS

We have been discussing so far the kind of material that interests an audience. However, one might mechanically follow all the suggestions made here and speak according to Cocker, and yet be vapid and dull. Catching and holding the interest of people is a delicate thing, a matter of feeling and spirit. It is not like operating a steam engine. No book of precise rules can be given for it.

Interest, be it remembered, is contagious. Your hearers are almost sure to catch it if you have a bad case of it yourself. A short time ago, a gentleman rose during a session of this course and warned his audience that if the present methods of catching rock fish were continued, the species would become extinct. And in a very few years! He felt his subject. It was important. He was in real earnest about it. Everything about his matter and manner showed that. When he arose to speak, I did not know that there was such an animal as a rock fish. I imagine that most of the audience shared my lack of knowledge and lack of interest. But before the speaker finished, all of us had caught something of his concern. All of us would probably have been willing to have signed a petition to the legislature to protect the rock fish by law.

I once asked Richard Washburn Child, then American Ambassador to Italy, the secret of his success as an interesting writer. He replied: "I am so excited about life that I cannot keep still. I just have to tell people about it." One cannot keep from being enthralled with a speaker or writer like that.

I recently went to hear a speaker in London: after he was through, one of our party, the late E.F. Benson, a well-known

English novelist, remarked that he enjoyed the last part of the talk far more than the first. When I asked him why, he replied: "The speaker himself seemed more interested in the last part, and I always rely on the speaker to supply the enthusiasm and interest."

Everyone does. Remember that.

Always have something to say. The man who has something to say, and who is known never to speak unless he has, is sure to be listened to.

—Lord Bryce

~

There is in all communication—written or spoken—a certain deadline of interest. If we can cross that deadline, we have the world with us—temporarily at least. If we cannot cross it, we may as well retire. The world will have none of us.

—H.A. Overstreet

~

My ultimate aim would be to captivate an audience, even just for a second.

—Tabrett Bethell

13

Capturing Your Audience At Once

A good teacher; like a good entertainer, first must hold his audiences attention, then he can teach his lesson.

—John Henrik Clarke

Several years ago a fuel and iron company was suffering from labour troubles. Shooting had taken place; there had been bloodshed. The air was electric with bitter hatreds. The very name of Rockefeller was anathema. Yet John D. Rockefeller Jr. wanted to talk to the employees of that concern. He wanted to explain, to persuade them to his way of thinking, to get them to accept his beliefs. He realized that in the very opening of his speech he must eradicate all ill-feeling, all antagonism. At the very outset, he did it beautifully and sincerely. Most public speakers can study his method with profit:

> This is a red-letter day in my life. It is the first time I have ever had the good fortune to meet the representatives of the employees of this great company, its officers and superintendents, together, and I can assure you that I am proud to be here, and

> that I shall remember this gathering for as long as I live. Had this meeting been held two weeks ago, I should have stood here a stranger to most of you, recognizing few faces. Having had the opportunity last week of visiting all the camps in the southern coalfields and of talking individually with practically all of the representatives, except those who were away; having visited in your homes, met many of your wives and children, we meet here not as strangers but as friends, and it is in this spirit of mutual friendship that I am glad to have this opportunity to discuss with you our common interests.
>
> Since this is a meeting of the officers of the company and the representatives of the employees, it is only by your courtesy that I am here, for I am not so fortunate as to be either one or the other; and yet I feel that I am intimately associated with you men, for, in a sense, I represent both the stockholders and the directors.

That is tact—supreme tact. And the speech, in spite of the bitter hatred that had existed, was successful. The men who had been striking and fighting for higher wages never said anything more about it after Rockefeller had explained all the facts in the situation.

A DROP OF HONEY AND TWO GUNMEN

"It is an old and true maxim 'That a drop of honey catches more flies than a gallon of gall.' So with men. If you would win a man to your cause, first convince him that you are his sincere friend. Therein is a drop of honey that catches his heart; which, say what he will, is the great high road to his reason, and when once gained, you will find but little trouble in convincing his judgment of the justice of your cause, if indeed that cause really be a just one."

That was Lincoln's plan. In 1858, during his campaign for the United States Senate, he was announced to speak in what was, at that time, the semi-barbarous part of Southern Illinois called "Egypt". They were a rough lot, the men in that section, and they carried ugly-looking knives and pistols strapped to their belts even on public occasions. Their hatred of all anti-slavery men was equalled only by their love of fighting and whiskey made from Indian corn. Southern men, some of them slave owners from Kentucky and Missouri, had crossed over the Mississippi and the Ohio to be on hand for the excitement and trouble. Plenty of it was in prospect, for the rougher elements had sworn that, if Lincoln tried to talk, they would "run the damned Abolitionist out of town", and "shoot him to fiddle strings".

Lincoln had heard these threats, and he knew the intense feeling that existed, the positive danger. "But if only they will give me a fair chance to say a few opening words," he declared, "I'll fix them all right." So, before beginning to talk, he had himself introduced to the ringleaders, and shook their hands cordially. He made one of the most tactful openings I have ever read:

> Fellow citizens of Southern Illinois, fellow citizens of the State of Kentucky, fellow citizens of Missouri—I am told there are some of you here present who would like to make trouble for me. I don't understand why they should. I am a plain, common man, like the rest of you and why should I not have as good a right to speak my sentiments as the rest of you?

> Why, good friends, I am one of you. I am not an interloper here. I was born in Kentucky, and raised in Illinois, just like most of you, and worked my way along by hard scratching. I know the people of Kentucky, and I know the people of Southern Illinois, and I think I know the Missourins. I am one of them, and therefore ought to know them; and they ought to know me better, and, if they did know me better, they would know that I am not disposed to make them trouble. Then, why should they, or any one of them, want to make trouble for me? Don't do any such foolish thing, fellow citizens. Let us be friends, and treat each other like friends. I am one of the humblest and most peaceful men in the world—would wrong no man, would interfere with no man's rights. And all I ask is that, having something to say, you give me a decent hearing. And, being Illinoisans, Kentuckians, and Missourians—brave and gallant people—I feel sure that you will do that. And now let us reason together, like the honest fellows we are.

As he spoke these words, his face was the very picture of good nature, and his voice vibrated with sympathetic earnestness. That tactful opening calmed the oncoming storm, silenced his enemies. In fact, it transformed many of them into friends. They cheered his speech and, later, those rough and rude "Egyptians" were among his most ardent supporters for the Presidency.

"Interesting," you remark, "but what has all this got to do with me? I am no Rockefeller; I am not going to address hungry strikers longing to strangle and batter the life out of me. I am no Lincoln; I am not going to talk to two gun desperadoes full of corn whiskey and hatred."

True, true, but aren't you, almost every day of your life, talking to people who differ from you on some subject under discussion? Aren't you constantly trying to win people to your way of thinking—at home, in the office, in the market place? Is there room for improvement in your methods? How do you begin? By showing Lincoln's tact? And Rockefeller's? If so, you are a person of rare finesse and extraordinary discretion. Most men begin, not by thinking about the other fellow's views and desires, not by trying to find a common ground of agreement, but by unloading their own opinions.

For example, I have heard hundreds of speeches on the hotly contested subject of prohibition. In almost every instance, the speaker, with all the tact of a bull in a china shop, opened with some positive and perhaps belligerent statement. He showed once and for all which direction he faced and under which flag he fought. He showed that his mind was made up so firmly that there was not the slightest chance of it being changed; yet he was expecting others to abandon their cherished beliefs and to accept his. The effect? About the same that results from all arguments: no one was convinced. Instantly, he lost by his blunt, aggressive opening the sympathetic attention of all who differed with him; instantly, they discounted all he said and would say; instantly, they challenged his statements; instantly, they held his opinions in contempt. His talk served but to entrench them more strongly behind the bulwark of their own beliefs.

You see, he made, at the very outset, the fatal mistake of prodding his listeners, of getting them bending backwards and saying through their shut teeth: "No! No! No!"

Is not that a very serious situation if one wishes to win converts to his way of thinking? A most illuminating statement on this point is the following quotation from Professor Overstreet's lectures before the School for Social Research.

"A 'No' response is a most difficult handicap to overcome. When a person has said 'No', all his pride of personality demands that he remain consistent with himself. He may later feel that the 'No' was ill advised; nevertheless, there is his precious pride to consider! Once having said a thing, he must stick to it. Hence it is of the very greatest importance that we start a person in the affirmative direction...." The skillful speaker gets at the outset a number of "yes-responses". He has thereby set the psychological processes of his listeners moving in the affirmative direction. It is like the movement of a billiard ball. Propel it in one direction, and it takes some force to deflect it; far more force to send it back in the opposite direction.

> The psychological patterns here are quite clear. When a person says "No" and really means it, he is doing far more than saying a word of two letters. His entire organism—glandular, nervous, muscular— gathers itself together into a condition of rejection. There is, usually in minute but sometimes in observable degree, a physical withdrawal, or readiness for withdrawal. The whole neuro-muscular system, in short, sets itself on guard against acceptance. Where, on the contrary, a person says "Yes", none of the withdrawing activities take place. The organism is in a forward-moving, accepting, open attitude. Hence the more "Yeses" we can, at the very outset, induce, the more likely we are to succeed in capturing the attention for our ultimate proposal.

> It is a very simple technique—this yes-response. And yet how much neglected! It often seems as if people get a sense of their own importance by antagonizing at the outset. The radical comes into a conference with his conservative brethren, and immediately he must make them furious! What, as a matter of fact, is the good of it? If he simply does it in order to get some pleasure out of it for himself, he may be pardoned. But if he expects to achieve something, he is only psychologically stupid.
>
> Get a student to say "No" at the beginning, or a customer, child, husband, or wife, and it takes the wisdom and the patience of angels to transform that bristling negative into an affirmative.

How is one going to get these desirable "yes-responses" at the very outset? Fairly simple. "My way of opening and winning an argument," confided Lincoln, "is to first find a common ground of agreement." Lincoln found it even when he was discussing the highly inflammable subject of slavery. "For the first half-hour," declared *The Mirror,* a neutral paper reporting one of his talks, "his opponents would agree with every word he uttered. From that point he began to lead them off, little by little, until it seemed as if he had got them all into his fold."

SENATOR LODGE'S WAY OF DOING IT

Shortly after the close of World War I, the late Senator Lodge and President Lowell of Harvard were scheduled to debate the League of Nations question before a Boston audience. Senator Lodge felt that most of the audience were hostile to his view, yet he must win them to his way of thinking. How? By a direct, frontal, aggressive attack on their convictions? Ah, no. The Senator was far too shrewd a psychologist to bungle his plea with such crude tactics. He began with supreme tact, with admirable finesse. The opening of his speech is quoted in the following paragraph. Note that even his most bitter opponents could not have differed with the sentiments expressed in his first dozen sentences. Note how he appeals to their emotion of patriotism in his salutation: "My Fellow Americans." Observe how he minimizes the differences in the views they are to defend, and how he deftly stresses the things they cherish in common.

See how he praises his opponent, how he insists upon the fact that they differ only on minor details of method, and not at all upon the vital question of the welfare of America and the peace of the world. He even goes further and admits that he is in favour of a League of Nations of some kind. So, in the last analysis, he differed from his opponent only in this: he felt that we ought to have a more ideal and efficacious League.

> Your Excellency, Ladies and Gentlemen, My Fellow Americans:
>
> I am largely indebted to President Lowell for this opportunity to address this great audience. He and I are friends of many years, both Republicans. He is the president of our great university, one of the most important and influential places in the United States. He is also an eminent student and historian of politics and government. He and I may differ as to methods in this great question now before the people, but I am sure that in regard to the security of

> the peace of the world and the welfare of the United States we do not differ in purposes.
>
> "I am going to say a single word, if you will permit me, as to my own position. I have tried to state it over and over again. I thought I had stated it in plain English. But there are those who find in misrepresentation a convenient weapon for controversy, and there are others, most excellent people, who perhaps have not seen what I have said and who possibly have misunderstood me. It has been said that I am against any League of Nations. I am not; far from it. I am anxious to have the nations, the free nations of the world, united in a league, as we call it, a society, as the French call it, but united, to do all that can be done to secure the future peace of the world and to bring about a general disarmament.

No matter how determined you were beforehand to differ with a speaker, an opening like that would make you soften and relent a bit, wouldn't it? Wouldn't it make you willing to listen to more? Wouldn't it tend to convince you of the speaker's fairmindedness?

What would have been the result had Senator Lodge set out immediately to show those who believed in the League of Nations that they were hopelessly in error, cherishing a delusion? The result would have been futile; the following quotation from Professor James Harvey Robinson's enlightening and popular book *The Mind in the Making* shows the psychological reason why such an attack would have been futile;

> We sometimes find ourselves changing our minds without any resistance or heavy emotion, but if we

are told we are wrong we resent the imputation and harden our hearts. We are incredibly heedless in the formation of our beliefs, but find ourselves filled with an illicit passion for them when anyone proposes to rob us of their companionship. It is obviously not the ideas themselves that are dear to us, but our self-esteem which is threatened.... The little word *my* is the most important one in human affairs, and properly to reckon with it is the beginning of wisdom. It has the same force whether it is *my* dinner, *my* dog and *my* house, or *my* faith, *my* country and *my* God. We not only resent the imputation that our watch is wrong, or our car shabby, but that our conception of the canals of Mars, of the pronunciation of 'Epictetus', of the medicinal value of salicine, or of the date of Sargon I, are subject to revision...We like to continue to believe what we have been accustomed to accept as true, and the resentment aroused when doubt is cast upon any of our assumptions leads us to seek every manner of excuse for clinging to it. The result is that most of our so-called reasoning consists in finding arguments for going on believing as we already do.

THE BEST ARGUMENT IS AN EXPLANATION

Is it not quite evident that the speaker who argues with his audience is merely arousing their stubbornness, putting them on the defensive, making it well nigh impossible for them to change their minds? Is it wise to start by saying, "I am going to prove so and so?" Aren't your hearers liable to accept that as a challenge and remark silently, "Let's see you do it."

Is it not much more advantageous to begin by stressing something that you and all of your hearers believe, and then to raise some pertinent question that everyone would like to have answered? Then take your audience with you in an earnest search for the answer. While on that search, present the facts as you see them so clearly that they will unconsciously be, led to accept your conclusions as their own. They will have much more faith in some truth that they believe they have discovered for themselves. "The best argument is that which seems merely an explanation."

In every controversy, no matter how wide and bitter the differences, there is always some common ground of agreement on which the speaker can invite everyone to assemble for the search after facts that he is going to conduct. To illustrate: even if the head of the Communist Party were addressing a convention of the Bankers' Association, he could find some mutual beliefs, some analogous desires to share with his hearers. Couldn't he? Let us see:

> Poverty has always been one of the cruel problems of human society. We have always felt it our duty to alleviate, whenever and wherever possible, the sufferings of the poor. We are a generous nation. No other people in all history have poured out their wealth so prodigally, so unselfishly to help the unfortunate. Now, with this same mental generosity and spiritual unselfishness that has characterized our givings in the past, let us examine together the facts of our industrial life and see if we can find some means, fair and just and acceptable to all, that will tend to prevent as well as to mitigate the evils of poverty.

Who could object to that? Could Father Coughlin, or Norman Thomas, or J. Pierpont Morgan? Hardly. Do we seem to be contradicting here the gospel of force and energy and enthusiasm? Hardly. There is a time for everything. But the time for force is seldom in the beginning of a talk. Tact is more likely to be needed then.

HOW PATRICK HENRY LAUNCHED HIS STORMY ADDRESS

Every schoolboy in the land is familiar with the fiery close of Patrick Henry's famous speech before the Virginia Convention of 1775:"Give me liberty or give me death." But few of them realize the comparative calm, the tactful manner in which Henry launched that stormy and emotional and history-making address. Should the American colonies separate from and go to war with England? The question was being debated with intense passion. Feelings flamed at white heat, yet Patrick Henry began by complimenting the abilities and praising the patriotism of those who opposed him. Note, in the second paragraph, how he gets his audience thinking with him by asking questions, by letting them draw their own conclusions:

> Mr. President: No man thinks more highly than I do of the patriotism, as well as abilities, of the very worthy gentlemen who have just addressed the house. But different men often see the same subject in different lights; and, therefore, I hope it will not be thought disrespectful to those gentlemen, if, entertaining as I do opinions of a character very opposite to theirs, I shall speak forth my sentiments freely, and without reserve. This is no time for ceremony. The question

> before the house is one of awful moment to the country. For my own part, I consider it as nothing less than a question of freedom or slavery. And in proportion to the magnitude of the subject ought to be the freedom of the debate. It is only in this way that we can hope to arrive at truth, and fulfill the great responsibility which we hold to God and our country. Should I keep back my opinions at such a time, through fear of giving offence, I should consider myself as guilty of treason towards my country, and of an act of disloyalty toward the Majesty of Heaven, which I revere above all earthly things.

Mr. President, it is natural to man to indulge in the illusions of hope. We are apt to shut our eyes against a painful truth, and listen to the song of that Siren till she transforms us into beasts. Is this the part of wise men, engaged in a great and arduous struggle for liberty? Are we disposed to be of the number of those who, having eyes see not, having ears hear not, the things which so nearly concern their temporal salvation? For my part, whatever anguish of spirit it may cost, I am willing to know the whole truth; to know the worst and to provide for it.

THE BEST SPEECH SHAKESPEARE WROTE

The most famous speech that Shakespeare put into the mouth of any of his characters—Mark Antony's funeral oration over the body of Julius Caesar—is a classic example of supreme tact.

This was the situation. Caesar had become dictator. Naturally, inevitably, a score of his political enemies were envious, and were eager to tear him down, to destroy him, to make his power their own. Twenty-three of them banded together under the leadership of Brutus and Cassius and thrust their daggers into his body.... Mark Antony had been Caesar's Secretary of State. He was a handsome chap, this Antony, a ready writer, a powerful speaker. He could represent the government well at public affairs. Small wonder Caesar had chosen him as his right hand man. Now, with Caesar out of the way, what should the conspirators do with Antony? Remove him? Kill him? There had been enough bloodshed already; there was enough to justify as it was. Why not win this Antony to their side, why not use his undeniable influence, his moving eloquence, to shield them and further their own ends? Sounded safe and reasonable, so they tried it. They saw him and went so far as to permit him to "say a few words" over the corpse of the man who had all but ruled the world....

Antony mounts the rostrum in the Roman Forum. Before him lies the murdered Caesar. A mob surges noisily and threateningly about Antony, a rabble friendly to Brutus, Cassius and the other assassins. Antony's purpose is to turn this popular enthusiasm into intense hatred, to stir the plebeians to rise in mutiny and slay those that had struck Caesar down. He raises his hands, the tumult ceases, he starts to speak. Note how ingeniously, how adroitly he begins, praising Brutus and the other conspirators:

For Brutus is an honorable man;
So are they all, all honorable men.

Observe that he does not argue. Gradually, unobtrusively, he presents certain facts about Caesar; tells how the ransom from his captives filled the general coffers, how he wept when the poor cried, how he refused a crown, how he willed his estates to the public. He presents the facts, asks the mob questions, and lets them draw their own conclusions. The evidence is presented, not as something new, but as something they had for the moment forgotten:

I tell you that which you yourselves do know.

And with a magic tongue through it all, he whipped up their feelings, stirred their emotions, aroused their pity, heated their anger. Antony's masterpiece of tact and eloquence is given here in its entirety. Search where you will, range through all the broad fields of literature and oratory, and I doubt if you will find half a dozen speeches to equal this. It merits the serious study of every man who aspires to excel in the fine art of influencing human nature. But there is another reason, entirely aside from the one we are considering now, why Shakespeare ought to be read and reread by businessmen; he possessed a larger vocabulary than did any other writer who ever lived; he used words more magically, more beautifully. No one can study *Macbeth* and *Hamlet* and *Julius Caesar* without unconsciously brightening and widening and refining his own diction.

Ant. Friends, Romans, countrymen, lend me your ears:
I come to bury Caesar, not to praise him.
The evil that men do lives after them;
The good is oft interred with their bones:
So let it be with Caesar. The noble Brutus hath told you
Caesar was ambitious:
If it were so, it was a grievous fault;
And grievously hath Caesar answer'd it.
Here, under leave of Brutus and the rest—

For Brutus is an honourable man;
So are they all, all honourable men—
Come I to speak in Caesar's funeral.
He was my friend, faithful and just to me:
But Brutus says he was ambitious;
And Brutus is an honourable man.
He hath brought many captives home to Rome,
Whose ransoms did the general coffers fill:
Did this in Caesar seem ambitious?
When that the poor have cried, Caesar hath wept:
Ambition should be made of sterner stuff:
Yet Brutus says he was ambitious;
And Brutus is an honourable man.
You all did see that on the Lupercal I thrice presented him a kingly crown,
Which he did thrice refuse. Was this ambition?
Yet Brutus says he was ambitious;
And, sure, he is an honourable man.
Speak not to disprove what Brutus spoke.
But here I am, to speak what I do know.
You all did love him once—not without cause;
What cause withholds you, then, to mourn for him?
O judgment, thou art fled to brutish beasts,
And men have lost their reason! Bear with me;
My heart is in the coffin there with Caesar,
And I must pause till it come back to me.
Cit. Methinks there is much reason in his sayings.
Cit. If thou consider rightly of the matter,
Caesar has had great wrong.
Cit. Has he not, masters?
I fear there will a worse come in his place.
Cit. Mark'd ye his words? He would not take the crown
Therefore 'tis certain he was not ambitious.

Cit. If it be found so, some will dear abide it.
Cit. Poor soul! his eyes are red as fire with weeping.
Cit. There's not a nobler man in Rome than Antony. *Cit.*
Now mark him; he begins again to speak.
Ant. But yesterday the word of Caesar might Have stood against the world: now lies he there,
And none so poor to do him reverence.
O masters, if I were dispos'd to stir
Your hearts and minds to mutiny and rage,
I should do Brutus wrong, and Cassius wrong,
Who, you all know, are honourable men.
I will not do them wrong: I rather choose To wrong the dead, to wrong myself, and you,
Than I will wrong such honourable men.
But here's a parchment with the seal of Caesar,—
I found it in his closet,— tis his will:
Let but the commons hear this testament (Which, pardon me, I do not mean to read),
And they would go and kiss dead Caesar's wounds,
And dip their napkins in his sacred blood;
Yea, beg a hair of him for memory,
And, dying, mention it within their wills,
Bequeathing it as a rich legacy Unto their issue.
4. *Cit.* We'll hear the will; read it, Mark Antony.
Citizens. The will, the will! We will hear Caesar's will.
Ant. Have patience, gentle friends; I must not read it:
It is not meet you know how Caesar lov'd you.
You are not wood, you are not stones, but men;
And, being men, hearing the will of Caesar,
It will inflame you, it will make you mad.
Tis good you know not that you are his heirs;
For, if you should, O what would come of it!

4. *Cit.* Read the will! we'll hear it, Antony;
You shall read us the will—Caesar's will!
Ant. Will you be patient? will you stay awhile?
I have o'ershot myself, to tell you of it.
I fear I wrong the honourable men
Whose daggers have stabb'd Caesar; I do fear it.
4. *Cit.* They were traitors: honourable men!
Citizens. The will! the testament!
4. *Cit.* They were villains, murderers. The will!
Read the will!
Ant. You will compel me, then, to read the will?
Then make a ring about the corpse of Caesar,
And let me show you him that made the will.
Shall I descend? And will you give me leave?
Citizens. Come down.
2. *Cit. Descend. [He comes down]*
3. *Cit.* You shall have leave.
4. *Cit.* A ring! Stand round.
1. *Cit.* Stand from the hearse; stand from the body
2. *Cit.* Room for Antony!—most noble Antony!
Ant. Nay, press not so upon me; stand far off.
Citizens. Stand back; room! bear back.
Ant. If you have tears, prepare to shed them now.
You all do know this mantle: I remember The first time ever Caesar put it on;
'Twas on a summer's evening, in his tent,
That day he overcame the Nervii.
Look, in this place ran Cassius' dagger through:
See what a rent the envious Casca made:
Through this the well-beloved Brutus stabb'd;
And, as he pluck'd his cursed steel away,
Mark how the blood of Caesar follow'd it,—

As rushing out of doors, to be resolv'd If Brutus so unkindly knock'd, or no;
For Brutus, as you know, was Caesar's angel:
Judge, O you gods, how dearly Caesar lov'd him!
This was the most unkindest cut of all;
For, when the noble Caesar saw him stab,
Ingratitude, more strong than traitors' arms,
Quite vanquish'd him: then burst his mighty heart; And, in his mantle muffling up his face,
Even at the base of Pompey's statue,
Which all the while ran blood, great Caesar fell.
O, what a fall was there, my countrymen!
Then I, and you, and all of us fell down,
Whilst bloody treason flourish'd over us.
O, now you weep; and, I perceive, you feel The dint of pity: these are gracious drops.
Kind souls, what, weep you, when you but behold Our Caesar's vesture wounded? Look you here,
Here is himself, marr'd, as you see, with traitors.
1 Cit. O piteous spectacle!
2. *Cit.* O noble Caesar!
3. *Cit.* O woeful day!
4. *Cit.* O traitors, villains!
1. *Cit.* O most bloody sight!
2. *Cit.* We will be reveng'd.
Citizens. Revenge—about—seek—burn—fire—kill slay—let not a traitor live!
Ant. Stay, countrymen.
1. *Cit.* Peace there! Hear the noble Antony.
2. *Cit.* We'll hear him, we'll follow him, we'll die with him.
Ant. Good friends, sweet friends, let me not stir you up
To such a sudden flood of mutiny.

They that have done this deed are honourable:
What private griefs they have, alas, I know not,
That made them don't; they're wise and honourable, And will, no doubt, with reasons answer you.
I come not, friends, to steal away your hearts:
I am no orator, as Brutus is;
But, as you know me all, a plain blunt man,
That love my friend; and that they know full well That gave me public leave to speak of him.
For I have neither wit, nor words, nor worth,
Action, nor utterance, nor the power of speech,
To stir men's blood: I only speak right on;
I tell you that which you yourselves do know;
Show you sweet Caesar's wounds, poor, poor dumb mouths,
And bid them speak for me: but were I Brutus,
And Brutus Antony, there were an Antony Would ruffle up your spirit, and put a tongue In every wound of Caesar, that should move The stones of Rome to rise and mutiny.
Citizens. We'll mutiny.
1. Cit. We'll burn the house of Brutus.
3. *Cit.* Away, then! come, seek the conspirators.
Ant. Yet hear me, countrymen; yet hear me speak.
Citizens. Peace, ho! Hear Antony; most noble Antony.
Ant. Why, friends, you go to do you know not what.
Wherein hath Caesar thus deserv'd your loves?
Alas, you know not; I must tell you, then:
You have forgot the will I told you of.
Citizens. Most true; the will!—Let's stay, and hear the will.
Ant. Here is the will, and under Caesars seal.
To every Roman citizen he gives.

To every several man, seventy-five drachmas.
2. *Cit.* Most noble Caesar!—We'll revenge his death.
3. *Cit.* O, royal Caesar!
Ant. Hear me with patience.
Citizens. Peace, ho!
Ant. Moreover, he hath left you all his walks,
His private arbours, and new-planted orchards,
On this side Tiber; he hath left them to you,
And to your heirs for ever; common pleasures,
To walk abroad, and recreate yourselves.
Here was a Caesar! When comes such another?
1 Cit. Never, never.—Come, away, away!
We'll burn his body in the holy place,
And with the brands fire the traitors' houses.
Take up the body.
2. Cit. Go, fetch fire.
3. *Cit.* Pluck down benches.
4. *Cit.* Pluck down forms, windows, anything.
[Exeunt Citizens with the body. Ant. Now let it work;
Mischief, thou art afoot,
Take thou what course thou wilt!]

You have to respect your audience. Without them, you're essentially standing alone, singing to yourself.

—K.D. Lang

~

If the audience knew what they wanted then they wouldn't be the audience, they would be the artist.

—Alan Moore

HOW TO ENJOY YOUR LIFE AND YOUR JOB

DALE CARNEGIE

Om Books International

PART I

WIN FRIENDS AND INFLUENCE PEOPLE

1

How To Make People Like You Instantly

I was waiting in line to register a letter in the post office at Thirty-third Street and Eighth Avenue in New York. I noticed that the clerk appeared to be bored with the job—weighing envelopes, handing out stamps, making change, issuing receipts—the same monotonous grind year after year. So I said to myself, "I am going to try to make that clerk like me. Obviously, to make him like me, I must say something nice, not about myself, but about him." So I asked myself, "What is there about him that I can honestly admire?" That is sometimes a hard question to answer, especially with strangers; but, in this case, it happened to be easy. I instantly saw something I admired no end.

So while he was weighing my envelope, I remarked with enthusiasm: "I certainly wish I had your head of hair."

He looked up, half-startled, his face beaming with smiles. "Well, it isn't as good as it used to be," he said modestly. I assured him that although it might have lost some of its pristine glory, nevertheless it was still magnificent. He was immensely pleased. We carried on a pleasant little conversation and the last thing he said to me was: "Many people have admired my hair."

I bet that person went out to lunch that day walking on air. I'll bet he went home that night and told his wife about it. I'll bet he looked in the mirror and said: "It is a beautiful head of hair."

I told this story once in public and a man asked me afterward: "What did you want to get out of him?"

What did I want to get out of him! What did I want to get out of him!

If we're are so contemptibly selfish that we can't radiate a little happiness and pass on a bit of honest appreciation without trying to get something out of the other person in return—if our souls are no bigger than sour crab apples, we shall meet with the failure we so richly deserve.

Oh yes, I did want something out of that chap. I wanted something priceless. And I got it. I got the feeling that I had done something for him without his being able to do anything whatever in return for me. That is a feeling that flows and sings in your memory long after the incident is past.

There is one all-important law of human conduct. If We obey that law, we shall almost never get into trouble. In fact, that law, if obeyed, will bring us countless friends and constant happiness. But the very instant we break the law, we shall get into endless trouble. The law is this: *Always make the other person feel important*. John Dewey said that the desire to be important is the deepest urge in human nature; and William James said: "The deepest principle in human nature is the craving to be appreciated." As I have already pointed out, it is this urge that differentiates us from the animals. It is this urge that has been responsible for civilization itself.

Philosophers have been speculating on the rules of human relationships for thousands of years, and out of all that speculation, there has evolved only one important precept. It is not new. It is as old as history. Zoroaster taught it to his followers in Persia twenty-five hundred years ago. Confucius preached it in China twenty-four centuries ago. Lao-tse, the founder of Taoism, taught it to his disciples in the Valley of the Han twenty-five centuries ago. Buddha preached it on the bank of the Holy Ganges five hundred years before Christ. The sacred books of Hinduism taught it a thousand years before that, Jesus taught it among the stony hills of Judea nineteen centuries ago. Jesus summed it up in one thought—probably the most important rule in the world: "Do unto others as you would have others do unto you."

You want the approval of those with whom you come in contact. You want recognition of your true worth. You want a feeling that you are important in your little world. You don't want to listen to cheap, insincere flattery, but you do crave sincere appreciation. You want your friends and associates to be, as Charles Schwab put it, "hearty in their approbation and lavish in their praise." All of us want that.

So let's obey the Golden Rule, and give unto others what we would have others give unto us.

How? When? Where? The answer is: All the time, everywhere.

David G. Smith of Eau Claire, Wisconsin, told one of our classes how he handled a delicate situation when he was asked to take charge of the refreshment booth at a charity concert.

"The night of the concert I arrived at the park and found two elderly ladies in a very bad humor standing next to the refreshment stand. Apparently each thought that she was in charge of this project. As I stood there pondering what to do, one of the members of the sponsoring committee appeared and handed me a cash box and thanked me for taking over the project. She introduced Rose and Jane as my helpers and then ran off.

"A great silence ensued. Realizing that the cash box was a symbol of authority (of sorts) I gave the box to Rose and explained that I might not be able to keep the money straight and that if she took care of it I would feel better. I then suggested to Jane that she show to teenagers who had been assigned to refreshments how to operate the soda machine, and I asked her to be responsible for that part of the project.

"The evening was very enjoyable, with Rose happily counting the money, Jane supervising the teenagers, and me enjoying the concert."

You don't have to wait until you are ambassador to France or chairman of the Clambake Committee of your lodge before you use this philosophy of appreciation. You can work magic with it almost every day.

If, for example, the waitress brings us mashed potatoes when we have ordered French fries, let's say: "I'm sorry to trouble you, but I prefer French fries." She'll probably reply, "No trouble at all" and will be glad to change the potatoes, because we have shown respect for her.

Little phrases such as "I'm sorry to trouble you," "Would you be so kind as to?" "Won't you please?" Would you mind?" "Thank you"—little courtesies like these relieve the monotonous grind of everyday life—and, incidentally, they are the hallmark of good breeding.

The unvarnished truth is that almost all the people you meet feel themselves superior to you in some way, and a sure way to their hearts is to let them realize in some subtle way that you recognize their importance, and recognize it sincerely.

Remember what Emerson said: "Every man I meet is my superior in some way. In that, I learn of him."

And the pathetic part of it is that, frequently, those who have the easy justification for a feeling of achievement bolster their egos by a show of tumult and conceit that is truly nauseating. As Shakespeare put it: "...man, proud man / Drest in a little brief authority / ...Plays such fantastic tricks before high heaven / As make the angels weep."

I am going to tell you how business people in my own courses have applied these principles with remarkable results. Let's take the case of a Connecticut attorney (because of his relatives, he prefers not to have his name mentioned).

Shortly after joining the course, Mr. R—drove to Long Island with his wife to visit some of her relatives. She left him to chat with an old aunt of hers and then rushed cf by herself to visit some of the younger relatives. Since he soon had to give a speech professionally on how he applied the principles of appreciation, he thought he would gain some worthwhile experience raiking with the elderly lady. So he locked around the house to see what he could honestly admire.

"This house was built in 1890, wasn't it?" he inquired.

"Yes," she replied, "that is precisely the year it was built."

"It reminds me of the house I was born in," he said. "It's beautiful. Well built. Roomy. You know, they don't build houses like this anymore."

"You're right," the old lady agreed. "The young folks nowadays don't care for beautiful homes. All they want is a small apartment, and then they go off gadding about in their automobiles.

"This is a dream house," she said in a voice vibrating with tender memories. "This house was built with love. My husband and I dreamed about it for years before we built it. We didn't have an architect. We planned it all ourselves." She showed Mr. R about the house, and he expressed his hearty admiration for the beautiful treasures she had picked up in her travels and cherished over a lifetime—paisley shawls, an old English tea set, Wedgwood china, French beds and chairs, Italian paintings, and silk draperies that had once hung in a French chateau.

After showing Mr. R.—through the house, she took him out to the garage, there, jacked up on blocks, was a Packard car—in mint condition.

"My husband bought that car for me shortly before he passed on," she said softly. "I have never ridden in it since his death... You appreciate nice things, and I'm going to give this car to you."

"Why, Aunty," he said, "you overwhelm me. I appreciate your generosity, of course; but I couldn't possibly accept it. I'm not even a relative of yours. I have a new car, and you have many relatives who would like to have that Packard."

"Relatives!" she exclaimed. "Yes, I have relatives who are just waiting till I die so they can get that car. But they are not going to get it."

"If you don't want to give it to them, you can very easily sell it to a secondhand dealer," he told her.

"Sell it!" she cried. "Do you think I would sell this car? Do you think I could stand to see strangers riding up and down the street in that car—that car that my husband bought for me? I wouldn't dream of selling it. I'm going to give it to you. You appreciate beautiful things."

He tried to get out of accepting the car, but he couldn't without hurting her feelings.

This lady, left all alone in a big house with her paisley shawls, her French antiques, and her memories, was starving for a little recognition. She had once been young and beautiful and sought after. She had once built a house, warm with love and had collected things from all over Europe to make it beautiful. Now, in the isolated loneliness of old age, she craved a little human warmth, a little genuine appreciation—and no one gave it to her. And when she found it, like a spring in the desert, her gratitude couldn't adequately express itself with anything less than the gift of her cherished Packard.

Let's take another case: Donald M. McMahon, who was superintendent of Lewis and Valentine, nurserymen and landscape architects in Rye, New York, related this incident: "Shortly after I attended the talk on 'How to Win Friends and Influence People,' I was landscaping the estate of a famous judge. The owner came out to give me a few instructions about where he wished to plant a mass of rhododendrons and azaleas.

"I said, 'Judge, you have a lovely hobby. I've been admiring your beautiful dogs. I understand you win a lot of blue ribbons every year at the show in Madison Square Garden.'

"The effect of this little expression of appreciation was striking.

"'Yes,' the judge replied, 'I do have a lot of fun with my dogs. Would you like to see my kennel?'

"He spent almost an hour showing me his dogs and the prizes they had won. He even brought out their pedigrees and explained about the bloodlines responsible for such beauty and intelligence.

"Finally, turning to me, he asked: 'Do you have any small children?'

"'Yes, I do,' I replied. 'I have a son.'

"'Well, wouldn't he like a puppy?' the judge inquired. "'Oh, yes, he'd be tickled pink.'

"'All right, I'm going to give him one,' the judge announced.

"He started to tell me how to feed the puppy. Then he paused. 'You'll forget it if I tell you. I'll write it out.' So the judge went in the house, typed out the pedigree and feeding instructions, and gave me a puppy worth several hundred dollars and one hour and fifteen minutes of his valuable time largely because I had expressed my honest admiration for his hobby and achievements."

George Eastman, of Kodak fame, invented the transparent film that made motion pictures possible, amassed a fortune of a hundred million dollars, and made himself one of the most famous businessmen on earth. Yet in spite of all these tremendous accomplishments, he craved a little recognition even as you and I.

To illustrate: When Eastman was building the Eastman School of Music and also Kilbourn Hall in Rochester, James Adamson, then president of the Superior Seating Company of New York, wanted to get the order to supply the theater chairs for these buildings. Phoning the architect, Mr. Adamson made an appointment to see Mr. Eastman in Rochester.

When Adamson arrived, the architect said: "I know you want to get this order, but I can tell you right now that you won't stand a ghost of a show if you take more than five minutes of George Eastman's time. He is a strict disciplinarian. He is very busy. So tell your story quickly and get out."

Adamson was prepared to do just that.

When he was ushered into the room, he saw Mr. Eastman bending over a pile of papers at his desk. Presently, Mr. Eastman looked up, removed his glasses, and walked toward the architect and Mr. Adamson, saying: "Good morning, gentlemen, what can I do for you?"

The architect introduced them, and then Mr. Adamson said: "While we've been waiting for you, Mr. Eastman, we've been admiring your office. I wouldn't mind working in a room like this myself. I'm in the interior-woodworking business, and I never saw a more beautiful office in all my life.

George Eastman replied: "You remind me of something I had almost forgotten. It is beautiful, isn't it? I enjoyed it a great deal when it was first built. But 1 come down here now with a lot of other things on my mind and sometimes don't even see the room for weeks at a time."

Adamson walked over and rubbed his hand across a panel. "This is English oak, isn't it? A little different in texture from kalian oak."

"Yes," Eastman replied. "Imported English oak. It was selected for me by a friend who specializes in fine woods."

Then Eastman showed him about the room, commenting on the proportions, the coloring, the hand carving, and other efforts he had helped to plan and execute.

While drifting about the room, admiring the woodwork, they paused before a window, and George Eastman, in his modest, soft-spoken way, pointed out some of the institutions through which he was trying to help humanity: the University of Rochester, the General Hospital, the Homeopathic Hospital, the Friendly Home, the Childrens Hospital. Mr, Adamson congratulated him warmly on the idealistic way he was using his wealth to alleviate the sufferings of humanity. Presently, George Eastman unlocked a glass case and pulled out the first camera be had ever owned—an invention he had bought from an Englishman.

Adamson questioned him at length about his early struggles to get started in business, and Mr. Eastman spoke with real feeling about the poverty of his childhood, telling how his widowed mother had kept a boardinghouse while he clerked in an insurance office. The terror of poverty haunted him day and night, and he resolved to make enough money so that his mother wouldn't have ro work. Mr. Adamson drew him out with further questions and listened, absorbed, while he related the story of his experiments with dry photographic plates. He told how he had worked in an office all day, and sometimes experimented all night, taking only brief naps while the chemicals were working and sleeping in his clothes for seventy-two hours at a stretch.

James Adamson had been ushered into Eastman's office at ten-fifteen and had been warned that he must not take more than five minutes; but an hour passed, then two hours passed. And they were still talking.

Finally, George Eastman turned to Adamson and said, "The last time I was in Japan I bought some chairs, brought them home, and put them in my sun porch. But the sun peeled the paint, so I went downtown the other day and bought some paint and painted the chairs myself. Would you like to see what sort of a job I can do painting chairs?

All right. Come up to my home and have lunch with me and I'll show you."

After lunch, Mr. Eastman showed Adamson the chairs he had brought from Japan, they weren't worth more than a few dollars, but George Eastman, now a multi-millionaire, was proud of them because he himself had painted them.

The order for the seats amounted to ninety thousand dollars. Who do you suppose got the order—James Adamson or one of his competitors? From the time of this story until Mr. Eastman's death, he and James Adamson were close friends.

Claude Marais, a restaurant owner in Rouen, France, used this principle and saved his restaurant the loss of a key employee. This woman had been in his employ for five years and was a vital link between M. Marais and his staff of twenty-one people. He was shocked to receive a registered letter from her advising him of her resignation.

M. Marais reported: "I was very surprised and, even more, disappointed, because I was under the impression that I had been fair to her and receptive to her needs. Inasmuch as she was a friend as well as an employee, I probably had taken her too much for granted and maybe was even more demanding of her than of other employees.

"I could not, of course, accept this resignation without some explanation, I took her aside and said, 'Paulette, you must understand that I cannot accept your resignation. You mean a great deal to me and to this company, and you are as important to the success of this restaurant as I am.' I repeated this in front of the entire staff, and I invited her to my home and reiterated my confidence in her with my family present.

"Paulette withdrew her resignation, and today I can rely on her as never before. I frequently reinforce this by expressing my appreciation for what she does and showing her how important she is to me and to the restaurant."

"Talk to people about themselves," said Disraeli, one of the shrewdest men who ever ruled the British Empire. "Talk to people about themselves and they will listen for hours."

Always make the other person feel important.

~

Inaction breeds doubt and fear. Action breeds confidence and courage. If you want to conquer fear, do not sit home and think about it. Go out and get busy.

2

Do This And You'll Be Welcome Anywhere

Why read this book to find out how to win friends? Why not study the technique of the greatest winner of friends the world has ever known? Who is he? You may meet him tomorrow coming down the street. When you get within ten feet of him, he will begin to wag his tail. If you stop and pat him, he will almost jump out of his skin to show you how much he likes you. And you know that behind this show of affection on his part, there are no ulterior motives: he doesn't want to sell you any real estate, and he doesn't want to marry you.

Did you ever stop to think that a dog is the only animal that doesn't have to work for a living? A hen has to lay eggs, a cow has to give milk, and a canary has to sing. But a dog makes his living by giving you nothing but love.

When I was five years old, my father bought a little yellow-haired pup for fifty cents. He was the light and joy of my childhood. Every afternoon about four-thirty, he would sit in the front yard with his beautiful eyes staring steadfastly at the path, and as soon as he heard my voice or saw me swinging my dinner pail through the buck brush, he was off like a shot, racing breathlessly up the hill to greet me with leaps of joy and barks of sheer ecstasy.

Tippy was my constant companion for five years. Then one tragic night—I shall never forget it—he was killed within ten feet of me, killed by lightning. Tippy's death was the tragedy of my boyhood.

You never read a book on psychology, Tippy. You didn't need to. You knew by some divine instinct that you can make more friends in two months by becoming genuinely interested in other people than you can in two years by trying to get other people interested in you. Let me repeat that. You can make more friends in two months by becoming interested in other people than you can in two years by trying to get other people interested in you.

Yet I know and you know people who blunder through life trying to wigwag other people into becoming interested in them.

Of course, it doesn't work. People are not interested in you. They are not interested in me. They are interested in themselves—morning, noon, and after dinner.

The New York Telephone Company made a detailed study of telephone conversations to find out which word is the most frequently used. You have guessed it: it is the personal pronoun "I." "I." "I." It was used 3,900 times in 500 telephone conversations. "I." "I." "I." "I."

When you see a group photograph that you are in, whose picture do you look for first?

If we merely try to impress people and get people interested in us, we will never have many true, sincere friends. Friends, real friends, are not made that way.

Napoleon tried it, and in his last meeting with Josephine he said: "Josephine, I have been as fortunate as any man ever was on this earth; and yet, at this hour, you are the only person in the world on whom I can rely." And historians doubt that he could rely even on her.

I once took a course in short-story writing at New York University, and during that course the editor of a leading magazine talked to our class. He said he could pick up any one of the dozens of stories that drifted across his desk every day and after reading a few paragraphs he could feel whether or not the author liked people. "If the author doesn't like people," he said, "people won't like his or her stories."

This hard-boiled editor stopped twice in the course of his talk on fiction writing and apologized for preaching a sermon. "I am telling you," he said, "the same things your preacher would tell you, but remember, you have to be interested in people if you want to be a successful writer of stories."

If that is true of writing fiction, you can be sure it is true of dealing with people face-to-face.

I spent an evening in the dressing room of Howard Thurston the last time he appeared on Broadway—Thurston was the acknowledged dean of magicians. For forty years he had traveled all over the world, time and again, creating illusions, mystifying audiences, and making people gasp with astonishment. More than 60 million people had paid admission to his show, and he had made almost $2 million in profit.

I asked Mr. Thurston to tell me the secret of his success. His schooling certainly had nothing to do with it, for he ran away from home as a small boy, became a hobo, rode in boxcars, slept in haystacks, begged his food from door to door, and learned to read by looking out of boxcars at signs along the railway.

Did he have a superior knowledge of magic? No, he told me hundreds of books had been written about legerdemain and scores of people knew as much about it as he did. But he had two things that the others didn't have. First, he had the ability to put his personality across the footlights. He was a master showman. He knew human nature. Everything he did, every gesture, every intonation of his voice, every lifting of an eyebrow had been carefully rehearsed, and his actions were timed to split seconds. But, in addition to that, Thurston had a genuine interest in people. He told me that many magicians would look at the audience and say to themselves, "Well, there is a bunch of suckers out there, a bunch of hicks; I'll fool them all right." But Thurston's method was totally different. He told me that every time he went on stage he said to himself: "I am grateful because these people came to see me. They make it possible for me to make my living in a very agreeable way. I'm going to give them the very best I possibly can."

He declared he never stepped in front of the footlights without first saying to himself over and over: "I love my audience, I love my audience." Ridiculous? Absurd? You are privileged to think anything you like. I am merely passing it on to you without comment as a recipe used by one of the most famous magicians of all time.

George Dyke of North Warren, Pennsylvania, was forced to retire from his service station business after thirty years when a new highway was constructed over the site of his station, it wasn't long before the idle days of retirement began to bore him, so he starred filling in his time trying to play music on his old fiddle. Soon he was traveling the area to listen to music and talk with many of the accomplished fiddlers. In his humble and friendly way he became generally interested in learning the background and interests of every musician he met. Although he was not a great fiddler himself, he made many friends in this pursuit. He attended competitions and soon became known to the country music fans in the eastern part of the United States as "Uncle George, the Fiddle Scraper from Kinzua County". When we heard Uncle George, he was seventy two and enjoying every minute of his life. By having a sustained interest in other people, he created a new life for himself at a time when most people consider their productive years over.

That, too, was one of the secrets of Theodore Roosevelt astonishing popularity. Even his servants loved him. His valet, James E. Amos, wrote a book about him entitled *Theodore Roosevelt, Hero to His Valet.* In that book Amos relates this illuminating incident:

> My wife one time asked the President about a bobwhite. She had never seen one and he described it to her fully. Sometime later, rhe telephone at our cottage rang. [Amos and his wife lived in a little cottage on the Roosevelt Estate at Oyster Bay.] My wife answered it and it was Mr. Roosevelt himself. He had called her, he said, to tell her that there was a bobwhite outside her window and that if she would look out she might see it. Little things like that were so characteristic of him. Whenever he went by our cottage, even though we were out of sight, we would hear him call out: "Oo-oo-oo, Annie?" or "Oo-oo-oo, James!" It was just a friendly greeting.

How could employees keep from liking a man like that? How could anyone keep from liking him?

Roosevelt called at the White House one day when the President and Mrs. Taft were away. His honest liking for humble people was shown by the fact that he greeted all the old White House servants by name, even the scullery maids.

"When he saw Alice, the kitchen maid," writes Archie Butt, "he asked her if she still made corn bread. Alice told him that she sometimes made it for the servants, but no one ate it upstairs.

"'They show bad taste,' Roosevelt boomed, 'and I'll tell the President so when I see him.'

Alice brought a piece to him on a plate, and he went over to the office eating it as he went and greeting gardeners and laborers as he passed...

"He addressed each person just as he had addressed them in the past. Ike Hoover, who had been head usher at the White House for forty years, said with tears in his eyes, 'It is the only happy day we had in nearly two years, and not one of us would exchange it for a hundred-dollar bill.'"

The same concern for the seemingly unimportant people helped sales representative Edward M. Sykes, Jr., of Chatham, New Jersey, retain an account. "Many years ago," he reported, "I called on customers for Johnson and Johnson in the Massachusetts area. One account was a drug store in Hingham. Whenever I went into this store I would always talk to the soda clerk and sales clerk for a few minutes before talking to the owner to obtain his order. One day I went up to the owner of the store, and he told me to leave as he was not interested in buying J&J products anymore because he felt they were concentrating their activities on food and discount stores to the detriment of the small drugstore. I left with my tail between my legs and drove around the town for several hours. Finally, I decided to go back and try at least to explain our position to the owner of the store.

"When I returned I walked in and as usual said hello to the soda clerk and sales clerk. When I walked up to the owner, he smiled at me and welcomed me back. He then gave me double the usual order. I looked at him with surprise and asked him what had happened since my visit only a few hours earlier. He pointed to the young man at the soda fountain and said that after I had left, the boy had come over and said that I was one of the few salespeople who called on the store who even bothered to say hello to him and to the others in the store. He told the owner that if any salesperson deserved his business, it was I. The owner agreed and remained a loyal customer. I never forgot that to be genuinely interested in other people is a most important quality for a salesperson to possess—for any person, for that matter."

I have discovered from personal experience that one can win the attention and time and cooperation of even the most sought-after people by becoming genuinely interested in them. Let me illustrate.

Years ago, I conducted a course in fiction writing at the Brooklyn Institute of Arts and Sciences, and we wanted distinguished and busy authors as Kathleen Norris, Fannie Hurst, Ida Tar bell, Albert Payson Terhune, and Rupert Hughes to come to Brooklyn and give us the benefit of their experience. So we wrote them, saying we admired their work and were deeply interested in getting their advice and learning the secrets of their success.

Each of these letters was signed by about 150 students. We said we realized that these authors were busy—too busy to prepare a lecture. So we enclosed a list of questions for them to answer about themselves and their methods of work. They liked that. Who wouldn't like it? So they left their homes and traveled to Brooklyn to give us a helping hand.

By using the same method, I persuaded Leslie M. Shaw, secretary of the treasury in Theodore Roosevelt's cabinet; George W. Wickersham, attorney general in Taft's cabinet; William Jennings Bryan; Franklin D. Roosevelt; and many other prominent men to come to talk to the students of my courses in public speaking.

All of us, be we workers in a factory, clerks in an office, or even a king upon his throne—all of us like people who admire us. Take the German kaiser, for example. At the close of World War I, he was probably the most savagely and universally despised man on this earth. Even his own nation turned against him when he fled over into Holland to save his neck. The hatred against him was so intense that millions of people would have loved to tear him limb from limb or burn him at the stake. In the midst of all this forest fire of fury, one little boy wrote the kaiser a simple, sincere letter glowing with kindliness and admiration. This little boy said that no matter what the others thought, he would always love Wilhelm as his emperor. The kaiser was deeply touched by his letter and invited the little boy to come see him. The boy came, so did his mother—and the kaiser married her. That little boy didn't need to read a book on how to win friends and influence people. He knew how instinctively.

If we want to make friends, let's put ourselves out to do things for other people—things that require time, energy, unselfishness, and thoughtfulness. When the Duke of Windsor was Prince of Wales, he was scheduled to tour South America, and before he started out on that tour he spent months studying Spanish so that he could make public talks in the language of the country; and the South Americans loved him for it.

For years I made it a point to find out the birthdays of my friends. How? Although I haven't the foggiest bit of faith in astrology, I began by asking the other whether he believed the date of one's birth has anything to do with character and disposition. I then asked him or her to tell me the month and day of birth. If he or she said November 24, for example, I kept repeating to myself, "November 24, November 24." The minute my friend's back was turned, I wrote down the name and birthday and later would transfer it to a birthday book. At the beginning of each year, I had these birthday dates scheduled in my calendar pad so that they came to my attention automatically. When the natal day arrived, there was my letter or telegram. What a hit it made! I was frequently the only person on earth who remembered.

If we want to make friends, let's greet people with animation and enthusiasm. When somebody calls you on the telephone use the same psychology. Say "Hello" in tones that bespeak how pleased you are to have the person call. Many companies train their telephone operators to greet all callers in a tone that radiates interest and enthusiasm. The callers feel the company is concerned about them. Let's remember that when we answer the telephone tomorrow.

Showing genuine interest in others not only wins friends for you, but may develop in its customers a loyalty to your company. In an issue of the publication of the National Bank of North America of New York, the following letter from Madeline Rosedale, a depositor, was published:

"I would like you to know how much I appreciate your staff. Everyone is so courteous, polite, and helpful. What a pleasure it is, after waiting in a long line, to have the teller greet you pleasantly.

"Last year my mother was hospitalized for five months. Frequently I went to Marie Petrucello, a teller. She was concerned about my mother and inquired about her 26."

Is there any doubt that Mrs. Rosedale will continue to use this bank?

Charles R. Walters, of one of the large banks in New York City, was assigned to prepare a confidential report on a certain corporation. He knew of only one person who possessed the facts he needed so urgently. As Mr. Walters was ushered into the president's office, a young woman stuck her head through a door and told the president that she didn't have any stamps for him that day.

"I am collecting stamps for my twelve-year-old son," the president explained to Mr. Walters.

Mr. Walters stated his mission and began asking questions. The president was vague, general, nebulous. He didn't want to talk, and apparently nothing could persuade him to talk. The interview was brief and barren.

"Frankly, I didn't know what to do," Mr. Walters said as he related the story to the class. "Then I remembered what his secretary had said to him—stamps, twelve-year-old son... And I also recalled that the foreign department of our bank collected stamps—stamps taken from letters pouring in from every continent washed by the seven seas.

"The next afternoon I called on this man and sent in word that I had some stamps for his boy. Was I ushered in with enthusiasm? Yes, Sir. He couldn't have shaken my hand with more enthusiasm if he had been running for Congress. He radiated smiles and good will. 'My George will love this one,' he kept saying as he fondled the stamps. 'And look at this! This is a treasure.'

"We spent half an hour talking stamps and looking at a picture of his boy, and he then devoted more than an hour of his time to giving me every bit of information I wanted—without my even suggesting that he do it. He told me all. He knew, and then called in his subordinates and questioned them. He telephoned some of his associates. He loaded me down with facts, figures, reports, and correspondence. In the parlance of newspaper reporters, I had a scoop."

Here is another illustration:

C. M. Knaphle, Jr., of Philadelphia, had tried for years to sell fuel to a large chain store organization. But the chain store company continued to purchase its fuel from an out-of-town dealer and haul it right past the door of Knaphle's office. Mr. Knaphle made a speech one night before one of my classes, pouring out his hot wrath upon chain stores, branding them as a curse on the nation.

And still he wondered why he couldn't sell them.

I suggested that he try different tactics. To put it briefly, this is what happened. We staged a debate between members of the course on whether the spread of the chain store is doing the country more harm than good.

Knaphle, at my suggestion, took the negative side; he agreed to defend the chain stores, and then went straight to an executive of the chain store organization that he despised and said: "I am not here to try to sell fuel. I have come to ask you to do me a favor." He then told about his debate and said, "I have come to you for help because I can't think of anyone else who would be more capable of giving me the facts I want. I'm anxious to win this debate, and I'll deeply appreciate whatever help you can give me." Here is the rest of the story in Mr. Knaphle's own words:

"I had asked this man for precisely one minute of his time. It was with this understanding that he consented to see me. After I had stated my case, he motioned me to a chair and talked to me for exactly one hour and forty-seven minutes. He called in another executive who had written a book about chain stores. He wrote to the National Chain Store Association and secured for me a copy of a debate on the subject. He feels that the chain store is rendering a real service to humanity. He is proud of what he is doing for hundreds of communities. His eyes fairly glowed as he talked, and I must confess that he opened my eyes to things I had never dreamed of. He changed my whole mental attitude.

"As I was leaving, he walked with me to the door, put his arm around my shoulder, wished me well in my debate, and asked me to stop in and see him again and let him know how I made out. The last words he said to me were; 'Please see me again later in the spring. I should like to place an order with you for fuel.'

"To me that was almost a miracle. Here he was offering to buy fuel without my even suggesting it. I had made more headway in two hours by becoming genuinely interested in him and his problems than I could have made in ten years trying ro get him interested in me and my product."

You didn't discover a new truth, Mr. Knaphle, for a long time ago, a hundred years before Christ was born, a Roman poet, Publilius Syrus, remarked: "We are interested in others when they are interested in us."

A show of interest, as with every other principle of human relations, must be sincere. It must pay off not only for the person showing the interest, but for the person receiving the attention, it is a two-way street—both parties benefit.

Martin Ginsberg, who took our course in Long Island, New York, reported how the special interest a nurse took in him profoundly affected his life:

"It was Thanksgiving Day and I was ten years old. I was in a welfare ward of a city hospital and was scheduled to undergo major orthopedic surgery the next day. I knew that I could only look forward to months of confinement, convalescence, and pain. My father was dead; my mother and I lived alone in a small apartment and we were on welfare. My mother was unable to visit me that day.

As the day went on, I became overwhelmed with the feeling of loneliness, despair, and fear, I knew my mother was home alone worrying about me, not having anyone to be with, not having anyone to eat with, and not even having enough money to afford a Thanksgiving Day dinner.

"The tears welled up in my eyes, and I stuck my head under the pillow and pulled the covers over it. I cried silently, but oh so bitterly, so much that my body racked with pain.

"A young student nurse heard my sobbing and came over to me. She took the covers off my face and started wiping my tears. She told me how lonely she was, having to work that day and not being able to be with her family. She asked me whether I would have dinner with her. She brought two trays of food: sliced turkey, mashed potatoes, cranberry sauce, and ice cream for dessert. She talked to me and tried to calm my fears. Even though she was scheduled to go off duty at 4:00 p.m., she stayed on her own time until almost 11:00 p.m.

She played games with me, talked to me, and stayed with me until I finally fell asleep.

"Many Thanksgivings have come and gone since I was ten, but one never passes without my remembering that particular one and my feelings of frustration, fear, loneliness, and the warmth and tenderness of the stranger who somehow made it all bearable."

If you want others to like you, if you want to develop real friendships, if you want to help others at the same time as you help yourself, keep this principle in mind:

If we want to make friends, let's greet people with animation and enthusiasm.

~

Keep on raging to stop the aging.

3

How To Deal With People

There is only one way under high heaven to get anybody to do anything. Did you ever stop to think of that? Yes, just one way. And that is by making the other person want to do it.

Remember, there is no other way.

Of course, you can make someone want to give you his watch by sticking a revolver in his ribs. You can make your employees give you cooperation—until your back is turned—by threatening to fire them. You can make a child do what you want it to do by a whip or a threat. But these crude methods have sharply undesirable repercussions.

The only way I can get you to do anything is by giving you what you want.

What do you want?

Sigmund Freud said that everything you and I do springs from two motives: the sex urge and the desire to be great.

John Dewey, one of America's most profound philosophers, phrased it a bit differently. Dr. Dewey said that the deepest urge in human nature is "the desire to be important." Remember that phrase: 'the desire to be important.' It is significant. You are going to hear a lot about it in this book.

What do you want? Not many things, but the few things that you do wish, you crave with an insistence that will nor be denied. Some of the things most people want include:

1. Health and the preservation of life
2. Food
3. Sleep
4. Money and the things money will buy
5. Life in the hereafter
6. Sexual gratification
7. The well-being of our children
8. A feeling of importance

Almost all these wants are usually gratified—all except one. But there is one longing—almost as deep, almost as imperious, as the desire for food or sleep—that is seldom gratified. It is what Freud calls "the desire to be great." It is what Dewey calls 'the desire to be important.'

Lincoln once began a letter saying: "Everybody likes a compliment." William James said: ""The deepest principle in human nature is the craving to be appreciated." He didn't speak, mind you, of the 'wish' or the 'desire' or the 'longing' to be appreciated. He said the 'craving' to be appreciated.

Here is a gnawing and unfaltering human hunger, and the rare individual who honestly satisfies this heart hunger will hold people in the palm of his or her hand and "even the undertaker will be sorry when he dies."

The desire for a feeling of importance is one of the chief distinguishing differences between mankind and the animals. To illustrate: When I was a farm boy out in Missouri, my father bred fine Duroc hogs and pedigreed white-faced cattle. We used to exhibit our hogs and white-faced cattle at the country fairs and livestock shows throughout the Middle West. We won first prizes by the score. My father pinned his blue ribbons on a sheet of white muslin, and when friends or visitors came to the house, he would get out the long sheet of muslin. He would hold once and would hold the other while he exhibited the blue ribbons.

The hogs didn't care about the ribbons they had won. But Father did. These prizes gave him a feeling of importance.

If our ancestors hadn't had this flaming urge for a feeling of importance, civilization would have been impossible. Without it, we should have been just about like animals.

It was this desire for a feeling of importance that inspired Dickens to write his immortal novels. This desire inspired Sir Christopher Wren to design his symphonies in stone. This desire made Rockefeller amass millions that he never spent! And this same desire made the richest family in your town build a house far too large for its requirements.

This desire makes you want to wear the latest styles, drive the latest cars, and talk about your brilliant children.

It is this desire that lures many boys and girls into joining gangs and engaging in criminal activities. The average young criminal, according to E. P. Mulroonev, one-time police commissioner of New York, is filled with ego, and his first request after arrest is for those lurid newspapers that make him a hero. The disagreeable prospect of serving time seems remote so long as he can gloat over his likeness sharing space with pictures of sports figures, movie and television stars and politicians.

If you tell me how you get your feeling of importance, I'll tell you what you are. That determines your character. That is the most significant thing about you. For example, John D. Rockefeller got his feeling of importance by giving money to erect a modern hospital in Peking, China, to care for millions of poor people whom he had never seen and never would see. Dillinger, on the other hand, got his feeling of importance by being a bandit, a bank robber and killer. When the FBI agents were hunting him, he dashed into a farmhouse up in Minnesota and said, "I'm Dillinger!" He was proud of the fact that he was Public Enemy Number One. "I'm not going to hurt you, but I'm Dillinger!" he said.

Yes, the one significant difference between Dillinger and Rockefeller is how they got their feeling of importance.

History sparkles with amusing examples of famous people struggling for a feeling of importance. Even George Washington wanted to be called "His Mightiness, the President of the United States"; and Columbus pleaded for the title "Admiral of the Ocean and Viceroy of India." Catherine the Great refused to open letters that were not addressed to "Her Imperial Majesty"; and Mrs. Lincoln, in the White House, turned upon Mrs. Grant like a tigress and shouted, "How dare you be seated in my presence until I invite you!"

Our millionaires helped finance Admiral Byrd's expedition to the Antarctic in 1928 with the understanding that ranges of icy mountains would be named after them; and Victor Hugo aspired to have nothing less than the city of Paris renamed in his honor. Even Shakespeare, mightiest of the mighty, tried to add luster to his name by procuring a coat of arms for his family.

People sometimes become invalids in order to win sympathy and attention, and get a feeling of importance. For example, take Mrs. McKinley. She got a feeling of importance by forcing her husband, the President of the United States, to neglect important affairs of state while he reclined on the bed beside her for hours at a time, his arm about her, soothing her to sleep. She fed her gnawing desire for attention by insisting that he remain with her while she was having her teeth fixed, and once created a stormy scene when he had to leave her alone with the dentist while he kept an appointment with John Hay, his secretary of state.

The writer Mary Roberts Rinehart once told me of a bright, vigorous young woman who became an invalid in order to get a feeling of importance. "One day," said Mrs. Rinehart, "this woman had been obliged to face something, her age perhaps. The lonely years were stretching ahead and there was little left for her to anticipate.

"She took to her bed; and for ten years her old mother traveled to the third floor and back, carrying trays, nursing her. Then one day the old mother, weary with service, lay down and died. For some weeks, the invalid languished; then she got up, put on her clothing, and resumed living again."

Some authorities declare that people may actually go insane in order to find, in the dreamland of insanity, the feeling of importance that has been denied them in the harsh world of reality. There are more patients suffering from mental diseases in the United States than from all other diseases combined.

What is the cause of insanity?

Nobody can answer such a sweeping question, but we know that certain diseases, such as syphilis, break down and destroy the brain cells and result in insanity. In fact, about one-half of all mental diseases can be attributed to such physical causes as brain lesions, alcohol, toxins, and injuries. But the other half—and this is the appalling part of the story—the other half of the people who go insane apparently have nothing organically wrong with their brain cells. In post-mortem examinations, when their brain tissues are studied under the highest-powered microscopes, these tissues are found to be apparently just as healthy as yours and mine.

Why do these people go insane?

I put that question to the head physician of one of our most important psychiatric hospitals. This doctor, who has received the highest honors and the most coveted awards for his knowledge of this subject, told me frankly that he didn't know why people went insane. Nobody knows for sure. But he did say that many people who go insane find in insanity a feeling of importance that they were unable to achieve in the world of reality. Then he told me this story:

"I have a patient right now whose marriage proved to be a tragedy. She wanted love, sexual gratification, children, and social prestige, but life blasted all her hopes. Her husband didn't love her. He refused even to eat with her and forced her to serve his meals in his room upstairs. She had no children, no social standing. She went insane; and, in her imagination, she divorced her husband and resumed her maiden name. She now believes she has married into English aristocracy, and she insists on being called Lady Smith.

"And as for children, she imagines now that she has had a new child every night. Each time I call on her she says: 'Doctor, I had a baby last night.'"

Life once wrecked all her dream ships on the sharp rocks of reality; but in the sunny, fantasy isles of insanity, all her barkentines race into port with canvas billowing and winds singing through the sails.

Tragic? Oh, I don't know. Her physician said to me: "If I could stretch out my hand and restore her sanity, I wouldn't do it. She's much happier as she is."

If some people are so hungry for a feeling of importance that they actually go insane to get it, imagine what miracle you and I can achieve by giving people honest appreciation this side of insanity.

One of the first people in American business to be paid a salary of over a million dollars a year (when there was no income tax and a person earning fifty dollars a week was considered well off) was Charles Schwab. He had been picked by Andrew Carnegie to become the first president of the newly formed United States Steel Company in 1921, when Schwab was only thirty-eight years old. (Schwab later left U.S. Steel to take over the then-troubled Bethlehem Steel Company, and he rebuilt it into one of the most profitable companies in America.)

Why did Andrew Carnegie pay a million dollars a year, or more than three thousand dollars a day, to Charles Schwab? Why? Because Schwab was a genius? No, Because he knew more about the manufacture of steel than other people? Nonsense. Charles Schwab told me himself that he had many men working for him who knew more about the manufacture of steel than he did.

Schwab says that he was paid this salary largely because of his ability to deal with people. I asked him how he did it. Here is his secret set down in his own words—words that ought to be cast in eternal bronze and hung in every home and school, every shop and office in the land; words that children ought to memorize instead of wasting their time memorizing the conjugation of Latin verbs or the amount of the annual rainfall in Brazil; words that will all but transform your life and mine if we will only live them:

"I consider my ability to arouse enthusiasm among my people," said Schwab, "the greatest asset I possess, and the way to develop the best that is in a person is by appreciation and encouragement.

"There is nothing else that so kills the ambitions of a person as criticisms from superiors. I never criticize anyone. I believe in giving a person incentive to work. So I am anxious to praise but loath to fault. If I like anything, I am hearty in my approbation and lavish in my praise."

That is what Schwab did. But what do average people do? The exact opposite. If they don't like a thing, they bawl out their subordinates; if they do like it, they say nothing. As the old couplet says: "Once I did bad and that I heard ever/Twice I did good, but that I heard never." "In my wide association in life, meeting with many and great people in various parts of the world," Schwab declared, "I have yet to find the person, however great and exalted his station, who did not do better work and put forth greater effort under a spirit of approval than he would ever do under a spirit of criticism."

That, he said frankly, was one of the outstanding reasons for the phenomenal success of Andrew Carnegie. Carnegie praised his associates publicly as well as privately.

Carnegie wanted to praise his assistants even on his tombstone. He wrote an epitaph for himself that read: "Here lies one who knew how to get around him men who were cleverer than himself."

Sincere appreciation was one of the secrets of John D. Rockefeller's success in handling men. For example, when one of his partners, Edward T. Bedford, lost a million dollars for the firm by a bad buy in South America, John D. might have criticized; but he knew Bedford had done his best—and the incident was closed. So Rockefeller found something to praise; he congratulated Bedford because he had been able to save sixty percent of the money he had invested. "That's splendid," said Rockefeller. "We don't always do as well as that upstairs."

I have among my clippings a story that I know never happened, but it illustrates a truth, so I'll repeat it:

According to this silly story, a farm woman, at the end of a heavy day's work, set before her menfolk a heaping pile of hay. And when they indignantly demanded whether she had gone crazy, she replied: "Why, how did I know you'd notice? I've been cooking for you men for the last twenty years and in all that time I ain't heard no word to let me know you wasn't just eating hay."

When a study was made a few years ago on runaway wives, what do you think was discovered to be the main reasons wives ran away? It was "lack of appreciation." And I'd bet that a similar study made of runaway husbands would come out the same way. We often take our spouses so much for granted that we never let them know we appreciate them.

Florenz Ziegfeld, the most spectacular producer who ever dazzled Broadway, gained his reputation by his subtle ability to "glorify the American girl." Time after time, he took drab litle creatures that no one ever looked at twice and transformed them on the stage into glamorous visions of mystery and seduction. Knowing the value of appreciation and confidence, he made women feel beautiful by the sheer power of his gallantry and consideration. He was practical: he raised the salary of chorus girls from $30 a week to as high as $175. And he was also chivalrous; on opening night at the Follies, he sent telegrams to the stars in the cast, and he deluged every chorus girl in the show with American Beauty roses.

I once succumbed to the fad of fasting and went for six days and nights without eating, it wasn't difficult. I was less hungry at the end of the sixth day than I was at the end of the second. Yet I know, as you know, people who would think they had committed a crime if they let their families or employees go for six days without food; but they will let them go for six days, and six weeks, and sometimes sixty years without giving them the hearty appreciation that they crave almost as much as they crave food.

When Alfred Lunt, one of the great actors of his time, played the leading role in *Reunion in Vienna*, he said, "There is nothing I need so much as nourishment for my self-esteem."

We nourish the bodies of our children and friends and employees, but how often do we nourish their self-esteem? We provide them with roast beef and potatoes to build energy, but we neglect to give them kind words of appreciation that would sing in their memories for years like the music of the morning stars.

Paul Harvey, in one of his radio broadcasts, "The Rest of the Story," told how showing sincere appreciation can change a person's life. He reported that years ago a tcacher in Detroit asked Stevie Morris to help her find a mouse that was lost in the classroom. You see, she appreciated the fact that nature had given Stevie something no one else in the room had. Nature had given Stevie a remarkable pair of ears to compensate for his blind eyes. But this was really the first time Stevie had been shown appreciation for those talented ears. Now, years later, he says that this act of appreciation was the beginning of a new life. You see, from that time on he developed his gift of hearing and went on to become, under the stage name of Stevie Wonder, one of *the* great pop singers and songwriters of the seventies.

Some readers are saying right now as they read these lines; "Oh, phooey! Flattery! Bear oil! I've tried that stuff. It doesn't work—not with intelligent people."

Of course, flattery seldom works with discerning people. It is shallow, selfish, and insincere. It ought to fail and it usually does. True, some people are so hungry, so thirsty, for appreciation that they will swallow anything, just as a starving man will eat grass and fishworms.

Even Queen Victoria was susceptible to flattery. Prime Minister Benjamin Disraeli confessed that he laid it on thick in dealing with the queen. To use his exact words, he said he "spread it on with a trowel." But Disraeli was one of the most polished, deft, and adroit men who ever ruled the far-flung British Empire. He was a genius in his line. What would work for him wouldn't necessarily work for you and me. In the long run, flattery will do you more harm than good. Flattery is counterfeit, and like counterfeit money, it will eventually get you into trouble if you pass it to someone else.

The difference between appreciation and flattery? That is simple. One is sincere and the other insincere. One comes from the heart; the other from the teeth. One is unselfish; the other selfish. One is universally admired; the other universally condemned.

I recently saw a bust of the Mexican hero General AJvaro Obregon in the Chapultepec palace in Mexico City. Below the bust are carved these wise words from General Obregon's philosophy: "Don't be afraid of enemies who attack you. Be afraid of friends who flatter you."

No! No! No! I am not suggesting flattery. Far from it. I'am talking about a new way of life. Let me repeat. *I am talking about a new way of life.*

King George V had a set of six maxims displayed on the walls of his study at Buckingham Palace. One of these maxims said: "Teach me neither to proffer nor receive cheap praise." That's all flattery is—cheap praise. I once read a definition of flattery that may be worth repeating: "Flattery is telling the other person precisely what he thinks about himself."

"Use what language you will," said Ralph Waldo Emerson, "you can never say anything but what you are." If all we had to do was flatter, everybody would catch on and we should all be experts in human relations.

When we are not engaged in thinking about some definite problem, we usually spend about ninety-five percent of our time thinking about ourselves. Now, if we stop thinking about ourselves for a while and begin to think of the other person's good points, we won't have to resort to flattery so cheap and false that it can be spotted almost before it is out of the mouth.

One of the most neglected virtues of our daily existence is appreciation. Somehow, we neglect to praise our son or daughter when he or she brings home a good report card, and we fail to encourage our children when they first succeed in baking a cake or building a birdhouse. Nothing pleases children more than this kind of parental interest and approval.

The next time you enjoy filet mignon at the club, send word to the chef that it was excellently prepared, and when a tired salesperson shows you unusual courtesy, please mention it.

Every minister, lecturer, and public speaker knows the discouragement of pouring himself or herself out to an audience and not receiving a single ripple of appreciative comment. What applies to professionals applies doubly to workers in offices, shops, and factories, and to our families and friends. In our interpersonal relations we should never forget that all our associates are human beings and hunger for appreciation. It is the legal tender that all souls enjoy.

Try leaving a friendly trail of little sparks of gratitude on your daily trips. You will be surprised how they will set small flames of friendship that will be rose beacons on your next visit.

Pamela Dunham of New Fairfield, Connecticut, had among her responsibilities on her job the supervision of a janitor who was doing a very poor job. The other employees would jeer at him and litter the hallways to show him what a bad job he was doing, (it was so bad, productive time was being lost in the shop.

Without success, Pam tried various ways to motivate this person. She noticed that occasionally he did a particularly good piece of work. She made a point to praise him for it in front of the other people. Each day the job he did all around got better, and pretty soon he started doing all his work efficiently. Now he does an excellent job and other people give him appreciation and recognition. Honest appreciation got results where criticism and ridicule failed.

Hurting people not only does not change them, it is never called for. There is an old saying that I have cut out and pasted on my mirror, where I cannot help but see it every day:

> I shall pass this way but once; any good, therefore, that I can do or any kindness that I can show to any human being, let me do it now. Let me not defer nor neglect it, for I shall not pass this way again.

Emerson said: "Every man I meet is my superior in some way. In that, I learn of him."

If that was true of Emerson, isn't it likely to be a thousand times more true of you and me? Let's cease thinking of our accomplishments, our wants. Let's try to figure out the other person's good points. Forget flattery. Give honest, sincere appreciation. Be "hearty in your approbation and lavish in your praise," and people will cherish your words and treasure them and repeat them over a lifetime—repeat them years after you have forgotten them,

One of the most neglected virtues of our daily existence is appreciation.

4

"He Who Can Do This Has The Whole World With Him. He Who Cannot Walks A Lonely Way"

I often went fishing up in Maine during the summer. Personally, I am very fond of strawberries and cream, but I have found that for some strange reason, fish prefer worms. So when I went fishing, I didn't think about what I wanted. I thought about what they wanted. 1 didn't bait the hook with strawberries and cream. Rather, I dangled a worm or a grasshopper in front of the fish and said: "Wouldn't you like to have that?"

Why not use the same common sense when fishing for people?

That is what Lloyd George, Great Britain's prime minister during World War I, did. When someone asked him how he managed to stay in power after the other wartime leaders—Wilson, Orlando, and Ciemenceau—had been forgotten, he replied that if his staying on top might be attributed to any one thing, it would be to his having learned that it was necessary to bait the hook to suit the fish.

Why talk about what we want? That is childish. Absurd. Of course, you are interested in what you want. You are eternally interested in it. But no one else is. The rest of us are just like you: we are interested in what we want.

So the only way on earth to influence other people is to talk about what they want and show them how to get it.

Remember that tomorrow when you are trying to get somebody to do something. If, for example, you don't want your children to smoke, don't preach at them, and don't talk about what you want; but show them that cigarettes may keep them from making the basketball team or winning the hundred-yard dash.

This is a good thing to remember regardless of whether you are dealing with children or calves or chimpanzees. For example: One day Ralph Waldo Emerson and his son tried to get a calf into a barn. But they made the common mistake of thinking only of what they wanted. Emerson pushed and his son pulled. But the calf was doing just what they were doing: he was thinking only of what he wanted; so he stiffened his legs and stubbornly refused to leave the pasture. The Irish housemaid saw their predicament. She couldn't write essays and books; but, on this occasion at least, she had more horse sense, or calf sense, than Emerson had. She thought of what the calf wanted; so she put her maternal finger in the calf's mouth and let the calf suck her finger as she gently led him into the barn.

Every act you have performed since the day you were born was performed because you wanted something. How about the time you gave a large contribution to the Red Cross? Yes, that is no exception to the rule. You gave the Red Cross the donation because you wanted to lend a helping hand: you wanted to do a beautiful, unselfish, divine act. "Inasmuch as ye have done it unto the least of these my brethren, ye have done it unto me."

If you hadn't wanted that feeling more than you wanted your money, you would not have made the contribution. Of course, you might have made the contribution because you were ashamed to refuse or because a customer asked you to do it. But one thing is certain. You made the contribution because you wanted something.

Harry A. Overstreet in his illuminating book *Influencing Human Behavior* said: "Action springs out of what we fundamentally desire... and the best piece of advice which can be given to would-be persuaders, whether in business, in the home, in the school, in politics, is: First, arouse in the other person an eager want. He who can do this has the whole world with him. He who cannot walks a lonely way."

Andrew Carnegie, the poverty-stricken Scotch lad who started to work at two cents an hour and finally gave away $365 million, learned early in life that the only way to influence people is to talk in terms of what the other person wants. He attended school only four years; yet he learned how to handle people.

An example of persuading comes from Stan Novak of Cleveland, Ohio, a participant in our course. Stan came home from work one evening to find his youngest son, Tim, kicking and screaming on the living room floor. He was to start kindergarten the next day and was protesting that he would not go. Stan's normal reaction would have been to banish the child to his room and tell him he'd just better make up his mind to go. He had no choice. But tonight, recognizing that this would not really help Tim start kindergarten in the best frame of mind, Stan sat down and thought, "If I were Tim, why would I be excited about going to kindergarten?" He and his wife made a list of all the fun things Tim would do such as finger-painting, singing songs, making new friends. Then they put them into action. "We all started finger-painting on the kitchen table—my wife, Lil, my other son, Bob, and myself, all having fun. Soon Tim was peeping around the corner. Next he was begging to participate. 'Oh, no! You have to go to kindergarten first to learn how to finger-paint.' With all the enthusiasm I could muster I went through the list talking in terms he could understand—telling him all the fun he would have in kindergarten. The next morning, I thought I was the first one up. I went downstairs and found Tim sitting sound asleep in the living room chair. 'What are you doing here?' I asked. Tim waiting to go to kindergarten. I don't want to be late.' The enthusiasm of our entire family had aroused in Tim an eager want that no amount of discussion or threat could have possibly accomplished."

Tomorrow you may want to persuade somebody to do something. Before you speak, pause and ask yourself: "How can I make this person want to do it?"

That question will stop us from rushing into a situation heedlessly, with futile chatter about our desires.

At one time, I rented the grand ballroom of a certain New York hotel for twenty nights in each season in order to hold a series of lectures.

At the beginning of one season, I was suddenly informed that I should have to pay almost three times as much rent as formerly. This news reached me after the tickets had been printed and distributed and all announcements had been made.

Naturally, I didn't want to pay the increase, but what was the use of talking to the hotel about what I wanted? They were interested only in what they wanted. So a couple of days later, I went to see the manager.

"I was a bit shocked when 1 got your letter," I said, "but I don't blame you at all. If I had been in your position, I should probably have written a similar letter myself. Your duty as the manager of the hotel is to make all the profit possible. If you don't do that, you will be fired and you ought to be fired. Now, let's take a piece of paper and write down the advantages and the disadvantages that will accrue to you, if you insist on this increase in rent."

Then I took a letterhead and ran a line through the center and headed one column "Advantages" and the other column "Disadvantages."

I wrote down under the head "Advantages" these words: "Ballroom free." Then I went on to say: "You will have the advantages of having the ballroom free to rent for dances and conventions. That is a big advantage, for affairs like that will pay you much more than you can get for a series of lectures. If I tie your ballroom up for twenty nights during the course of the season, it is sure to mean a loss of some very profitable business to you.

"Now, let's consider the disadvantages. First, instead of increasing your income from me, you are going to decrease it. In fact, you are going to wipe it out because I cannot pay the rent you are asking. I shall be forced to hold these lectures at some other place.

"There's another disadvantage to you also. These lectures attract crowds of educated and cultured people to your hotel. That is good advertising for you, isn't it? In fact, if you spent five thousand dollars advertising in the newspapers, you couldn't bring as many people to look at your hotel as I can bring by these lectures. That is worth a lot to a hotel, isn't it?"

As I talked, I wrote these two "disadvantages" under the proper heading, and handed the sheet of paper to the manager, saying: "1 wish you would carefully consider both the advantages and the disadvantages that are going to accrue to you and then give me your final decision."

I received a letter the next day, informing me that my rent would be increased only fifty percent instead of three hundred percent.

Mind you, I got this reduction without saying a word about what I wanted. I talked all the time about what the other person wanted and how he could get it.

Suppose I had done the human, natural thing; suppose I had stormed into his office and said, "What do you mean by raising my rent three hundred percent when you know the tickets have been printed and the announcements made? Three hundred percent! Ridiculous! Absurd! I won't pay it!"

What would have happened then? An argument would have begun to steam and boil and sputter—and you know how arguments end. Even if I had convinced him that he was wrong, his pride would have made it difficult for him to back down and give in.

Here is one of the best bits of advice ever given about the fine art of human relationships. "If there is any one secret of success," said Henry Ford, "it lies in the ability to get the other person's point of view and see things from that person's angle as well as from your own."

That is so good, I want to repeat it: "If there is any one secret of success, it lies in the ability to get the other person's point of view and see things from that person's angle as well as from your own."

That is so simple, so obvious, that anyone ought to see the truth of it at a glance; yet ninety percent of the people on this earth ignore it ninety percent of the time.

An example? Look at the letters that come across your desk tomorrow morning, and you will find that most of them violate this important canon of common sense. Take this one, a letter written by the head of rhe radio department of an advertising agency with offices scattered across the continent. This letter was sent to the managers of local radio stations throughout the country. (I have set down, in brackets, my reactions to each paragraph.)

Mr. John Blank,
Blankville,
Indiana

Dear Mr. Blank,

The company desires to retain its position in advertising agency leadership in the radio field.

[Who cares what your company desires? I am worried about my own problems. The bank is foreclosing the mortgage on my house, the bugs are destroying the hollyhocks, the stock market tumbled yesterday. I missed the eight-fifteen this morning, I wasn't invited to the Joneses' dance last night, the doctor tells me I have high blood pressure and neuritis and dandruff. And then what happens? I come down to the office this morning worried, open my mail, and here is some little whippersnapper off in New York yapping about what his company wants. Bah! If he only realized what sort of impression his letter makes, he would get out of the advertising business and start manufacturing sheep dip.]

This agency's national advertising accounts were the bulwark of the network. Our subsequent clearances of station time have kept us at the top of agencies year after year.

[You are big and rich and right at the top, aren't you? So what? I don't give two whoops in Hades if you are as big as General Motors and General Electric and the General Staff of the U.S. Army all combined. If you had as much sense as a half-witted hummingbird, you would realize that I am interested in how big I am—not how big you are. All this talk about your enormous success makes me feel small and unimportant.]

We desire to service our accounts with the last word on radio station information.

[You desire! You desire. You unmitigated ass. I'm not interested in what you desire or what the President of the United States desires. Let me tell you once and for all that I am interested in what I desire—and you haven't said a word about that yet in this absurd letter of yours.]

Will you, therefore, put the—company on your preferred list for weekly station information—every single detail that will be useful to an agency in booking time.

["Preferred list." You have your nerve! You make me feel insignificant by your big talk about your company—and then you ask me to put you on a "preferred" list, and you don't even say "please" when you ask it.]

A prompt acknowledgment of this letter, giving us yout latest "doings," will be mutually helpful.

[You fool! You mail me a cheap form letter, a letter scattered far and wide like the autumn leaves, and you have the gall to ask me, when I am worried about the mortgage and the hollyhocks and my blood pressure, to sit down and dictate a personal note acknowledging your form letter—and you ask me to do it "promptly." What do you mean, "promptly"? Don't you know I am just as busy as you are—or, at least, I like to think I am. And while we are on the subject, who gave you the lordly right to order me around? You say it will be "mutually helpful." At last, at last, you have begun to see my viewpoint. But you are vague about how it will be to my advantage.]

Very truly yours,
John Doe
Manager, Radio Department

P.S. The enclosed reprint from the *Blankville* journal will be of interest to you, and you may want *to broadcast it over your station.*

[Finally, down here in the postscript, you mention something that may help me solve one of my problems. Why didn't you begin your letter with—but what's the use? Any advertising man who is guilty of perpetrating such drivel as you have sent me has something wrong with his medulla oblongata. You don't need a letter giving our latest doings. What you need is a quart of iodine in your thyroid gland.]

Now, if people who devote their lives to advertising and who pose as experts in the art of influencing people to buy—if they write a letter like that, what can we expect from the butcher and baker or the auto mechanic?

Here is another letter, written by the superintendent of a large freight terminal to a student of this course, Edward Vermylen. What effect did this letter have on the man to whom it was addressed? Read it and then I'll tell you.

A. Zeregas Sons, Inc.
28 Front Street
Brooklyn, N.Y. 11201
Attention: Mr. Edward Vermylen

Gentlemen,

'The operations at our outbound-rail-receiving station are handicapped because a material percentage of the total business is delivered us in the late afternoon. This condition results in congestion, overtime on the part of our forces, delays to trucks, and in some cases delays to freight. On November 10, we received from your company a lot of 510 pieces, which reached here at 4:20 p.m.

We solicit your cooperation toward overcoming the undesirable effects arising from late receipt of freight. May we ask that, on days on which you ship the volume which was received on the above date, effort be made either to get the truck here earlier or to deliver us part of the freight during the morning?

The advantage that would accrue to you under such an arrangement would be that of more expeditious discharge of your trucks and the assurance that your business would go forward on the date of its receipt.

Very truly yours,
J— B—, Supt.

After reading this letter, Mr. Vermylen, Sales Manager for A. Zerega's Sons, Inc., sent it to me with the following comment:

This letter had the reverse effect from that which was intended. The letter begins by describing the Terminal's difficulties, in which we are nor interested, generally speaking. Our cooperation is then requested without any thought as to whether it would inconvenience us, and then, finally, in the last paragraph, the fact is mentioned that if we do cooperate it will mean more expeditious discharge of our trucks with the assurance that our freight will go forward on the date of its receipt.

> In other words, that in which we are most interested is mentioned last and the whole effect is one of raising a spirit of antagonism rather than of cooperation.

Let's see if we can't rewrite and improve this letter. Let's not waste any time talking about our problems. As Henry Ford admonishes, let's "get the other person's point of view and see things from that person's angle, as well as from our own."

Here is one way of revising the letter. It may not be the best way, but isn't it an improvement?

> Mr. Edward Vermylen
> c/o A. Zerega's Sons, Inc.
> 28 Front St.
> Brooklyn, N.Y. 11201
>
> Dear Mr. Vermylen,
>
> Your company has been one of our good customers for fourteen years. Naturally, we are very

grateful for your patronage and are eager to give you the speedy, efficient service you deserve. However, we regret to say that it isn't possible for us to do that when your trucks bring us a large shipment late in the afternoon, as they did on November 10. Why? Because many other customers make late-afternoon deliveries also. Naturally, that causes congestion. That means your trucks are held up unavoidably at the pier and sometimes even your freight is delayed.

That's bad, but it can be avoided. If you make your deliveries at the pier in the morning when possible, your trucks will be able to keep moving, your freight will get immediate attention, and our workers will get home early at night to enjoy a dinner of the delicious macaroni and noodles that you manufacture.

Regardless of when your shipments arrive, we shall always cheerfully do all in our power to serve you promptly.

You are busy. Please don't trouble to answer this note.

Very truly yours,
J— B—, Supt.

Barbara Anderson, who worked in a bank in New York, desired to move to Phoenix, Arizona, because of the health of her son. Using the principles she had learned in our course, she wrote the following letter to twelve banks in Phoenix:

Dear Sir,

My ten years of bank experience should be of interest to a rapidly growing bank like yours.

In various capacities in bank operations with the Bankers Trust Company in New York, leading to my present assignment as branch manager, I have acquired skills in all phases of banking, including depositor relations, credits, loans, and administration.

I will be relocating to Phoenix in May and I am sure I can contribute to your growth and profit. I will be in Phoenix the week of April 3 and would appreciate the opportunity to show you how I can help your bank meet its goals.

Sincerely,
Barbara L. Anderson

Do you think Mrs. Anderson received any response from that letter? Eleven of the twelve banks invited her to be interviewed, and she had a choice of which bank's offer to accept. Why? Mrs. Anderson did not state what *she* wanted, but wrote in the letter how she could help them, and focused on *their* wants, not her own.

Thousands of salespeople are pounding the pavements today, tired, discouraged, and underpaid. Why? Because they are always thinking only of what they want. They don't realize that neither you nor I want to buy anything. If we did, we would go out and buy it. But both of us are eternally interested in solving our problems. And if salespeople can show us how their services or merchandise will help us solve our problems, they won't need to sell us. We'll buy. And customers like to feel that they are buying—not being sold.

Yet many salespeople spend a lifetime in selling without seeing things from the customer's angle. For example, for many years I lived in Forest Hills, a little community of private homes in the center of Greater New York. One day as I was rushing to the station, I chanced to meet a real estate operator who had bought and sold property in that area for many years. He knew Forest Hiils well, so I hurriedly asked him whether or not my stucco house was built with metal lath or hollow tile. He said he didn't know and told me what I already knew—that I could find out by calling the Forest Hills Garden Association. The following morning, I received a letter from him. Did he give me the information I wanted? He could have gotten it in sixty seconds by a telephone call. But he didn't. He told me again that I could get it by telephoning, and then asked me to let him handle my insurance.

He was not interested in helping me. He was interested only in helping himself.

J. Howard Lucas of Birmingham, Alabama, tells how two salespeople from the same company handled the same type of situation. He reported:

"Several years ago, I was on the management team of a small company. Headquartered near us was the district office of a large insurance company. Their agents were assigned territories, and our company was assigned to two agents, who I shall refer to as Carl and John.

"One morning, Carl dropped by our office and casually mentioned that his company had just introduced a new life insurance policy for executives and thought we might be interested later on and he would get back to us when he had more information on it.

"The same day, John saw us on the sidewalk while returning from a coffee break, and he shouted: 'Hey, Luke, hold up, I have some great news for you fellows.' He hurried up and very excitedly told us about an executive life insurance policy his company had introduced that very day. (It was the same policy that Carl had casually mentioned.) He wanted us to have one of the first issued. He gave us a few important facts about the coverage and ended saying, "The policy is so new, I'm going to have someone from the home office come out tomorrow and explain it. Now, in the meantime, let's get the applications signed and on the way so he can have more information to work with." His enthusiasm aroused in us an eager want for this policy even though we still did not have details. When they were made available to us, they confirmed Johns initial understanding of the policy, and he not only sold each of us a policy, but later doubled our coverage.

"Carl could have had those sales, but he made no effort to arouse in us any desire for the policies."

The world is full of people who are grabbing and self-seeking. So the fair individual who unselfishly tries to serve others has an enormous advantage. He has little competition. Owen D. Young, a noted lawyer and one of Americas great business leaders, once said: "People who can put themselves in the place of other people, who can understand the workings of their minds, need never worry about what the future has in store for them."

If out of reading this book you get just one thing—an increased tendency to think always in terms of other people's point of view, and see things from their angle—if you get that one thing out of this book, it may easily prove to be one of the building blocks of your career.

Looking at the other persons point of view and arousing an eager want for something is not to be construed as manipulating that person to do something that is only for your benefit and his or her detriment. Each party should gain from the negotiation. In the letters to Mr. Vermylen, both the sender and the receiver of the correspondence gained by implementing what was suggested. Won by her letter, the bank obtained a valuable employee, and Mrs. Anderson a suitable job. And in the example of John's sale of insurance to Mr. Lucas, both gained through the transaction.

Another example in which everybody gains through this principle of arousing an eager want comes from Michael E. Whidden of Warwick, Rhode Island, who is a territory salesman for the Shell Oil Company. Mike wanted to become the number-one salesperson in his district, but one service station was holding back. It was run by an older man who could not be motivated to clean up his station. It was in such poor shape that sales were declining significantly.

The manager would not listen to any of Mikes pleas to upgrade the station. After many exhortations and heart- to-heart talks—all of which had no impact—Mike decided to invite the manager to visit the newest Shell station in his territory.

The manager was so impressed by the facilities at the new station that when Mike visited him the next time, his station was cleaned up and had recorded a sales increase. This enabled Mike to reach the number-one spot in his district. All his talking and discussion hadn't helped, but by arousing an eager want in the manager, by showing him the modern station, he had accomplished his goal, and both the manager and Mike benefited.

Most people go through college and learn to read Virgil and master the mysteries of calculus without ever discovering how their own minds function. For instance, I once gave a course in Effective Speaking for the young college graduates who were entering the employ of the Carrier Corporation, the large air-conditioner manufacturer. One of the participants wanted to persuade the others to play basketball in their free time, and this is about what he said, "If I want you to come out and play basketball. I like to play basketball, but the last few times I've been to the gymnasium, there haven't been enough people to get up a game. Two or three of us got to throwing the ball around the other night—and T got a black eye. I wish all of you would come down tomorrow night. I want to play basketball."

Did he talk about anything you want? You don't want to go to a gymnasium that no one else goes to, do you? You don't care about what he wants. You don't want to get a black eye.

Could he have shown you how to get the things you want by using the gymnasium? Surely. More pep. Keener edge to the appetite. Clearer brain. Fun. Games. Basketball.

To repeat Professor Overstreets wise advice: First, arouse in the other person an eager want. He who can do this has the whole world with him. He who cannot walks a lonely way.

One of the students in the training course was worried about his little boy. The child was underweight and refused to eat properly. They scolded and nagged. "Mother wants you to eat this and that." "Father wants you to grow up to be a big man."

Did the boy pay any attention to these pleas? Just about as much as you would pay to one fleck of sand on a sandy beach.

No one with a trace of horse sense would expect a child three years old to react to the viewpoint of a father thirty years old. Yet that was precisely what that father had expected, it was absurd. He finally saw that. So he said to himself: "What does that boy want? How can I tie up what I want to what he wants?"

It was easy for the father when he started thinking about it. His boy had a tricycle that he loved to ride up and down the sidewalk in front of the house in Brooklyn. A few doors down the street lived a bully—a bigger boy who would pull the little boy off his tricycle and ride it himself.

Naturally, the little boy would run screaming to his mother, and she would have to come out and take the bully off the tricycle and put her little boy on again. This happened almost every day.

What did the little boy want? It didn't take a Sherlock Holmes to answer that one. His pride, his anger, his desire for a feeling of importance—all the strongest emotions in his makeup—goaded him to get revenge, to smash the bully in the nose. And when his father explained that the boy would be able to wallop the daylights out of the bigger kid someday if he would only eat the things his mother wanted him to eat—when his father promised him that—there was no longer any problem of dietetics. That boy would have eaten spinach, sauerkraut, salt mackerel—anything in order to be big enough to whip the bully who had humiliated him so often.

After solving that problem, the parents tackled another: the boy had the unholy habit of wetting the bed.

He slept with his grandmother. In the morning, his grandmother would wake up and feel the sheet and say: "Look, Johnny, what you did again last night."

He would say: "No, 1 didn't do it. You did it." Scolding, spanking, shaming him, reiterating that the parents didn't want him to do it—none of these things kept the bed dry. So the parents asked: "How can we make this boy want to stop wetting his bed?".

What were his wants? First, he wanted to wear pajamas like Daddy instead of wearing a nightgown like

Grandmother. Grandmother was getting fed up with his nocturnal iniquities, so she gladly offered to buy him a pair of pajamas if he would reform. Second, he wanted a bed of his own. Grandma didn't object.

His mother took him to a department store in Brooklyn, winked at the salesgirl, and said: "Here is a little gentleman who would like to do some shopping." The salesgirl made him feel important by saying: "Young man, what can I show you?"

He stood a couple of inches taller and said: "I want to buy a bed for myself."

When he was shown the one his mother wanted him to buy, she winked at the salesgirl and the boy was persuaded to buy it.

The bed was delivered the next day; and that night, when Father came home, the little boy ran to the door shouting; "Daddy! Daddy! Come upstairs and see my bed that I bought!"

The father, looking at the bed, obeyed Charles Schwab's injunction: he was "hearty in his approbation and lavish in his praise."

"You are not going to wet this bed, are you?" the father said.

"Oh, no, no! I am not going to wet this bed." The boy kept his promise, for his pride was involved. That was his bed. He and he alone had bought it. And he was wearing pajamas now like a little man. He wanted to act like a man. And he did.

Another father, K. T. Dutschmann, a telephone engineer, a student of the training course, couldn't get his three-year-old daughter to eat breakfast. The usual scolding, pleading, coaxing methods had all ended in futility. So the parents asked themselves: "How can we make her want to do it?"

The little girl loved to imitate her mother, to feel big and grown up; so one morning they put her on a chair and let her make the breakfast. At the psychological moment, Father drifted into the kitchen while she was stirring the cereal and she said: "Oh, look, Daddy, I am making the cereal this morning."

She ate two helpings of the cereal without any coaxing, because she was interested in it. She had achieved a feeling of importance; she had found in making the cereal an avenue of self-expression.

William Winter once remarked that "self-expression is the dominant necessity of human nature." Why can't we adapt this same psychology to business dealings? When we have a brilliant idea, instead of making others think it is ours, why not let them cook and stir the idea themselves? They will then regard it as their own; they will like it and maybe eat a couple of helpings of it.

Remember: "First, arouse in the other person an eager want. He who can do this has the whole world with him. He who cannot walks a lonely way."

Look at things from the other persons vantage as well as your own.

~

Instead of worrying about what people say of you, why not spend time trying to accomplish something they will admire.

5

"If You Want To Gather Honey, Don't Kick Over The Beehive"

On May 7, 1931, the most sensational manhunt New York City had ever known had come to its climax. After weeks of search, "Two Gun" Crowley—the killer, the gunman who didn't smoke or drink—was at bay, trapped in his sweetheart's apartment on West End Avenue.

One hundred and fifty policemen and detectives laid siege to his top-floor hideaway. They chopped holes in the roof; they tried to smoke out Crowley, the "cop killer" with reargas. Then they mounted their machine guns on surrounding buildings, and for more than an hour, one of New Yorks fine residential areas reverberated with the crack of pistol fire and the rat-tat-tat of machine guns. Crowley, crouching behind an overstuffed chair, fired incessantly at the police. Ten thousand excited people watched the battle. Nothing like it had ever been seen before on the sidewalks of New York.

When Crowley was captured, Police Commissioner E. P. Mulrooney declared that the two-gun desperado was one of the most dangerous criminals ever encountered in the history of New York. "He will kill," said the commissioner, "at the drop of a feather."

But how did "Two Gun" Crowley regard himself? We know, because while the police were firing into the apartment, he wrote a letter addressed "To whom it may concern." And, as he wrote, the blood flowing from his wounds left a crimson trail on the paper. In this letter Crowley said: "Under my coat is a weary heart, but a kind one—one that would do nobody any harm."

A short time before this, Crowley had been having a party with his girlfriend on a country road out on Long Island. Suddenly a policeman walked up to the car and said: "Let me see your license."

Without saying a word, Crowley drew his gun and cut the policeman down with a shower of lead. As rhe dying officer fell, Crowley leaped out of the car, grabbed the officer's revolver, and fired another bullet into the prostrate body. And the killer said, "Under my coat is a weary heart, but a kind one—one that would do nobody any harm."

Crowley was sentenced to the electric chair. When he arrived at the death house in Sing Sing, did he say, "This is what I get for killing people?" No, he said: "This is what I get for defending myself."

The point of the story is this: Crowley didn't blame himself for anything.

Is that an unusual attitude among criminals? If you think so, listen to this:

"I have spent the best years of my life giving people the lighter pleasures, helping them have a good time, and all I get is abuse, the existence of a hunted man."

That's Al Capone speaking. Yes, America's most notorious Public Enemy—the most sinister gang leader who ever shot up Chicago. Capone didn't condemn himself. He actually regarded himself as a public benefactor—an unappreciated and misunderstood public benefactor.

And so did Dutch Schultz before he crumpled up under gangster bullets in Newark. Dutch Schultz, one of New York's most notorious rats, said in a newspaper interview that he was a public benefactor. And he believed it.

I have had some interesting correspondence with Lewis Lawes, who was warden of New Yorks infamous Sing Sing prison for many years, on this subject, and he declared that "few of the criminals in Sing Sing regard themselves as bad men. They are just as human as you and I. So they rationalize, they explain. They can tell you why they had to crack a safe or be quick on the trigger finger. Most of them attempt by a form of reasoning, fallacious or logical, to justify their antisocial acts even to themselves, consequently stoutly maintaining that they should never have been imprisoned at all."

If Al Capone, "Two Gun" Crowley, Dutch Schultz and the desperate men and women behind prison walls don't blame themselves for anything—what about the people with whom you and I come in contact?

John Wanamaker, founder of the stores that bear his name, once confessed: "I learned thirty years ago that it is foolish to scold. I have enough trouble overcoming my own limitations without fretting over the fact that God has not seen fit to distribute evenly the gift of intelligence."

Wanamaker learned this lesson early, but I personally had to blunder through this old world for a third of a century before it even began to dawn upon me that ninety-nine times out of a hundred, people don't criticize themselves for anything, no matter how wrong it may be.

Criticism is futile because it puts a person on the defensive and usually makes him strive to justify himself. Criticism is dangerous, because it wounds a person's precious pride, hurts his sense of importance, and arouses resentment.

B. F. Skinner, the world-famous psychologist, proved through his experiments that an animal rewarded for good behavior will learn much more rapidly and retain what it learns far more effectively than an animal punished for bad behavior. Later studies have shown that the same applies to humans. By criticizing, we do not make lasting changes and often incur resentment.

Hans Selye, another great psychologist, said, "As much as we thirst for approval, we dread condemnation."

The resentment that criticism engenders can demoralize employees, family members, and friends, and still not correct the situation that has been condemned.

George B. Johnston of Enid, Oklahoma, is the safety coordinator for an engineering company. One of his responsibilities is to see that employees wear their hard hats whenever they are on the job in the field. He reported that whenever he came across workers who were not wearing hard hats, he would tell them with a lot of authority of the regulation and that they must comply. As a result he would get sullen acceptance, and often after he left, the workers would remove the hats.

He decided to try a different approach. The next time he found some of the workers not wearing their hard hats, he asked if the hats were uncomfortable or did not fit properly. Then he reminded the men in a pleasant tone of voice that the hat was designed to protect them from injury and suggested that it always be worn on the job. The result was increased compliance with the regulation with no resentment or emotional upset.

You will find examples of the futility of criticism bristling on a thousand pages of history. Take, for example, the famous quarrel between Theodore Roosevelt and President Taft—a quarrelsome chat split the Republican party, put Woodrow Wilson in the White House, and wrote bold, luminous lines across the First World War and altered the flow of history Let's review the facts quickly. When Theodore Roosevelt stepped out of the White House in 1908, he supported Taft, who was elected president. Then Theodore Roosevelt went off to Africa to shoot lions. When he returned, he exploded. He denounced lift for his conservatism, tried to secure the nomination for a third term himself, formed the Bull Moose party, but demolished the GOP. In the election that followed, William Howard Taft and the Republican party carried only two states, Vermont and Utah—the most disastrous defeat the party had ever known.

Theodore Roosevelt blamed Taft, but did President Taft blame himself? Of course not. With tears in his eyes, Taft said: "I don't see how I could have done any differently from what I have."

Who was to blame? Roosevelt or Taft? Frankly, I don't know, and I don't care. The point I am trying to make is that all of Theodore Roosevelt's criticism didn't persuade Taft that he was wrong, it merely made Taft strive to justify himself and to reiterate with tears in his eyes: "I don't see how I could have done any differently from what I have."

Or, take the Teapot Dome oil scandal. It kept the newspapers ringing with indignation in the early 1920s. It rocked the nation! Within the memory of living men, nothing like it had ever happened before in American public life. Here are the bare facts of the scandal: Albert B. Fall, secretary of the interior in Hardings cabinet, was entrusted with the leasing of government oil reserves at Elk Hill and Teapot Dome—oil reserves that had been set aside for the future use of the Navy. Did Secretary Fall permit competitive bidding? No sir. He handed the fat, juicy contract outright to his friend Edward I. Dohenv. And what did Doheny do? He gave Secretary Fall what he was pleased to call a "loan" of one hundred thousand dollars. Then in a high-handed manner, Secretary Fall ordered United States Marines into the district to drive off competitors whose adjacent wells were sapping oil out of the Elk Hill reserves. These competitors, driven off their ground at the ends of guns and bayonets, rushed into court—and blew the lid off the Teapot Dome scandal. A stench arose so vile that it ruined the Harding administration, nauseated an entire nation, threatened to wreck the Republican party, and put Albert B. Fall behind prison bars.

Fall was condemned viciously—condemned as few men in public life have ever been. Did he repent? Never! Years later, Herbert Hoover intimated in a public speech that President Harding's death had been due to mental anxiety and worry because a friend had betrayed him. When Mrs. Fall heard that, she sprang from her chair, she wept, she shook her fists at fate and screamed; "What? Harding betrayed by Fall? No! My husband never betrayed anyone. This whole house full of gold would not tempt my husband to do wrong. He is the one who has been betrayed and led to the slaughter and crucified."

There you are; human nature in action, wrongdoers, blaming everybody but themselves. We are all like that. So when you and I are tempted to criticize someone tomorrow, let's remember Al Capone, "Two Gun" Crowley, and Albert Fall. Let's realize that criticisms are like homing pigeons. They always return home. Let's realize that the person we are going to correct and condemn will probably justify himself or herself, and condemn us in return; or, like the gentle Taft, will say: "I don't see how I could have done any differently from what I have."

On the morning of April 15, 1865, Abraham Lincoln lay dying in a hall bedroom of a cheap lodging house directly across the street from Ford's Theater, where John Wilkes Booth had shot him. Lincolns long body lay stretched diagonally across a sagging bed that was too short for him. A cheap reproduction of Rosa Ronheur's famous painting *The Horse Fair* hung above the bed, and a dismal gas jet flickered yellow light.

As Lincoln lay dying, Secretary of War Stanton said, "There lies the most perfect ruler of men that the world has ever seen."

What was the secret of Lincoln's success in dealing with people? I studied the life of Abraham Lincoln for ten years and devoted all of three years to writing and rewriting a book entitled *Lincoln the Unknown*. I believe I have made as detailed and exhaustive a study of Lincoln's personality and home life as it is possible for any being to make. I made a special study of Lincoln's method of dealing with people. Did he indulge in criticism? Oh, yes. As a young man in the Pigeon Creek Valley of Indiana, he not only criticized but also wrote letters and poems ridiculing people and dropped these letters on the country roads where they were sure to be found. One of these letters aroused resentments that burned for a lifetime.

Even after Lincoln had become a practising lawyer in Springfield, Illinois, he attacked his opponents openly in letters published in the newspapers. But he did this just once too often.

In the autumn of 1842, he ridiculed a vain, pugnacious politician by the name of James Shields. Lincoln lampooned him through an anonymous letter published in the *Springfield* journal. The town roared with laughter. Shields, sensitive and proud, boiled with indignation. He found out who wrote the letter, leaped on his horse, started after Lincoln, and challenged him to fight a duel. Lincoln didn't want to fight. He was opposed to dueling, but he couldn't get out of it and save his honor. He was given the choice of weapons. Since he had very long arms, he chose cavalry broadswords and took lessons in sword fighting from a West Point graduate. On the appointed day, he and Shields met on a sandbar in the Mississippi River, prepared to fight to the death, but at the last minute, their seconds interrupted and stopped the duel.

That was the most lurid personal incident in Lincoln's life. It taught him an invaluable lesson in the art of dealing with people. Never again did he write an insulting letter. Never again did he ridicule anyone. And from that time on, he almost never criticized anybody for anything.

Time after time, during the Civil War, Lincoln put a new general at the head of the Army of the Potomac, and each one in turn—McClellan, Pope, Burnside, Hooker, Meade—blundered tragically and drove Lincoln to pacing the floor in despair. Half the nation savagely condemned these incompetent generals, but Lincoln, "with malice toward none, with charity for all," held his peace. One of his favorite quotations was "Judge not, that ye be not judged."

And when Mrs. Lincoln and others spoke harshly of the southern people, Lincoln replied: "Don't criticize them; they are just what we would be under similar circumstances."

Yet if any man ever had occasion to criticize, surely it was Lincoln. Let's take just one illustration:

The Battle of Gettysburg was fought during the first three days of July 1863. During the night of July 4, Lee began to retreat southward while storm clouds deluged the country with rain. When Lee reached the Potomac with his defeated army, he found a swollen, impassible river in front of him, and a victorious Union Army behind him. Lee was in a trap. He couldn't escape. Lincoln saw that. Here was a golden, heaven-sent opportunity—the opportunity to capture Lees army and end the war immediately. So, with a surge of high hope, Lincoln ordered Meade not to call a council of war but to attack Lee immediately. Lincoln telegraphed his orders and then sent a special messenger to Meade demanding immediate action.

And what did General Meade do? He did the very opposite of what he was told to do. He called a council of war in direct violation of Lincoln's orders. He hesitated. He procrastinated. He telegraphed all manner of excuses. He refused point-blank to attack Lee. Finally the waters receded and Lee escaped over the Potomac with his forces.

Lincoln was furious. "What does this mean?" Lincoln cried to his son Robert. "Great God! What does this mean? We had them within our grasp, and had only to stretch forth our hands and they were ours; yet nothing I could say or do could make the army move. Under rhe circumstances, almost any general could have defeated Lee. If I had gone up there, I could have whipped him myself."

In bitter disappointment, Lincoln sat down and wrote Meade this letter. And remember, at this period of his life Lincoln was extremely conservative and restrained in his phraseology. So this letter coming from Lincoln in 1863 was tantamount to the severest rebuke.

My dear General,

I do not believe you appreciate the magnitude of the misfortune involved in Lee's escape. He was within our easy grasp, and to have closed upon him would, in connection with our other late successes, have ended the war. As it is, the war will be prolonged indefinitely. If you could not safely attack Lee last Monday, how can you possibly do so south of the river, when you can take with you very few—no more than two-thirds of the force you then had in hand? It would be unreasonable to expect and I do not expect that you can now effect much. Your golden opportunity is gone, and I am distressed immeasurably because of it.

What do you suppose Meade did when he read the letter?

Meade never saw that letter. Lincoln never mailed it. It was found among his papers after his death.

My guess is—and this is only a guess—that after writing that letter, Lincoln looked out of the window and said to himself, "just a minute. Maybe I ought not to be so hasty. It is easy enough for me to sit here in the quiet of the White House and order Meade to attack; but if I had been up at Gettysburg, and if I had seen as much blood as Meade has seen during the last week, and if my ears had been pierced with the screams and shrieks ol the wounded and dying, maybe I wouldn't be so anxious to attack either. If I had Meade's timid temperament, perhaps I would have done just what he had done. Anyhow, it is water under the bridge now. If I send this letter, it will relieve my feelings, but it will make Meade try to justify himself It will make him condemn me. It will arouse hard feelings, impair all his further usefulness as a commander, and perhaps force him to resign from the army."

So, as I have already said, Lincoln put the letter aside, for he had learned by bitter experience that sharp criticisms and rebukes almost invariably end in futility.

Theodore Roosevelt said that when he, as president, was confronted with a perplexing problem, he used to lean back and look up at a large painting of Lincoln that hung above his desk in the White House and ask himself, "What would Lincoln do if he were in my shoes? How would he solve this problem?"

The next time we are tempted to admonish somebody, let's pull a five-dollar bill out of our pocket, look at Lincoln's picture on the bill, and ask, "How would Lincoln handle this problem if he had it?"

Mark Twain lost his temper occasionally and wrote letters that turned the paper brown. For example, he once wrote to a man who had aroused his ire: "The thing for you is a burial permit. You have only to speak and I will see that you get it." On another occasion he wrote to an editor about a proofreader's attempts to "improve my spelling and punctuation." He ordered: "See, the matter according to my copy hereafter and see that the proofreader retains his suggestions in the mush of his decayed brain."

The writing of these stinging letters made Mark Twain feel better. They allowed him to blow off steam, and the letters didn't do any real harm, because Mark's wife secretly lifted them out of the mail. They were never sent.

Do you know someone you would like to change and regulate and improve? Good! This is fine. I am all in favor of it. But why not begin on yourself? From a purely selfish standpoint, that is a lot more profitable than trying to improve others—yes, and a lot less dangerous. "Don't complain about the snow on your neighbor's roof," said Confucius, "when your own doorstep is unclean."

When I was still young and trying hard to impress people, I wrote a foolish letter to Richard Harding Davis, an author who once loomed large on the literary horizon of America. I was preparing a magazine article about authors, and I asked Davis to tell me about his method of work. A few weeks earlier, I had received a letter from someone with this notation at the bottom: "Dictated but not read." I was quite impressed. I felt that the writer must be very big and busy and important. I wasn't the slightest bit busy, but I was eager to make an impression on Richard Harding Davis, so I ended my short note with the words: "Dictated but not read."

He never troubled to answer the letter. He simply returned it to me with this scribbled across the bottom: "Your bad manners are exceeded only by your bad manners." True, I had blundered, and perhaps I deserved this rebuke. But, being human, I resented it. I resented it so sharply that when I read of the death of Richard Harding Davis ten years later, the one thought that still persisted in my mind—I am ashamed to admit—was the hurt he had given me.

If you and I want to stir up a resentment tomorrow that may rankle across the decades and endure until death, just let us indulge in a little stinging criticism.

When dealing with people, let us remember we are not dealing with creatures of logic. We are dealing with creatures of emotion, creatures bristling with prejudices and motivated by pride and vanity.

Bitter criticism caused the sensitive Thomas Hardy, one of the finest novelists ever to enrich English literature, to give up forever the writing of fiction. Criticism drove Thomas Chatterton, the English poet, to suicide.

Benjamin Franklin, tactless in his youth, became so diplomatic, so adroit at handling people, that he was made American ambassador to France. The secret of his success? "I will speak ill of no man," he said, and speak all the good I know of everybody."

Any fool can criticize, condemn, and complain—and most fools do.

But it takes character and self-control to be understanding and forgiving.

"A great man shows his greatness," said Carlyle, "by the way he treats little men."

Bob Hoover, a famous test pilot and frequent performer at air shows, was returning to his home in Los Angeles from an air show in San Diego. As described in the magazine *Flight Operations,* at three hundred feet in the air, both engines suddenly stopped. By deft maneuvering he managed to land the plane, but it was badly damaged although nobody was hurt.

Hoover's first act after the emergency landing was to inspect the airplane's fuel. Just as he suspected, the World War II propeller plane he had been flying had been fueled with jet fuel rather than gasoline.

Upon returning to the airport, he asked to see the mechanic who had serviced his airplane. The young man was sick with the agony of his mistake. Tears streamed down his face as Hoover approached. He had just caused the loss of a very expensive plane and could have caused the loss of three lives as well.

You can imagine Hoover's anger. One could anticipate the tongue-lashing that this proud and precise pilot would unleash for that carelessness. But Hoover didn't scold the mechanic; he didn't even criticize him. Instead, he put his big arm around the man's shoulder and said, "To show you I'm sure that you'll never do this again, I want you to service my F-51 tomorrow."

Often parents are tempted to criticize their children. You would expect me to say "Don't." But I will not. I am merely going to say, "Before you criticize them, read one of the classics of American journalism, 'Father Forgets.'" It originally appeared as an editorial in the *People's Home Journal*. We are reprinting it here with the author's permission, as condensed in the *Reader's Digest*.

"Father Forgets" is one of those little pieces that—dashed off in a moment of sincere feeling—strikes an echoing chord in so many readers as to become a perennial reprint favorite. Since its first appearance, "Father Forgets" has been reproduced, writes the author, W. Livingston Larned, "in hundreds of magazines and house organs, and in newspapers the country over. It has been reprinted almost as extensively in many foreign languages. I have given personal permission to thousands who wished to read it from school, church, and lecture platforms. It has been 'on the air' on countless occasions and programs. Oddly enough, college periodicals have used it, and high-school magazines. Sometimes a little piece seems mysteriously to 'click.' This one certainly did."

FATHER FORGETS
W. Livingston Larned

Listen, son: I am saying this as you lie asleep, one little paw crumpled under your cheek and the blond curls stickily wet on your damp forehead. I have stolen into your room alone. Just a few minutes ago, as I sat reading my paper in the library, a stifling wave of remorse swept over me. Guiltily I came to your bedside.

There are the things I was thinking, son: I had been cross to you. I scolded you as you were dressing for school because you gave your face merely a dab with a towel. I took you to task for not cleaning your shoes. I called out angrily when you threw some of your things on the floor.

At breakfast I found fault, too. You spilled things. You gulped down your food. You put your elbows on the table. You spread butter too thick on your bread. And as you started off to play and I made for my train, you turned and waved a hand and called, "Goodbye, Daddy!" and I frowned, and said in reply, "Hold your shoulders back!"

Then it began all over again in the late afternoon. As I came up the road I spied you, down on your knees, playing marbles. There were holes in your stockings. I humiliated you before your boyfriends by marching you ahead of me to the house. Stockings were expensive—and if you had to buy them you would be more careful! Imagine that, son, from a father!

Do you remember, later, when I was reading in the library, how you came in timidly, with a sort of hurt look in your eyes? When I glanced up over my paper, impatient at the interruption, you hesitated at the door. "What is it you want?" I snapped.

You said nothing, but ran across in one tempestuous plunge, and threw your arms around my neck and kissed me, and your small arms tightened with an affection that God had set blooming in your heart and which even neglect could not wither. And then you were gone, pattering up the stairs.

Well, son, it was shortly afterwards that my paper slipped from my hands and a terrible sickening fear came over me. What has habit been doing to me? The habit of finding fault, of reprimanding—this was my reward to you for being a boy. It was not that I did not love you; it was that I expected too much of youth. I was measuring you by the yardstick of my own years.

And there was so much that was good and fine and true in your character. The little heart of yours was as big as the dawn itself over the wide hills. This was shown by your spontaneous impulse to rush in and kiss me good night. Nothing else matters tonight, son. I have come to your bedside in the darkness, and I have knelt there, ashamed!

It is a feeble atonement; I know you would not understand these things if I told them to you during your waking hours. But tomorrow I will be a real daddy! I will chum with you, and suffer when you suffer, and laugh when you laugh. I will bite my tongue when impatient words come. I will keep saying as if it were a ritual: "He is nothing but a boy—a little boy!"

I am afraid I have visualized you as a man. Yet as I see you now, son, crumpled and weary in your cot, I see that you are still a baby. Yesterday you were in your mother's arms, your head on her shoulder. I have asked too much, too much.

Instead of condemning people, let's try to understand them. Let's try to figure out why they do what they do. That's a lot more profitable and intriguing than criticism; and it breeds sympathy, tolerance, and kindness. "To know all is to forgive all."

As Dr. Johnson said: "God himself, sir, does not propose to judge man until the end of his days."

Why should you and I?

Instead of condemning people, try to understand them.

6

The High Road To Reason

If your temper is aroused and you tell them a thing or two, you will have a fine time unloading your feelings. But what about the other person? Will he share your pleasure? Will your belligerent tones, your hostile attitude, make it easy for him to agree with you?

"If you come at me with your fists doubled," said Woodrow Wilson, "I think I can promise you that mine will double as fast as yours; but if you come to me and say, 'Let us sit down and take counsel together, and, if we differ from each other, understand why it is that we differ, just what the points at issue are,' we will presently find that we are not so far apart after all, that the points on which we differ are few and the points on which we agree are many, and that if we only have the patience and the candor and the desire to get together, we will get together."

Nobody appreciated the truth of Woodrow Wilson's statement more than John D. Rockefeller, Jr. Back in 1915, Rockefeller was the most fiercely despised man in Colorado. One of the bloodiest strikes in the history of American industry had been shocking the state for two terrible years. Irate, belligerent miners were demanding higher wages from the Colorado Fuel and Iron Company; Rockefeller controlled that company. Property had been destroyed, troops had been called out. Blood had been shed. Strikers had been shot, their bodies riddled with bullets.

At a time like that, with the air seething with hatred, Rockefeller wanted to win the strikers to his way of thinking. And he did it. How? Here's the story. After weeks spent in making friends, Rockefeller addressed the representatives of the strikers. This speech, in its entirety, is a masterpiece. It produced astonishing results. It calmed the tempestuous waves of hate that threatened to engulf Rockefeller. It won him a host of admirers. It presented facts in such a friendly manner that the strikers went back to work without saying another word about the increase in wages for which they had fought so violently.

The opening of that remarkable speech follows. Note how it fairly glows with friendliness. Rockefeller, remember, was talking to men who, a few days previously, had wanted to hang him by the neck to a sour apple tree; yet he couldn't have been more gracious, more friendly if he had addressed a group of medical missionaries. His speech was radiant with such phrases as, I am proud to be here, having visited in your homes, met many of your wives and children, we meet here not as strangers, but as friends...spirit of mutual friendship, our common interests, it is only by your courtesy that I am here.

"This is a red-letter day in my life," Rockefeller began. "It is the first time I have ever had the good fortune to meet the representatives of the employees of this great company, its officers and superintendents, together, and I can assure you that I am proud to be here, and that I shall remember this gathering as long as I live. Had this meeting been held two weeks ago, I should have stood here a stranger to most of you, recognizing a few faces. Having had the opportunity last week of visiting all the camps in the southern coal field and of talking individually with practically all of the representatives, except those who were away; having visited in your homes, met many of your wives and children, we meet here not as strangers, but as friends, and it is in that spirit of mutual friendship that I am glad to have this opportunity to discuss with you our common interests.

"Since this is a meeting of the officers of the company and the representatives of the employees, it is only by your courtesy that I am here, for I am not so fortunate as to be either one or the other; and yet I feel that I am intimately associated with you men, for, in a sense, I represent both the stockholders and the directors."

Isn't that a superb example of the fine art of making friends out of enemies?

Suppose Rockefeller had taken a different tact. Suppose he had argued with these miners and hurled devastating facts in their faces. Suppose he had told them by his tone and insinuations that they were wrong. Suppose that, by all the rules of logic, he had proved that they were wrong. What would have happened? More anger would have been stirred up, more hatred, more revolt.

If a man's heart is rankling with discord and ill feeling towards you, you can't win him to your way of thinking with all the logic in Christendom. Scolding parents and domineering bosses and husbands and nagging wives ought to realize that people don't want to change their minds. They can't be forced or driven to agree with you or me. But they may possibly be led to, if we are gentle and friendly, ever so gentle and ever so friendly.

Lincoln said that, in effect, over a hundred years ago. Here are his words:

It is an old and true maxim that "a drop of honey catches more flies than a gallon of gall." So with men, if you would win a man to your cause, first convince him that you are his sincere friend. Therein is a drop of honey that catches his heart; which, say what you will, is the great high road to his reason.

Business executives have learned that it pays to be friendly to strikers. For example, when twenty-five hundred employees in the White Motor Company's plant struck for higher wages and a union shop, Robert F. Black, then president of the company, didn't lose his temper and condemn and threaten and talk of tyranny and communists. He actually praised the strikers. He published an advertisement in the Cleveland papers, complimenting them on "the peaceful way in which they laid down their tools." Finding the strike pickets idle, he bought them a couple of dozen baseball bats and gloves and invited them to play ball on vacant lots. For those who preferred bowling, he rented a bowling alley.

This friendliness on Mr. Black's part did what friendliness always does: it begot friendliness. So the strikers borrowed brooms, shovels, and rubbish carts, and began picking up matches, papers, cigarette stubs, and cigar butts around the factory. Imagine it! Imagine strikers tidying up the factory grounds while battling for higher wages and recognition of the union. Such an event had never been heard of before in the long, tempestuous history of American labor wars. That strike ended with a compromise settlement within a week—ended without any ill feeling or rancor.

Daniel Webster, who looked like a god and talked like Jehovah, was one of the most successful advocates who ever pleaded a case; yet he ushered in his most powerful arguments with such friendly remarks as; "It will be for the jury to consider," "This may, perhaps, be worth thinking of,"

"Here are some facts that I trust you will not lose sight of," or "You, with your knowledge of human nature, will easily see the significance of these facts." No bulldozing. No high-pressure methods. No attempt to force his opinions on others. Webster used the soft-spoken, quiet, friendly approach, and it helped to make him famous.

You may never be called upon to settle a strike or address a jury, but you may want to get your rent reduced. Will the friendly approach help you then? Let's see.

O. L. Straub, an engineer, wanted to get his rent reduced. And he knew his landlord was hard-boiled. "I wrote to him," Mr. Straub said in a speech before the class, "notifying him that I was vacating my apartment as soon as my lease expired. The truth was, I didn't want to move. I wanted to stay if I could get my rent reduced. But the situation seemed hopeless. Other tenants had tried—and failed. Everyone told me that the landlord was extremely difficult to deal with. But I said to myself, 'I am studying a course in how to deal with people, so I'll try it on him—and see how it works.'

"He and his secretary came to see me as soon as he got my letter. I met him at the door with a friendly greeting. I fairly bubbled with good will and enthusiasm. I didn't begin talking about how high the rent was. I began talking about how much I liked his apartment house. Believe me, I was hearty in my approbation and lavish in my praise.' I complimented him on the way he ran the building and told him I should like so much to stay for another year but I couldn't afford it.

"He had evidently never had such a reception from a tenant. He hardly knew what to make of it.

"Then he started to tell me his troubles. Complaining tenants. One had written him fourteen letters, some of them positively insulting. Another threatened to break his lease unless the landlord kept the man on the floor above from snoring. 'What a relief it is,' he said, 'to have a satisfied tenant like you.' And then, without my even asking him to do it, he offered to reduce my rent a little. I wanted more, so I named the figure I could afford to pay, and he accepted without a word.

"As he was leaving, he turned to me and asked, 'What decorating can I do for you?'

"If I had tried to get the rent reduced by the methods the other tenants were using, I am positive I should have met the same failure they encountered. It was the friendly, sympathetic, appreciative approach that won."

Dean Woodcock of Pittsburgh, Pennsylvania, is the superintendent of a department of the local electric company. His staff was called upon to repair some equipment on top of a pole. This type of work had formerly been performed by a different department and had only recently been transferred to Woodcock's section. Although his people had been trained in the work, this was the first time they had ever actually been called upon to do it. Everybody in the organization was interested in seeing if and how they could handle it. Mr. Woodcock, several of his subordinate managers, and members of other departments of the utility went to see the operation. Many cars and trucks were there, and a number of people were standing around watching the two lone men on top of the pole.

Glancing around, Woodcock noticed a man up the street getting out of his car with a camera. He began taking pictures of the scene. Utility people are extremely conscious of public relations, and suddenly Woodcock realized what this setup looked like to the man with the camera—overkill, dozens of people being called out to do a two-person job. He strolled up the street to the photographer.

"I see you're interested in our operation."

"Yes, and my mother will be more than interested. She owns stock in your company. This will be an eye-opener for her. She may even decide her investment was unwise. I've been telling her for years there's a lot of waste motion in companies like yours. This proves it. The newspapers might like these pictures, too."

"It does look like it, doesn't it? I'd think the same thing in your position. But this is a unique situation," and Dean Woodcock went on to explain how this was the first job of this type for his department and how everyone from executives down was interested. He assured the man that under normal conditions two people could handle the job. The photographer put away his camera, shook Woodcock's hand, and thanked him for taking the time to explain the situation to him.

Dean Woodcock's friendly approach saved his company much embarrassment and bad publicity.

Another member of one of our classes, Gerald H. Winn of Littleton, New Hampshire, reported how, by using a friendly approach, he obtained a very satisfactory settlement on a damage claim.

"Early in the spring," he reported, "before the ground had thawed from winter freezing, there was an unusually heavy rainstorm and the water, which normally would have run off to nearby ditches and storm drains along the road, took a new course onto a building lot where I had just built a new home.

"Not being able to run off, the water pressure built up around the foundation of the house. The water forced itself under the concrete basement floor, causing it to explode, and the basement filled with water. This ruined the furnace and the hot-water heater. The cost to repair this damage was in excess of two thousand dollars. I had no insurance to cover this type of damage.

"However, I soon found out that the owner of the subdivision had neglected to put in a storm drain near the house which could have prevented this problem. I made an appointment to see him. During the twenty-five-minute trip to his office, I carefully reviewed the situation and, remembering the principles I learned in this course, I decided that showing my anger would not serve any worthwhile purpose. When I arrived, I kept very calm and started by talking about his recent vacation to the West Indies; then, when I felt the timing was right, I mentioned the 'little' problem of water damage. He quickly agreed to do his share in helping to correct the problem.

"A few days later he called and said he would pay for the damage and also put in a storm drain to prevent the same thing from happening in the future.

"Even though it was the fault of the owner of the subdivision, if I had not begun in a friendly way, there would have been a great deal of difficulty in getting him to agree to the total liability."

Years ago, when I was a barefoot boy walking through the woods to a country school out in northwest Missouri, I read a fable by Aesop about the sun and the wind. They quarreled about which was the stronger, and the wind said, "I'll prove I am. See the old man down there with a coat? I bet I can get his coat off him quicker than you can."

So the sun went behind a cloud, and the wind blew until it was almost a tornado, but the harder it blew, the tighter the old man clutched his coat to him.

Finally, the wind calmed down and gave up, and then the sun came out from behind the clouds and smiled kindly on the old man. Presently, he mopped his brow and pulled off his coat. The sun then told the wind that gentleness and friendliness were always stronger than fury and force.

The use of gentleness and friendliness is demonstrated day after day by people who have learned that a drop of honey catches more flies than a gallon of gall. F. Gale Connor of Lutherville, Maryland, proved this when he had to take his four-month-old car to the service department of the car dealer for the third time. He told our class: "It was apparent that talking to, reasoning with, or shouting at the service manager was not going to lead to a satisfactory resolution of my problems.

"I walked over to the showroom and asked to see the agency owner, Mr. White. After a short wait, I was ushered into Mr. White's office. I introduced myself and explained to him that I had bought my car from his dealership because of the recommendations of friends who had had previous dealings with him. I was told that his prices were very competitive and his service was outstanding. He smiled with satisfaction as he listened to me. I then explained the problem I was having with the service department. 'I thought you might want to be aware of any situation that might tarnish your fine reputation,' I added. He thanked me for calling this to his attention and assured me that my problem would be taken care of. Not only did he personally get involved, but he also lent me his car to use while mine was being repaired."

Aesop was a Greek slave who lived at the court of Croesus and spun immortal fables six hundred years before Christ. Yet the truths he taught about human nature are just as true in Boston and Birmingham now as they were twenty-six centuries ago in Athens. The sun can make you take off your coat more quickly than the wind; and kindliness, the friendly approach, and appreciation can make people change their minds more readily than all the bluster and storming in the world.

Remember what Lincoln said: "A drop of honey catches more flies than a gallon of gall."

Be friendly.

~

It isn't what you have, or who you are, or where you are, or what you are doing that makes you happy or unhappy. It is what you think about.

7

How To Get Cooperation

Don't you have much more faith in ideas that you discover for yourself than in ideas that are handed to you on a silver platter? If so, isn't it bad judgment to try to ram your opinions down the throats of other people? Isn't it wiser to make suggestions—and let the other person think out the conclusion?

Adolph Seitz of Philadelphia, sales manager in an automobile showroom and a student in one of my courses, suddenly found himself confronted with the necessity of injecting enthusiasm into a discouraged and disorganized group of automobile salespeople. Calling a sales meeting, he urged his people to tell him exactly what they expected from him. As they talked, he wrote their ideas on the blackboard. He then said: "I'll give you all these qualities you expect from me. Now I want you to tell me what I have a right to expect from you." The replies came quick and fast: loyalty, honesty, initiative, optimism, teamwork, eight hours a day of enthusiastic work. The meeting ended with a new courage, a new inspiration—one salesperson volunteered to work fourteen hours a day—and Mr. Seitz reported to me that the increase of sales was phenomenal.

"The people had made a sort of moral bargain with me," said Mr. Seitz, "and as long as I lived up to my part in it, they were determined to live up to theirs. Consulting them about their wishes and desires was just the shot in the arm they needed."

No one likes to feel that he or she is being told something or told to do a thing. We much prefer to feel that we are buying of our own accord or acting on our own ideas. We like to be consulted about our wishes, our wants, our thoughts.

Take the case of Eugene Wesson. He lost countless thousands of dollars in commissions before he learned this truth. Mr. Wesson sold sketches for a studio that created designs for stylists and textile manufacturers. Mr. Wesson had called on one of the leading stylists in New York once a week, every week for three years. "He never refused to see me," said Mr. Wesson, "but he never bought. He always looked over my sketches very carefully and then said: 'No, Wesson, I guess we don't get together today.'"

After 150 failures, Wesson realized he must be in a mental rut, so he resolved to devote one evening a week to the study of influencing human behavior, to help him develop new ideas and generate new enthusiasm.

He decided on this new approach. With half a dozen unfinished artists' sketches under his arm, he rushed over to the buyer's office. "I want you to do me a little favor, if you will," he said. "Here are some uncompleted sketches. Won't you please tell me how we could finish them up in such a way that you could use them?"

The buyer looked at the sketches for a while without uttering a word. Finally he said: "Leave these with me for a few days, Wesson, and then come back and see me."

Wesson returned three days later, got his suggestions, took the sketches back to the studio, and had them finished according to the buyer's ideas. The result? All accepted.

After that, this buyer ordered scores of other sketches from Wesson, all drawn according to the buyers ideas. "I realized why I had failed for years to sell him," said Mr. Wesson. "I had urged him to buy what I thought he ought to have. Then I changed my approach completely. I urged him to give me his ideas. This made him feel that he was creating the designs. And he was. I didn't have to sell him. He bought."

Letting the other person feel that the idea is his or hers not only works in business and politics, it works in family life as well. Paul M. Davis of Tulsa, Oklahoma, told his class how he applied this principle:

"My family and I enjoyed one of the most interesting sightseeing vacation trips we have ever taken. I had long dreamed of visiting such historic sites as the Civil War battlefield in Gettysburg, Independence Hall in Philadelphia, and our nation's capital. Valley Forge, Jamestown, and the restored colonial village of Williamsburg were high on the list of things I wanted to see.

"In March my wife, Nancy, mentioned that she had ideas for our summer vacation which included a tour of the western states, visiting points of interest in New Mexico, Arizona, California, and Nevada. She had wanted to make this trip for several years. But we couldn't, obviously, make both trips.

"Our daughter, Anne, had just completed a course in U.S. history in junior high school and had become very interested in the events that shaped our country's growth. I asked her how she would like to visit the places she had learned about on our next vacation. She said she would love to.

"Two evenings later as we sat around the dinner table, Nancy announced that if we all agreed, the summer's vacation would be to the eastern states, that it would be a great trip for Anne and thrilling for all of us. We all concurred."

This same psychology was used by an X-ray manufacturer to sell his equipment to one of the largest hospitals in Brooklyn. This hospital was building an addition and preparing to equip it with the finest X-ray department in America. Dr. L—, who was in charge of the X-ray department, was overwhelmed with sales representatives, each caroling the praises of his own company's equipment.

One manufacturer, however, was more skillful. He knew far more about handling human nature than the others did. He wrote a letter something like this:

> Our factory has recently completed a new line of X-ray equipment. The first shipment of these machines has just arrived at our office. They are not perfect. We know that, and we want to improve them. So we should be deeply obligated to you if you could find time to look them over and give us your ideas about how they can be made more serviceable to your profession. Knowing how occupied you are, I shall be glad to send my car for you at any hour you specify.

"I was surprised to get that letter," Dr. L—said as he related the incident before the class. "I was both surprised and complimented. I had never had an X-ray manufacturer seeking my advice before. It made me feel important. I was busy every night that week, but I canceled a dinner appointment in order to look over the equipment. The more I studied it, the more I discovered for myself how much I liked it.

"Nobody had tried to sell it to me. I felt that the idea of buying that equipment for the hospital was my own. I sold myself on its superior qualities and ordered it installed."

Ralph Waldo Emerson in his essay "Self-Reliance" stated: "In every work of genius we recognize our own rejected thoughts; they come back to us with a certain alienated majesty."

Colonel Edward M. House wielded an enormous influence in national and international affairs while Woodrow Wilson occupied the White House. Wilson leaned upon Colonel House for secret counsel and advice more than he did upon even members of his own cabinet.

What method did the colonel use in influencing the President? Fortunately, we know, for House himself revealed it to Arthur D. Howden Smith, and Smith quoted House in an article in *The Saturday Evening Post.*

"After I got to know the President, House said, "I learned the best way to convert him to an idea was to plant it in his mind casually, but so as to interest him in it—so as to get him thinking about it on his own account. The first time this worked it was an accident. I had been visiting him at the White House and urged a policy on him which he appeared to disapprove. But several days later, at the dinner table, I was amazed to hear him trot out my suggestion as his own."

Did House interrupt him and say, "That's not your idea. That's mine"? Oh, no. Not House. He was too adroit for that. He didn't care about credit. He wanted results. So he let Wilson continue to feel that the idea was his. House did even more than that. He gave Wilson public credit for these ideas.

Let's remember that everyone we come in contact with is just as human as Woodrow Wilson. So let's use Colonel House's technique.

A man up in the beautiful Canadian province of New Brunswick used this technique on me and won my patronage. I was planning at the time to do some fishing and canoeing in New Brunswick. So I wrote the tourist bureau for information. Evidently my name and address were put on a mailing list, for I was immediately overwhelmed with scores of letters and booklets and printed testimonials from camps and guides. I was bewildered. I didn't know which to choose. Then one camp owner did a clever thing. He sent me the names and telephone numbers of several New York people who had stayed at his camp and he invited me to telephone them and discover for myself what he had to offer.

I found to my surprise that I knew one of the men on his list. I telephoned him, found out what his experience had been, and then wired the camp the date of my arrival.

The others had been trying to sell me their service, but one let me sell myself. That organization won.

Twenty-five centuries ago, Lao-tse, a Chinese sage, said some things that readers of this book might use today: "The reason why rivers and seas receive the homage of a hundred mountain streams is that they keep below them. Thus they are able to reign over all the mountain streams. So the sage, wishing to be above men, putteth himself below them; wishing to be before them, he putteth himself behind them. Thus, though his place be above men, they do not feel his weight; though his place be before them, they do not count it an injury."

Let the other person feel that the idea is his or hers.

~

Men of age object too much, consult too long, adventure too little, repent too soon, and seldom drive business home to the fullperiod, but content themselves with a mediocrity of success.

8

An Appeal That Everybody Likes

I was reared on the edge of the Jesse James country out in Missouri, and I visited the James farm at Kearney, Missouri, where the son of Jesse James was then living.

His wife told me stories of how Jesse robbed trains and held up banks and then gave money to the neighboring farmers to pay off their mortgages.

Jesse James probably regarded himself as an idealist at heart, just as Dutch Schultz, "Two Gun" Crowley, Al Capone, and many other organized crime "godfathers" did generations later. The fact is that all people you meet have a high regard for themselves and like to be fine and unselfish in their own estimation.

J. Pierpont Morgan observed, in one of his analytical interludes, that a person usually has two good reasons for doing a thing: one that sounds good and a real one. The person himself will think of the real reason. You don't need to emphasize that. But all of us, being idealists at heart, like to think of motives that sound good. So, in order to change people, appeal to the nobler motives.

Is that too idealistic to work in business? Let's see. Let's take the case of Hamilton J. Farrell of the Farrell-Mitchell Company of Glenolden, Pennsylvania. Mr. Farrell had a disgruntled tenant who threatened to move. The tenant's lease still had four months to run; nevertheless, he served notice that he was vacating immediately, regardless of lease.

"These people had lived in my house all winter—the most expensive part of the year," Mr. Farrell said as he told the story to the class, "and I knew it would be difficult to rent the apartment again before fall. I could see all that rent income going over the hill and believe me, I saw red.

"Now, ordinarily, I would have waded into that tenant and advised him to read his lease again. I would have pointed out that if he moved, the full balance of his rent would fall due at once—and that I could, *and would,* take steps to collect.

"However, instead of flying off the handle and making a scene, I decided to try other tactics. So I started like this: 'Mr. Doe,' I said, 'I have listened to your story, and I still don't believe you intend to move. Years in the renting business have taught me something about human nature, and I sized you up in the first place as being a man of your word. In fact, I'm so sure of it that I'm willing to take a gamble.

"'Now, here's my proposition. Lay your decision on the table for a few days and think it over. If you come back to me between now and the first of the month, when the rent is due, and tell me you still intend to move, I give you my word I will accept your decision as final. I will give you the privilege of moving and admit to myself I've been wrong in my judgment. But I still believe you're a man of your word and will live up to your contract. For after all, we are either men or monkeys—and the choice usually lies with ourselves!'

"Well, when the new month came around, this gentleman came to see me and paid his rent in person. He and his wife had talked it over, he said—and decided to stay. They had concluded that the only honorable thing to do was to live up to their lease."

When the late Lord Northcliffe found a newspaper using a picture of him which he didn't want published, he wrote the editor a letter. But did he say, "Please do not publish that picture of me anymore; I don't like it"? No, he appealed to a nobler motive. He appealed to the respect and love that all of us have for motherhood. He wrote, "Please do not publish that picture of me anymore. My mother doesn't like it."

When John D. Rockefeller, Jr. wished to stop newspaper photographers from snapping pictures of his children, he, too, appealed to the nobler motives. He didn't say; "I don't want the pictures published." No, he appealed to the desire, deep in all of us, to refrain from harming children. He said; "You know how it is, boys. You've got children yourselves, some of you. And you know it's not good for youngsters to get too much publicity."

When Cyrus H.K. Curtis, a poor boy from Maine, was starting on the meteoric career which was destined to make him millions as owner of *The Saturday Evening Post* and the *Ladies Home Journal,* he couldn't afford to pay his contributors the prices that other magazines paid. He couldn't afford to hire first-class authors to write for money alone. So he appealed to their nobler motives. For example, he persuaded even Louisa May Alcott, the immortal author of *Little Women,* to write for him when she was at the flood tide of her fame; and he did it by offering to send a check for a hundred dollars, not to her, but to her favorite charity.

Right here the skeptic may say: "Oh, that stuff is all right for Northcliffe and Rockefeller or a sentimental novelist. But I'd like to see you make it work with the tough babies I have to collect bills from!"

You may be right. Nothing will work in all cases—and nothing will work with all people. If you are satisfied with the results you are getting, why change? If you are not satisfied, why not experiment?

At any rate, I think you will enjoy reading this true story told by James L. Thomas, a former student of mine:

Six customers of a certain automobile company refused to pay their bills for servicing. None of the customers protested the entire bill, but each claimed that some one charge was wrong. In each case, the customer had signed for the work done, so the company knew it was right—and said so. That was the first mistake.

Here are the steps the credit department took to collect these overdue bills. Do you suppose they succeeded?

They called on the customers and told them bluntly that they had come to collect a bill that was long past due.

They made it very plain that the company was absolutely and unconditionally right; therefore, the customer was absolutely and unconditionally wrong.

They intimated that they, the company, knew more about automobiles than the customer could ever hope to know. So what was the argument about?

Result: They argued.

Did any of these methods reconcile the customer and settle the account? You can answer that one yourself.

At this stage of affairs, the credit manager was about to open fire with a battery of legal talent, when fortunately the matter came to the attention of the general manager. The manager investigated these defaulting clients and discovered that they all had the reputation of paying their bills promptly. Something was wrong here—something was drastically wrong about the method of collection. So he called in James

L. Thomas and told him to collect these "uncollectible" accounts.

Here, in his words, are the steps Mr. Thomas took:

"My visit to each customer was likewise to collect a bill long past due—a bill that we knew was absolutely right. But I didn't say a word about that. I explained I had called to find out what it was the company had done, or failed to do.

"I made it clear that, until I heard the customer's story, I had no opinion to offer. I told him the company made no claims to being infallible.

"I told him I was interested only in his car, and that he knew more about his car than anyone else in the world; that he was the authority on the subject.

"I let him talk, and I listened to him with all the interest and sympathy that he wanted—and expected.

"Finally, when the customer was in a reasonable mood, I put the whole thing up to his sense of fair play. I appealed to the nobler motives. 'First,' I said, 'I want you to know I also feel this matter has been badly mishandled. You've been inconvenienced and annoyed and irritated by one of our representatives. That should never have happened. I'm sorry and, as a representative of the company, I apologize. As I sat here and listened to your side of the story, I could not help being impressed by your fairness and patience. And now, because you are fair-minded and patient, I am going to ask you do to something for me. It's something that you can do better than anyone else, something you know more about than anyone else. Here is your bill; I know it is safe for me to adjust it, just as you would do if you were the president of my company. I am going to leave it all up to you. Whatever you say goes.' "Did he adjust the bill? He certainly did, and got quite a kick out of it. The bills ranged from $150 to $400—

but did the customer give himself the best of it? Yes, one of them did! One of them refused to pay a penny of the disputed charge; but the other five all gave the company the best of it! And here's the cream of the whole thing: we delivered new cars to all six of these customers within the next two years!"

"Experience has taught me," says Mr. Thomas, "that when no information can be secured about the customer, the only sound basis on which to proceed is to assume that he or she is sincere, honest, truthful, and willing and anxious to pay the charges, once convinced they are correct. To put it differently and perhaps more clearly, people are honest and want to discharge their obligations. The exceptions to that rule are comparatively few, and I am convinced that the individuals who are inclined to chisel will in most cases react favorably if you make them feel that you consider them honest, upright, and fair."

In order to change people, appeal to the nobler motives.

~

Most of the important things in the world have been accomplished by people who have kept on trying when there seemed to be no hope at all.

9

A Sure Way Of Making Enemies And How To Avoid It

When Theodore Roosevelt was in the White House, he confessed that if he could be right seventy-five percent of the time, he would reach the highest measure of his expectation.

If that was the highest rating that one of the most distinguished men of the twentieth century could hope to obtain, what about you and me?

If you can be sure of being right only fifty-five per cent of the time, you can go down to Wall Street and make a million dollars a day. If you can't be sure of being right even fifty-five per cent of the time, why should you tell other people they are wrong?

You can tell people they are wrong by a look or an intonation or a gesture just as eloquently as you can in words—and if you tell them they are wrong, do you make them want to agree with you? Never! For you have struck a direct blow at their intelligence, judgment, pride, and self-respect. That will make them want to strike back. But it will never make them want to change their minds. You may then hurl at them all the logic of a Plato or an Immanuel Kant, but you will not alter their opinions, for you have hurt their feelings.

Never begin by announcing, "I am going to prove so-and-so to you." That's bad. That's tantamount to saying: "I'm smarter than you are. I'm going to tell you a thing or two and make you change your mind."

That is a challenge. It arouses opposition and makes the listener want to battle with you before you even start. It is difficult, under even the most benign conditions, to change people's minds. So why make it harder? Why handicap yourself?

Well, I can't hope to be any smarter than Socrates, so I have quit telling people they are wrong. And I find that it pays.

If a person makes a statement that you think is wrong—yes, even that you know is wrong—isn't it better to begin by saying: "Well, now, look. I thought otherwise, but I may be wrong. I frequently am. And if I am wrong, I want to be put right. Let's examine the facts."

There's magic, positive magic, in such phrases as: "I may be wrong. I frequently am. Let's examine the facts." Nobody in the heavens above or on the earth will ever object to your saying: "I may be wrong. Let's examine the facts."

One of our class members who used this approach in dealing with customers was Harold Reinke, a Dodge dealer in Billings, Montana. He reported that because of the pressures of the automobile business, he was often hard-boiled and callous when dealing with customers complaints. This caused flared tempers, loss of business, and general unpleasantness.

He told his class: "Recognizing that this was getting me nowhere fast, I tried a new tack. I would say something like this: 'Our dealership has made so many mistakes that I am frequently ashamed. We have erred in your case. Tell me about it.'

"This approach becomes quite disarming, and by the time the customer releases his feelings, he is usually much more reasonable when it comes to settling the matter. In fact, several customers have thanked me for having such an understanding attitude. And two of them have even brought in friends to buy new cars. In this highly competitive market, we need more of this type of customer, and I believe that showing respect for all customer's opinions and treating them diplomatically and courteously will help beat the competition."

You will never get into trouble by admitting that you may be wrong. That will stop all argument and inspire your opponent to be just as fair and open and broadminded as you are. It will make him want to admit that he, too, may be wrong.

If you know positively that a person is wrong, and you bluntly tell him or her so, what happens? Let me illustrate. Mr. S., a young New York attorney, once argued a rather important case before the United States Supreme Court (Lustgarten v. Fleet Corporation 280 U.S. 320). The case involved a considerable sum of money and an important question of law. During the argument, one of the Supreme Court justices said to him: "The statute of limitations is six years, is it not?"

Mr. S. stopped, stared at the justice for a moment, and then said bluntly, "Your Honor, there is no statute of limitations in admiralty."

"A hush fell on the court," said Mr. S., as he related his experience to one of the author's classes, "and the temperature in the room seemed to drop to zero. I was right. Justice was wrong. And I had told him so. But did that make him friendly? No. I still believe that I had the law on my side. And I know that I spoke better than I ever spoke before. But

I didn't persuade. I made the enormous blunder of telling a very learned and famous man that he was wrong."

Few people are logical. Most of us are prejudiced and biased. Most of us are blighted with preconceived notions, with jealousy, suspicion, fear, envy, and pride. And most citizens don't want to change their minds about their religion or their haircut or communism or their favorite movie star.

Carl Rogers, the eminent psychologist, wrote in his book *On Becoming a Person*:

> I have found it of enormous value when I can permit myself to understand the other person. The way in which I have worded this statement may seem strange to you. Is it necessary to permit oneself to understand another? I think it is. Our first reaction to most of the statements [which we hear from other people] is an evaluation or judgment, rather than an understanding of it. When someone expresses some feeling, attitude or belief, our tendency is almost immediately to feel "that's right," or "that's stupid," "that's abnormal," "that's unreasonable," "that's incorrect," "that's not nice." Very rarely do we permit ourselves to *understand* precisely what the meaning of the statement is to the other person.

I once employed an interior decorator to make some draperies for my home. When the bill arrived, I was dismayed.

A few days later, a friend dropped in and looked at the draperies. The price was mentioned, and she exclaimed with a note of triumph: "What? That's awful. I am afraid he put one over on you."

True? Yes, she had told the truth, but few people like to listen to truths that reflect on their judgment. So, being human, I tried to defend myself. I pointed out that the best is eventually the cheapest, that one can't expect to get quality and artistic taste at bargain-basement prices, and so on and on.

The next day, another friend dropped in, admired the draperies, bubbled over with enthusiasm, and expressed a wish that she could afford such exquisite creations for her home. My reaction was totally different. "Well, to tell the truth,' I said, "I can't afford them myself. I paid too much. I'm sorry I ordered them."

When we are wrong, we may admit it to ourselves. And if we are handled gently and tactfully, we may admit it to others and even take pride in our frankness and broad-mindedness. But not if someone else is trying to ram the unpalatable fact down our esophagus.

Horace Greeley, the most famous editor in America during the time of the Civil War, disagreed violently with Lincoln's policies. He believed that he could drive Lincoln into agreeing with him by a campaign of argument, ridicule, and abuse. He waged this bitter campaign month after month, year after year. In fact, he wrote a brutal, bitter, sarcastic, and personal attack on President Lincoln the night Booth shot him.

But did all this bitterness make Lincoln agree with Greeley? Not at all. Ridicule and abuse never do.

If you want some excellent suggestions about dealing with people and managing yourself and improving your personality, read Benjamin Franklin's autobiography—one of the most fascinating life stories ever written, one of the classics of American literature. Ben Franklin tells how he conquered the iniquitous habit of argument and transformed himself into one of the most able, suave, and diplomatic men in American history.

One day, when Ben Franklin was a blundering youth, an old Quaker friend took him aside and lashed him with a few stinging truths, something like this:

> Ben, you are impossible. Your opinions have a slap in them for everyone who differs with you. They have become so offensive that nobody cares for them. Your friends find they enjoy themselves better when you are not around. You know so much that no man can tell you anything. Indeed, no man is going to try, for the effort would lead only to discomfort and hard work. So you are not likely ever to know any more than you do now, which is very little.

One of the finest things I know about Ben Franklin is the way he accepted that smarting rebuke. He was big enough and wise enough to realize that it was true, to sense that he was headed for failure and social disaster. So he made a right-about-face. He began immediately to change his insolent, opinionated ways.

"I made it a rule," said Franklin, "to forbear all direct contradiction to the sentiment of others, and all positive assertion of my own. I even forbade myself the use of every word or expression in the language that imported a fix'd opinion, such as 'certainly,' 'undoubtedly,' etc., and I adopted, instead of them, 'I conceive,' 'I apprehend,' or 'I imagine' a thing to be so or so, or 'it so appears to me at present.' When another asserted something that I thought an error, I deny'd myself the pleasure of contradicting him abruptly, and of showing immediately some absurdity in his proposition: and in answering I began by observing that in certain cases or instances his opinion would be right, but in the present case there appear'd or seem'd to me some difference, etc.

I soon found the advantage of this change in my manner; the conversations I engag'd in went on more pleasantly. The modest way in which I propos'd my opinions procur'd them a readier reception and less contradiction; I had less mortification when I was found to be in the wrong, and I more easily prevail'd with others to give up their mistakes and join with me when I happened to be in the right.

"And this mode, which I at first put on with some violence to natural inclination, became at length so easy, and so habitual to me, that perhaps for these fifty years past no one has ever heard a dogmatical expression escape me. And to this habit (after my character of integrity) I think it principally owing that I had earned so much weight with my fellow citizens when I proposed new institutions, or alterations in the old, and so much influence in public councils when I became a member; for I was but a bad speaker, never eloquent, subject to much hesitation in my choice of words, hardly correct in language, and yet I generally carried my points."

How do Ben Franklin's methods work in business? Let's take two examples.

Katherine A. Allred of Kings Mountain, North Carolina, is an industrial engineering supervisor for a yarn-processing plant. She told one of our classes how she handled a sensitive problem before and after taking our training:

"Part of my responsibility," she reported, "deals with setting up and maintaining incentive systems and standards for our operators so they can make more money by producing more yarn. The system we were using had worked fine when we had only two or three different types of yarn, but recently we had expanded our inventory and capabilities to enable us to run more than twelve different varieties. The present system was no longer adequate to pay the operators fairly for the work being performed and give them an incentive to increase production. I had worked up a new system which would enable us to pay the operator by the class of yarn she was running at any one particular time. With my new system in hand, I entered the meeting determined to prove to the management that my system was the right approach. I told them in detail how they were wrong and showed where they were being unfair and how I had all the answers they needed. To say the least, I failed miserably! I had become so busy defending my position on the new system that I had left them no opening to graciously admit their problems on the old one. The issue was dead.

"After several sessions of this course, I realized all too well where I had made my mistakes. I called another meeting and this time I asked where they felt their problems were. We discussed each point, and I asked them their opinions on which was the best way to proceed. With a few low-keyed suggestions, at proper intervals, I let them develop my system themselves. At the end of the meeting when I actually presented my system, they enthusiastically accepted it.

"I am convinced now that nothing good is accomplished and a lot of damage can be done if you tell a person straight out that he or she is wrong. You only succeed in stripping that person of self-dignity and making yourself an unwelcome part of any discussion."

Let's take another example—and remember these cases I am citing are typical of the experiences of thousands of other people. R.V. Crowley was a salesman for a lumber company in New York. Crowley admitted that he had been telling hard-boiled lumber inspectors for years that they were wrong. And he had won the arguments too. But it hadn't done any good. "For these lumber inspectors," said

Mr. Crowley, "are like baseball umpires. Once they make a decision, they never change it."

Mr. Crowley saw that his firm was losing thousands of dollars through the arguments he won. So while taking my course, he resolved to change tactics and abandon arguments. With what results? Here is the story as he told it to the fellow members of his class:

"One morning, the phone rang in my office. A hot and bothered person at the other end proceeded to inform me that a car of lumber we had shipped into his plant was entirely unsatisfactory. His firm had stopped unloading and requested that we make immediate arrangements to remove the stock from their yard. After about one-fourth of the car had been unloaded, their lumber inspector reported that the lumber was running fifty-five per cent below grade. Under the circumstances, they refused to accept it.

"I immediately started for his plant and on the way turned over in my mind the best way to handle the situation. Ordinarily, under such circumstances, I should have quoted grading rules and tried, as a result of my own experience and knowledge as a lumber inspector, to convince the other inspector that the lumber was actually up to grade, and that he was misinterpreting the rules in his inspection. However, I thought I would apply the principles learned in this training.

"When I arrived at the plant, I found the purchasing agent and the lumber inspector in a wicked humor, both set for an argument and a fight. We walked out to the car that was being unloaded, and I requested that they continue to unload so that I could see how things were going. I asked the inspector to go right ahead and lay out the rejects, as he had been doing, and to put the good pieces in another pile.

"After watching him for a while it began to dawn on me that his inspection actually was much too strict and that he was misinterpreting the rules. This particular lumber was white pine, and I knew the inspector was thoroughly schooled in hard woods but not a competent, experienced inspector on white pine. White pine happened to be my own strong suit, but did I offer any objection to the way he was grading the lumber? None whatever. I kept on watching and gradually began to ask questions as to why certain pieces were not satisfactory. I didn't for one instant insinuate that the inspector was wrong. I emphasized that my only reason for asking was in order that we could give his firm exactly what they wanted in future shipments.

"By asking questions in a very friendly, cooperative spirit, and insisting continually that they were right in laying out boards not satisfactory to their purpose, I got him warmed up, and the strained relations between us began to thaw and melt away. An occasional carefully put remark on my part gave birth to the idea in his mind that possibly some of these rejected pieces were actually within the grade that they had bought, and that their requirements demanded a more expensive grade. I was very careful, however, not to let him think I was making an issue of this point.

"Gradually, his whole attitude changed. He finally admitted to me that he was not experienced on white pine and began to ask me questions about each piece as it came out of the car. I would explain why such a piece came within the grade specified, but kept on insisting that we did not want him to take it if it was unsuitable for their purpose. He finally got to the point where he felt guilty every time he put a piece in the rejected pile. And at last, he saw that the mistake was on their part for not having specified as good a grade as they needed.

"The ultimate outcome was that he went through the entire carload again after I left, accepted the whole lot, and we received a check in full.

"In that one instance alone, a little tact, and the determination to refrain from telling the other man he was wrong, saved my company a substantial amount of cash, and it would be hard to place a money value on the good will that was saved."

Martin Luther King, Jr., was asked how, as a pacifist, he could be an admirer of Air Force General Daniel "Chappie" James, then the nation's highest-ranking black officer. Dr. King replied, "I judge people by their own principles—not by my own."

In a similar way, General Robert E. Lee once spoke to the president of the Confederacy, Jefferson Davis, in the most glowing terms about a certain officer under his command. Another officer was astonished. "General," he said, "do you not know that the man of whom you speak so highly is one of your bitterest enemies who misses no opportunity to malign you?" "Yes," replied General Lee, "but the president asked my opinion of him; he did not ask for his opinion of me."

By the way, I am not revealing anything new in this chapter. Two thousand years ago, Jesus said: "Agree with thine adversary quickly."

And twenty-two hundred years before Christ was born, Pharaoh Akhtoi of Egypt gave his son some shrewd advice—advice that is sorely needed today. "Be diplomatic," counseled the pharaoh. "It will help you gain your point."

In other words, don't argue with your customer or your spouse or your adversary. Don't tell them they are wrong, don't get them stirred up. Use a little diplomacy.

Be diplomatic.

~

Most of us have far more courage than we ever dreamed possible.

10

How To Criticize And Not Be Hated For It

Charles Schwab was passing through one of his steel mills one day at noon when he came across some of his employees smoking. Immediately above their heads was a sign that said No Smoking. Did Schwab point to the sign and say, "Can't you read?" Oh, no, not Schwab. He walked over to the men, handed each one a cigar, and said, "I'll appreciate it, boys, if you will smoke these on the outside." They knew that he knew that they had broken a rule—and they admired him because he said nothing about it and gave them a little present and made them feel important. Couldn't keep from loving a man like that, could you?

John Wanamaker used the same technique. Wanamaker used to make a tour of his great store in Philadelphia every day. Once he saw a customer waiting at a counter. No one was paying the slightest attention to her. The salespeople? Oh, they were in a huddle at the far end of the counter laughing and talking among themselves. Wanamaker didn't say a word. Quietly slipping behind the counter, he waited on the woman himself and then handed the purchase to the sales people to be wrapped as he went on his way.

Public officials are often criticized for not being accessible to their constituents. They are busy people, and the fault sometimes lies in overprotective assistants who don't want to overburden their bosses with too many visitors. Carl Langford, who had been mayor of Orlando, Florida, the home of Disney World, for many years, frequently admonished his staff to allow people to see him. He claimed he had an "open-door" policy; yet the citizens of his community were blocked by secretaries and administrators when they called.

Finally the mayor found the solution. He removed the door from his office! His aides got the message, and the mayor had a truly open administration from the day his door was symbolically thrown away.

Simply changing one three-letter word can often spell the difference between failure and success in changing people without giving offense or arousing resentment.

Many people begin their criticism with sincere praise followed by the word "but" and ending with a critical statement. For example, in trying to change a child's careless attitude toward studies, we might say, "We're really proud of you, Johnnie, for raising your grades this term. *But* if you had worked harder on your algebra, the results would have been better."

In this case, Johnnie might feel encouraged until he heard the word "but." He might then question the sincerity of the original praise. To him, the praise might seem only to be a contrived lead in to a critical inference of failure. Credibility would be strained, and we probably would not achieve our objective of changing Johnnie's attitude toward his studies.

This could be easily overcome by changing the word "but" to "and." "We're really proud of you, Johnnie, for raising your grades this term, *and* if you continue the same conscientious efforts next term, your algebra grade can be up with all the others."

Now, Johnnie would accept the praise because there was no follow-up of an inference of failure. We have called his attention to the behavior we wished to change indirectly, and the chances are he will try to live up to our expectations.

Calling attention indirectly to someone's mistakes works wonders with sensitive people who may resent bitterly any direct criticism. Marge Jacob of Woonsocket, Rhode Island, told one of our classes how she convinced some sloppy construction workers to clean up after themselves when they were building additions to her house.

For the first few days of the work, when Mrs. Jacob returned from her job, she noticed that the yard was strewn with the cut ends of lumber. She didn't want to antagonize the builders, because they did excellent work. So after the workers had gone home, she and her children picked up and neatly piled all the lumber debris in a corner. The following morning she called the foreman to one side and said, "I'm really pleased with the way the front lawn was left last night; it is nice and clean and does not offend the neighbors." From that day forward, the workers picked up and piled the debris to one side, and the foreman came in each day seeking approval of the condition the lawn was left in after a day's work.

One of the major areas of controversy between members of the army reserves and their regular army trainers is haircuts. The reservists consider themselves civilians (which they are most of the time) and resent having to cut their hair short.

Master Sergeant Harley Kaiser of the 542nd USAR School addressed himself to this problem when he was working with a group of reserve non-commissioned officers. As an old-time regular-army master sergeant, he might have been expected to yell at his troops and threaten them. Instead he chose to make his point indirectly.

"Gentlemen," he started, "you are leaders. You will be most effective when you lead by example. You must be the example for your men to follow. You know what the army regulations say about haircuts. I am going to get my hair cut today, although it is still much shorter than some of yours. You look at yourself in the mirror, and if you feel you need a haircut to be a good example, we'll arrange time for you to visit the post barber shop."

The result was predictable. Several of the candidates did look in the mirror and went to the barber shop that afternoon and received "regulation" haircuts. Sergeant Kaiser commented the next morning that he already could see the development of leadership qualities in some of the members of the squad.

On March 8, 1887, the eloquent Henry Ward Beecher died. The following Sunday, Lyman Abbott was invited to speak in the pulpit left silent by Beecher's passing. Eager to do his best, he wrote, rewrote, and polished his sermon with the meticulous care of a Flaubert. Then he read it to his wife. It was poor—as most written speeches are. She might have said, if she had had less judgment, "Lyman, that is terrible. That'll never do. You'll put people to sleep. It reads like an encyclopedia. You ought to know better than that after all the years you have been preaching. For heaven's sake, why don't you talk like a human being? Why don't you act natural? You'll disgrace yourself if you ever read that stuff."

That's what she *might* have said. And, if she had, you know what would have happened. And she knew too. So, she merely remarked that it would make an excellent article for the *North American Review.* In other words, she praised it and at the same time subtly suggested that it wouldn't do as a speech. Lyman Abbott saw the point, tore up his carefully prepared manuscript, and preached without even using notes.

Don't call attention to people's mistakes directly.

~

Most of us have far more courage than we ever dreamed we possessed.

11

No One Likes To Take Orders

I once had the pleasure of dining with Mrs. Ida Tarbell, the dean of American biographers. When I told her I was writing this book, we began discussing this all-important subject of getting along with people, and she told me that while she was writing her biography of Owen D. Young, she interviewed a man who had sat for three years in the same office with Mr. Young. This man declared that during all that time he had never heard Owen D. Young give a direct order to anyone. He always gave suggestions, not orders. Owen D. Young never said, for example, "Do this or do that," or "Don't do this or don't do that." He would say, "You might consider this," or "Do you think that would work?" Frequently he would say, after he had dictated a letter, "What do you think of this?" In looking over a letter of one of his assistants, he would say, "Maybe if we were to phrase it this way it would be better." He always gave people the opportunity to do things themselves; he never told his assistants to do things; he let them do them, let them learn from their mistakes.

A technique like that makes it easy for a person to correct errors. A technique like that saves a person's pride and gives him or her a feeling of importance. It encourages cooperation instead of rebellion.

Resentment caused by a brash order may last a long time—even if the order was given to correct an obviously bad situation. Dan Santatelli, a teacher at a vocational school in Wyoming, Pennsylvania, told one of our classes how one of his students had blocked the entraceway to one of the school's shops by illegally parking his car in it. One of the other instructors stormed into the classroom and asked in an arrogant tone, "Whose car is blocking the driveway?" When the student who owned the car responded, the instructor screamed: "Move that car and move it right now, or I'll wrap a chain around it and drag it out of there."

Now that student was wrong. The car should not have been parked there. But from that day on, not only did that student resent the instructor's action, but all the students in the class did everything they could to give the instructor a hard time and make his job unpleasant.

How could he have handled it differently? If he had asked in a friendly way, "Whose car is in the driveway?" and then suggested that if it were moved, other cars could get in and out, the student would have gladly moved it and neither he nor his classmates would have been upset and resentful.

Asking questions not only makes an order more palatable; it often stimulates the creativity of the persons whom you ask. People are more likely to accept an order if they have had a part in the decision that caused the order to be issued.

When Ian Macdonald of Johannesburg, South Africa, the general manager of a small manufacturing plant specializing in precision machine parts, had the opportunity to accept a very large order, he was convinced that he would not meet the promised delivery date. The work already scheduled in the shop and the short completion time needed for this order made it seem impossible for him to accept the order.

Instead of pushing his people to accelerate their work and rush the order through, he called everybody together, explained the situation to them, and told them how much it would mean to the company and to them if they could make it possible to produce the order on time. Then he started asking questions:

"Is there anything we can do to handle this order?" "Can anyone think of different ways to process it through the shop that will make it possible to take the order?"

"Is there any way to adjust our hours or personnel assignments that would help?"

The employees came up with many ideas and insisted that he take the order. They approached it with a "We can do it" attitude, and the order was accepted, produced, and delivered on time.

An effective leader will...

Make people part of the decision.

~

An old man was asked what had robbed him of joy in his life. His reply was, "Things that never happened."

12

Let The Other Person Save Face

Years ago the General Electric Company was faced with the delicate task of removing Charles Steinmetz from the head of a department. Steinmetz, a genius of the first magnitude when it came to electricity, was a failure as the head of the calculating department. Yet the company didn't dare offend the man. He was indispensable—and highly sensitive. So they gave him a new title. They made him consulting engineer of the General Electric Company—a new title for work he was already doing—and let someone else head the department.

Steinmetz was happy.

So were the officers of G.E. They had gently maneuvered their most temperamental star, and they had done it without a storm—by letting him save face.

Letting someone save face! How important, how vitally important, that is! And how few of us ever stop to think of it! We ride roughshod over the feelings of others, getting our own way, finding fault, issuing threats, criticizing a child or an employee in front of others, without even considering the hurt to the other person's pride. Whereas a few minutes' thought, a considerate word or two, a genuine understanding of the other person's attitude, would go so far toward alleviating the sting!

Let's remember this the next time we are faced with the distasteful necessity of discharging or reprimanding an employee.

"Firing employees is not much fun. Getting fired is even less fun." (I'm quoting now from a letter written to me by Marshall A. Granger, a certified public accountant.) "Our business is mostly seasonal. Therefore, we have to let a lot of people go when the income tax rush is over.

"It's a byword in our profession that no one enjoys wielding the ax. Consequently, the custom has developed of getting it over as soon as possible, and usually in the following way: 'Sit down, Mr. Smith. The season's over, and we don't seem to see any more assignments for you. Of course, you understand you were employed only for the busy season anyhow, etc., etc.'

"The effect on these people is one of disappointment and a feeling of being 'let down.' Most of them are in the accounting field for life, and they retain no particular love for the firm that drops them so casually.

"I recently decided to let our seasonal personnel go with a little more tact and consideration. So I call each one in only after carefully thinking over his or her work during the winter. And I've said something like this: 'Mr. Smith, you've done a fine job (if he has). That time we sent you to Newark, you had a tough assignment. You were on the spot, but you came through with flying colors, and we want you to know the firm is proud of you. You've got the stuff-—you're going a long way, wherever you're working. This firm believes in you, and is rooting for you, and we don't want you to forget it.' "Effect? The people go away feeling a lot better about being fired. They don't feel 'let down'. They know that if we had work for them, we'd keep them on. And when we need them again, they come to us with a keen personal affection."

At one session of our course, two class members discussed the negative effects of fault-finding versus the positive effects of letting the other person save face.

Fred Clark of Harrisburg, Pennsylvania, told of an incident that occurred in his company: "At one of our production meetings, a vice-president was asking very pointed questions of one of our production supervisors regarding a production process. His tone of voice was aggressive and aimed at pointing out faulty performance on the part of the supervisor. Not wanting to be embarrassed in front of his peers, the supervisor was evasive in his responses. This caused the vice-president to lose his temper, berate the supervisor, and accuse him of lying.

"Any working relationship that might have existed prior to this encounter was destroyed in a few brief moments. This supervisor, who was basically a good worker, was useless to our company from that time on. A few months later, he left our firm and went to work for a competitor, where I understand he is doing a fine job."

Another class member, Anna Mazzone, related how a similar incident had occurred at her job—but what a difference in approach and results! Ms. Mazzone, a marketing specialist for a food packer, was given her first major assignment—the test marketing of a new product. She told the class: "When the results of the test came in, I was devastated. I had made a serious error in my planning, and the entire test had to be done all over again. To make this worse, I had no time to discuss it with my boss before the meeting in which I was to make my report on the project.

"When I was called on to give the report, I was shaking with fright. I had all I could do to keep from breaking down, but I resolved I would not cry and have all those men make remarks about women not being able to handle an assignment because they are too emotional. I made my report briefly and stated that due to an error I would repeat the study before the next meeting. I sat down, expecting my boss to blow up.

"Instead, he thanked me for my work and remarked that it was not unusual for a person to make an error on a new project and that he had confidence that the repeat survey would be accurate and meaningful to the company. He assured me, in front of my colleagues, that he had faith in me and knew I had done my best, and that my lack of experience, not my lack of ability, was the reason for the failure.

"I left that meeting with my head up in the air and with the determination that I would never let that boss of mine down again."

Even if we are right and the other person is definitely wrong, we only destroy ego by causing someone to lose face. The legendary French aviation pioneer and author Antoine de Saint-Exupéry wrote: "I have no right to say or do anything that diminishes a man in his own eyes. What matters is not what I think of him, but what he thinks of himself. Hurting a man in his dignity is a crime."

Let people save face.

13

Talk About Your Own Mistakes First

My niece, Josephine Carnegie, had come to New York to be my secretary. She was nineteen, had graduated from high school three years previously, and her business experience was a trifle more than zero. She became one of the most proficient secretaries west of Suez, but in the beginning, she was—well, susceptible to improvement. One day when I started to criticize her, I said to myself: "Just a minute, Dale Carnegie, just a minute. You are twice as old as Josephine. You have ten thousand times as much business experience. How can you possibly expect her to have your viewpoint, your judgment, your initiative—mediocre though they may be? And just a minute, Dale, what were you doing at nineteen? Remember the asinine mistakes and blunders you made? Remember the time you did this...and that...?"

After thinking the matter over, honestly and impartially, I concluded that Josephine's batting average at nineteen was better than mine had been—and that, I'm sorry to confess, isn't paying Josephine much of a compliment.

So after that, when I wanted to call Josephine's attention to a mistake, I used to begin by saying, "You have made a mistake, Josephine, but the Lord knows, it's no worse than many I have made. You were not born with judgment. That comes only with experience, and you are better than I was at your age. I have been guilty of so many stupid, silly things myself, I have very little inclination to criticize you or anyone. But don't you think it would have been wiser if you had done so and so?"

It isn't nearly so difficult to listen to a recital of your faults if the person criticizing begins by humbly admitting that he, too, is far from impeccable.

E.G. Dillistone, an engineer in Brandon, Manitoba, Canada, was having problems with his new secretary. Letters he dictated were coming to his desk for signature with two or three spelling mistakes per page. Mr. Dillistone reported how he handled this:

"Like many engineers, I have not been noted for my excellent English or spelling. For years, I have kept a little black thumb-index book for words I had trouble spelling. When it became apparent that merely pointing out the errors was not going to cause my secretary to do more proofreading and dictionary work, I resolved to take another approach. When the next letter came to my attention that had errors in it, I sat down with the typist and said:

"'Somehow this word doesn't look right. It's one of the words I always have had trouble with. That's the reason I started this spelling book of mine. (I opened the book to the appropriate page.) Yes, here it is. I'm very conscious of the spelling now because people do judge us by our letters, and misspellings make us look less professional.'

"I don't know whether she copied my system or not, but since that conversation, her frequency of spelling errors has been significantly reduced."

The polished Prince Bernhard von Bülow learned the sharp necessity of doing this back in 1909. Von Bülow was then the imperial chancellor of Germany, and on the throne sat Wilhelm II—Wilhelm, the haughty; Wilhelm, the arrogant; Wilhelm, the last of the German kaisers, building an army and navy that he boasted could whip their weight in wildcats.

Then an astonishing thing happened. The kaiser said things, incredible things, things that rocked the continent and started a series of explosions heard around the world. To make matters worse, the kaiser made silly, egotistical, absurd announcements in public. He made them while he was a guest in England, and he gave his royal permission to have them printed in the *Daily Telegraph*. For example, he declared that he was the only German who felt friendly toward the English; that he was constructing a navy against the menace of Japan; that he, and he alone, had saved England from being humbled in the dust by Russia and France; that it had been *his* campaign plan that enabled England's Lord Roberts to defeat the Boers in South Africa, and so on and on.

No other such amazing words had ever fallen from the lips of a European king in peacetime within a hundred years. The entire continent buzzed with the fury of a hornet's nest. England was incensed. German statesmen were aghast. And in the midst of all this consternation, the kaiser became panicky and suggested to Prince von Bülow, the imperial chancellor, that he take the blame. Yes, he wanted von Biilow to announce that it was all his responsibility, that he had advised his monarch to say these incredible things.

"But Your Majesty," von Bülow protested, "it seems to me utterly impossible that anybody either in Germany or England could suppose me capable of having advised Your Majesty to say any such thing."

The moment those words were out of von Bülow's mouth, he realized he had made a grave mistake. The Kaiser blew up.

"You consider me a donkey," he shouted, "capable of blunders you yourself could never have committed."

Von Bülow knew that he ought to have praised before he condemned; but since it was too late, he did the next best thing. He praised after he had criticized. And it worked a miracle.

"I'm far from suggesting that," he answered respectfully. "Your Majesty surpasses me in many respects; not only, of course, in naval and military knowledge, but above all, in natural science. I have often listened in admiration when Your Majesty explained the barometer, or wireless telegraphy, or the Roentgen rays. I am shamefully ignorant of all branches of natural science, have no notion of chemistry or physics, and am quite incapable of explaining the simplest of natural phenomena. But," von Billow continued, "in compensation, I possess some historical knowledge and perhaps certain qualities useful in politics, especially in diplomacy."

The kaiser beamed. Von Bülow had praised him. Von Bülow had exalted him and humbled himself. The kaiser could forgive anything after that. "Haven't I always told you," he exclaimed with enthusiasm, "that we complete one another famously? We should stick together, and we will!"

He shook hands with von Bülow, not once, but several times. And later in the day, he waxed so enthusiastic that he exclaimed with doubled fists, "If anyone says anything to me against Prince von Bülow, *I shall punch him in the nose!*'

Von Bülow saved himself in time—but, canny diplomat that he was, he nevertheless had made one error: he should have *begun* by talking about his own shortcomings and Wilhelm's superiority—not by intimating that the kaiser was a half-wit in need of a guardian.

If a few sentences humbling oneself and praising the other party can turn a haughty, insulted kaiser into a staunch friend, imagine what humility and praise can do for you and me in our daily contacts. Rightly used, they will work veritable miracles in human relations.

Admitting one's own mistakes—even when one hasn't corrected them—can help convince somebody to change his or her behavior. This was illustrated more recently by Clarence Zerhusen of Timonium, Maryland, when he discovered his fifteen-year-old son was experimenting with cigarettes.

"Naturally, I didn't want David to smoke," Mr. Zerhusen told us, "but his mother and I smoked cigarettes; we were giving him a bad example all the time. I explained to Dave how I started smoking at about his age and how the nicotine had gotten the best of me and now it was nearly impossible for me to stop. I reminded him how irritating my cough was and how he had been after me to give up cigarettes not many years before. I didn't exhort him to stop or make threats or warn him about their dangers. All I did was point out how I was hooked on cigarettes and what it had meant to me.

"He thought about it for a while and decided he wouldn't smoke until he had graduated from high school. As the years went by, David never did start smoking and has no intention of ever doing so.

"As a result of that conversation, I made the decision to stop smoking myself, and with the support of my family, I have succeeded."

Admit to your own faults before pointing the finger at others.

~

One of the most tragic things I know about human nature is that all of us tend to put off living. We are all dreaming of some magical rose garden over the horizon instead of enjoying the roses that are blooming outside our windows today.

PART II

STOP WORRYING

14

Four Good Working Habits That Will Help Prevent Fatigue And Worry

GOOD WORKING HABIT NO. 1

Clear your desk of all papers except those relating to the immediate problem at hand.

Roland L. Williams, President of the Chicago and Northwestern Railway, once said, "A person with his desk piled high with papers on various matters will find his work much easier and more accurate if he clears that desk of all but the immediate problem on hand. I call this good housekeeping, and it is the number-one step toward efficiency."

If you visit the Library of Congress in Washington, D.C., you will find five words painted on the ceiling— five words written by the poet Pope:

"Order is Heaven's first law."

Order ought to be the first law of business, too. But is it? No, the average desk is cluttered up with papers that haven't been looked at for weeks. In fact, the publisher of a New Orleans newspaper once told me that his secretary cleared up one of his desks and found a typewriter that had been missing for two years!

The mere sight of a desk littered with unanswered mail and reports and memos is enough to breed confusion, tension, and worries. It is much worse than that. The constant reminder of a million things to do and no time to do them" can worry you not only into tension and fatigue, but also into high blood pressure, heart trouble, and stomach ulcers.

Dr. John H. Stokes, Professor, Graduate School of Medicine, University of Pennsylvania, read a paper before the National Convention of the American Medical Association—a paper entitled "Functional Neuroses as Complications of Organic Disease." In that paper, Dr. Stokes listed eleven conditions under the title: "What to Look for in the Patient's State of Mind." Here is the first item on that list:

> The sense of must or obligation; the unending stretch of things ahead that simply have to be done.

But how can such an elementary procedure as clearing your desk and making decisions help you avoid this high pressure, this sense of *must,* this sense of an "unending stretch of things ahead" that simply have to be done? Dr. William L. Sadler, the famous psychiatrist, told of a patient who, by using this simple device, avoided a nervous breakdown. The man was an executive in a big Chicago firm. When he came to Dr. Sadler's office, he was tense, nervous, worried. He knew he was heading for a tailspin, but he couldn't quit work. He had to have help.

"While this man was telling me his story," Dr. Sadler says, "my telephone rang. It was the hospital calling, and instead of deferring the matter, I took time right then to come to a decision. I always settle questions, if possible, right on the spot. I had no sooner hung up than the phone rang again. Again an urgent matter, which I took time to discuss. The third interruption came when a colleague of mine came to my office for advice on a patient who was critically ill. When I had finished with him, I turned to my caller and began to apologize for keeping him waiting. But he had brightened up. He had a completely different look on his face."

"Don't apologize, doctor!" this man said to Sadler. "In the last ten minutes, I think I've got a hunch as to what is wrong with me. I'm going back to my office and revise my working habits... But before I go, do you mind if I take a look in your desk?"

Dr. Sadler opened up the drawers of his desk. All empty—except for supplies. "Tell me," said the patient, "where do you keep your unfinished business?" "Finished!" said Sadler.

"And where do you keep your unanswered mail?" "Answered!" Sadler told him. "My rule is never to lay down a letter until I have answered it. I dictate the reply to my secretary at once."

Six weeks later, this same executive invited Dr. Sadler to come to his office. He was changed—and so was his desk. He opened the desk drawers to show there was no unfinished business inside of the desk. "Six weeks ago," this executive said, "I had three different desks in two different offices—and was snowed under by my work. I was never finished. After talking to you, I came back here and cleared out a wagonload of reports and old papers. Now I work at one desk, settle things as they come up, and don't have a mountain of unfinished business nagging at me and making me tense and worried. But the most astonishing thing is I've recovered completely. There is nothing wrong anymore with my health!"

Charles Evans Hughes, former Chief Justice of the United States Supreme Court, said: "Men do not die from overwork. They die from dissipation and worry." Yes, from dissipation of their energies—and worry because they never seem to get their work done.

GOOD WORKING HABIT NO. 2

Do things in the order of their importance.

Henry L. Doherty, founder of the nationwide Cities Service Company, said that regardless of how much salary he paid, there were two abilities he found it almost impossible to find.

Those two priceless abilities; first, the ability to think. Second, the ability to do things in the order of their importance.

Charles Luckman, the lad who started from scratch and climbed in twelve years to president of the Pepsodent Company, got a salary of a hundred thousand dollars a year, and made a million dollars besides—that lad declared that he owed much of his success to developing the two abilities that Henry L. Doherty said he found almost impossible to find. Charles Luckman said: "As far back as I can remember, I have gotten up at five o'clock in the morning because I can think better then than any other time—I can think better then and plan my day, plan to do things in the order of their importance."

Frank Bettger, one of Americas most successful insurance salesmen, didn't wait until five o'clock in the morning to plan his day. He planned it the night before—set a goal for himself—a goal to sell a certain amount of insurance that day. If he failed, that amount was added to his next day—and so on.

I know from long experience that one is not always able to do things in the order of their importance, but I also know that some kind of plan to do first things first is infinitely better than extemporizing as you go along.

If George Bernard Shaw had not made it a rigid rule to do first things first, he would probably have failed as a writer and might have remained a bank cashier all his life. His plan called for writing five pages each day for nine heartbreaking years, even though he made a total of thirty dollars in those nine years—about a penny a day. Even Robinson Crusoe wrote out a schedule of what he would do each hour of the day.

GOOD WORKING HABIT NO. 3

When you face a problem, solve it then and there if you have the facts necessary to make a decision. Don't keep putting off decisions.

One of my former students, the late H.P. Howell, told me that when he was a member of the board of directors of U.S. Steel, the meetings of the board were often long-drawn-out affairs—many problems were discussed, few decisions were made. The result: each member of the board had to carry home bundles of reports to study.

Finally, Mr. Howell persuaded the board of directors to take up one problem at a time and come to a decision. No procrastination—no putting off. The decision might be to ask for additional facts; it might be to do something or to do nothing. But a decision was reached on each problem before passing on to the next. Mr. Howell told me that the results were striking and salutary: the docket was cleared. The calender was clean. No longer was it necessary for each member to carry home a bundle of reports. No longer was there a worried sense of unresolved problems.

A good rule, not only for the board of directors of U.S. Steel, but for you and me.

GOOD WORKING HABIT NO. 4

Learn to organize, deputize and supervise.

Many business persons are driving themselves to premature graves because they have never learned to delegate responsibility to others, insisting on doing everything themselves. Result: details and confusion overwhelm them. They are driven by a sense of hurry, worry, anxiety and tension. It is hard to learn to delegate responsibilities. I know. It was hard for me, awfully hard. I also know from experience the disasters that can be caused by delegating authority to the wrong people. But difficult as it is to delegate authority, executives must do it if they are to avoid worry, tension and fatigue.

Executives who build up big businesses and don't learn to organize, deputize and supervise usually pop off with heart trouble in their fifties or early sixties—heart trouble caused by tension and worries. Want a specific instance? Look at the death notices in your local paper.

Our fatigue is often caused not by work, but by worry, frustration and resentment.

~

Only the prepared speaker deserves to be confident.

15

How To Banish The Boredom That Produces Fatigue, Worry And Resentment

One of the chief causes of fatigue is boredom. To illustrate, let's take the case of Alice, an executive who lives on your street. Alice came home one night utterly exhausted. She *acted* fatigued. She *was* fatigued. She had a headache. She had a backache. She was so exhausted, she wanted to go to bed without waiting for dinner. Her mother pleaded... She sat down at the table. The telephone rang. The boyfriend! An invitation to a dance! Her eyes sparkled. Her spirits soared. She rushed upstairs, put on her Alice-Blue gown, and danced until three o'clock in the morning; and when she finally did get home, she was not the slightest bit exhausted. She was, in fact, so exhilarated she couldn't fall asleep.

Was Alice really and honestly tired eight hours earlier, when she looked and acted exhausted? Sure, she was. She was exhausted because she was bored with her work, perhaps bored with life. There are millions of Alices. You may be one of them.

It is a well-known fact that your emotional attitude usually has far more to do with producing fatigue than has physical exertion. A few years ago, Joseph E. Barmack, Ph.D., published in the *Archives of Psychology* a report of some of his experiments, showing how boredom produces fatigue. Dr. Barmack put a group of students through a series of tests in which, he knew, they could have little interest. The result? The students felt tired and sleepy, complained of headaches and eyestrain, felt irritable. In some cases, even their stomachs were upset. Was it all "imagination"? No. Metabolism tests were taken of these students. These tests showed that the blood pressure of the body and the consumption of oxygen actually decrease when a person is bored, and that the whole metabolism picks up immediately as soon as he begins to feel interest and pleasure in his work!

We rarely get tired when we are doing something interesting and exciting. For example, I recently took a vacation in the Canadian Rockies up around Lake Louise. I spent several days trout fishing along Corral Creek, fighting my way through brush higher than my head, stumbling over logs, struggling through fallen timber—yet after eight hours of this, I was not exhausted. Why? Because I was excited, exhilarated. I had a sense of high achievement: six cut-throat trout. But suppose I had been bored by fishing, then how do you think I would have felt? I would have been worn out by such strenuous work at an altitude of seven thousand feet.

Even in such exhausting activities as mountain climbing, boredom may tire you far more than the strenuous work involved. For example, Mr. S.H. Kingman, president of the Farmers and Mechanics Savings Bank of Minneapolis, told me of an incident that is a perfect illustration of that statement. In July, 1953, the Canadian government asked the Canadian Alpine Club to furnish guides to train the members of the Prince of Wales Rangers in mountain climbing. Mr. Kingman was one of the guides chosen to train these soldiers. He told me how he and the other guides—men ranging from forty-two to fifty-nine years of age—took these young army men on long hikes across glaciers and snowfields and up a sheer cliff of forty feet, where they had to climb with ropes and tiny footholds and precarious handholds. They climbed Michael's Peak, the Vice-President Peak, and other unnamed peaks in the Little Yoho Valley in the Canadian Rockies. After fifteen hours of mountain climbing, these young men, who were in the pink of condition (they had just finished a six-week course in tough Commando training), were utterly exhausted.

Was their fatigue caused by using muscles that had not been hardened by Commando training? Anyone who had ever been through Commando training would hoot at such a ridiculous question! No, they were utterly exhausted because they were bored by mountain climbing. They were so tired that many of them fell asleep without waiting to eat. But the guides—men who were two and three times as old as the soldiers—were they tired? Yes, but not exhausted. The guides ate dinner and stayed up for hours, talking about the day's experiences. They were not exhausted because they were interested.

When Dr. Edward Thorndike of Columbia was conducting experiments in fatigue, he kept young men awake for almost a week by keeping them constantly interested. After much investigation, Dr. Thorndike is reported to have said: "Boredom is the only real cause of diminution of work."

If you are a mental worker, it is seldom the amount of work you do that makes you tired. You may be tired by the amount of work you do *not* do. For example, remember the day last week when you were constantly interrupted. No letters answered. Appointments broken. Trouble here and there. Everything went wrong that day. You accomplished nothing whatever, yet you went home exhausted—and with a splitting head.

The next day, everything clicked at the office. You accomplished forty times more than you did the previous day. Yet you went home fresh as a snowy-white gardenia. You have had that experience. So have I.

The lesson to be learned? Just this: our fatigue is often caused not by work, but by worry, frustration, and resentment.

While writing this chapter, I went to see a revival of Jerome Kern's delightful musical comedy *Show Boat.* Captain Andy, captain of the *Cotton Blossom,* says in one of his philosophical interludes: "The lucky folks are the ones that get to do things they enjoy doing." Such folk are lucky because they have more energy, more happiness, less worry and less fatigue. Where your interests are, there is your energy also. Walking ten blocks with a nagging wife or husband can be more fatiguing than walking ten miles with an adoring sweetheart.

And so what? What can you do about it? Well, here is what one stenographer did about it—a stenographer working for an oil company in Tulsa, Oklahoma. For several days each month, she had one of the dullest jobs imaginable: filling out printed forms for oil leases, inserting figures and statistics. This task was so boring that she resolved, in self-defense, to make it interesting. How? She had a daily contest with herself. She counted the number of forms she filled out each morning, and then tried to excel that record in the afternoon. She counted each day's total and tried to better it the next day. Result? She was soon able to fill out more of these dull printed forms than any other stenographer in her division. And what did all this get her? Praise? No... Thanks? No... Promotion? No... Increased pay? No... But it did help to prevent the fatigue that is spawned by boredom. It did give her a mental stimulant. Because she had done her best to make a dull job interesting, she had more energy, more zest, and got far more happiness out of her leisure hours.

I happen to know this story is true, because I married that girl.

Here is the story of another stenographer who found it paid to act *as if* her work were interesting. She used to fight her work. But no more. She is Miss Vallie G. Golden, of Elmhurst, Illinois. Here is her story, as she wrote it to me:

"There are four stenographers in my office and each of us is assigned to take letters from several men. Once in a while, we get jammed up in these assignments. One day, when an assistant department head insisted that I do a long letter over, I started to rebel. I tried to point out to him that the letter could be corrected without being retyped—and he retorted that if I didn't do it over, he would find someone else who would! I was absolutely fuming! But as I started to retype this letter, it suddenly occurred to me that there were a lot of other people who would jump at the chance to do the work I was doing. Also, that I was being paid a salary to do just that work. 1 began to feel better. I suddenly made up my mind to do my work as if I actually enjoyed it—even though I despised it. Then I made this important discovery: if I do my work *as if* I really enjoy it, then I do enjoy it to some extent. I also found I can work faster when I enjoy my work. So there is seldom any need now for me to work overtime. This new attitude of mine gained me the reputation of being a good worker. And when one of the department superintendents needed a private secretary, he asked for me for the job—because, he said, I was willing to do extra work without being sulky! This matter of the power of a changed mental attitude," wrote Miss Golden, "has been a tremendously important discovery to me. It has worked wonders!"

Miss Golden used the wonder-working "as if" philosophy of Professor Hans Vaihinger. He taught us to act "as if" we were happy—and so on.

If you act "as if" you are interested in your job, that bit of acting will tend to make your interest real. It will also tend to decrease your fatigue, your tensions, and your worries.

A few years ago, Harlan A. Howard made a decision that completely altered his life. He resolved to make a dull job interesting—and he certainly had a dull one: washing plates, scrubbing counters, and dishing out ice cream in the high-school lunchroom while the other boys were playing ball or kidding the girls. Harlan Howard despised his job—but since he had to stick to it, he resolved to study ice cream—how it was made, what ingredients were used, why some ice creams were better than others. He studied the chemistry of ice cream, and became a whiz in the high-school chemistry course. He was so interested now in food chemistry that he entered the Massachusetts State College and majored in the field of "food technology." When the New York Cocoa Exchange offered a hundred-dollar prize for the best paper on uses of cocoa and chocolate—a prize open to all college students—who do you suppose won it? That's right. Harlan Howard.

When he found it difficult to get a job, he opened a private laboratory in the basement of his home in Amherst, Massachusetts. Shortly after that, a new law was passed. The bacteria in milk had to be counted. Harlan A. Howard was soon counting bacteria for the fourteen milk companies in Amherst—and he had to hire two assistants.

Where will he be twenty-five years from now? Well, the men who are now running the business of food chemistry will be retired then, or dead; and their places will be taken by young lads who are now radiating initiative and enthusiasm. Twenty-five years from now, Harlan A. Howard will probably be one of the leaders in his profession, while some of his classmates to whom he used to sell ice cream over the counter will be sour, unemployed, cussing the government, and complaining that they never had a chance. Harlan A. Howard might never have had a chance, either, if he hadn't resolved to make a dull job interesting.

Years ago, there was another young man who was bored with his dull job of standing at a lathe, turning out bolts in a factory. His first name was Sam. Sam wanted to quit, but he was afraid he couldn't find another job. Since he had to do this dull work, Sam decided he would make it interesting. So he ran a race with the mechanic operating a machine beside him. One of them was to trim off the rough surfaces on his machine, and the other was to trim the bolts down to the proper diameter. They would switch machines occasionally and see who could turn out the most bolts. The foreman, impressed with Sam's speed and accuracy, soon gave him a better job. That was the start of a whole series of promotions. Thirty years later, Sam—Samuel Vauclain—was president of the Baldwin Locomotive Works. But he might have remained a mechanic all his life if he had not resolved to make a dull job interesting.

H.V. Kaltenborn—the famous radio news analyst—once told me how he made a dull job interesting. When he was twenty-two years old, he worked his way across the

Atlantic on a cattle boat, feeding and watering the steers. After making a bicycle tour of England, he arrived in Paris, hungry and broke. Pawning his camera for five dollars, he put an ad in the Paris edition of *The New York Herald* and got a job selling stereopticon machines. I can remember those old-fashioned stereoscopes that we used to hold up before our eyes to look at two pictures exactly alike. As we looked, a miracle happened. The two lenses in the stereoscope transformed the two pictures into a single scene with the effect of a third dimension. We saw distance. We got an astounding sense of perspective.

Well, as I was saying, Kaltenborn started out selling these machines from door to door in Paris—and he couldn't speak French. But he earned five thousand dollars in commissions the first year, and made himself one of the highest-paid salesmen in France that year. H.V. Kaltenborn told me that this experience did as much to develop within him the qualities that make for success as did any single year of study at Harvard. Confidence? He told me himself that after that experience, he felt he could have sold *The Congressional Record* to French housewives.

That experience gave him an intimate understanding of French life that later proved invaluable in interpreting, on the radio, European events.

How did he manage to become an expert salesman when he couldn't speak French? Well, he had his employer write out his sales talk in perfect French, and he memorized it. He would ring a doorbell, a housewife would answer, and Kaltenborn would begin repeating his memorized sales talk with an accent so terrible, it was funny. He would show the housewife his pictures, and when she asked a question, he would shrug his shoulders and say, "An American...an

American." He would then take off his hat and point to a copy of the sales talk in perfect French that he had pasted in the top of his hat. The housewife would laugh, he would laugh—and show her more pictures. When H.V. Kaltenborn told me about this, he confessed that the job had been far from easy. He told me that there was only one quality that pulled him through: his determination to make the job interesting. Every morning before he started out, he looked into the mirror and gave himself a pep talk: "Kaltenborn, you have to do this if you want to eat. Since you have to do it—why not have a good time doing it? Why not imagine every time you ring a doorbell that you are an actor before the footlights and that there's an audience out there looking at you? After all, what you are doing is just as funny as something on the stage. So why not put a lot of zest and enthusiasm into it?"

Mr. Kaltenborn told me that these daily pep talks helped him transform a task that he had once hated and dreaded into an adventure that he liked and made highly profitable.

When I asked Mr. Kaltenborn if he had any advice to give to the young men of America who are eager to succeed, he said: "Yes, go to bat with yourself every morning. We talk a lot about the importance of physical exercise to wake us up out of the half-sleep in which so many of us walk around. But we need, even more, some spiritual and mental exercises every morning to stir us into action. Give yourself a pep talk every day."

Is giving yourself a pep talk every day silly, superficial, childish? No, on the contrary, it is the very essence of sound psychology. "Our life is what our thoughts make it." These words are just as true today as they were eighteen centuries ago when Marcus Aurelius first wrote them in his book on *Meditations:* "Our life is what our thoughts make it."

By talking to yourself every hour of the day, you can direct yourself to think thoughts of courage and happiness, thoughts of power and peace. By talking to yourself about the things you have to be grateful for, you can fill your mind with thoughts that soar and sing.

By thinking the right thoughts, you can make any job less distasteful. Your boss wants you to be interested in your job so that he or she will make more money. But let's forget about what the boss wants. Think only of what getting interested in your job will do for you. Remind yourself that it may double the amount of happiness you get out of life, for you spend about one half of your waking hours at your work, and if you don't find happiness in your work, you may never find it anywhere. Keep reminding yourself that getting interested in your job will take your mind off your worries, and, in the long run, will probably bring promotion and increased pay. Even if it doesn't do that, it will reduce fatigue to a minimum and help you enjoy your hours of leisure.

People rarely succeed unless they have fun in what they are doing.

~

Remember happiness doesn't depend upon who you are or what you have; it depends solely on what you think.

16

Find Yourself And Be Yourself

I have a letter from Mrs. Edith Allred, of Mount Airy, North Carolina: "As a child, I was extremely sensitive and shy," she says in her letter. "I was always overweight and my cheeks made me look even fatter than I was. I had an old-fashioned mother who thought it was foolish to make clothes look pretty. She always said: 'Wide will wear while narrow will tear'; and she dressed me accordingly. I never went to parties; never had any fun; and when I went to school, I never joined the other children in outside activities, not even athletics. I was morbidly shy. I felt I was 'different' from everybody else and entirely undesirable.

"When I grew up, I married a man who was several years my senior. But I didn't change. My in-laws were a poised and self-confident family. They were everything I should have been but simply was not. I tried my best to be like them, but I couldn't. Every attempt they made to draw me out of myself only drove me further into my shell. I became nervous and irritable. I avoided all friends. I got so bad I even dreaded the sound of the doorbell ringing! I was a failure. I knew it; and I was afraid my husband would find it out. So, whenever we were in public, I tried to be gay, and overacted my part. I knew I overacted; and I would be miserable for days afterwards.

At last I became so unhappy that I could see no point in prolonging my existence. I began to think of suicide."

What happened to change this unhappy woman's life? Just a chance remark!

"A chance remark," Mrs. Allred continued, "transformed my whole life. My mother-in-law was talking one day of how she brought her children up, and she said, 'No matter what happened, I always insisted on their being themselves.' ...'On being themselves.' ...That remark is what did it! In a flash, I realized I had brought all this misery on myself by trying to fit myself into a pattern to which I did not conform.

"I changed overnight! I started being myself. I tried to make a study of my own personality. Tried to find out *what I was.* I studied my strong points. I learned all I could about colors and styles, and dressed in a way that I felt was becoming to me. I reached out to make friends. I joined an organization—a small one at first—and was petrified with fright when they put me on a program. But each time I spoke, I gained a little courage. It took a long while—but today I have more happiness than I ever dreamed possible. In rearing my own children, I have always taught them the lesson I had to learn from such bitter experience: *No matter what happens, always be yourself.*'

This problem of being unwilling to be yourself is "as old as history," says Dr. James Gordon Gilkey, "and as universal as human life." This problem of being unwilling to be yourself is the hidden spring behind many neuroses and psychoses and complexes. Angelo Patri has written thirteen books and thousands of syndicated newspaper articles on the subject of child training, and he says: "Nobody is so miserable as he who longs to be somebody and something other than the person he is in body and mind."

This craving to be something you are not is especially rampant in Hollywood. Sam Wood, one of Hollywood's best-known directors, said the greatest headache he has with aspiring young actors is exactly this problem: to make them be themselves. They all want to be second- rate Lana Turners or third-rate Clark Gables. "The public has already had that flavor," Sam Wood keeps telling them: "Now it wants something else."

Before he started directing such pictures as *Goodbye, Mr. Chips* and *For Whom the Bell Tolls,* Sam Wood spent years in the real-estate business, developing sales personalities. He declares that the same principles apply in the business world as in the world of moving pictures. You won't get anywhere playing the ape. You can't be a parrot. "Experience has taught me," says Sam Wood, "that it is safest to drop, as quickly as possible, people who pretend to be what they aren't."

I asked Paul Boynton, then employment director for a major oil company, what is the biggest mistake people make in applying for jobs. He ought to know: he has interviewed more than sixty thousand job seekers; and he has written a book entitled *6 Ways to Get a Job.* He replied: "The biggest mistake people make in applying for jobs is in not being themselves. Instead of taking their hair down and being completely frank, they often try to give you the answers they think you want." But it doesn't work, because nobody wants a phony. Nobody ever wants a counterfeit coin.

A certain daughter of a streetcar conductor had to learn that lesson the hard way. She longed to be a singer. But her face was her misfortune. She had a large mouth and protruding buck teeth. When she first sang in public—in a New Jersey night club—she tried to pull down her upper lip to cover her teeth. She tried to act "glamorous." The results? She made herself ridiculous. She was headed for failure.

However, there was a man in this night club who heard the girl sing and thought she had talent. "See here," he said bluntly, "I've been watching your performance and I know what it is you're trying to hide. You're ashamed of your teeth!" The girl was embarrassed, but the man continued, "What of it? Is there any particular crime in having buck teeth? Don't try to hide them! Open your mouth, and the audience will love you when they see you're not ashamed. Besides," he said shrewdly, "those teeth you're trying to hide may make your fortune!"

Cass Daley took his advice and forgot about her teeth. From that time on, she thought only about her audience. She opened her mouth wide and sang with such gusto and enjoyment that she became a top star in movies and radio. Other comedians tried to copy her!

The renowned William James was speaking of people who had never found themselves when he declared that the average person develops only ten percent of his or her latent mental abilities. "Compared to what we ought to be," he wrote, "we are only half awake. We are making use of only a small part of our physical and mental resources. Stating the thing broadly, human individuals thus far live within their limits. They possess powers of various sorts which they habitually fail to use."

You and I have such abilities, so let's not waste a second worrying because we are not like other people. You are something new in this world. Never before, since the beginning of time, has there ever been anybody exactly like you; and never again throughout all the ages to come will there ever be anybody exactly like you again. The science of genetics informs us that you are what you are largely as a result of twenty-four chromosomes contributed by your father and twenty-four chromosomes contributed by your mother. These forty-eight chromosomes comprise everything that determines what you inherit. In each chromosome there may be, says Amram Scheinfeld, "anywhere from scores to hundreds of genes—with a single gene, in some cases, able to change the whole life of an individual." Truly, we are "fearfully and wonderfully" made.

Even after your mother and father met and mated, there was only one chance in 300,000 billion that the person who is specifically you would be born! In other words, if you had 300,000 billion brothers and sisters, they might all have been different from you. Is all this guesswork? No. It is a scientific fact. If you would like to read more about it, consult *You and Heredity*, by Amram Scheinfeld.

I can talk with conviction about this subject of being yourself because I feel deeply about it. I know what I am talking about. I know from bitter and costly experience. To illustrate: when I first came to New York from the cornfields of Missouri, I enrolled in the American Academy of Dramatic Arts. I aspired to be an actor. I had what I thought was a brilliant idea, a shortcut to success, an idea so simple, so foolproof, that I couldn't understand why thousands of ambitious people hadn't already discovered it. It was this: I would study how the famous actors of that day—John Drew, Walter Hampden, and Otis Skinner—got their effects. Then I would imitate the best points of each one of them and make myself into a shining, triumphant combination of all of them. How silly! How absurd! I had to waste years of my life imitating other people before it penetrated through my thick Missouri skull that I had to be myself, and that I couldn't possibly be anyone else.

That distressing experience ought to have taught me a lasting lesson. But it didn't. Not me. I was too dumb. I had to learn it all over again. Several years later, I set out to write what I hoped would be the best book on public speaking for businessmen that had ever been written. I had the same foolish idea about writing this book that I had formerly had about acting: I was going to *borrow* the ideas of a lot of other writers and put them all in one book—a book that would have everything. So I got scores of books on public speaking and spent a year incorporating their ideas into my manuscript. But it finally dawned on me once again that I was playing the fool. This hodgepodge of other men's ideas that I had written was so synthetic, so dull, that no businessman would ever plod through it. So I tossed a year's work into the wastebasket and started all over again. This time I said to myself: "You've got to be Dale Carnegie, with all his faults and limitations. You can't possibly be anybody else." So I quit trying to be a combination of other men, and rolled up my sleeves and did what I should have done in the first place: I wrote a textbook on public speaking out of my own experiences, observations, and convictions as a speaker and a teacher of speaking. I learned—for all time, I hope—the lesson that Sir Walter Raleigh learned. (I am *not* talking about the Sir Walter who threw his coat in the mud for the queen to step on. I am talking about the Sir Walter Raleigh who was professor of English literature at Oxford back in 1904.) "I can't write a book commensurate with Shakespeare," he said, "but I can write a book by me."

Be yourself. Act on the sage advice that Irving Berlin gave the late George Gershwin. When Berlin and Gershwin first met, Berlin was famous but Gershwin was a struggling young composer working for thirty-five dollars a week in Tin Pan Alley. Berlin, impressed by Gershwin's ability, offered Gershwin a job as his musical secretary at almost three times the salary he was then getting. "But don't take the job," Berlin advised. "If you do, you may develop into a second-rate Berlin. But if you insist on being yourself, someday you'll become a first-rate Gershwin."

Gershwin heeded that warning and slowly transformed himself into one of the significant American composers of his generation.

Charlie Chaplin, Will Rogers, Mary Margaret McBride, Gene Autry, and millions of others had to learn the lesson I am trying to hammer home in this chapter. They had to learn the hard way—just as I did.

When Charlie Chaplin first started making films, the director of the picture insisted on Chaplin's imitating a popular German comedian of that day. Charlie Chaplin got nowhere until he acted himself. Bob Hope had a similar experience: spent years in a singing-and-dancing act—and got nowhere until he began to wisecrack and be himself. Will Rogers twirled a rope in vaudeville for years without saying a word. He got nowhere until he discovered his unique gift for humor and began to talk as he twirled his rope.

When Mary Margaret McBride first went on the air, she tried to be an Irish comedian and failed. When she tried to be just what she was—a plain country girl from Missouri—she became one of the most popular radio stars in New York.

When Gene Autry tried to get rid of his Texas accent and dressed like city boys and claimed he was from New York, people merely laughed behind his back. But when he started twanging his banjo and singing cowboy ballads, Gene

Autry started out on a career that made him the world's most popular cowboy both in pictures and on the radio.

You are something new in this world. Be glad of it. Make the most of what nature gave you. In the last analysis, all art is autobiographical. You can sing only what you are. You can paint only what you are. You must be what your experiences, your environment, and your heredity have made you. For better or for worse, you must cultivate your own little garden. For better or for worse, you must play your own little instrument in the orchestra of life.

As Emerson said in his essay on "Self-Reliance": "There is a time in every man's education when he arrives at the conviction that envy is ignorance; that imitation is suicide; that he must take himself for better, for worse, as his portion; that though the wide universe is full of good, no kernel of nourishing corn can come to him but through his toil bestowed on that plot of ground which is given to him to till. The power which resides in him is new in nature, and none but he knows what that is which he can do, nor does he know until he has tried."

That is the way Emerson said it. But here is the way a poet—the late Douglas Malloch—said it:

If you can't be a pine on the top of the hill

Be a scrub in the valley—but be The best little scrub by the side of the rill;

Be a bush, if you can't be a tree.

If you can't be a bush, be a bit of the grass,

And some highway happier make;

If you cant be a muskie, then just be a bass—

But the liveliest bass in the lake!

We can't all be captains, we've got to be crew,

There's something for all of us here.

There's big work to do and there's lesser to do

And the task we must do is the near.

If you can't be a highway, then just be a trail,

If you can't be the sun, be a star;

It isn't by size that you win or you fail—

Be the best of whatever you are!

Speakers who talk about what life has taught them never fail to keep the attention of their listeners.

~

Success is getting what you want. Happiness is wanting what you get.

17

How To Overcome Tiredness

Here is an astounding and significant fact: Mental work alone can't make you tired. Sounds absurd. But a few years ago, scientists tried to find out how long the human brain could labor without reaching "a diminished capacity for work," the scientific definition of fatigue. To the amazement of these scientists, they discovered that blood passing through the brain, when it is active, shows no fatigue at all! If you took blood from the veins of a day laborer while he was working, you would find it full of "fatigue toxins" and fatigue products. But if you took a drop of blood from the brain of an Albert Einstein, it would show no fatigue toxins whatever at the end of the day.

So far as the brain is concerned, it can work "as well and as swiftly at the end of eight or even twelve hours of effort as at the beginning." The brain is utterly tireless... So what makes you tired?

Psychiatrists declare that most of our fatigue derives from our mental and emotional attitudes. One of England's most distinguished psychiatrists, J.A. Hadfield, says in his book *The Psychology of Power*. "The greater part of the fatigue from which we suffer is of mental origin; in fact exhaustion of purely physical origin is rare."

One of America's most distinguished psychiatrists. Dr. A.A. Brill, goes even further. He declares, "One hundred percent of the fatigue of the sedentary worker in good health is due to psychological factors, by which we mean emotional factors."

What kinds of emotional factors tire the sedentary (or sitting) worker? Joy? Contentment? No! Never! Boredom, resentment, a feeling of not being appreciated, a feeling of futility, hurry, anxiety, worry—those are the emotional factors that exhaust the sitting worker, make him susceptible to colds, reduce his output, and send him home with a nervous headache. Yes, we get tired because our emotions produce nervous tensions in the body.

The Metropolitan Life Insurance Company pointed that out in a leaflet on fatigue: "Hard work by itself," said this great life insurance company, "seldom causes fatigue which cannot be cured by a good sleep or rest... Worry, tenseness, and emotional upsets are three of the biggest causes of fatigue. Often they are to blame when physical or mental work seems to be the cause... Remember that a tense muscle is a working muscle. Ease up! Save energy for important duties."

Stop now, right where you are, and give yourself a checkup. As you read these lines, are you scowling at the book? Do you feel a strain between the eyes? Are you sitting relaxed in your chair? Or are you hunching up your shoulders? Are the muscles of your face tense? Unless your entire body is as limp and relaxed as an old rag doll, you are at this very moment producing nervous tensions and muscular tensions. *You are producing nervous tensions and nervous fatigue!*

Why do we produce these unnecessary tensions in doing mental work? Daniel W. Josselyn said, "I find that the chief obstacle ...is the almost universal belief that hard work requires a feeling of effort, else it is not well done." So we scowl when we concentrate. We hunch up our shoulders. We call on our muscles to make the motion of *effort,* which in no way assists our brain in its work.

Here is an astonishing and tragic truth: millions of people who wouldn't dream of wasting dollars go right on wasting and squandering their energy with the recklessness of seven drunken sailors in Singapore.

What is the answer to this nervous fatigue? Relax! Relax! Relax! Learn to relax while you are doing your work!

Easy? No. You will probably have to reverse the habits of a lifetime. But it is worth the effort, for it may revolutionize your life! William James said, in his essay "The Gospel of Relaxation": "The American overtension and jerkiness and breathlessness and intensity and agony of expression... are *bad habits,* nothing more or less." Tension is a habit. Relaxing is a habit. And bad habits can be broken, good habits formed.

How do you relax? Do you start with your mind, or do you start with your nerves? You don't start with either. You always begin to relax with your muscles!

Let's give it a try. To show how it is done, suppose we start with your eyes. Read this paragraph through, and when you've reached the end, lean back, close your eyes, *and say to your eyes* silently, "Let go. Let go. Stop straining, stop frowning. Let go. Let go." Repeat that over and over very slowly for a minute

Didn't you notice that after a few seconds the muscles of the eyes *began to obey*? Didn't you feel as though some hand had wiped away the tension? Well, incredible as it seems, you have sampled in that one minute the whole key and secret to the art of relaxing. You can do the same thing with the jaw, with the muscles of the face, with the neck, with the shoulders, the whole of the body. But the most important organ of all is the eye. Dr. Edmund Jacobson of the University of Chicago has gone so far as to say that if you can completely relax the muscles of the eyes, you can forget all your troubles! The reason the eyes are so important in relieving nervous tension is that they burn up one fourth of all the nervous energies consumed by the body. That is also why so many people with perfectly sound vision suffer from "eyestrain." They are tensing the eyes.

Vicki Baum, the famous novelist, said that when she was a child, she met an old man who taught her one of the most important lessons she ever learned. She had fallen down and cut her knees and hurt her wrist. The old man picked her up. He had once been a circus clown, and as he brushed her off, he said, "The reason you injured yourself was because you don't know how to relax. You have to pretend you are as limp as a sock, as an old crumpled sock. Come, I'll show you how to do it."

That old man taught Vicki Baum and the other children how to fall, how to do flip-flops, and how to turn somersaults. And always he insisted, "Think of yourself as an old crumpled sock. Then you've *got* to relax!"

You can relax in odd moments, almost anywhere you are. Only don't make an effort to relax. *Relaxation is the absence of all tension and effort.* Think ease and relaxation. Begin by thinking relaxation of the muscles of your eyes and your face, saying over and over, "Let go...let go...let go and relax." Feel the energy flowing out of your facial muscles to the center of your body. Think of yourself as being as free from tension as a baby.

That is what Galli-Curci, the great soprano, used to do. Helen Jepson told me that she used to see Galli-Curci before a performance, sitting in a chair with all her muscles relaxed and her lower jaw so limp it actually sagged. An excellent practice—it kept her from becoming too nervous before her stage entrance; it prevented fatigue.

Here are four suggestions that will help you learn to relax:

1. Relax in odd moments. Let your body go limp like an old sock. I keep an old, maroon-colored sock on my desk as I work—keep it there as a reminder of how limp I ought to be. If you haven't got a sock, a cat will do. Did you ever pick up a kitten sleeping in the sunshine? If so, both ends sagged like a wet newspaper. Even the yogis in India say that if you want to master the art of relaxation, study the cat. I never saw a tired cat, a cat with a nervous breakdown, or a cat suffering from insomnia, worry, or stomach ulcers. You will probably avoid these disasters if you learn to relax as the cat does.
2. Work, as much as possible, in a comfortable position. Remember that tensions on the body produce aching shoulders and nervous fatigue.
3. Check yourself four or five times a day and say to yourself, "Am I making my work harder than it actually is? Am I using muscles that have nothing to do with the work I am doing?" This will help you form the *habit* of relaxing, and as Dr. David Harold Fink says, "Among those who know psychology best, it is habits two to one."
4. Test yourself again at the end of the day, by asking yourself, "Just how tired am I? If I am tired, it is not because of the mental work I have

done, but the way I have done it." "I measure my accomplishments," said Daniel W. Josselyn, "not by how tired I am at the end of the day, or when irritability proves that my nerves are tired, I know beyond question that it has been an inefficient day both as to quantity and quality." If every businessperson in America would learn that same lesson, our death rate from "hypertension" diseases would drop overnight. And we would stop filling up our sanitariums and asylums with people who have been broken by fatigue and worry.

Take a chance! All life is a chance. The man who goes farthest is generally the one who is willing to do and dare.

18

Do This And Criticism Can't Hurt You

I once interviewed Major General Smedley Butler—old "Gimlet-Eye." Old "Hell-Devil" Butler! Remember him? One of the most colorful, swashbuckling generals who ever commanded the United States Marines.

He told me that when he was young, he was desperately eager to be popular, wanted to make a good impression on everyone. In those days the slightest criticism smarted and stung. But he confessed that thirty years in the Marines had toughened his hide. "I have been berated and insulted," he said, "and denounced as a yellow dog, a snake, and a skunk. I have been cursed by the experts. I have been called every possible combination of unprintable, cuss words in the English language. Bother me? Huh! When I hear somebody cussing me now, I never turn my head to see who is talking."

Maybe old "Gimlet-Eye" Butler was too indifferent to criticism, but one thing is sure: most of us take the little jibes and javelins that are hurled at us far too seriously. I remember the time, years ago, when a reporter from the *New York Sun* attended a demonstration meeting of my adult-education classes and lampooned me and my work. Was I burned up? I took it as a personal insult. I telephoned Gil Hodges, the chairman of the Executive Committee of the *Sun* and practically demanded that he print an article stating the facts—instead of ridicule. I was determined to make the punishment fit the crime.

I am ashamed now of the way I acted. I realize now that half the people who bought the paper never saw that article. Half of those who read it regarded it as a source of innocent merriment. Half of those who gloated over it forgot all about it in a few weeks.

I realize now that people are not thinking about you and me or caring what is said about us. They are thinking about themselves—before breakfast, after breakfast, and right on until ten minutes past midnight. They would be a thousand times more concerned about a slight headache of their own than they would about the news of your death or mine.

Even if you and I are lied about, ridiculed, double-crossed, knifed in the back, and sold down the river by one out of every six of our most intimate friends—let's not indulge in an orgy of self-pity. Instead, let's remind ourselves that that's precisely what happened to Jesus. One of His twelve most intimate friends turned traitor for a bribe that would amount, in our modern money, to about nineteen dollars. Another one of His twelve most intimate friends openly deserted Jesus the moment He got into trouble, and declared three times that he didn't even know Jesus—and swore as he said it. One out of six! That is what happened to Jesus. Why should you and I expect a better score?

I discovered years ago that although I couldn't keep people from criticizing me unjustly, I could do something infinitely more important: I could determine whether I would let the unjust condemnation disturb me.

Let's be clear about this: I am not advocating ignoring all criticism. Far from it. I am talking about *ignoring only unjust criticism.* I once asked Eleanor Roosevelt how she handled unjust criticism—and Allah knows she had a lot of it. She probably had more ardent friends and more violent enemies than any other woman who ever lived in the White House.

She told me that as a young girl she was almost morbidly shy, afraid of what people might say. She was so afraid of criticism that one day she asked her aunt, Theodore Roosevelt's sister, for advice. She said: "Auntie, I want to do so-and-so. But I'm afraid of being criticized."

Teddy Roosevelt's sister looked her in the eye and said: "Never be bothered by what people say, as long as you know in your heart you are right." Eleanor Roosevelt told me that that bit of advice proved to be her Rock of Gibraltar years later, when she was in the White House. She told me that the only way we can avoid all criticism is to be like a Dresden-china figure and stay on a shelf. "Do what you feel in your heart to be right—for you'll be criticized, anyway. You'll be damned if you do, and damned if you don't.'" That is her advice.

When the late Matthew C. Brush was president of the American International Corporation, I asked him if he was ever sensitive to criticism, and he replied, "Yes, I was very sensitive to it in my early days. I was eager then to have all the employees in the organization think I was perfect. If they didn't, it worried me. I would try to please first one person who had been sounding off against me; but the very thing I did to patch it up with him would make someone else mad. Then when I tried to fix it up with this person, I would stir up a couple of other bumblebees. I finally discovered that the more I tried to pacify and to smooth over injured feelings in order to escape personal criticism, the more certain I was to increase my enemies. So finally I said to myself, 'If you get your head above the crowd, you're going to be criticized.

So get used to the idea.' That helped me tremendously. From that time on I made it a rule to do the very best I could and then put up my old umbrella and let the rain of criticism drain off me instead of run down my neck."

Deems Taylor went a bit further: he let the rain of criticism run down his neck and had a good laugh over it—in public. When he was giving his comments during the intermission of the Sunday-afternoon radio concerts of the New York Philharmonic Symphony Orchestra, one woman wrote him a letter calling him "a liar, a traitor, a snake, and a moron." Mr. Taylor says in his book, *Of Men and Music.* "I have a suspicion that she didn't care for that talk." On the following week's broadcast, Mr. Taylor read this letter over the radio to millions of listeners—and received another letter from the same lady a few days later, "expressing her unaltered opinion," says Mr. Taylor, "that I was *still* a liar, a traitor, a snake, and a moron." We can't keep from admiring a man who takes criticism like that. We admire his serenity, his unshaken poise, and his sense of humor.

When Charles Schwab was addressing the student body at Princeton, he confessed that one of the most important lessons he had ever learned was taught to him by an old German who worked in Schwab's steel mill. This old German got involved in a hot wartime argument with the other steelworkers, and they tossed him into the river. "When he came into my office," Mr. Schwab said, "covered with mud and water, I asked him what he had said to the men who had thrown him into the river, and he replied, 'I just laughed.'"

Mr. Schwab declared that he had adopted that old German's words as his motto: "Just laugh."

That motto is especially good when you are the victim of unjust criticism. You can answer the man who answers you back, but what can you say to the man who "just laughs"?

Lincoln might have broken under the strain of the Civil War if he hadn't learned the folly of trying to answer all the vitriolic condemnations hurled at him. His description of how he handled his critics has become a literary gem—a classic. General MacArthur had a copy of it hanging above his headquarters desk during the war, and Winston Churchill had a framed copy of it on the wall of his study at Chartwell. It goes like this: "If I were to try to read, much less to answer, all the attacks made on me, this shop might as well be closed for any other business. I do the very best I know how—the very best I can; and I mean to keep on doing so until the end. If the end brings me out all right, then what is said against me won't matter; if the end brings me out wrong, then ten angels swearing I was right would make no difference."

If you want to gather honey, don't kick over the beehive.

19

Would You Take A Million Dollars For What You Have?

I have known Harold Abbott for years. He lived in Webb City, Missouri. He used to be my lecture manager. One day, he and I met in Kansas City and he drove me down to my farm at Belton, Missouri. During that drive, 1 asked him how he kept from worrying, and he told me an inspiring story that I shall never forget.

"I used to worry a lot," he said, "but one spring day in 1934, I was walking down West Dougherty Street in Webb City when I saw a sight that banished all my worries. It all happened in ten seconds, but during those ten seconds, I learned more about how to live than I had learned in the previous ten years. For two years, I had been running a grocery store in Webb City." Harold Abbott said, as he told me the story, "I had not only lost all my savings, but I had incurred debts that took me seven years to pay back. My grocery store had been closed the previous Saturday, and now I was going to the Merchants and Miners Bank to borrow money so I could go to Kansas City to look for a job. I walked like a beaten man. I had lost all my fight and faith. Then suddenly I saw coming down the street a man who had no legs. He was sitting on a little wooden platform equipped with wheels from roller skates. He propelled himself along the street with a block of wood in each hand. I met him just after he had crossed the street and was starting to lift himself up a few inches over the curb to the sidewalk. As he tilted his little wooden platform to an angle, his eyes met mine. He greeted me with a grand smile. 'Good morning, sir. It is a fine morning, isn't it?' he said with spirit. As I stood looking at him, I realized how rich I was. I had two legs. I could walk. I felt ashamed of my self-pity. I said to myself, if he can be happy, cheerful, and confident without legs, I certainly can with legs. I could already feel my chest lifting. I had intended to ask the Merchants and Miners Bank for only one hundred dollars. But now I had courage to ask for *two* hundred. I had intended to say that I wanted to go to Kansas City to *try* to get a job. But now I announced confidently that I wanted to go to Kansas City to *get* a job. I got the loan, and I got the job.

I now have the following words pasted on my bathroom mirror, and I read them every morning as I shave;

I had the blues because I had no shoes,
Until upon the street, I met a man who had no feet.

I once asked Eddie Rickenbacker what was the biggest lesson he had learned from drifting about with his companions in life rafts for twenty-one days, hopelessly lost in the Pacific. "The biggest lesson I learned from that experience," he said, "was that if you have all the fresh water you want to drink and all the food you want to eat, you ought never to complain about anything."

Time ran an article about a sergeant who had been wounded on Guadalcanal. Hit in the throat by a shell fragment, this sergeant had had seven blood transfusions. Writing a note to his doctor, he asked: "Will I live?" The doctor replied: "Yes." He wrote another note, asking, "Will I be able to talk?" Again the answer was yes. He then wrote another note, saying: "Then what in the hell am I worrying about?"

Why don't you stop right now and ask yourself, "What in the hell am I worrying about?" You will probably find that it is comparatively unimportant and insignificant.

About ninety per cent of the things in our lives are right and about ten per cent are wrong. If we want to be happy, all we have to do is to concentrate on the ninety percent that are right and ignore the ten percent that are wrong. If we want to be worried and bitter and have stomach ulcers, all we have to do is to concentrate on the ten per cent that are wrong and ignore the ninety per cent that are glorious.

The words "Think and Thank" are inscribed in many of the Cromwellian churches of England. These words ought to be inscribed on our hearts, too: "Think and Thank." Think of all we have to be grateful for, and thank God for all our boons and bounties.

Jonathan Swift, author of *Gulliver's Travels*, was the most devastating pessimist in English literature. He was so sorry that he had been born that he wore black and fasted on his birthdays, yet, in his despair, this supreme pessimist of English literature praised the great health-giving powers of cheerfulness and happiness. "The best doctors in the world," he declared, "are Doctor Diet, Doctor Quiet, and Doctor Merryman."

You and I may have the services of "Doctor Merryman" free every day by keeping our attention fixed on all the incredible riches we possess—riches exceeding by far the fabled treasures of Ali Baba. Would you sell both your eyes for a billion dollars? What would you take for your two legs?

Your hands? Your hearing? Your children? Your family? Add up your assets, and you will find that you won't sell what you have for all the gold ever amassed by the Rockefellers, the Fords, and the Morgans combined.

But do we appreciate all this? Ah, no. As Schopenhauer said: "We seldom think of what we have but always of what we lack." Yes, the tendency to "seldom think of what we have but always of what we lack" is the greatest tragedy on earth. It has probably caused more misery than all the wars and diseases in history.

It caused John Palmer to turn "from a regular guy into an old grouch," and almost wrecked his home. I know because he told me so.

Mr. Palmer lived in Paterson, New Jersey. "Shortly after I returned from the Army," he said, "I started in business for myself. I worked hard day and night. Things were going nicely. Then trouble started. I couldn't get parts and materials. I was afraid I would have to give up my business. I worried so much that I changed from a regular guy into an old grouch. I became so sour and cross that—well, I didn't know it then but I now realize that I came very near to losing my happy home. Then one day, a young, disabled veteran who works for me said, 'Johnny, you ought to be ashamed of yourself. You take on as if you were the only person in the world with troubles. Suppose you do have to shut up shop for a while—so what? You can start up again when things get normal. You've got a lot to be thankful for. Yet you are always growling. Boy, how I wish I were in your shoes! Look at me. I've got only one arm, and half of my face is shot away, and yet I am not complaining. If you don't stop your growling and grumbling, you will lose not only your business, but also your health, your home, and your friends!'

"Those remarks stopped me dead in my tracks. They made me realize how well off I was. I resolved then and there that I would change and be my old self again—and I did."

A friend of mine, Lucile Blake, had to tremble on the edge of tragedy before she learned to be happy about what she had instead of worrying over what she lacked.

I met Lucile years ago, when we were both studying short-story writing in the Columbia University School of Journalism. Some years ago, she got the shock of her life. She was living then in Tucson, Arizona. She had—well, here is the story as she told it to me:

"I had been living in a whirl: studying the organ at the University of Arizona, conducting a speech clinic in town, and teaching a class in musical appreciation at the Desert Willow Ranch, where I was staying. I was going in for parties, dances, horseback rides under the stars. One morning, I collapsed. My heart! 'You will have to lie in bed for a year of complete rest,' the doctor said. He didn't encourage me to believe I would ever be strong again.

"In bed for a year! To be an invalid—perhaps to die! I was terror-stricken! Why did all this have to happen to me? What had I done to deserve it? I wept and wailed. I was bitter and rebellious. But I did go to bed as the doctor advised. A neighbor of mine, Mr. Rudolf, an artist, said to me, 'You think now that spending a year in bed will be a tragedy. But it won't be. You will have time to think and get acquainted with yourself. You will make more spiritual growth in these next few months than you have made during all your previous life.' I became calmer, and tried to develop a new sense of values. I read books of inspiration. One day, I heard a radio commentator say: 'You can express only what is in your own consciousness.' I had heard words like these many times before, but now they reached down inside me and took root. I resolved to think only the thoughts I wanted to live by: thoughts of joy, happiness, health. I forced myself each morning, as soon as I awoke, to go over all the things I had to be grateful for. No pain. A lovely young daughter. My eyesight. My hearing. Lovely music on the radio. Time to read. Good food. Good friends. I was so cheerful and had so many visitors that the doctor put up a sign saying that only one visitor at a time would be allowed in my cabin—and only at certain hours.

"Many years have passed since then, and I now lead a full, active life. I am deeply grateful now for that year I spent in bed. It was the most valuable and the happiest year I spent in Arizona. The habit I formed then of counting my blessings each morning still remains with me. It is one of my most precious possessions. I am ashamed to realize that I never really learned to live until I feared I was going to die."

My dear Lucile Blake, you may not realize it, but you learned the same lesson that Dr. Samuel Johnson learned two hundred years ago. "The habit of looking on the best side of every event," said Dr. Johnson, "is worth more than a thousand pounds a year."

Those words were uttered, mind you, not by a professional optimist, but by a man who had known anxiety, rags, and hunger for twenty years—and finally became one of the most eminent writers of his generation and the most celebrated conversationalist of all time.

Logan Pearsall Smith packed a lot of wisdom into a few words when he said: "There are two things to aim at in life: first, to get what you want; and, after that, to enjoy it. Only the wisest of mankind achieve the second." Would you like to know how to make even dishwashing at the kitchen sink a thrilling experience? If so, read an inspiring book of incredible courage by Borghild Dahl. It is called *I Wanted to See.*

This book was written by a woman who was practically blind for half a century. "I had only one eye," she writes, "and it was so covered with dense scars that I had to do all my seeing through one small opening in the left of the eye. I could see a book only by holding it up close to my face and by straining my one eye as hard as I could to the left."

But she refused to be pitied, refused to be considered "different." As a child, she wanted to play hopscotch with other children, but she couldn't see the markings. So after the other children had gone home, she got down on the ground and crawled along with her eyes near the marks. She memorized every bit of the ground where she and her friends played and soon became an expert at running games. She did her reading at home, holding a book of large print so close to her eyes that her eyelashes brushed the pages. She earned two college degrees: a B.A. from the University of Minnesota and a Master of Arts from Columbia University.

She started teaching in the tiny village of Twin Valley, Minnesota, and rose until she became professor of journalism and literature at Augustana College in Sioux Falls, South Dakota. She taught there for thirteen years, lecturing before women's clubs and giving radio talks about books and authors. "In the back of my mind," she writes, "there had always lurked a fear of total blindness. In order to overcome this, I had adopted a cheerful, almost hilarious, attitude toward life."

Then in 1943, when she was fifty-two years old, a miracle happened: an operation at the famous Mayo Clinic. She could now see forty times as well as she had ever been able to see before.

A new and exciting world of loveliness opened before her. She now found it thrilling even to wash dishes in the kitchen sink. "I begin to play with the white fluffy suds in the dishpan," she writes. "I dip my hands into them and I pick up a ball of tiny soap bubbles. I hold them up against the light, and in each of them I can see the brilliant colors of a miniature rainbow."

As she looked through the window above the kitchen sink, she saw "the flapping gray-black wings of the sparrows flying through the thick, falling snow."

She found such ecstasy looking at the soap bubbles and sparrows that she closed her book with these words: "'Dear Lord,' I whisper. Our Father in Heaven, I thank Thee. I thank Thee.'"

Imagine thanking God because you can wash dishes and see rainbows in bubbles and sparrows flying through the snow!

You and I ought to be ashamed of ourselves. All the days of our years we have been living in a fairyland of beauty, but we have been too blind to see, too satiated to enjoy.

Tell the audience what you're going to say, say it; then tell them what you've said.

~

The essence of all art is to have pleasure in giving pleasure.